THE AGE OF FRENCH IMPRESSIONISM

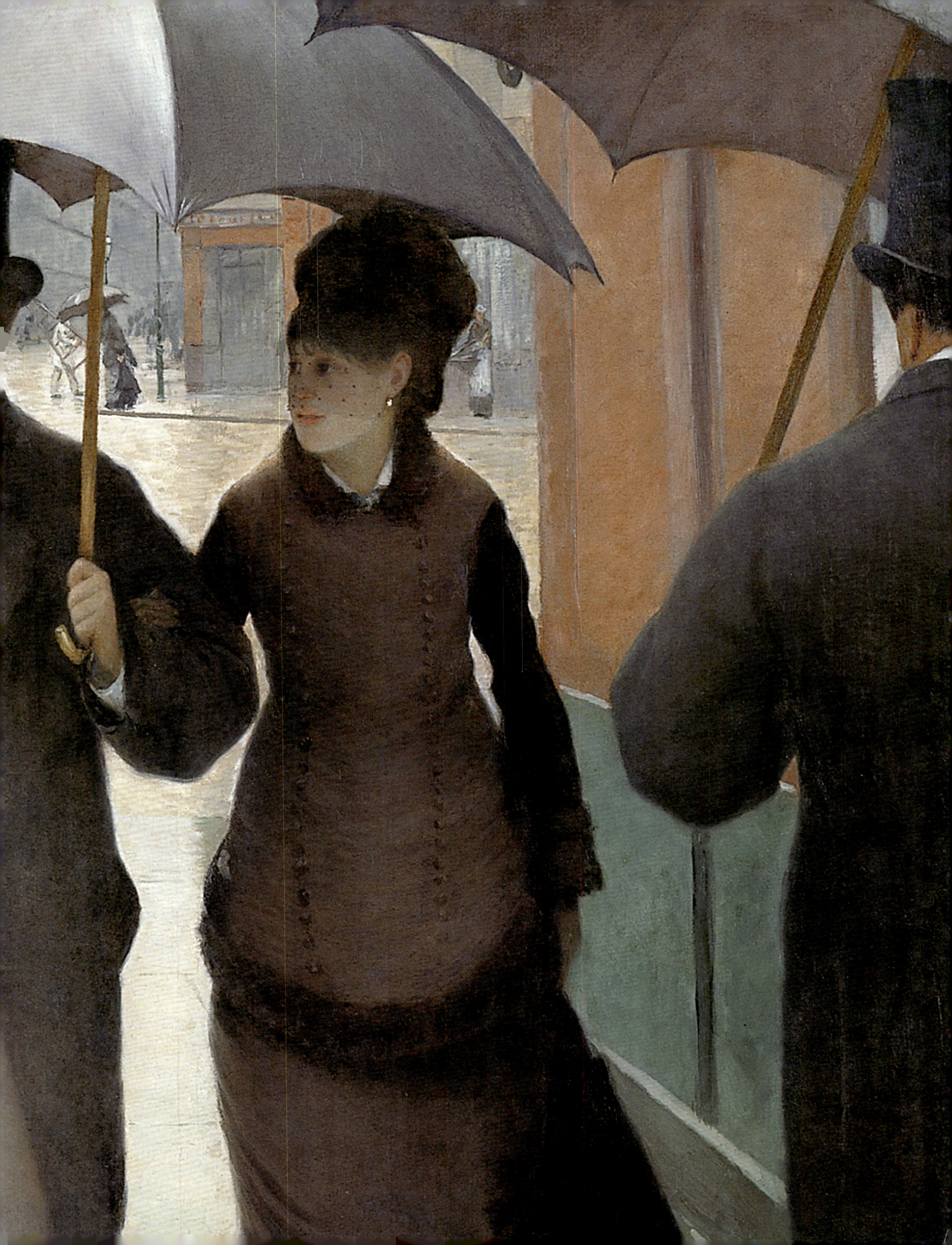

The Age of French Impressionism

Masterpieces from the Art Institute of Chicago

GLORIA GROOM AND DOUGLAS DRUICK

WITH THE ASSISTANCE OF DOROTA CHUDZICKA AND JILL SHAW

THE ART INSTITUTE OF CHICAGO

YALE UNIVERSITY PRESS, NEW HAVEN AND LONDON

This book is a revised and expanded edition of *The Age of Impressionism at the Art Institute of Chicago*, published in 2008 by the Art Institute of Chicago.

Printed in Italy

Library of Congress Control Number: 2010904626
ISBN: 978-0-300-16780-1 (cloth)
ISBN: 978-0-86559-240-7 (paper)

Published by
The Art Institute of Chicago
111 South Michigan Avenue
Chicago, Illinois 60603-6404
www.artic.edu

Distributed by
Yale University Press
302 Temple Street
P. O. Box 209040
New Haven, Connecticut 06520-9040
www.yalebooks.com

Produced by the Publications Department of the Art Institute of Chicago, Robert V. Sharp, Executive Director

Edited by Susan E. Weidemeyer with Susan F. Rossen

Production by Sarah E. Guernsey, Carolyn Ziebarth, and Kate Kotan

Photography research by Joseph Mohan

Designed and typeset by Joan Sommers Design, Chicago, Illinois

Separations by Professional Graphics, Rockford, Illinois

Printing and binding by Mondadori, Verona, Italy

COVER IMAGES:

Front: Georges Seurat. *A Sunday on La Grande Jatte—1884* (cat. 63) (detail), 1884–86.

Back: Edgar Degas. *Yellow Dancers (In the Wings)* (cat. 46), 1874/76.

DETAILS:

Frontispiece: Gustave Caillebotte. *Paris Street; Rainy Day* (cat. 24), 1877.

Page 6: Claude Monet. *Vétheuil* (cat. 95), 1901.

Page 8: Vincent van Gogh. *Fishing in Spring, the Pont de Clichy (Asnières)* (cat. 67), 1887.

Page 10: Pierre-Auguste Renoir. *Two Sisters (On the Terrace)* (cat. 34), 1881.

Page 27: Édouard Manet. *The Races at Longchamp* (cat. 8), 1866.

Page 47: Berthe Morisot. *Woman at Her Toilette* (cat. 25), 1875/80.

Page 107: Henri de Toulouse-Lautrec. *At the Moulin Rouge* (cat. 75), 1892/95.

Page 169: Claude Monet. *Waterloo Bridge, Sunlight Effect* (cat. 100), 1903.

Page 194: Pierre-Auguste Renoir. *Near the Lake* (cat. 33), 1879/80.

Page 198: Vincent van Gogh. *Self-Portrait* (cat. 69), 1887.

CONTENTS

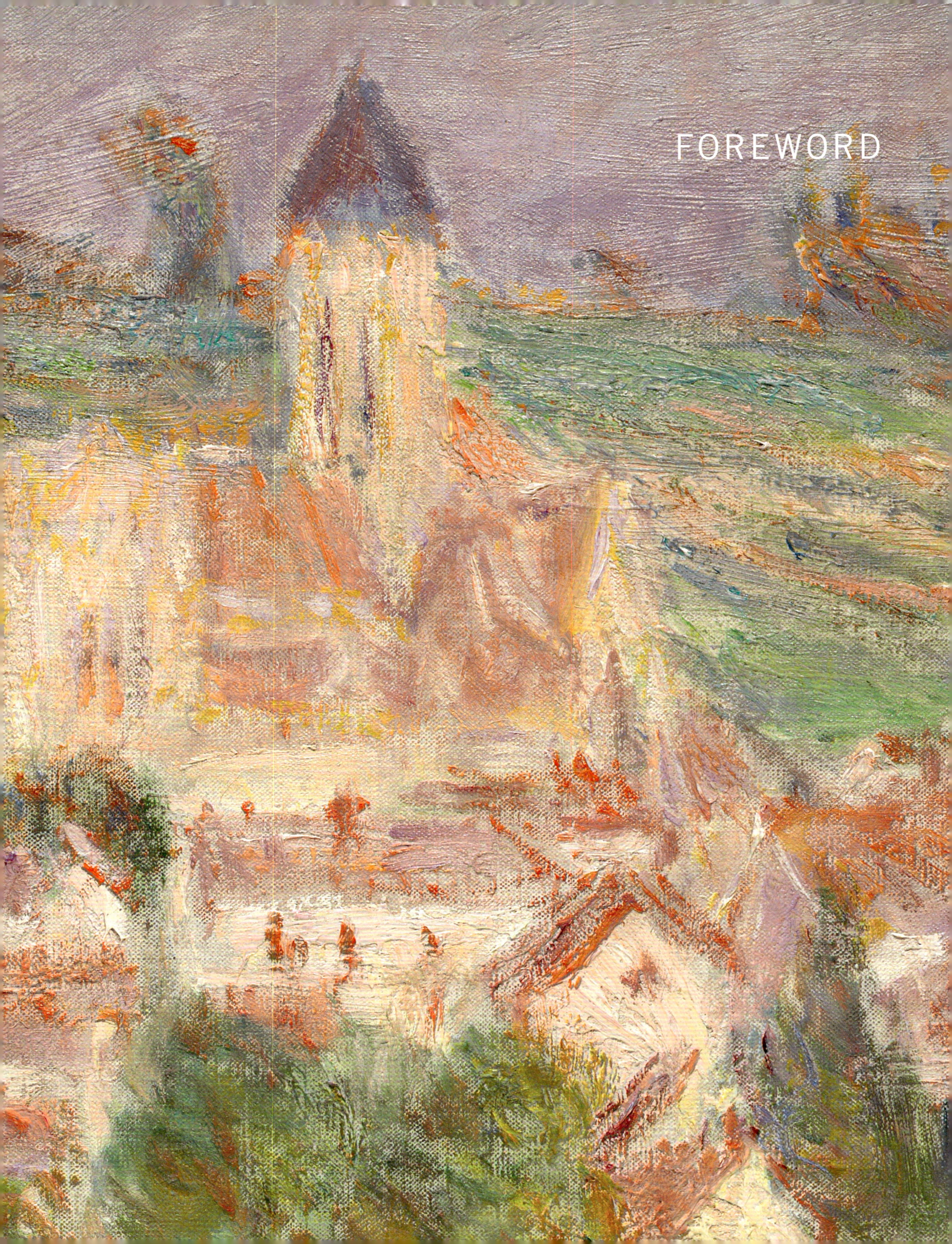

FOREWORD

The Art Institute of Chicago's holdings of Impressionist and Post-Impressionist paintings are among the very finest outside of France. We take great pride in this collection, which is beloved by all who visit the Art Institute. Indeed, it plays a central role in the history of both the museum and the city. And it reminds us that the Art Institute has always been dedicated to the art of its time.

The history of Chicago is well known. It was virtually destroyed by a great fire in 1871 and—with the development of new technologies that allowed for tall, steel-frame structures—rebuilt itself into a thriving metropolis in time for the World's Columbian Exposition of 1893. In 1889 the Art Institute's first director and president, William M. R. French (1843–1914), traveled with a group of civic leaders to Paris to attend the Exposition Universelle, the highlight of which was Gustave Eiffel's great iron tower. They were intent on evaluating the fair in anticipation of Chicago's own upcoming exposition, and while there, they also looked for recent works of art for the Art Institute's collection. Impressionist painting had been shown in increasingly popular exhibitions in Paris from 1874 to 1886. At the same time, commercial galleries were displaying contemporary art on a scale never before seen in the French capital. This art would be represented in an exhibition at the Columbian Exposition, thanks in particular to two of Chicago's earliest collectors of modern European art, Potter and Bertha Honoré Palmer. The generosity of the Palmers, and others whose names are included in the credit lines of the works that appear in this publication (among them, Frederic Clay Bartlett, Mrs. Lewis Larned Coburn, Mr. and Mrs. Martin A. Ryerson, and Charles H. and Mary F. S. Worcester), resulted in the Art Institute's encyclopedic representation of nineteenth-century French art.

Over the past fifty years, several generations of directors, curators, and conservators at the Art Institute have continued the commitment to the research, care, development, and presentation of this important part of the collection. Major monographic and group exhibition projects have forged notable relationships between scholars, conservators, and scientists, uncovering new information about the working and creative processes of many of the artists featured in this catalogue, including Frédéric Bazille, Gustave Caillebotte, Paul Cézanne, Edgar Degas, Paul Gauguin, Vincent van Gogh, Édouard Manet, Claude Monet, Pierre-Auguste Renoir, Georges Seurat, and Henri de Toulouse-Lautrec, as well as other major Post-Impressionist artists such as Pierre Bonnard, Odilon Redon, and Édouard Vuillard.

The Art Institute has also remained attentive to the display of our world-class collection, and in December 2008, we opened newly renovated and reinstalled Impressionist and Post-Impressionist galleries. Designed by the Chicago firm Vinci/Hamp Architects, Inc., long associated with the Art Institute and the preservation of Chicago's landmark buildings, the elegant reinstallation of these galleries has provided visitors and scholars with the opportunity to experience our extraordinary collection afresh, alongside a selection of sculpture and decorative arts from the same historical moment.

This publication highlights the history and importance of the Art Institute's collection of French Impressionist and Post-Impressionist art. The creation of the book has been the task of Gloria Groom, David and Mary Winton Green Curator of Nineteenth-Century European Painting and Sculpture, and Douglas Druick, Searle Curator and Chair of Medieval through Modern European Painting and Sculpture and Prince Trust Curator and Chair of Prints and Drawings, who work most closely with the collection and have published and lectured widely on it. We are deeply grateful to them for their devotion to the project, which has brought new research to bear upon well-known and well-loved works. This catalogue celebrating our collection's strengths builds upon our past accomplishments and incorporates newly acquired conservation information. It also serves as a prelude to a comprehensive and systematic analysis of the entire collection of nineteenth-century paintings, which we are undertaking for the first time since our founders began to acquire them for the Art Institute and the citizens of Chicago and beyond.

James Cuno
President and Eloise W. Martin Director
The Art Institute of Chicago

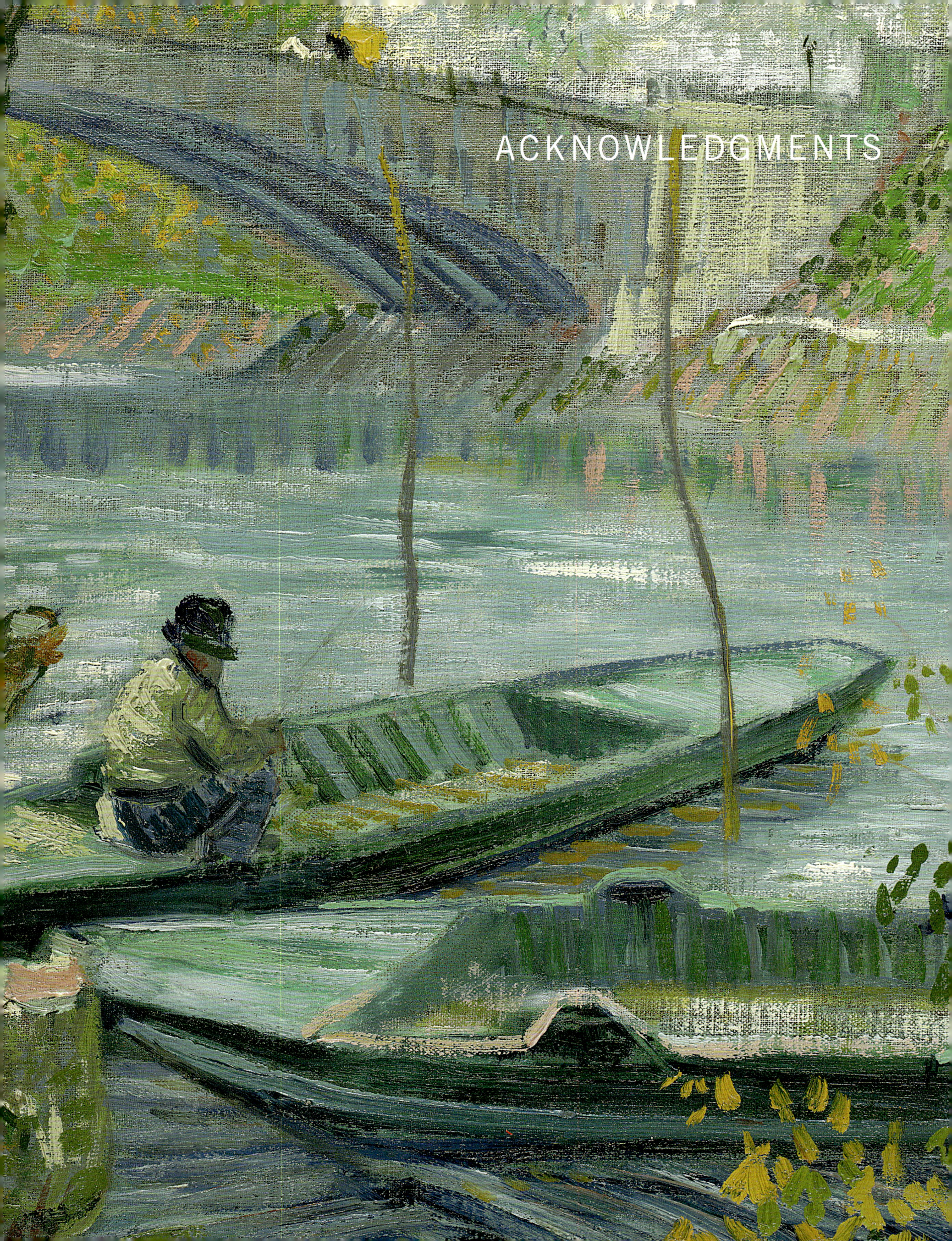

ACKNOWLEDGMENTS

This project was conceived under the direction of James Cuno, President and Eloise W. Martin Director of the Art Institute of Chicago. We thank him, along with Meredith Mack, former Deputy Director and Chief Operating Officer, and Dorothy Schroeder, Vice President for Exhibitions and Museum Administration, for their invaluable support.

Many other people in several departments in the museum are owed special thanks. The catalogue was produced in collaboration with a wonderful team in the Publications Department, headed by Robert V. Sharp, Executive Director of Publications. The task of organizing and editing the text for this book was beautifully handled by Susan Weidemeyer, an editor in the Publications Department, assisted by Susan F. Rossen, former Executive Director of Publications. Led by Sarah Guernsey, Director of Production, Carolyn Ziebarth, Kate Kotan, and Joseph Mohan were responsible for the book's visual elements and high production value. Photography was provided by the Department of Imaging: Director Christopher Gallagher, along with Robert Hashimoto, Caroline Nutley, and Amy Zavaleta, all of whom are under the direction of Sam Quigley, Vice President for Collections Management, Imaging, and Information Technology. The book owes its handsome design to Joan Sommers of Joan Sommers Design.

In the Art Institute's Archives, we owe particular thanks to Bart Ryckbosch for his assistance in unearthing important information on the museum's history for the illustrated chronology. We also thank Mary Woolever and Deborah Webb in that department. For their additional review of the chronology, we thank Jack Perry Brown, Executive Director of Libraries, and Robert V. Sharp. For their help with archival photography research, we acknowledge Mary Lou Perkins of the Woman's Board and Jane Allen, Paul Florian, and Randy White.

In the Department of Medieval through Modern European Painting and Sculpture, special thanks go to Jill Shaw and former department member Dorota Chudzicka, without whom this book would not have been possible. We are also grateful to current and former department members Geri Banik, Darren Burge, Robert Burnier, Stephanie D'Alessandro, Rachel Drescher, Adrienne Jeske, Jennifer Paoletti, Aza Quinn-Brauner, and Martha Wolff, as well as to our former interns Renee Inouye, Caroline Neely, and Anastasia Standa. In the Department of Conservation, Frank Zuccari, Grainger Executive Director of Conservation, and Kirk Vuillemot provided their expertise for the reframing of a number of featured paintings. We also acknowledge the efforts of Kelly Keegan, Allison Langley, Kristin Lister, Kim Muir, and Faye Wrubel, who, in addition to her diligent examination of the works, was always willing to share her knowledge of painting techniques with us. In the Department of Prints and Drawings, we want to acknowledge Rachel Freeman, Suzanne Folds McCullagh, Harriet Stratis, Emily Vokt, and Peter Zegers. We also wish to thank the following current and former Art Institute employees: in Museum Registration, Darrell Green, Patricia Loiko, Mary Solt, and John Molini and our art packers and handlers; in the Office of the General Counsel and Corporation Secretary, Julia E. Getzels and Maria Simon; in Museum Finance, Dawn Koster and Jeanne Ladd; in Marketing and Public Affairs, Carrie Heinonen, Erin Hogan, and Chai Lee; in Protection Services, Michelle Lehrman-Jenness; and in Graphic Design, Lyn DelliQuadri.

For this project, we have drawn upon the scholarship of authors who have previously published on the Art Institute's Impressionist and Post-Impressionist collection. We wish to acknowledge the work of Jean Sutherland Boggs, Richard Brettell, the late Andrew Forge, John Goodman, Sally Ruth May, Britt Salvesen, and Belinda Thomson. Research for this book went far beyond what is included in the selected bibliography. The important work of scholars we could not mention here will be fully credited in the upcoming scholarly catalogues on the Art Institute's collection of nineteenth-century European paintings.

Nonetheless, we would like to acknowledge the contribution of those individuals who helped us to address a number of questions still posed by these familiar works: Stephen Eisenman, Jodi Hauptman, Jean-François Heim, Robert Herbert, Joachim Pissarro, Susan Stein, Vérane Tesseau, Jayne Warman, and Mary Weaver Chapin. Special thanks go to Jill DeVonyar, an independent art historian, and Richard Kendall at the Sterling and Francine Clark Art Institute, Williamstown, Massachusetts; Aileen Ribeiro at the Courtauld Institute of Art, London; Richard Thomson at the University of Edinburgh; Louis van Tilborgh at the Van Gogh Museum, Amsterdam; and Juliet Wilson-Bareau, an independent art historian in London, all of whom generously shared their research and tirelessly responded to our inquiries. Finally, our thanks go to Jean Coyner, an independent art historian in Paris, for contributing her translation skills to the project.

Gloria Groom and Douglas Druick

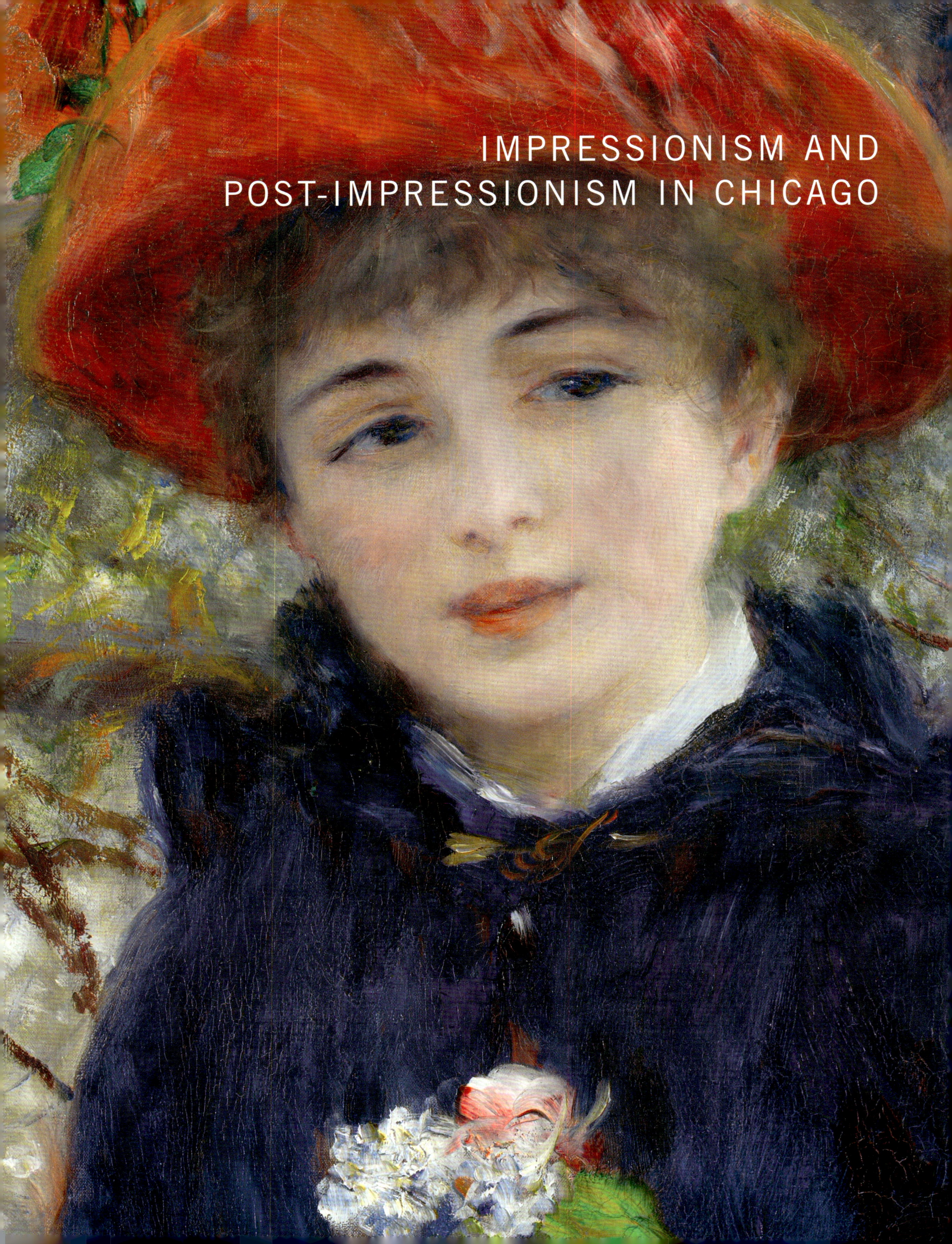
IMPRESSIONISM AND
POST-IMPRESSIONISM IN CHICAGO

BY JILL SHAW AND DOROTA CHUDZICKA

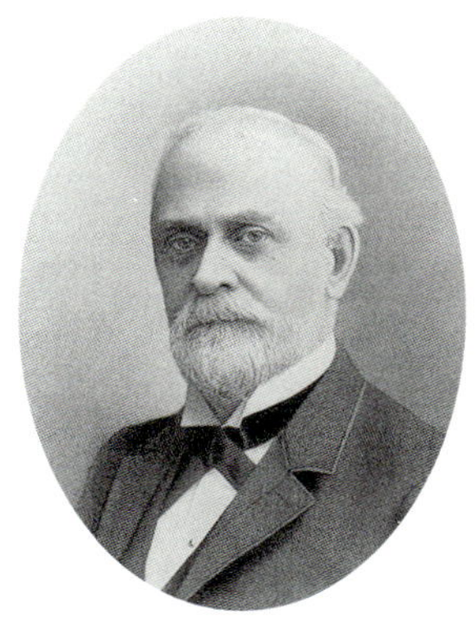

Potter Palmer (1826–1902).

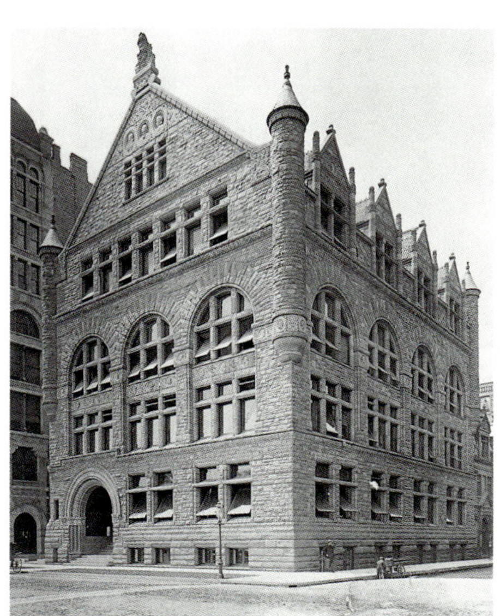

From 1887 to 1893, the Art Institute occupies a building designed by architects Burnham and Root. It is located at Michigan Avenue and Van Buren Street.

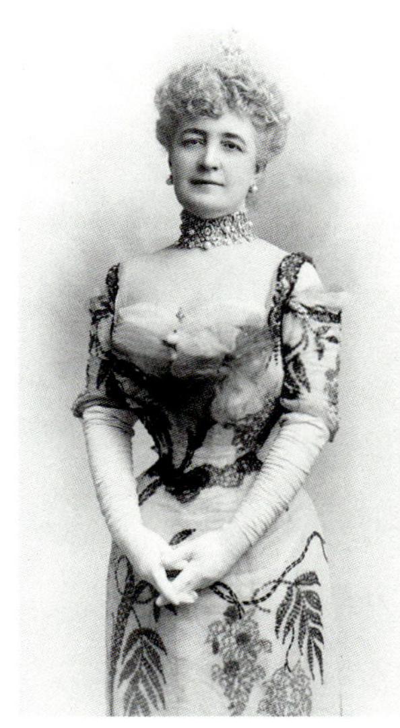

Bertha Honoré Palmer (1849–1918).

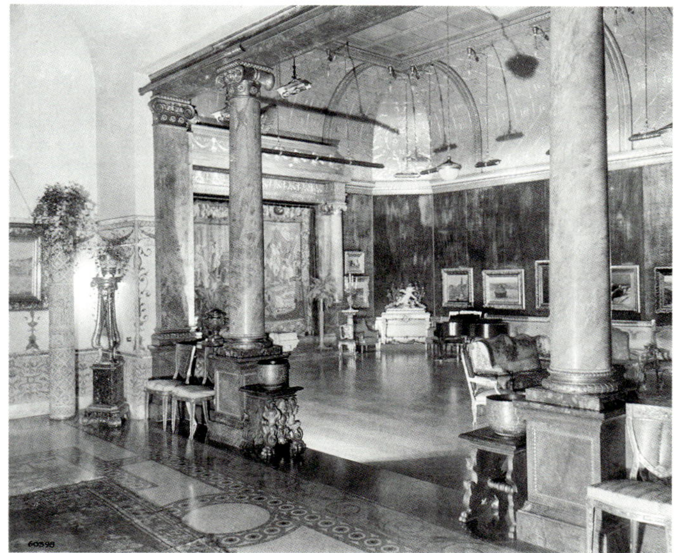

Interior of the Palmers' residence with paintings by Claude Monet, including *Stack of Wheat* (cat. 92), arranged along the far wall.

1879

On May 24, the Chicago Academy of Fine Arts is created from the Academy of Design, an institution established by a group of artists in 1866. In December 1882, the Academy will undergo a change in name, becoming the Art Institute of Chicago.

1888

In November the Thurber Gallery, Chicago, exhibits works by Claude Monet, Camille Pissarro, and Alfred Sisley. The exhibition is the earliest documented display of French Impressionist art in Chicago.

1889

Chicagoans Potter Palmer (1826–1902), a hotelier and real-estate developer, and his wife, Bertha Honoré Palmer (1849–1918), begin collecting works by Impressionist artists. Through their friendship with the artist Mary Cassatt and the art consultant Sara Tyson Halloway, the Palmers quickly become enthusiastic supporters of "the new painting." Among their first purchases is a pastel by Edgar Degas (*On the Stage*, 1876–77; Art Institute of Chicago), acquired from the dealer Paul Durand-Ruel in Paris.

1890

On September 3, the Inter-State Industrial Exposition of Chicago opens in a building located on the future site of the Art Institute. The exposition includes a fine-arts section with nearly five hundred oils, watercolors, and pastels gathered together by Sara Tyson Halloway, the secretary of its art department. Works by Eugène-Louis Boudin, Henri Fantin-Latour, Degas, Monet, Pissarro, Pierre-Auguste Renoir, and Sisley, among others, are exhibited.

1891

Martin A. Ryerson (1856–1932) makes his first purchase of Monet's work, probably *The "Red Road" near Menton* (1884; private collection), from the Durand-Ruel Gallery, New York. The painting will enter the Art Institute's collection with the Ryerson bequest in 1933 and will be deaccessioned in 1983. Ryerson, a trustee of the Art Institute from 1890 to 1924 and its vice president for many years, and his wife, Carrie Hutchinson Ryerson (1859–1937), will become the museum's greatest single donors.

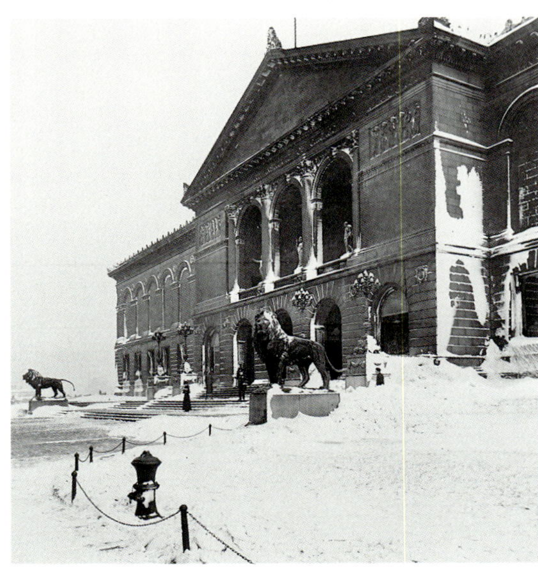

View of the Art Institute's new home on Michigan Avenue, c. 1894, after Mrs. Henry Field commissions and donates two bronze lions by Edward Kemeys to stand at the entrance.

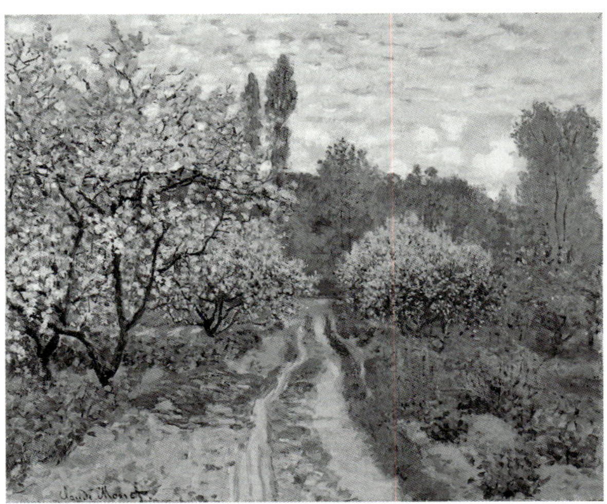

Claude Monet. *Pommiers en fleurs (Le Printemps)*, 1872. Collection of the Union League Club of Chicago. This work is shown in an 1895 Monet exhibition at the Art Institute.

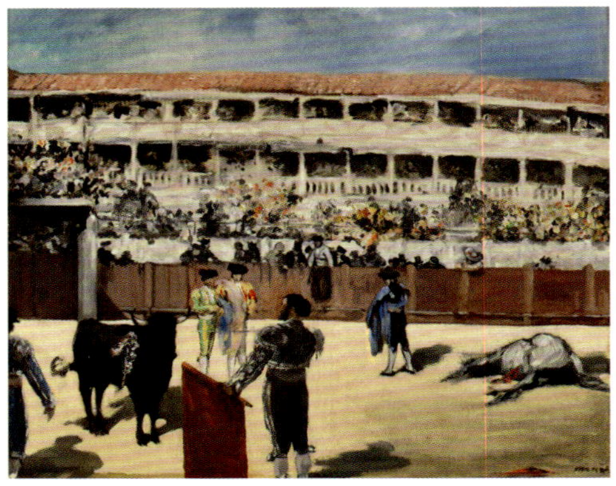

Édouard Manet. *Bullfight*, 1865/66 (cat. 9). This painting is included in an 1895 Manet exhibition and the 1913 Armory Show.

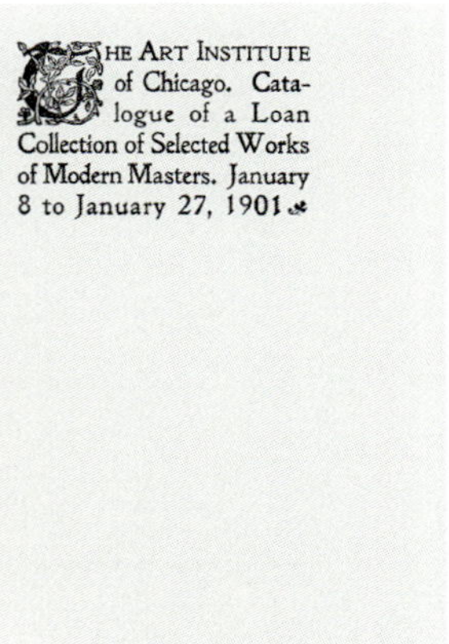

The Art Institute of Chicago. Catalogue of a Loan Collection of Selected Works of Modern Masters. January 8 to January 27, 1901.

Catalogue cover for the 1901 exhibition *Loan Collection of Selected Works of Modern Masters*, on view at the Art Institute.

1892

In February construction begins on a new building on Michigan Avenue at Adams Street. Designed by the Boston architectural firm of Shepley, Rutan, and Coolidge and planned in cooperation with the 1893 World's Columbian Exposition, the Allerton Building, as it will later be named, is first occupied by the World's Congress Auxiliary of the Columbian Exposition. After the exposition closes, on October 31, 1893, the Art Institute takes possession of the building, which formally opens on December 8. Surrounded by later wings, it continues to serve as the main entrance to the museum.

In May the Palmers attend the opening of a Renoir exhibition at the Durand-Ruel Gallery, Paris. In the weeks before the show, they acquire ten Renoirs from the dealer. At the same exhibition, they see Monet, and by the end of 1892, they own a number of his works, including at least eight canvases from his series *Stacks of Wheat*. They display their collection prominently on the red velvet-covered walls of their residence at 1350 North Lake Shore Drive, Chicago.

1893

Bertha Honoré Palmer is the president of the Board of Lady Managers of the World's Columbian Exposition. Among its myriad displays is *Loan Collection: Foreign Masterpieces Owned in the United States*; most of the 126 works featured are by nineteenth-century French artists. The Palmers lend fifteen paintings, including canvases by Pissarro and Sisley.

1895

Between March 18 and March 28, the Art Institute hosts Monet's first-ever one-man exhibition held in a museum. Comprised of twenty paintings, it is one of a series of shows mounted this year by Durand-Ruel in order to introduce the artist's work to the American public. *Pommiers en fleurs (Le Printemps)* is purchased from the exhibition and enters the collection of the Union League Club of Chicago.

On May 29, *15 Works by Édouard Manet* opens at the Art Institute. A number of the featured paintings had been shown earlier this year at the Durand-Ruel Gallery, New York. Édouard Manet's *Bullfight* (cat. 9), exhibited at the New York venue, will be acquired from Durand-Ruel by Martin A. Ryerson in 1911 and later bequeathed to the Art Institute.

1901

Loan Collection of Selected Works of Modern Masters is held at the Art Institute from January 8 to January 27. It includes examples by a number of Impressionist artists—such as Boudin, Monet, Pissarro, and Sisley—lent by Durand-Ruel. Ryerson loans a painting by Stanislas Lépine, a contemporary of the Impressionists, and Potter Palmer lends works by Jean-Charles Cazin to the exhibition.

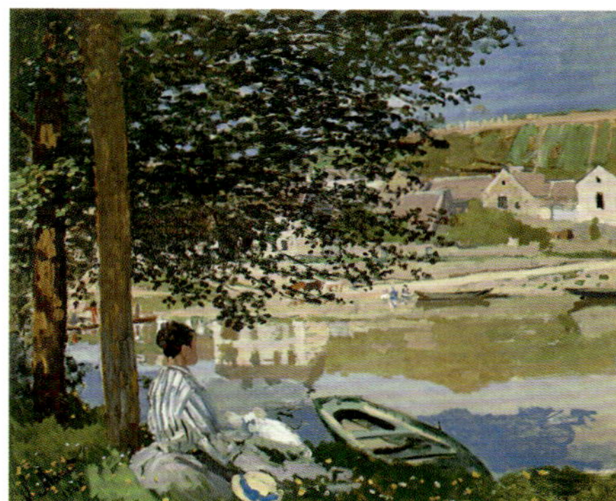

Claude Monet. *On the Bank of the Seine, Bennecourt*, 1868 (cat. 17). This painting is featured in a 1905 Boston show and a 1910 Chicago exhibition.

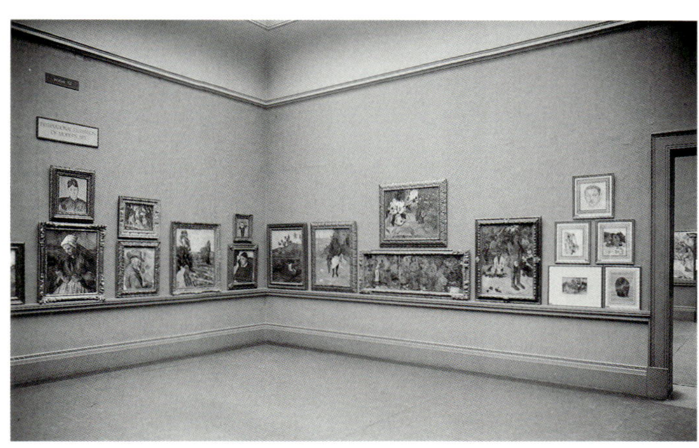

Room 52 of the Chicago installation of the 1913 Armory Show, including works by Paul Cézanne and Paul Gauguin. Four of Gauguin's drawings and watercolors (at right) will eventually enter the Art Institute's collection.

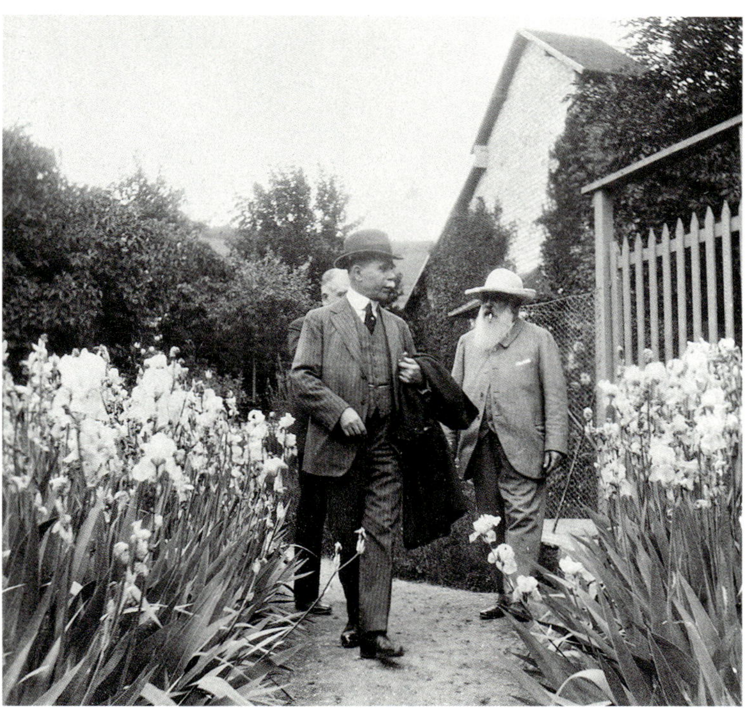

Martin A. Ryerson (1856–1932) with Monet (at right) and possibly Joseph Durand-Ruel at Giverny, France, June 1920.

1903

In February the Art Institute becomes the first American museum to acquire a work by Monet. It will deaccession the painting, *Pourville in Bad Weather* (1896; private collection), purchased from Durand-Ruel, in 1930.

1905

In March the Copley Society, Boston, hosts an exhibition of ninety-five paintings by Monet (along with eleven sculptures by Auguste Rodin) that is heralded as "the largest collection of works of the famous French Impressionist ever brought together in the United States." The greatest single lender is James F. Sutton of the American Art Association, but loans come from collectors throughout the country, including Chicagoans Mrs. John Jay Borland, the Palmers (who loan seven Monets, including *On the Bank of the Seine, Bennecourt* [cat. 17]), and Martin A. Ryerson.

1910

Paintings from the Collection of Mrs. Potter Palmer, on view at the Art Institute from May to August, features fifty-three works from this groundbreaking collection. Nine are by Monet, including *On the Bank of the Seine, Bennecourt* (cat. 17), *Stacks of Wheat (Sunset, Snow Effect)* (cat. 90), and *Bordighera* (cat. 56).

1913

From March 24 to April 16, the Art Institute hosts the controversial International Exhibition of Modern Art, better known as the Armory Show. Exhibited the previous month at the 69th Regiment Armory, New York, it is the most comprehensive assemblage of European modern art held in the United States to date and attracts 188,650 visitors in Chicago. Manet's *Bullfight* (cat. 9) is lent by Ryerson to the New York exhibition.

1920

On June 4, Joseph Durand-Ruel, the Ryersons, and Mrs. Charles (Frances) Hutchinson (1857–1936), the wife of the president of the Art Institute's Board of Trustees, visit Monet at Giverny. They travel there in order to see the artist's recent *Water Lilies* murals and buy them for the Art Institute. Although this transaction is not realized, the Ryersons have acquired seventeen Monets by this time.

The Art Institute stages an exhibition of work by Degas from March 9 to April 1. It includes four paintings, fifteen pastels, and twenty-three drawings.

Pierre-Auguste Renoir. *Acrobats at the Cirque Fernando (Francisca and Angelina Wartenberg)*, 1879 (cat. 32).

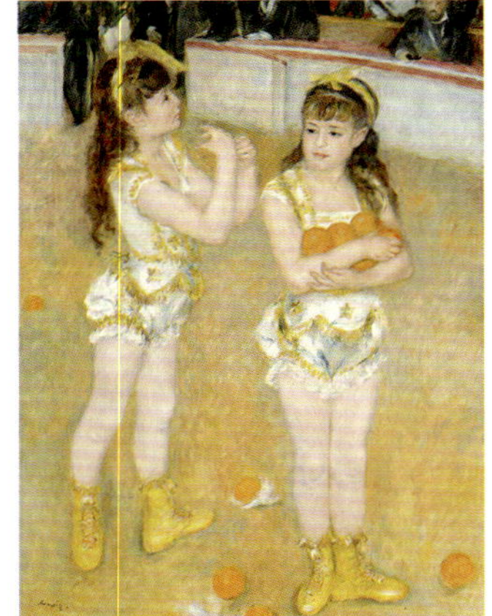

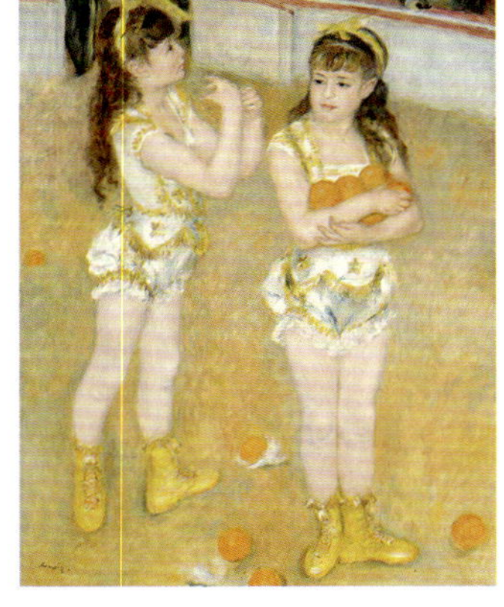

Lucie Bru Cousturier in front of *La Grande Jatte* (cat. 63), early 1920s. Frederic Clay Bartlett will buy the painting from her in 1924.

The actor Kirk Douglas next to the Art Institute's *Self-Portrait* (cat. 69) by Vincent van Gogh, a work in the Joseph Winterbotham Collection. Douglas will play the role of Van Gogh in the 1956 film *Lust for Life*.

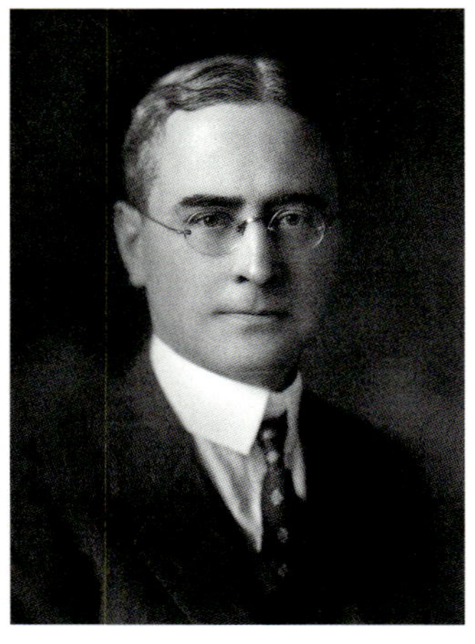

Potter Palmer II (1875–1943).

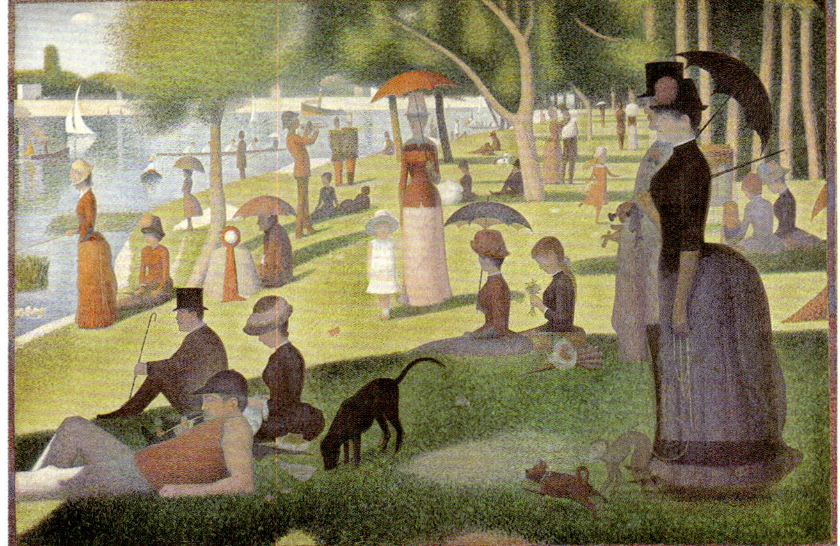

Georges Seurat. *A Sunday on La Grande Jatte—1884*, 1884–86 (cat. 63).

1921

Joseph Winterbotham (1852–1925) makes an initial gift of $50,000 to the Art Institute with an unusual stipulation: the money will be invested and the museum will use the interest to build a collection of thirty-five European paintings. Once the first group of thirty-five is assembled, any of these can be sold or exchanged to ensure that "the purchase of paintings, as time goes on, is toward superior works of art and of greater merit and continuous improvement." Paintings such as Paul Gauguin's *Woman in Front of a Still Life by Cézanne* (cat. 78), Vincent van Gogh's *Self-Portrait* (cat. 69), and Henri de Toulouse-Lautrec's *Equestrienne (At the Cirque Fernando)* (cat. 73) will all become part of the Joseph Winterbotham Collection at the Art Institute.

1922

Four years after Bertha Honoré Palmer's death, her sons, Honoré (1874–1964) and Potter II (1875–1943), together with Robert Harshe, the Art Institute's director from 1921 to 1938, and several trustees, select works from her collection and acquire them with money bequeathed to the museum in her will. At the same time, Honoré and Potter II present the Art Institute with additional works that they have inherited from their mother. Along with examples by French Romantic and Barbizon artists, the Palmer gift brings the first major group of French Impressionist art to the museum's collection. Of these works, Renoir's *Acrobats at the Cirque Fernando (Francisca and Angelina Wartenberg)* (cat. 32) was Mrs. Palmer's favorite; she took it with her on her European trips and visits to the East Coast. Potter II will serve as the museum's president from 1925 to 1943.

1924

In June Robert Harshe receives news from the artist and trustee Frederic Clay Bartlett (1873–1953) that he has acquired "almost by a miracle . . . the finest modern picture in France." He acquires Georges Seurat's *A Sunday on La Grande Jatte—1884* (cat. 63) from the artist Lucie Bru Cousturier, whose father had purchased it in 1900.

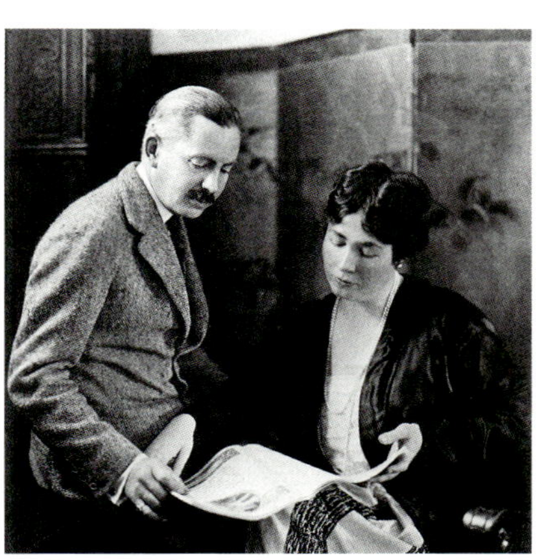

Frederic Clay (1873–1953) and Helen Birch Bartlett (1883–1925), c. 1923.

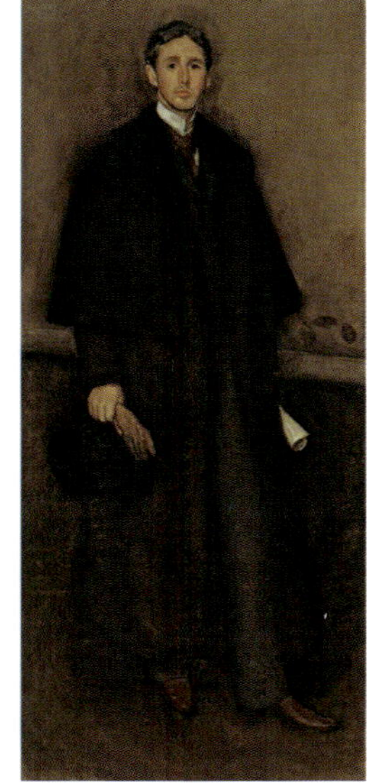

James McNeill Whistler (American, 1834–1903). *Arrangement in Flesh Color and Brown: Portrait of Arthur Jerome Eddy*, 1894. The Art Institute of Chicago, Arthur Jerome Eddy Memorial Collection, 1931.501.

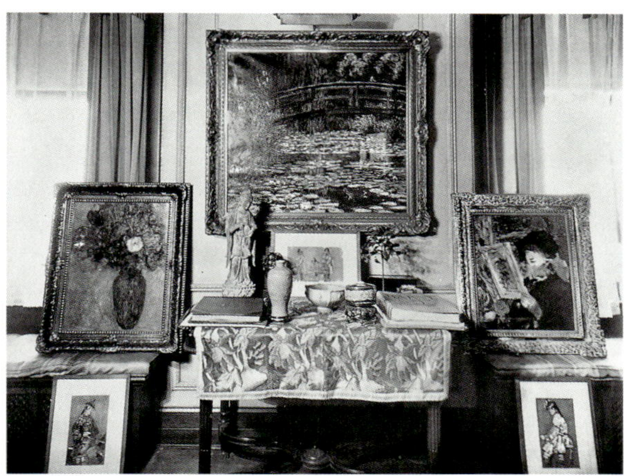

A view of Mrs. Lewis Larned Coburn's Blackstone Hotel apartment showing her casual, eccentric display of artwork, including Manet's *Woman Reading* (cat. 27) and Monet's *Water Lily Pond* (cat. 103).

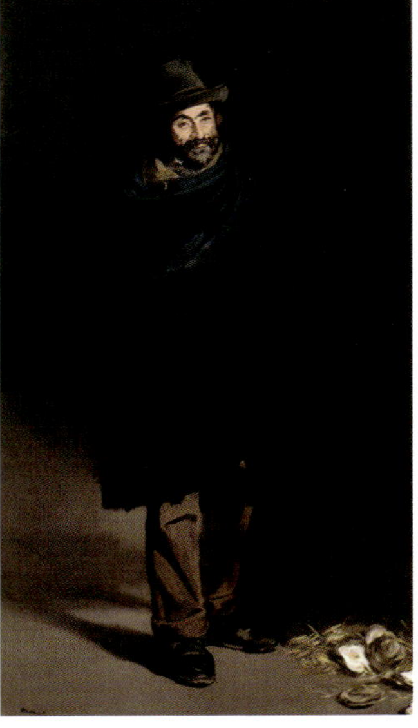

Édouard Manet. *Beggar with Oysters (Philosopher)*, 1865/67 (cat. 2). This canvas is acquired from the estate of Arthur Jerome Eddy (1859–1920) in 1931.

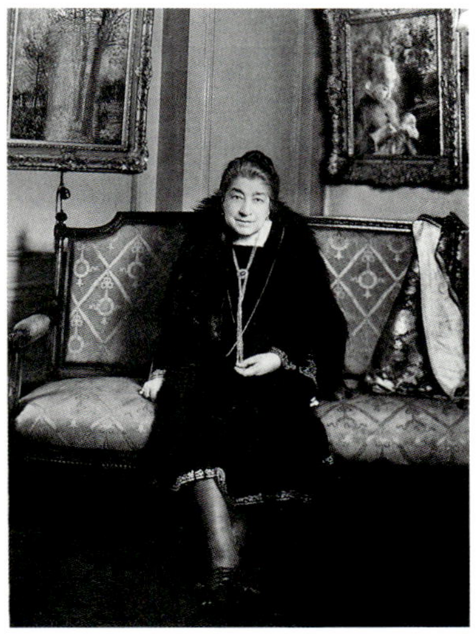

Mrs. Lewis Larned Coburn (1856–1932) with Renoir's *Young Woman Sewing* (cat. 35) at upper right.

1926

As a memorial to his second wife, Helen Birch (1883–1925), Frederic Clay Bartlett presents the Art Institute with *La Grande Jatte* (cat. 63), along with over twenty other significant Post-Impressionist paintings by artists such as Paul Cézanne (cat. 80), Gauguin (cat. 84), and Van Gogh (cats. 66 and 70). Proposed in December 1925, the Helen Birch Bartlett Memorial Collection officially enters the museum in 1926. Bartlett will make several additions and deletions to the collection in the late 1920s, finally adding Lautrec's *Ballet Dancers* (1885–86) in 1931. He considers this collection of key Post-Impressionist pictures to be a way for the Art Institute to increase its representation of modern art, previously exemplified largely by the Impressionists.

1930

The Art Institute opens a loan exhibition of over 250 works—including paintings, drawings, prints, and posters—by Lautrec.

1931

The Art Institute receives twenty-three objects, including Manet's *Beggar with Oysters (Philosopher)* (cat. 2), from the estate of Arthur Jerome Eddy (1859–1920), a prominent Chicago lawyer. In addition to being a pioneering champion of modern art, Eddy wrote several books, including *Cubists and Post-Impressionism* (1914), which was the first comprehensive text published in English on the subject. He was also instrumental in bringing the 1913 Armory Show to Chicago and acquired many paintings and sculptures from it.

1932

The exhibition *Mrs. L. L. Coburn Collection of Modern Paintings and Watercolors* is displayed at the Art Institute from April 6 to October 9. Annie Swan Coburn (1856–1932) had initially purchased American art, gradually expanding her collection to include French Impressionist paintings. Upon her death, nearly two months after the opening of this exhibition, her will reveals a gift to the museum of over one hundred paintings, pastels, and watercolors, many of which are important Impressionist and Post-Impressionist works; they will be officially accessioned in 1933.

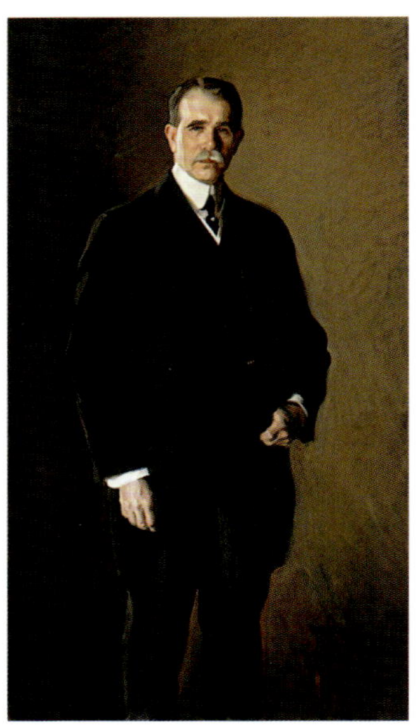

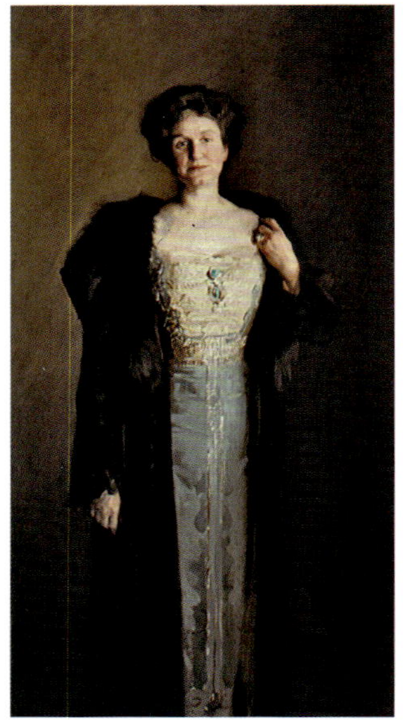

Far left: Louis Betts (American, 1873–1961). *Martin A. Ryerson,* 1913. The Art Institute of Chicago, Mr. and Mrs. Martin A. Ryerson Collection, 1933.1183.

Left: Louis Betts. *Mrs. Martin A. Ryerson,* 1912. The Art Institute of Chicago, Mrs. Martin A. Ryerson Collection, 1935.433.

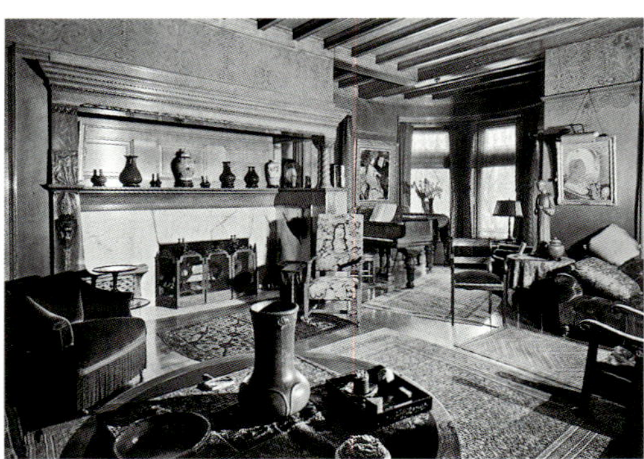

Interior of the Ryersons' Chicago home with Renoir's *Woman at the Piano* (cat. 30) hanging over the piano. This was Mrs. Ryerson's favorite painting.

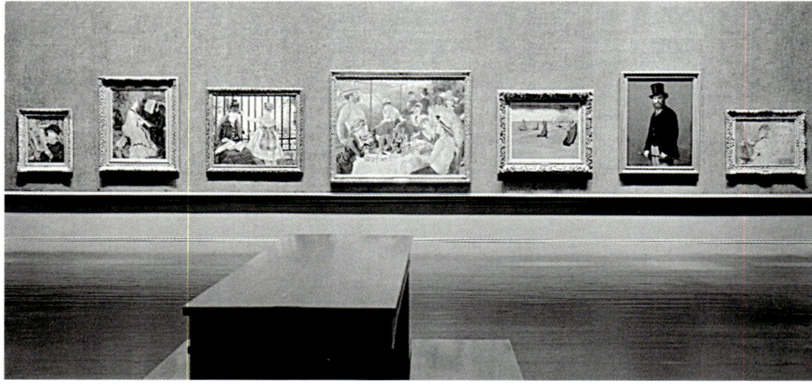

A gallery at the 1933 Century of Progress Exhibition of Paintings and Sculpture at the Art Institute. Among the works on view are, left to right, Manet's *Woman Reading* (cat. 27), Renoir's *Woman at the Piano* (cat. 30), Manet's *Steamboat Leaving Boulogne* (cat. 10), Henri Fantin-Latour's *Édouard Manet* (cat. 6), and Berthe Morisot's *Woman at Her Toilette* (cat. 25). In the center hangs Renoir's famous *Luncheon of the Boating Party* (1880–81; Phillips Collection, Washington, D.C.).

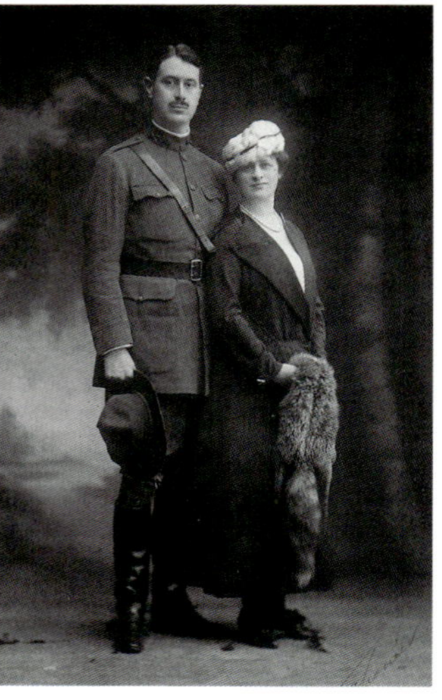

Colonel Robert R. (1880–1955) and Amy Irwin McCormick (1880–1939).

1933

Upon Martin A. Ryerson's death, the Art Institute receives the initial bequest of the Mr. and Mrs. Martin A. Ryerson Collection. This unprecedented gift—totaling over two hundred European and American paintings, in addition to textiles, European decorative arts, sculptures, prints, and drawings—remains the greatest single donation of art in the museum's history. A number of works will stay in the Ryerson home until Mrs. Ryerson's death in 1937.

In conjunction with the Century of Progress Exposition commemorating Chicago's centennial, the Art Institute organizes an exhibition of over one thousand works of art from the early Renaissance to the present. It runs from June 1 to November 1. Assembled primarily from North American collections, the show illuminates the progress of art collecting on this side of the Atlantic. The Century of Progress Exposition proves so popular that it will reopen the following year, to which the Art Institute will respond by staging a second loan exhibition, from June 1 to November 1, 1934.

Prior to the two Century of Progress exhibitions, the Art Institute's collections had been organized according to donor. These exhibitions prompt the museum to reinstall its permanent collection chronologically, an arrangement that has continued to the present day.

1940

The Art Institute stages an exhibition of paintings from the collection of Colonel and Mrs. Robert R. McCormick from April 17 to June 2. The show features nineteen primarily nineteenth- and twentieth-century French paintings, as well as four works painted by Mrs. McCormick (1880–1939). A great-nephew of the inventor and businessman Cyrus McCormick, the colonel (1880–1955) is the publisher of the *Chicago Tribune*. In addition to seven other works of art, he will give Cézanne's *The Bathers* (cat. 81) and Degas's *Two Dancers* (cat. 51) to the Art Institute in 1942 as part of the Amy McCormick Memorial Collection.

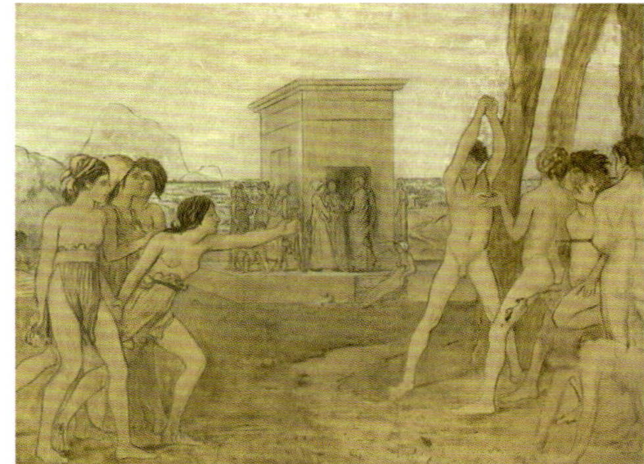

Edgar Degas. *Young Spartan Girls Challenging Boys*, c. 1860 (cat. 44). This painting will be purchased in 1961 through funds provided by the Worcesters.

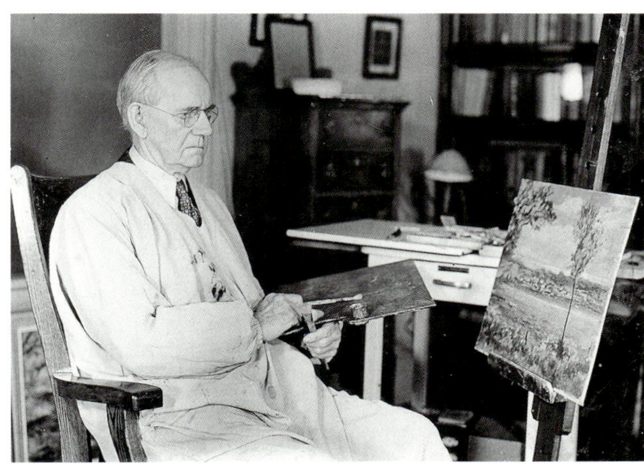

Charles H. Worcester (1864–1956) at his easel.

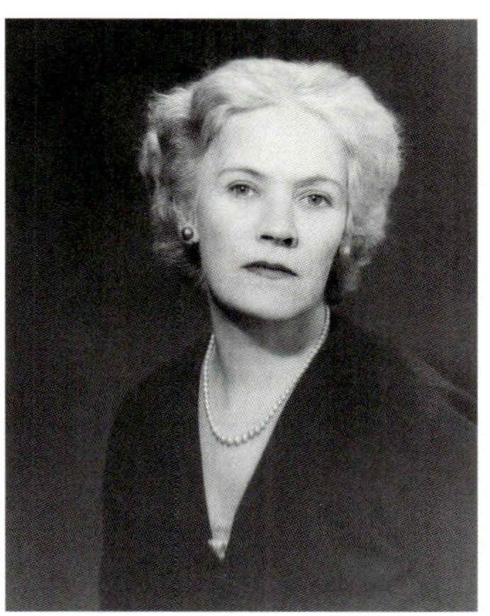

Kate Lancaster Brewster (1879–1947) as photographed by Man Ray (American, 1890–1976) in 1930 (Art Institute of Chicago, 1964.409).

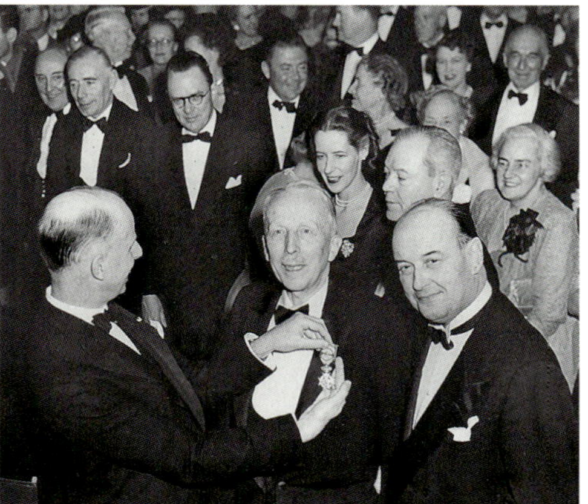

Vincent W. van Gogh (front row, center), the artist's nephew, at the 1950 Van Gogh exhibition opening. Behind him to the left is the Art Institute's director, Daniel Catton Rich.

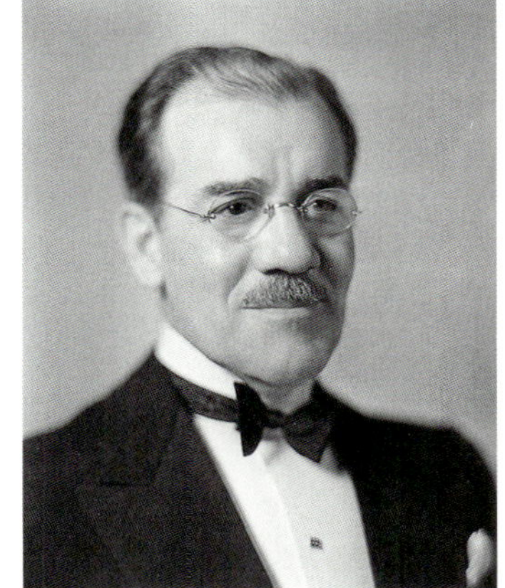

Walter S. Brewster (1872–1954).

1941

A monumental loan exhibition of 272 primarily nineteenth-century French paintings, watercolors, and drawings from over twenty European institutions and many private collections opens at the Art Institute in April. Organized by the French government, it traveled to South America in May 1939. When World War II broke out in Europe, the De Young Museum, San Francisco, arranged for the exhibition to tour the United States. Portions of the show are seen at the De Young and the Metropolitan Museum of Art, New York. The Art Institute is the first American venue to display the entire exhibition.

1944

For financial reasons, the Art Institute's Board of Trustees directs the administration to sell many works—including Old Master, Barbizon, and Impressionist paintings—at two auctions at Parke-Bernet Galleries, New York.

1947

Charles H. (1864–1956) and Mary F. S. (1861–1954) Worcester present seventy paintings, drawings, and sculptures from their wide-ranging collection to the Art Institute; the donation includes Monet's *Boats on the Beach at Étretat* (cat. 58) and Renoir's *The Laundress* (cat. 31). They also leave funds that will allow the museum to purchase Gustave Caillebotte's *Paris Street; Rainy Day* (cat. 24) and Degas's *Young Spartan Girls Challenging Boys* (cat. 44).

1950

A comprehensive exhibition of Van Gogh's work opens at the Art Institute on February 1. Co-organized with the Metropolitan Museum of Art, the Chicago show features over 150 works. Nearly fifty paintings and many drawings are lent by Vincent W. van Gogh, the artist's nephew, who attends the Chicago opening.

An exhibition of sixty-three paintings, sculptures, prints, and drawings recently donated to the Art Institute as part of the bequest of Kate Lancaster Brewster (1879–1947) goes on view. Kate Brewster was the president of the Chicago Public School Art Society, and her husband, Walter S. Brewster (1872–1954), a stockbroker, was a museum trustee. He contributes greatly to the Art Institute, including donations of funds, his collection of Whistleriana, and other gifts and bequests to the Department of Prints and Drawings.

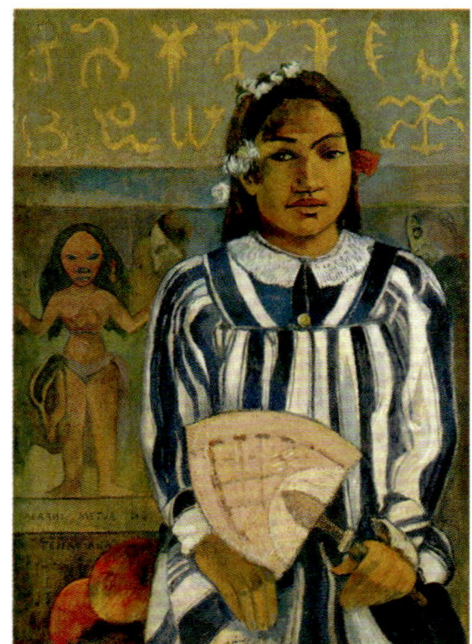

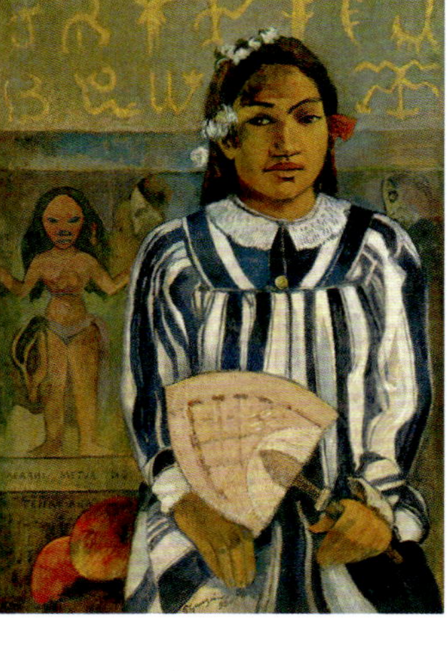

Paul Gauguin. *The Ancestors of Tehamana*, 1893 (cat. 83). This work is in a 1955 exhibition organized by the Art Institute in memory of Chauncey McCormick.

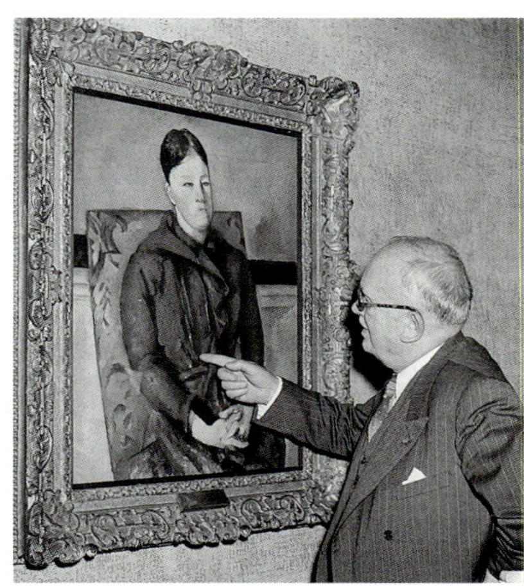

Vincent Auriol, president of France, in front of *Madame Cézanne in a Yellow Chair* (cat. 77), which appears in a 1952 Cézanne exhibition at the Art Institute.

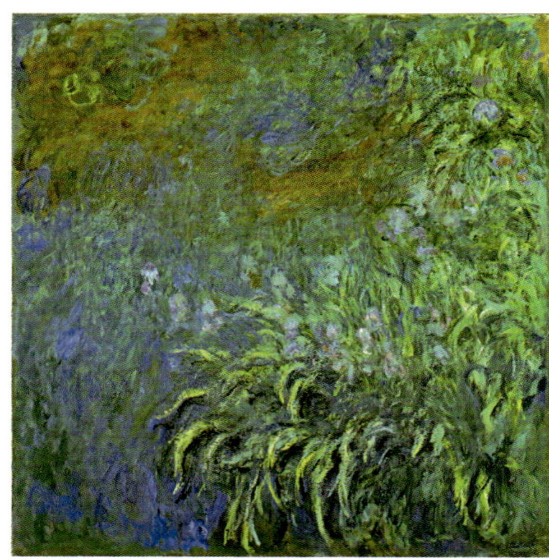

Monet's *Iris* (1922/26) is purchased by the Art Institute in 1956.

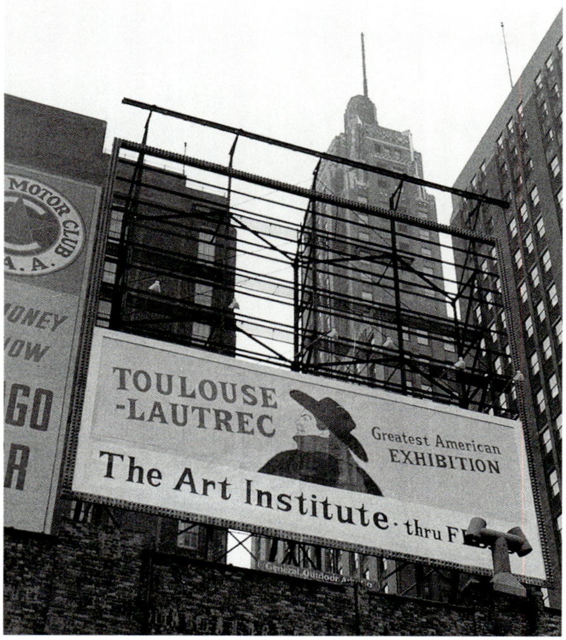

Billboard in the Chicago Loop advertising the Art Institute's 1956 Lautrec exhibition.

1952

In collaboration with the Metropolitan Museum of Art, the Art Institute holds an exhibition of over one hundred of Cézanne's paintings, watercolors, and drawings from February 7 to March 16. This retrospective includes loans from museums and collectors across four continents.

1955

From January 20 to February 20, the Art Institute exhibits *Great French Paintings: An Exhibition in Memory of Chauncey McCormick*. Chauncey McCormick (1884–1954), president of the Art Institute from 1944 to 1954, made a number of gifts to the museum, together with his wife, Marion Deering McCormick (1886–1965). Mrs. McCormick and her sister, Barbara Deering Danielson (1888–1987), also donated numerous masterpieces of Spanish painting that had belonged to their father, Charles Deering (1852–1927). The nearly forty works on view in this loan exhibition include Gauguin's *The Ancestors of Tehamana* (cat. 83). The McCormicks' son Charles Deering McCormick will present this painting to the museum in 1980. He, along with his brothers, Brooks and Roger McCormick, will make many other gifts to the Art Institute, including Van Gogh's *Fishing in Spring* (cat. 67).

1956

Nearly 250 paintings, drawings, prints, and posters by Lautrec are exhibited at the Art Institute from January 10 to February 15. This comprehensive show is organized in collaboration with the Philadelphia Museum of Art and the Albi Museum, France (now known as the Musée Toulouse-Lautrec).

Katharine Kuh, Art Institute publicist, educator, and curator from 1943 to 1959, facilitates the purchase of Monet's *Iris* from Katia Granoff's gallery in Paris. The painting, one of the canvases left in the artist's Giverny studio after his death, had recently been put on the market by his son Michel. This purchase, along with other late Monet works that will enter public and private collections around the same time, initiates a reevaluation of Monet's art, especially his *Water Lilies* series, now seen as the culmination of his career. Alfred H. Barr, Jr., director of the Museum of Modern Art, New York, is equally interested in buying *Iris*, but he fails to persuade Kuh to give up acquiring the painting for the Art Institute.

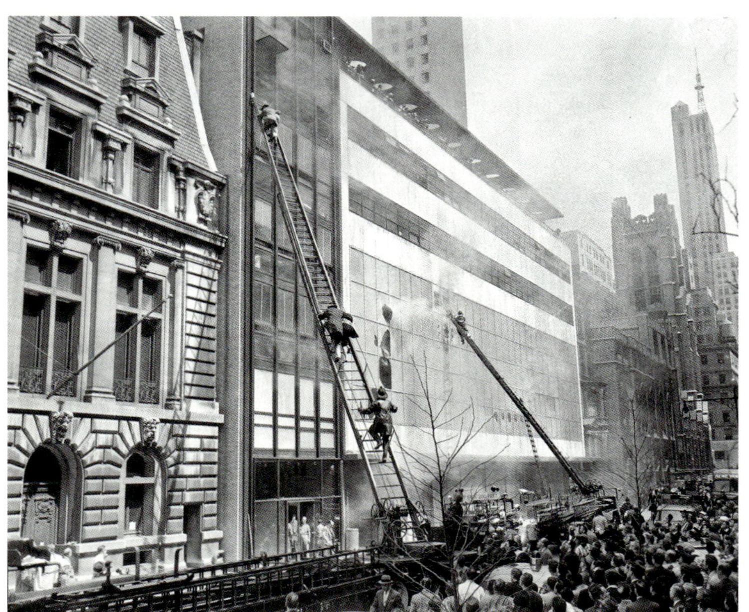

Fire at the Museum of Modern Art, New York, on April 15, 1958, during a Seurat exhibition, to which the Art Institute has loaned *La Grande Jatte* (cat. 63).

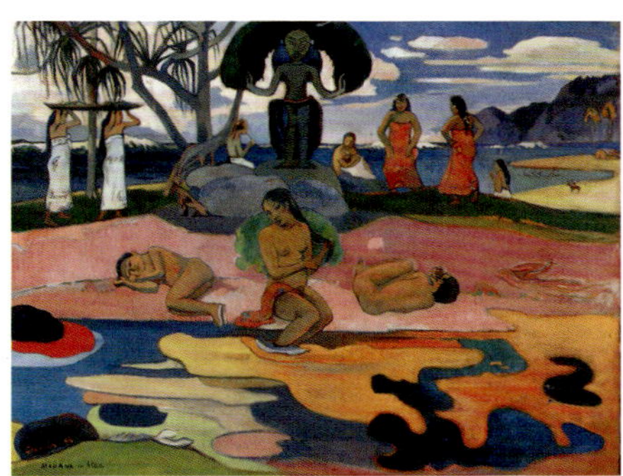

Paul Gauguin. *Day of the God (Mahana no Atua)*, 1894 (cat. 84). This painting is included in a 1959 Gauguin exhibition at the Art Institute.

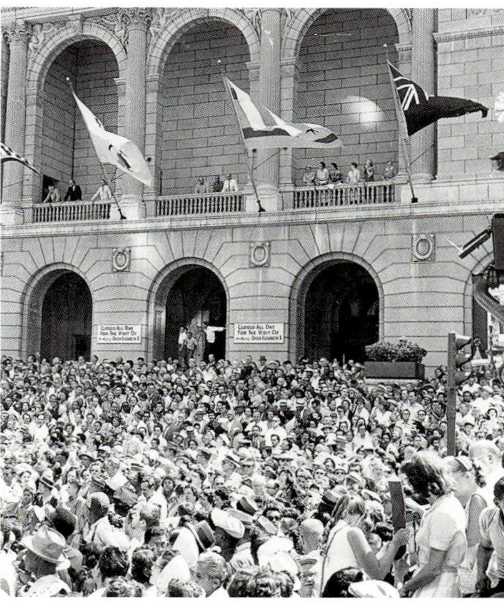

Crowd in front of the Art Institute during Queen Elizabeth's 1959 visit to Chicago.

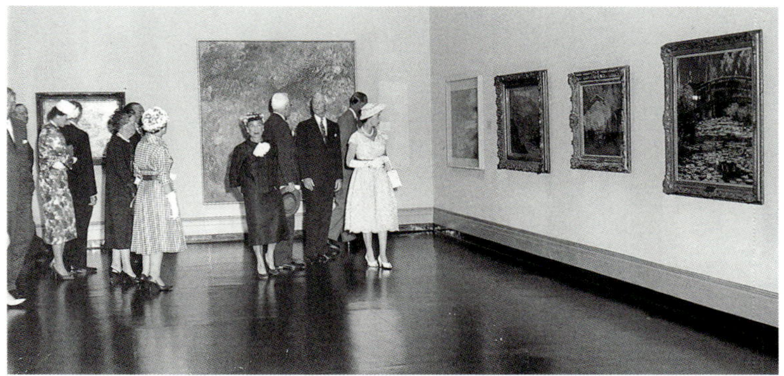

At the Art Institute, the queen tours a gallery of paintings by Monet. On the far wall is *Iris*; on the right wall are such canvases as *Arrival of the Normandy Train, Gare Saint-Lazare* (cat. 22) and *Water Lily Pond* (cat. 103). To the queen's right are board president William McCormick Blair and curator Katharine Kuh.

1957

Inspired by the acquisition of Monet's *Iris* the previous year, the Art Institute holds the exhibition *The Paintings of Monet* from April to mid-June. The show includes all thirty works by the artist in the museum's collection.

1958

A major retrospective of the art of Seurat is organized by Daniel Catton Rich, the Art Institute's director from 1938 to 1958. Featuring some 150 drawings and paintings, including *A Sunday on La Grande Jatte—1884* (cat. 63), the show also travels to the Museum of Modern Art. During the exhibition at MoMA, a fire breaks out in the galleries. Although the painting is unharmed, the Art Institute's trustees decide never to let it leave the museum again.

1959

An exhibition of work by Gauguin opens on February 12. Organized with the Metropolitan Museum of Art, it features paintings, drawings, watercolors, prints, and sculptures. The Art Institute is the single largest lender.

During a trip to Canada for the official opening of the St. Lawrence Seaway on June 26, Queen Elizabeth II comes to Chicago, the only United States stop on her itinerary. Arriving on July 6 aboard their royal yacht—accompanied by American, British, and Canadian destroyers—Queen Elizabeth and Prince Philip tour the city. Over two million Chicago spectators gather to catch a glimpse of the couple, who visit the Art Institute, among other sites.

1963–64

During a renovation of its galleries, the Museum of Modern Art loans *Reflections of Clouds on the Water-Lily Pond* (c. 1920) by Monet to the Art Institute for several months. The monumental triptych, nearly forty-two feet long and over six feet high, is installed in a second-floor gallery of the Morton Wing.

1964

John Maxon, the Art Institute's director from 1958 to 1965, purchases Caillebotte's masterpiece *Paris Street; Rainy Day* (cat. 24), which quickly becomes an Art Institute favorite. Maxon will also serve as the museum's Associate Director (1965–72) and Vice President of Collections and Exhibitions (1972–77).

Pierre-Auguste Renoir. *Lunch at the Restaurant Fournaise (The Rowers' Lunch)*, 1875 (cat. 29). This painting is shown in the Art Institute's 1973 Renoir exhibition.

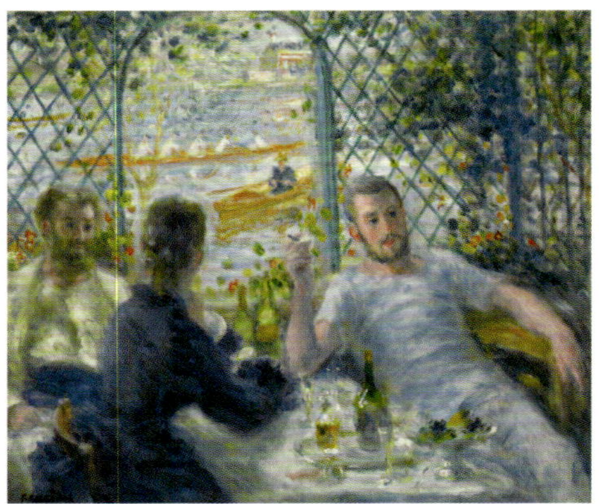

James N. Wood (center) discusses Monet's *Water Lily Pond* (cat. 103) with a museum visitor.

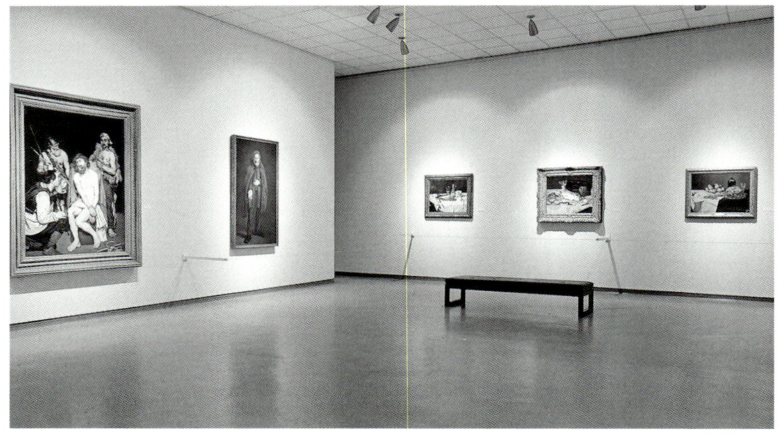

Installation view of a 1967 Manet exhibition at the Art Institute, including (from left) *Jesus Mocked by the Soldiers* (cat. 4), *Beggar with a Duffle Coat (Philosopher)* (cat. 3), and *Fish (Still Life)* (cat. 1).

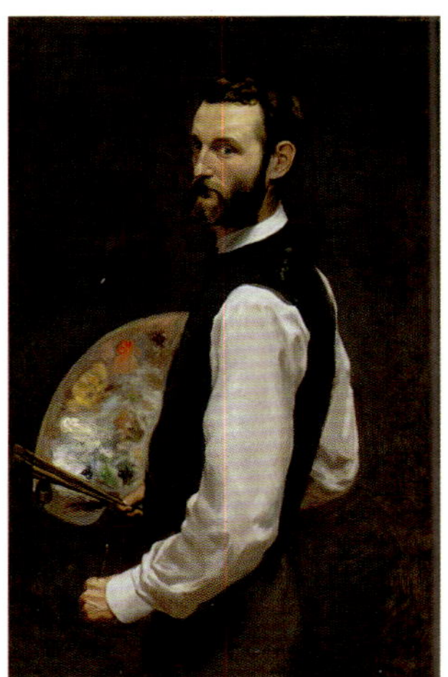

Frédéric Bazille. *Self-Portrait*, 1865/66 (cat. 7). This canvas is exhibited in the Art Institute's 1978 Bazille show.

1967

In collaboration with the Philadelphia Museum of Art, from January 13 to February 19, the Art Institute stages the most extensive exhibition of Manet's work in the United States to date. The show features approximately two hundred paintings, drawings, and works on paper from some eighty private and museum collections.

1973

The Art Institute holds a Renoir exhibition from February 3 to April 1. Shown only in Chicago, it is put together with the help of the artist's son Jean, the art historian François Daulte, and Charles Durand-Ruel, grandson of the dealer Paul Durand-Ruel. By the end of its two-month run, 354,169 visitors have seen it. This sets an attendance record for paid loan exhibitions at the Art Institute.

1975

An exhibition of over one hundred paintings from all phases of Monet's career is held at the Art Institute from March 15 to May 11.

1978

J. Patrice Marandel, Curator of Classical Art and European Painting at the Art Institute from 1974 to 1979, organizes *Frédéric Bazille and Early Impressionism*, on view from March 4 to April 30. Comprising nearly fifty paintings, as well as drawings, it introduces the work of this relatively unknown artist to the American public. Also included in the show are paintings by Bazille's close colleagues Manet, Monet, Renoir, and Sisley, among others.

1979

An exhibition of 109 paintings by Lautrec, organized by the Art Institute, is on view from October 4 to December 2. Forty works come from the Musée Toulouse-Lautrec, Albi. In exchange for this generous loan, in 1980 the Art Institute will lend the Albi museum fifty-nine French and American nineteenth-century paintings for the exhibition *Trésors impressionnistes du Musée de Chicago*.

1980

James N. Wood becomes Director and President of the Art Institute of Chicago, a position he will hold until 2004. During his long tenure, the museum will organize and host a number of major international loan exhibitions of Impressionist and Post-Impressionist art. He will also initiate the renovation of the Art Institute's Allerton Building, the construction of the Rice Building, and the planning of the Modern Wing.

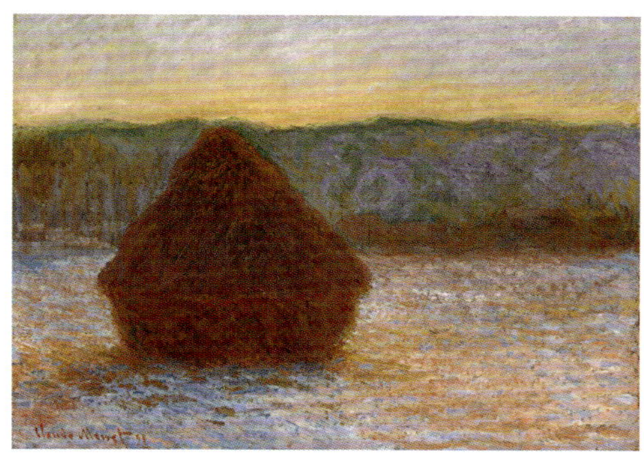

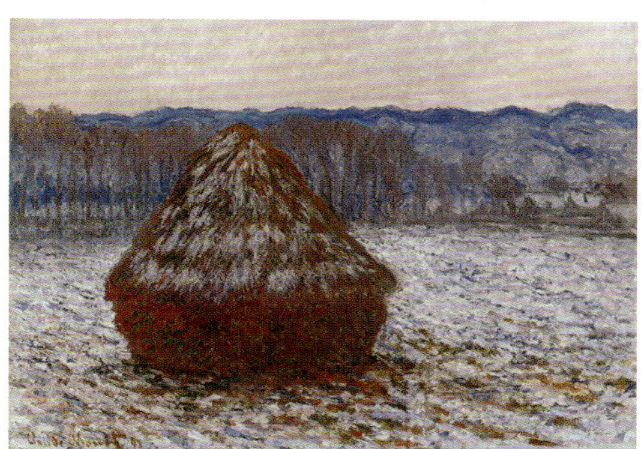

Claude Monet. *Stack of Wheat (Thaw, Sunset)*, 1890/91 (cat. 93); *Stack of Wheat*, 1890/91 (cat. 92); *Stacks of Wheat (End of Summer)*, 1890/91 (cat. 88). These canvases enter the Art Institute's collection in 1983 and 1985.

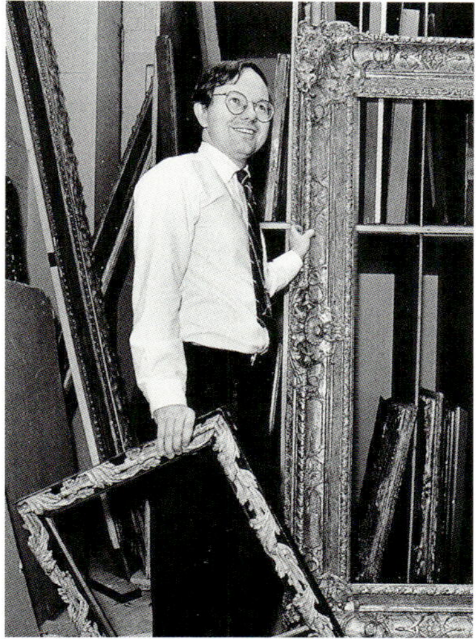

Richard Brettell in the Art Institute's frame storage area.

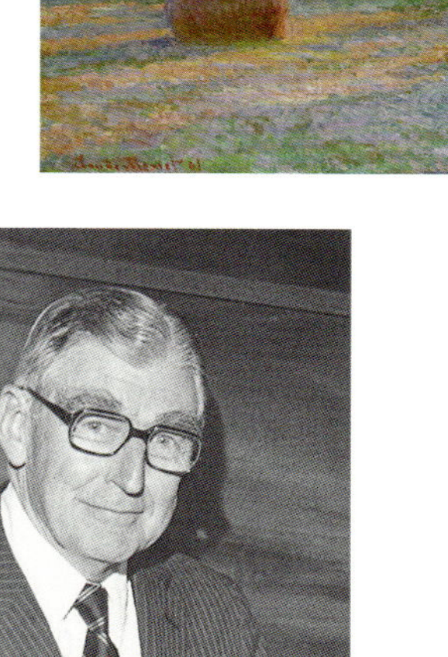

Arthur M. Wood, Sr. (1913–2006).

1983

The Art Institute acquires two paintings from Monet's *Stacks of Wheat* series. Mr. and Mrs. Daniel Searle are instrumental in both acquisitions, donating *Stack of Wheat (Thaw, Sunset)* (cat. 93) and providing additional funds for the purchase of *Stack of Wheat* (cat. 92).

1984

To celebrate Degas's 150th birthday, Richard Brettell, Searle Curator of European Painting from 1980 to 1988, and Suzanne Folds McCullagh, in the Department of Prints and Drawings since 1975 and Anne Vogt Fuller and Marion Titus Searle Curator of Earlier Prints and Drawings since 2001, mount an exhibition of ninety-one paintings, sculptures, prints, drawings, pastels, and monotypes by Degas owned by the Art Institute, supplemented by rarely seen works from Chicago-area collections. This show inaugurates a series of publications and loan exhibitions featuring the museum's holdings of a single artist's work in various media.

An unprecedented international loan exhibition of over 130 French Impressionist landscape paintings organized by Richard Brettell opens at the Art Institute on October 23. Including works by seventeen Impressionist and Post-Impressionist artists, *A Day in the Country: Impressionism and the French Landscape* is groundbreaking in its focus on landscapes as reflections of contemporary social, economic, and technical developments, such as expanding railroad lines, suburbanization, and industrialization. The exhibition is organized by the Los Angeles County Museum of Art in collaboration with the Art Institute and the Réunion des Musées Nationaux, Paris.

1985

Arthur M. Wood, Sr. (1913–2006), trustee of the Art Institute for several decades and chairman of the board from 1978 to 1981, donates Monet's *Stacks of Wheat (End of Summer)* (cat. 88) to the Art Institute in honor of his late wife, Pauline Palmer Wood (1917–1984). Mrs. Wood was the daughter of Potter Palmer II and Pauline Kohlsaat Palmer and a granddaughter of Potter and Bertha Honoré Palmer. This gift adds a sixth *Stacks of Wheat* canvas to the Art Institute's collection, making it the largest group from a single series to be owned by any museum in the world.

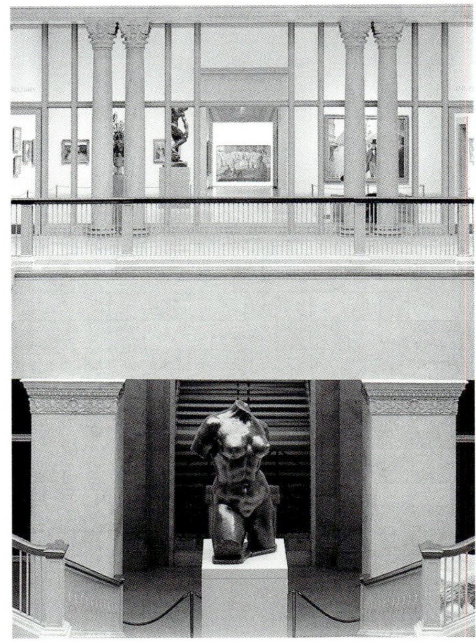

Installation view of the Art Institute's renovated galleries looking through Gallery 201 onto Seurat's *A Sunday on La Grande Jatte—1884* (cat. 63) in Gallery 240, 1987.

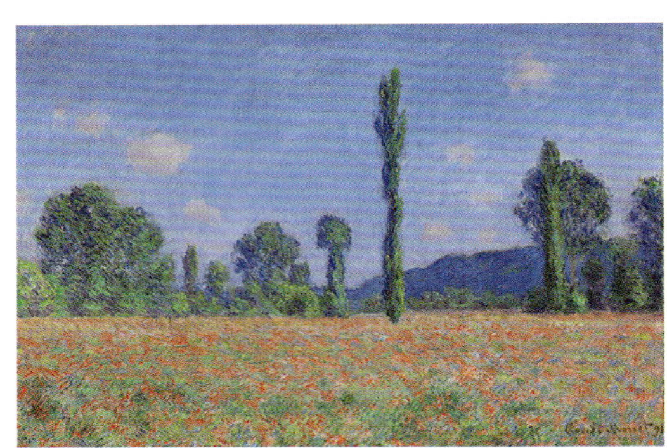

Claude Monet. *Poppy Field*, 1890–91 (cat. 87). This painting is included in the 1990 exhibition *Monet in the '90s: The Series Paintings.*

A sign in the Seibu Museum of Art, Tokyo, promoting the 1985–86 exhibition *The Impressionist Tradition: Masterpieces from The Art Institute of Chicago.*

View of the installation of the Art Institute's 1988 Gauguin exhibition.

1985–86

During a renovation of its galleries, the Art Institute loans sixty-five important Impressionist and Post-Impressionist paintings to Japan. *The Impressionist Tradition: Masterpieces from The Art Institute of Chicago* travels to three museums in Japan, attracting large crowds.

1987

The Art Institute's galleries of European Art reopen to the public after a two-year renovation overseen by Chicago architectural firm Skidmore, Owings and Merrill. With the reinstallation, works on paper can be exhibited in the corridor galleries adjacent to the daylit spaces where paintings and sculptures are displayed. This allows viewers to appreciate the work of an artist in a variety of media. The project also includes a renovation of the Art Institute's lobby and Grand Staircase by Chicago architect John Vinci.

1988

The Art of Paul Gauguin opens at the Art Institute in September, organized by Richard Brettell and Charles Stuckey, Frances and Thomas Dittmer Curator of Twentieth-Century Painting and Sculpture from 1987 to 1995. They are assisted by Gloria Groom, in the Department of European Painting since 1984 and David and Mary Winton Green Curator of Nineteenth-Century European Painting since 1999; and Peter Zegers, in the Department of Prints and Drawings since 1986 and Rothman Family Research Curator since 1996. Five years in the making, this comprehensive exhibition features over 250 paintings, sculptures, ceramics, prints, and drawings from the artist's early Impressionist phase to his time in Brittany, Tahiti, and the Marquesas. Co-organized by the Art Institute, the National Gallery of Art, Washington, D.C., and the Réunion des Musées Nationaux, this show inaugurates Regenstein Hall, the exhibition space in the Art Institute's new Daniel F. and Ada L. Rice Building.

1990

Organized by the Museum of Fine Arts, Boston, *Monet in the '90s: The Series Paintings* opens in Chicago on May 19. This exhibition brings together approximately ninety works related to the series Monet executed between 1889 and 1900, including *Poppy Field, Stacks of Wheat*, and *Water Lily Pond* (cats. 87, 88–93, and 103). The Chicago presentation is facilitated by Douglas Druick, Prince Trust Curator of Prints and Drawings since 1985 and recently appointed Searle Curator and head of the Department of European Painting.

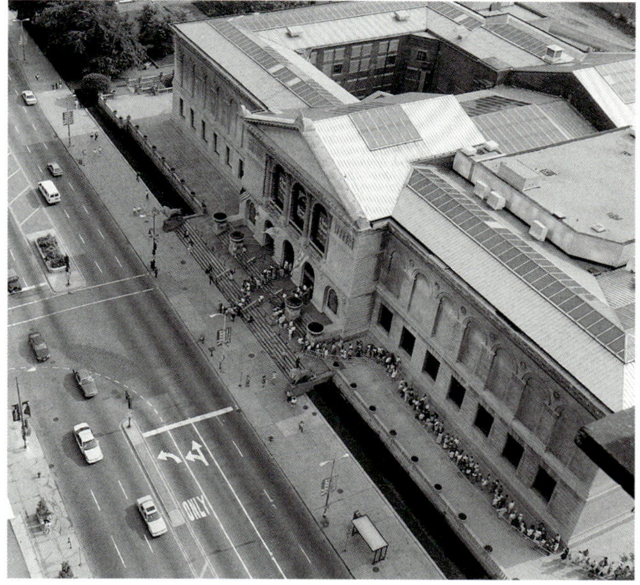

A long line of visitors waiting to enter the Art Institute to see a 1995 Monet exhibition.

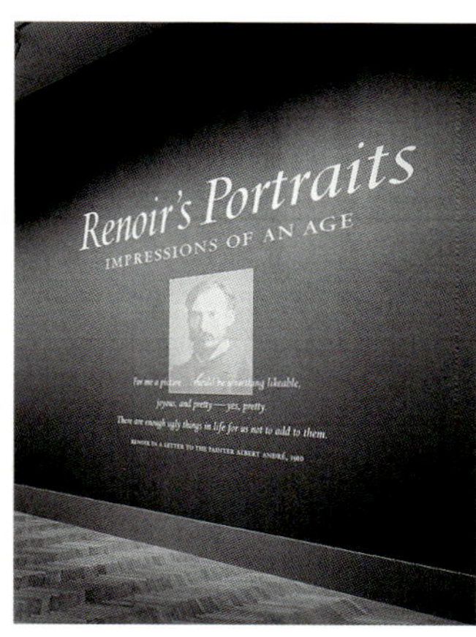

Title wall for the 1997 exhibition *Renoir's Portraits* at the Art Institute.

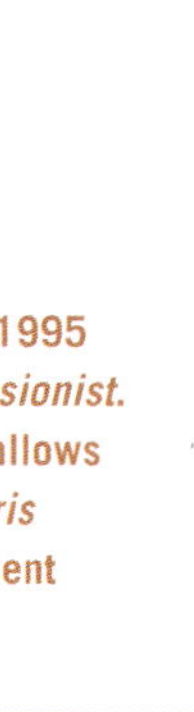

View of the installation of the Art Institute's 1995 exhibition *Gustave Caillebotte: Urban Impressionist.* A cutout in the wall of the exhibition space allows viewers to catch a glimpse of the artist's *Paris Street; Rainy Day* (cat. 24) while in an adjacent gallery of related drawings.

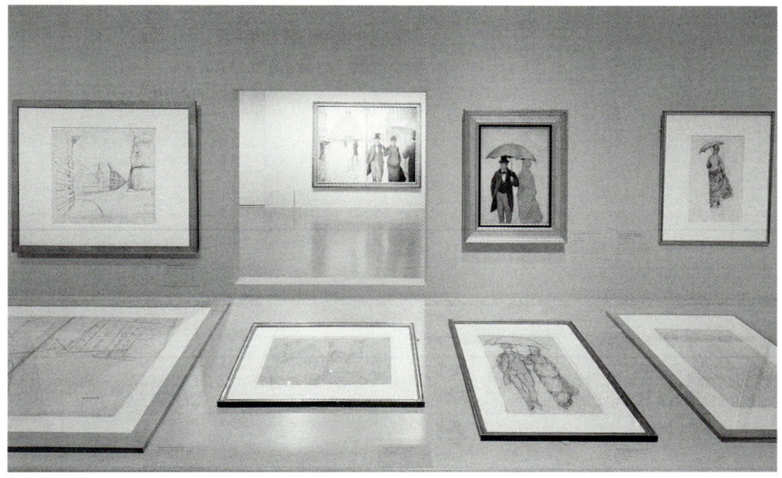

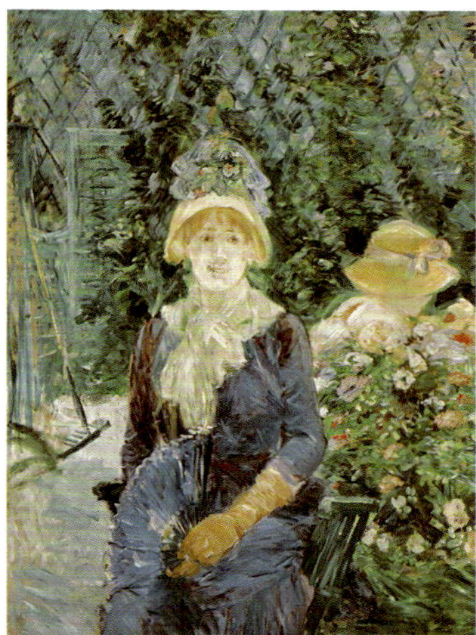

Berthe Morisot. *Woman in a Garden,* 1882/83 (cat. 26). This work is part of the Millennium Gift of Sara Lee Corporation.

1995

In recognition of the one hundredth anniversary of Caillebotte's 1894 death, the Art Institute collaborates with the Réunion des Musées Nationaux and the Musée d'Orsay, Paris, to present a major international retrospective of the artist, patron, and collector. *Gustave Caillebotte: Urban Impressionist* features over one hundred works. Following the exhibition, the Art Institute acquires Caillebotte's *Calf's Head and Ox Tongue* (cat. 43) directly from the artist's family.

The largest and most comprehensive exhibition ever devoted to the art of Monet is held exclusively at the Art Institute. *Claude Monet: 1840–1926* brings together over 150 works from international public and private collections. Nearly one million people visit the exhibition between July 22 and November 26.

1996

Co-organized with the National Gallery, London, *Degas: Beyond Impressionism* opens at the Art Institute. It is the first in-depth exhibition devoted to the artist's late years, focusing on the period between 1886, the date of the last Impressionist exhibition, and 1917, the year of his death.

1997

The Art Institute presents the first major survey of Renoir's portraits. Organized by the National Gallery of Canada, Ottawa, in conjunction with the Art Institute and the Kimbell Art Museum, Fort Worth, *Renoir's Portraits: Impressions of an Age* reflects all phases of the artist's career and attests to the rich relationships he had with family, friends, patrons, and fellow artists.

1998

Sara Lee Corporation announces that it will donate fifty-two works from its art collection (assembled by its founder, Nathan Cummings) to forty museums around the world. The Art Institute receives twelve (they will officially enter the collection in 1999), including Berthe Morisot's *Woman in a Garden* (cat. 26) and Pissarro's *Woman Bathing Her Feet in a Brook* (cat. 55). Before the collection is dispersed, it will tour the world in the exhibition *Monet to Moore: The Millennium Gift of Sara Lee Corporation*. The show will visit the Art Institute in 2000.

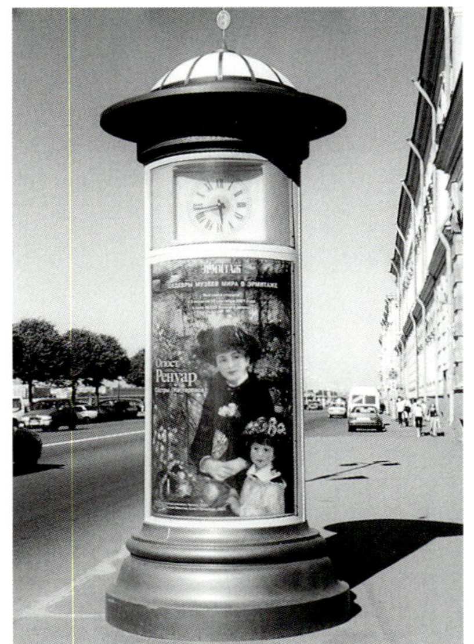

Kiosk outside the State Hermitage Museum, St. Petersburg, promoting the Art Institute's 2001 loan of Renoir's *Two Sisters* (cat. 34).

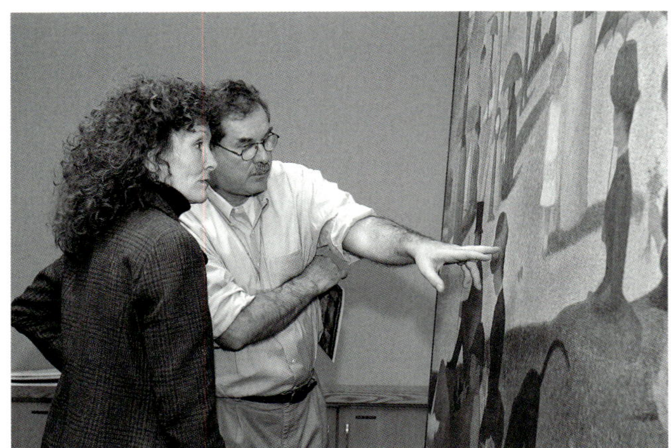

Gloria Groom and Frank Zuccari, Grainger Executive Director of Conservation at the Art Institute, examine *La Grande Jatte* (cat. 63) in the conservation laboratory.

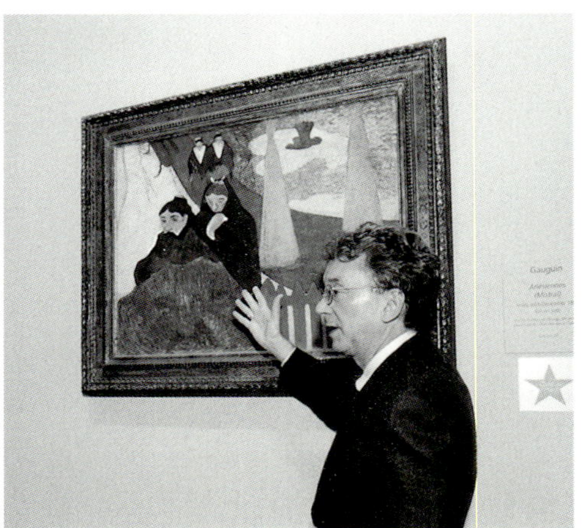

Douglas Druick speaking about Gauguin's *Arlésiennes (Mistral)* (cat. 72) at the 2001 opening gala for the exhibition *Van Gogh and Gauguin: The Studio of the South.*

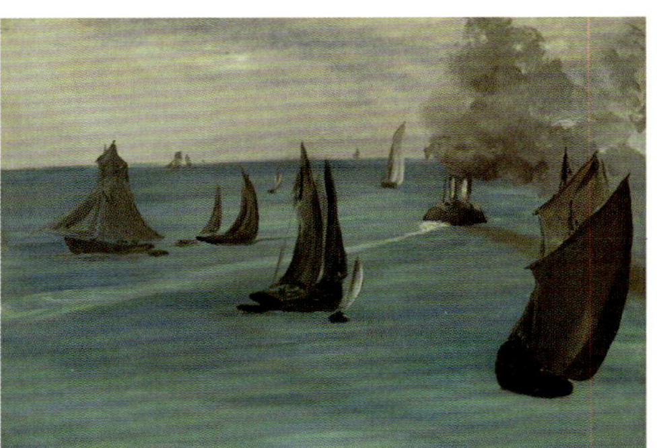

Édouard Manet. *Steamboat Leaving Boulogne*, 1864 (cat. 10). This painting appears in the 2003 *Manet and the Sea* exhibition.

2001

Organized by Art Institute curator Gloria Groom, in collaboration with the Metropolitan Museum of Art, *Beyond the Easel: Decorative Painting by Bonnard, Vuillard, Denis, and Roussel, 1890–1930* opens in February. It is the first exhibition to explore the mural-size paintings of these Post-Impressionist artists.

The Art Institute loans Renoir's *Two Sisters (On the Terrace)* (cat. 34) to the State Hermitage Museum, St. Petersburg, as the star work in an exhibition in their series *Masterpieces from the World's Museums in the Hermitage*.

In September, Art Institute curators Douglas Druick and Peter Zegers present the groundbreaking exhibition *Van Gogh and Gauguin: The Studio of the South*. Many years in the making, this show explores the complicated personal and professional relationship between this pair of artists. Co-organized with the Van Gogh Museum, Amsterdam, it brings together paintings, works on paper, ceramics, and sculptures from public and private collections worldwide. It also incorporates new evidence for dating works and understanding their development that has come to light from technical investigations into the artists' working practices.

2003

Opening in October, *Manet and the Sea*, the first major exhibition exploring the marine paintings of Manet, is organized with the Philadelphia Museum of Art and the Van Gogh Museum. This show traces Manet's innovative interpretations of the sea and demonstrates how he approached the theme and, in turn, influenced other artists painting this subject. The organizing curator for Philadelphia, Joseph Rishel, was a curator in the Art Institute's paintings department from 1968 to 1971.

2004

James Cuno becomes President and Eloise W. Martin Director of the Art Institute. Previously he had served as Professor and Director of the Courtauld Institute of Art, University of London, and as Professor and Director of the Harvard University Art Museums, Cambridge, Massachusetts, both of which are known for their Impressionist collections.

Seurat's masterwork *A Sunday on La Grande Jatte—1884* (cat. 63) is the focus of the exhibition *Seurat and the Making of "La Grande Jatte,"* which opens in June. The show brings together many of the numerous studies (see cat. 62) for the artist's magnum opus, helping to trace the painting's conception and evolution. Research by the Art Institute's conservation, curatorial, and imaging staff plays a critical role in elucidating the stages of the painting's development, as well as in analyzing the exact nature of its discoloration.

James Cuno with Dorothy Schroeder, Vice President for Exhibitions and Museum Administration at the Art Institute, at the opening gala for *Cézanne to Picasso: Ambroise Vollard, Patron of the Avant-Garde*, 2007.

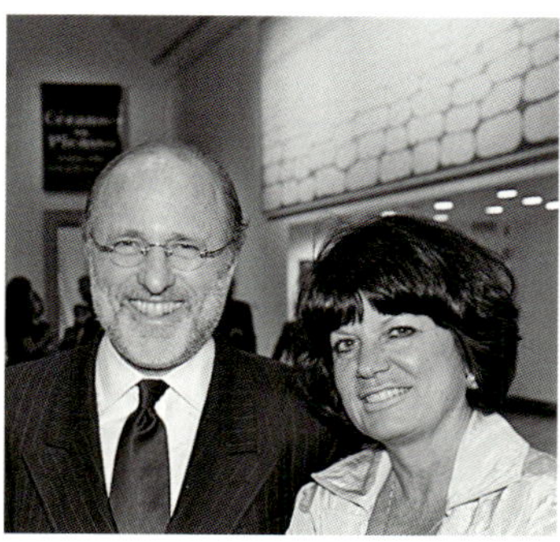

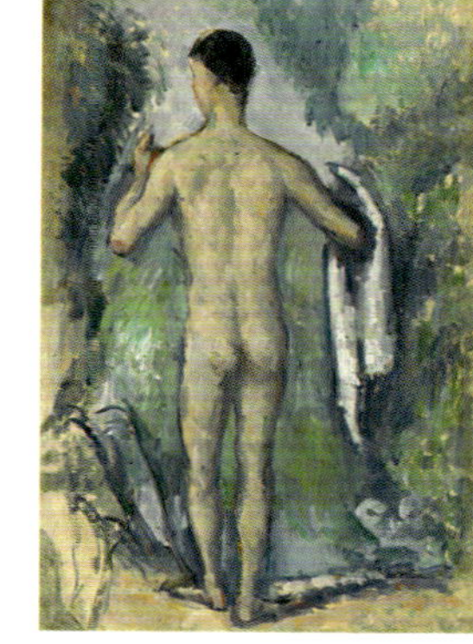

Paul Cézanne. *Standing Bather, Seen from the Back*, 1879/82. The Art Institute of Chicago, bequest of Brooks McCormick, 2007.289.

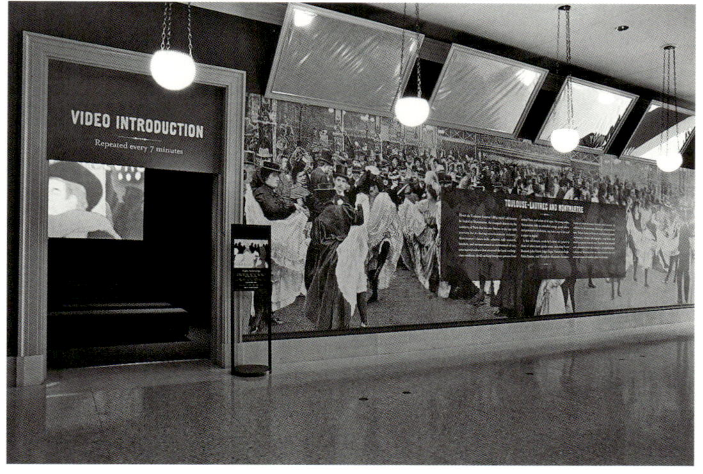

Entryway of the 2005 exhibition *Toulouse-Lautrec and Montmartre* at the Art Institute.

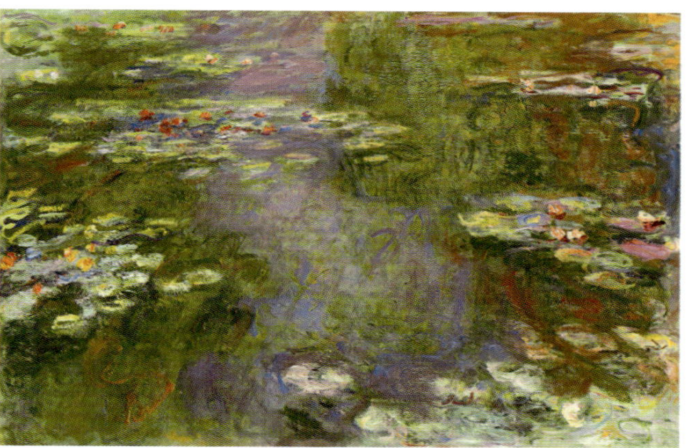

Claude Monet. *Water Lily Pond*, 1917–22 (cat. 105). This painting is given to the Art Institute by Mrs. Harvey (Ruth) Kaplan.

2005

Organized with the National Gallery of Art, Washington, D.C., the Art Institute presents *Toulouse-Lautrec and Montmartre*, which features over 250 works in various media by Lautrec and nearly fifty other artists.

The Art Institute acquires the late Monet painting *Water Lily Pond* (cat. 105) upon the death of Mrs. Harvey (Ruth) Kaplan (1910–2005). A Life Member and distinguished benefactor of the museum, she had announced the gift in 1982 but kept the painting until her death. This donation allows the Art Institute to fully represent the evolution of Monet's motif of the water-lily pond.

2007

Cézanne to Picasso: Ambroise Vollard, Patron of the Avant-Garde is shown at the Art Institute. This exhibition, co-organized with the Metropolitan Museum of Art, the Musée d'Orsay, and the Réunion des Musées Nationaux, explores the career of the legendary art dealer and publisher Ambroise Vollard. The Chicago exhibition features nearly 250 paintings, sculptures, prints, ceramics, and books—by artists like Cézanne, Gauguin, and Renoir—that Vollard handled, commissioned, exhibited, or owned.

The Art Institute receives a generous bequest from Brooks McCormick (1917–2006), a trustee of the museum from 1954 to 1987 and vice chairman of the board for many years. Included in this gift is Cézanne's *Standing Bather, Seen from the Back*, which joins another painting on this theme, *The Bathers* (cat. 81), bequeathed to the museum by one of McCormick's relatives in 1942.

2008

During the renovation of the European Painting and Sculpture galleries, ninety-two Impressionist and Post-Impressionist masterpieces from the Art Institute travel to the Kimbell Art Museum for the exhibition *The Impressionists: Master Paintings from the Art Institute of Chicago*, which is on view from June to November.

In December the Art Institute's Impressionist and Post-Impressionist paintings, along with European paintings and sculptures from the Middle Ages through 1900, reopen in a resplendent suite of galleries refurbished by Vinci/Hamp Architects, Inc., Chicago, on the Allerton Building's second floor.

2009

Building on past research, Art Institute curators and conservators begin for the first time a comprehensive, systematic analysis of the entire collection of nineteenth-century paintings.

Landscape and Figure Painting: New Approaches

TRADITION AND INNOVATION

MANET: RACES AND BULLFIGHTING

SEA AND SKY

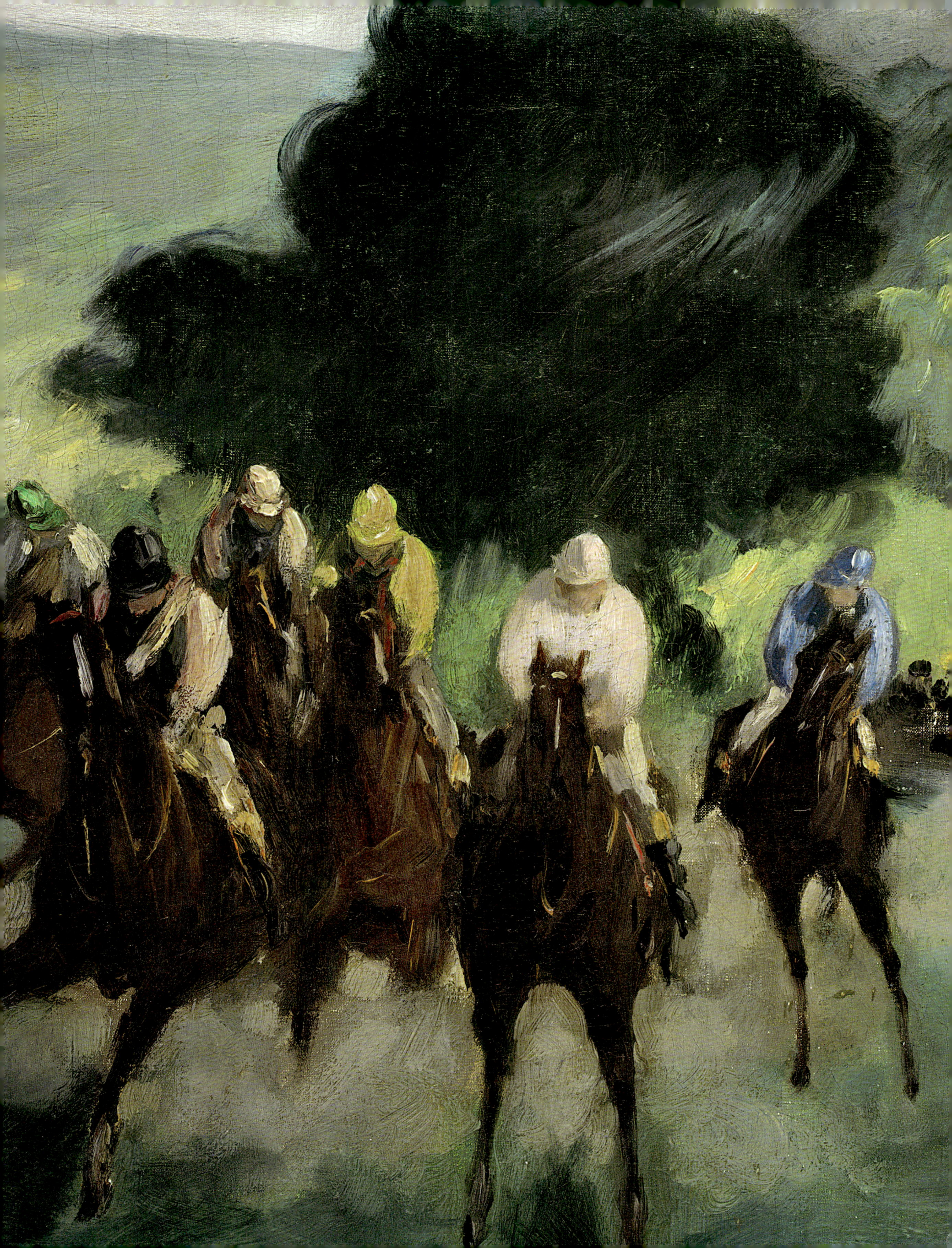

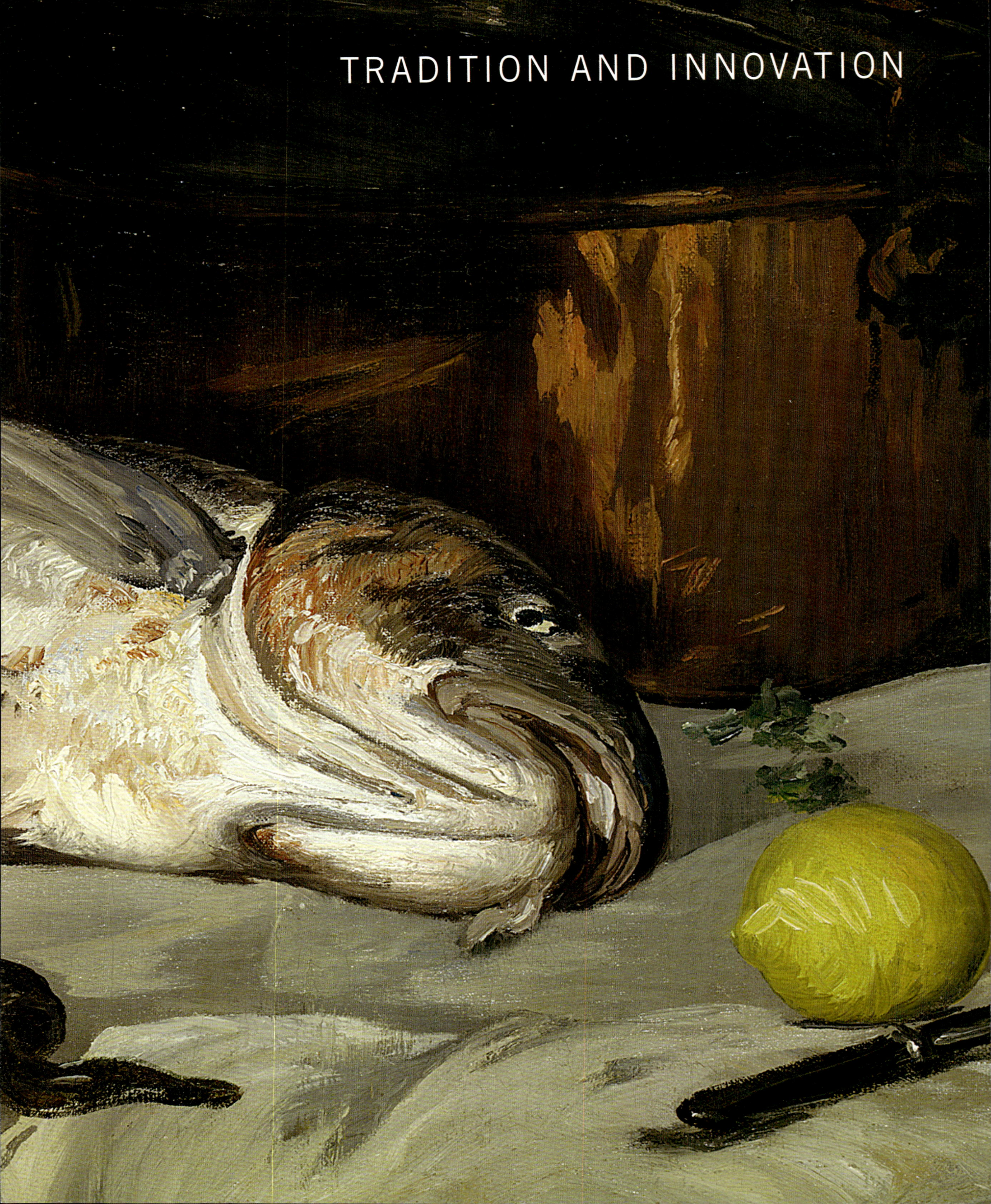
TRADITION AND INNOVATION

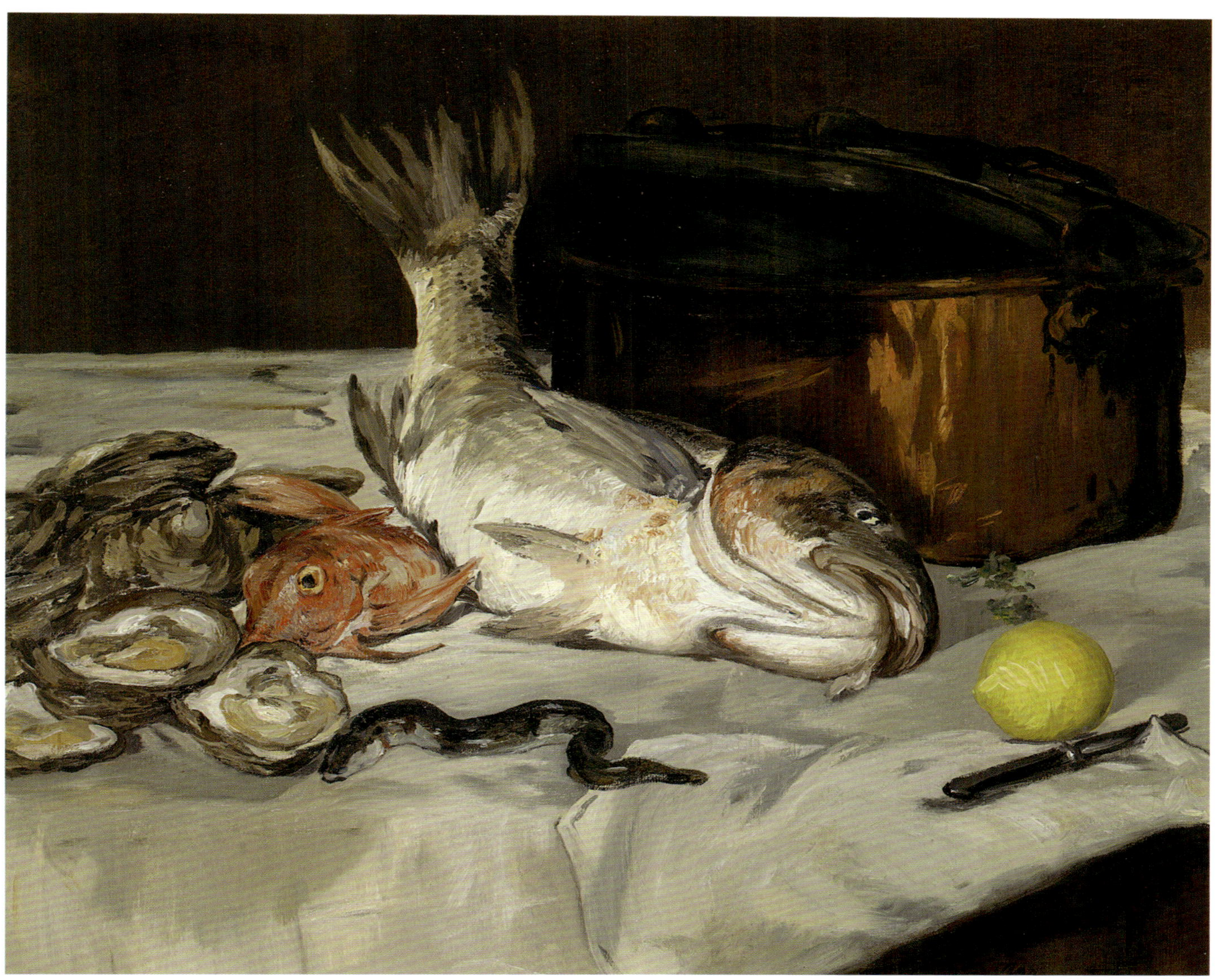

1

Fish (Still Life), 1864

Oil on canvas; 73.4 x 92.1 cm (28⅞ x 36¼ in.)
Mr. and Mrs. Lewis Larned Coburn Memorial Collection, 1942.311
Signed lower right: *Manet*

By age thirty, Édouard Manet had garnered recognition at the state-sponsored Salon exhibition in Paris and established himself as the artist to watch, producing works that translated Old Master painting into a modern idiom. In its subject, light, and handling, *Fish (Still Life)* recalls the work of seventeenth-century Dutch still-life painters, the *bodegones* of the Spanish Baroque masters, and especially the humble kitchen arrangements of the eighteenth-century French painter Jean-Baptiste Chardin, all of which had gained new currency by the mid-nineteenth century among artists of the Realist school.

This imposing arrangement of carp, red mullet, eel, oysters, lemon, stockpot, and knife is one of numerous still lifes that Manet painted in 1864, the year of his most intense engagement with the genre. Having been vilified for his Salon submissions that year, Manet may have found *nature morte* (literally "dead nature") an easily accessible and therapeutic alternative to working with live models on history paintings, which were subjected to stricter academic standards for technique and finish. The resulting composition, however, is anything but mild. In this and smaller variants, Manet created a pulse-quickening sense of immediacy and instability by raising the tail of the central fish and strategically positioning elements along the diagonal of the tablecloth so that they seem to slide forward into the viewer's space. This feeling of slipperiness is further suggested by the precariously balanced knife, the still-slithering eel, and above all, the painterly rendering of the oiliness of the fish and oysters, whose watery trail has soaked through the crisp white tablecloth.

Manet never submitted any of his still lifes to the official Salon, preferring instead to exhibit them through the burgeoning network of Parisian art galleries, such as Galerie Cadart, where *Fish (Still Life)* was probably first shown in 1865.

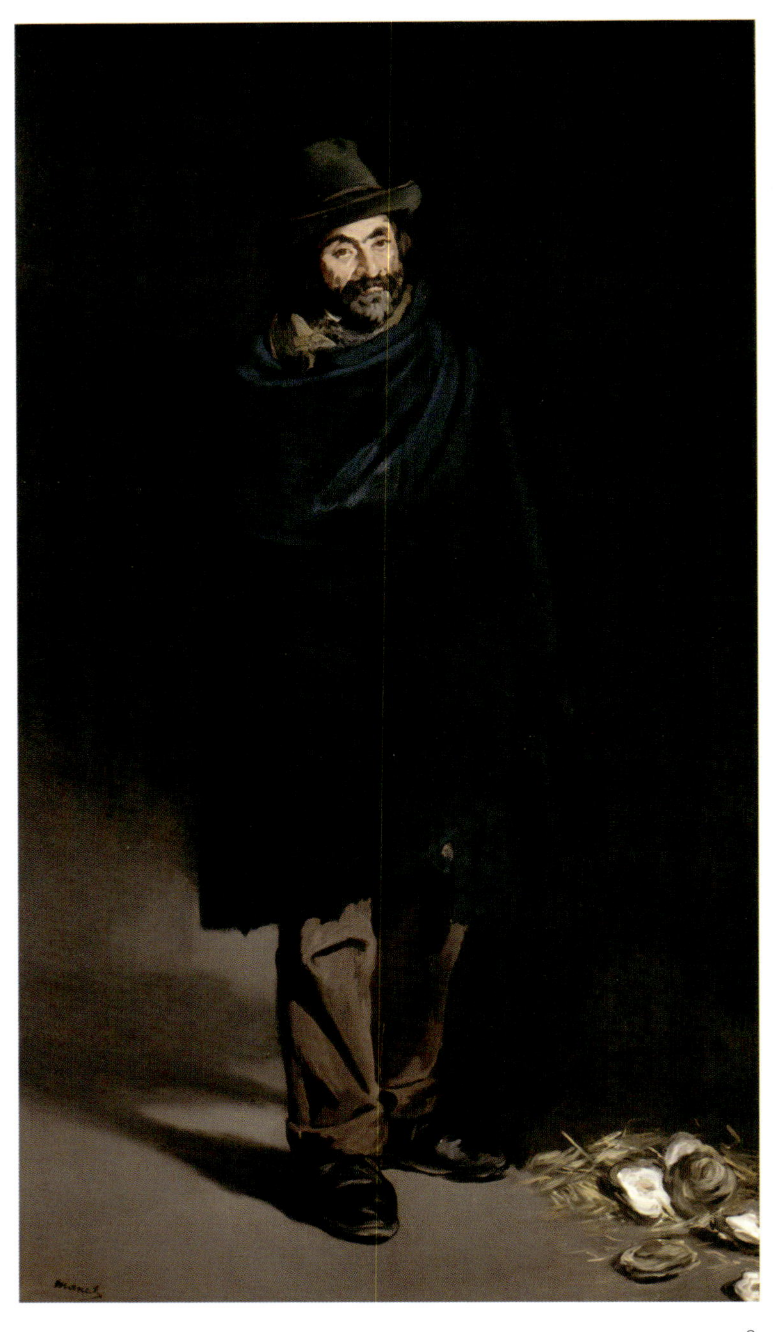

2

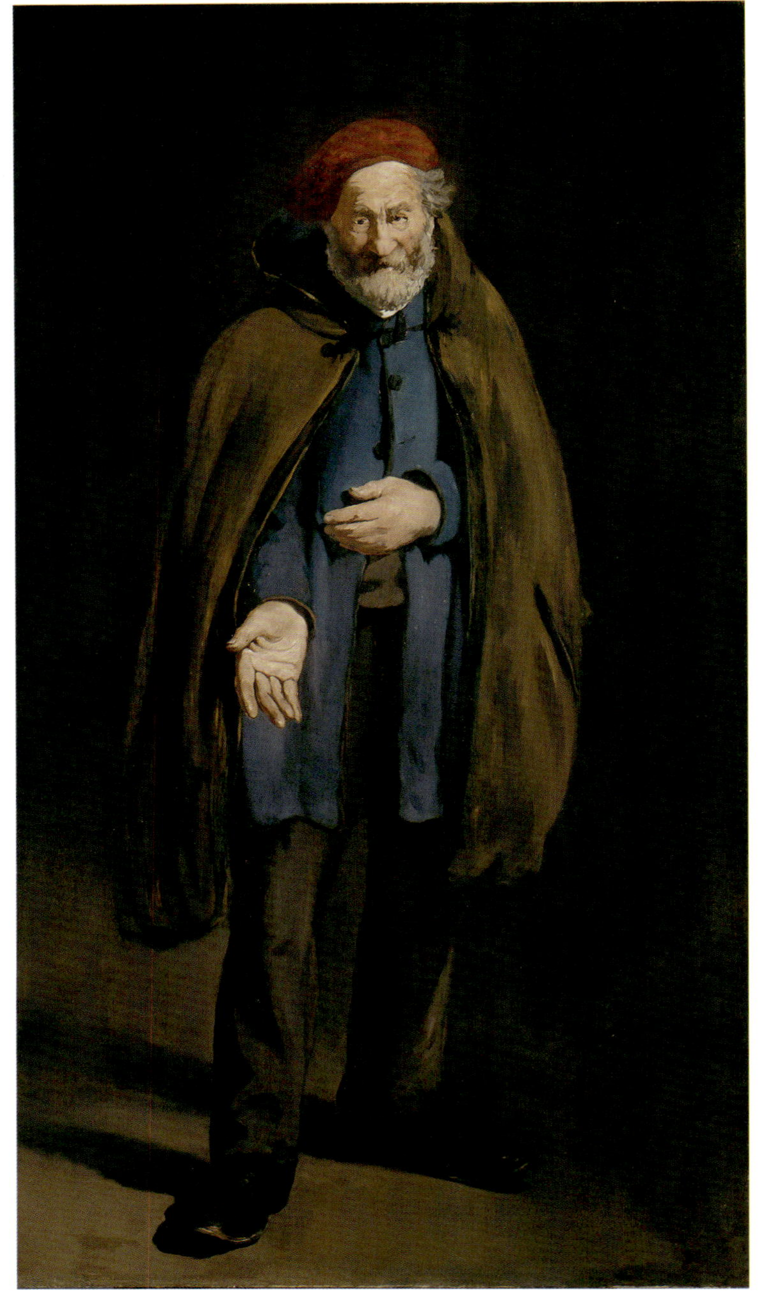

3

2

Beggar with Oysters (Philosopher), 1865/67

Oil on canvas; 187.3 x 108 cm (73¾ x 42½ in.)
Arthur Jerome Eddy Memorial Collection, 1931.504
Signed lower left: *Manet.*

3

Beggar with a Duffle Coat (Philosopher), 1865/67

Oil on canvas; 187.7 x 109.9 cm (73⅞ x 43¼ in.)
A. A. Munger Collection, 1910.304
Signed lower right: *Manet*

Édouard Manet's fascination with Spanish art reflects a passion among the French for all things Spanish (*espagñolisme*), which was stimulated by the court of Empress Eugénie, Napoleon III's Spanish wife. Nonetheless, the artist's depictions of Spanish singers, bullfighters, and bullfights were highly criticized. Because his unorthodox compositions and rough, vigorous brushwork ran so counter to the detailed and polished paintings of the French academicians, his works found little favor when they were exhibited. Indeed, Manet may have embarked on a long-contemplated trip to Spain in 1865 to recover from the devastating reviews of the two paintings he submitted to the Salon that year—one of which was the infamous *Olympia* (1863; Musée d'Orsay, Paris). At the Museo del Prado, Madrid, he was overwhelmed by the works of the Baroque artist Diego Velázquez, commenting in particular on his life-size portrayals of Aesop and Menippus (both c. 1638). Undoubtedly as a result of that encounter, upon his return to Paris, Manet began work on these two similarly scaled canvases depicting beggar-philosophers.

Probably conceived as pendants, the paintings were shown together for the first time in 1867, along with *Absinthe Drinker* (1858/59; Ny Carlsberg Glyptotek, Copenhagen). By 1872 Manet had grouped these and an additional canvas, *Ragpicker* (1865/70; Norton Simon Museum, Pasadena), under the collective title *Philosophers*. In the Art Institute's canvases, Manet paid special homage to the subjects, stark compositions, earth-toned palette, and vigorous brushwork of Velázquez, whose ancient Greek philosophers Manet updated with these equally impoverished, world-weary, and dignified members of what the French called the *classe dangereuse*. Like the ancient stoics, whose poverty is associated with wisdom, Manet's beggar-philosophers fit into the popular notion of the social outcast as a seer possessing rare insight. Beggars and ragpickers (nocturnal scavengers of garbage unsuitable for resale) held a particular fascination for Realist artists and writers, who saw these figures as resourceful, proud, and appealingly nonconformist types threatened by government "regularization" projects intended to drive them out of the city.

In *Beggar with Oysters*, the pose of the dark-bearded man, a ragged mantle (or blanket) thrown over his shoulders, suggests an element of rugged independence. The oysters at his feet—some opened, some not—remain mysterious, since it is not clear why or how he obtained them. When the painting was shown in 1867, its hint of unpleasant confrontation inspired one cartoonist to draw the beggar holding a knife behind his cloak. This disturbing ambiguity is more explicitly felt in *Beggar with a Duffle Coat*, which features a man with narrowed eyes sporting a beret and *caban* (a duffle coat often worn by mariners) and soliciting alms with his crudely rendered hand extended provocatively to the viewer. As is the case with many of his early figure paintings, Manet's beggar-philosophers reflect historical precedents that the artist made modern, thus creating a new imagery for contemporary types and events that confronts and confounds easy categorization.

By a remarkable coincidence, at the turn of the twentieth century, these two closely related works found their way by very different means to the Art Institute's collection, where they can again be viewed as they were originally in 1867.

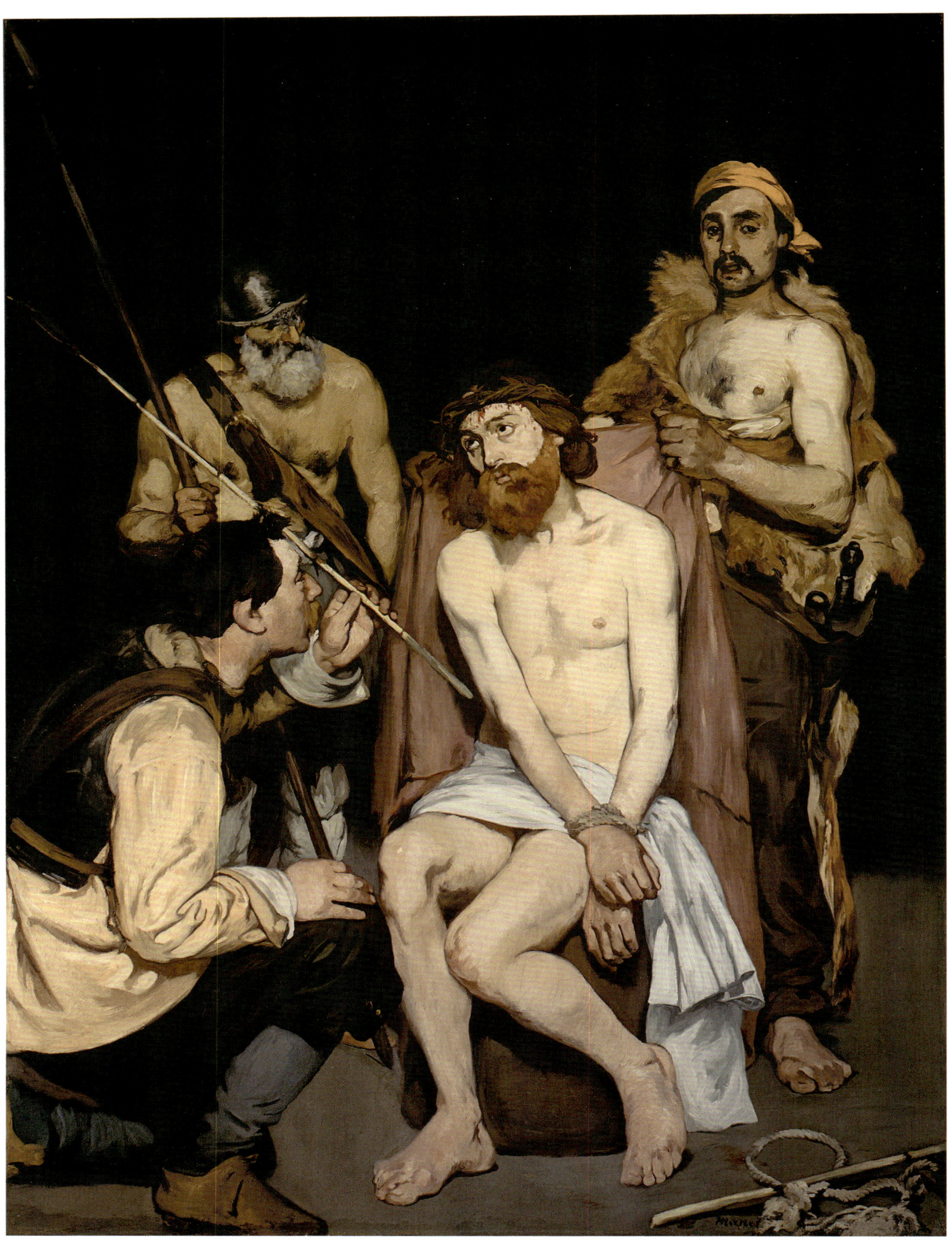

ÉDOUARD MANET French, 1832–1883

4

Jesus Mocked by the Soldiers, 1865

Oil on canvas; 190.8 x 148.3 cm (75 1/8 x 58 3/8 in.)
Gift of James Deering, 1925.703

Throughout his career, Édouard Manet managed to shock and confound the public with his bold technique and unorthodox approach to subject matter. Perhaps the most startling feature of his great religious composition *Jesus Mocked by the Soldiers* is that it was painted at all. After the advent of the Realist movement—grounded in the here and now—in early-nineteenth-century French painting, and with the breakdown of the authority formally held by the Catholic Church in France, avant-garde artists moved away from religious themes. Yet, while Manet was most certainly a painter of secular subjects—indeed, he was particularly urbane in his themes and lifestyle—he was also interested in the biblical narratives that had compelled artists for many centuries. It is likely that there is a connection between this interest and the popular contemporary biography *Vie de Jésus* (*Life of Jesus*) (1863) by the French philosopher and historian Joseph-Ernest Renan, a controversial work that emphasized Christ's humanity. Even the use of Jesus's name in the title of that book, instead of the more formal title Christ (a Greek term meaning "the anointed one"), underscores his earthly identification.

In this painting, Manet portrayed Jesus as very human and vulnerable by presenting him frontally, his bound hands held between his legs; making him seem submissive, almost limp; and surrounding him with figures that range from stern (the standing man at right) to supplicating (the kneeling man at left, whose spear, gingerly held between two fingers, seems more of an offering than a weapon). The canvas's visible brushstrokes and almost monochromatic tonality create an insistent sense of materiality that further evokes a palpable, unidealized Christ. The work depicts the moment when Jesus's captors mock the "King of the Jews" by crowning him with thorns and covering him with a robe. Although, according to the Gospel story, this taunting was followed by beatings, Manet's would-be tormentors appear ambivalent as they surround the pale, denuded figure. Thus, the artist managed to present a traditional subject in a contemporary, challenging light.

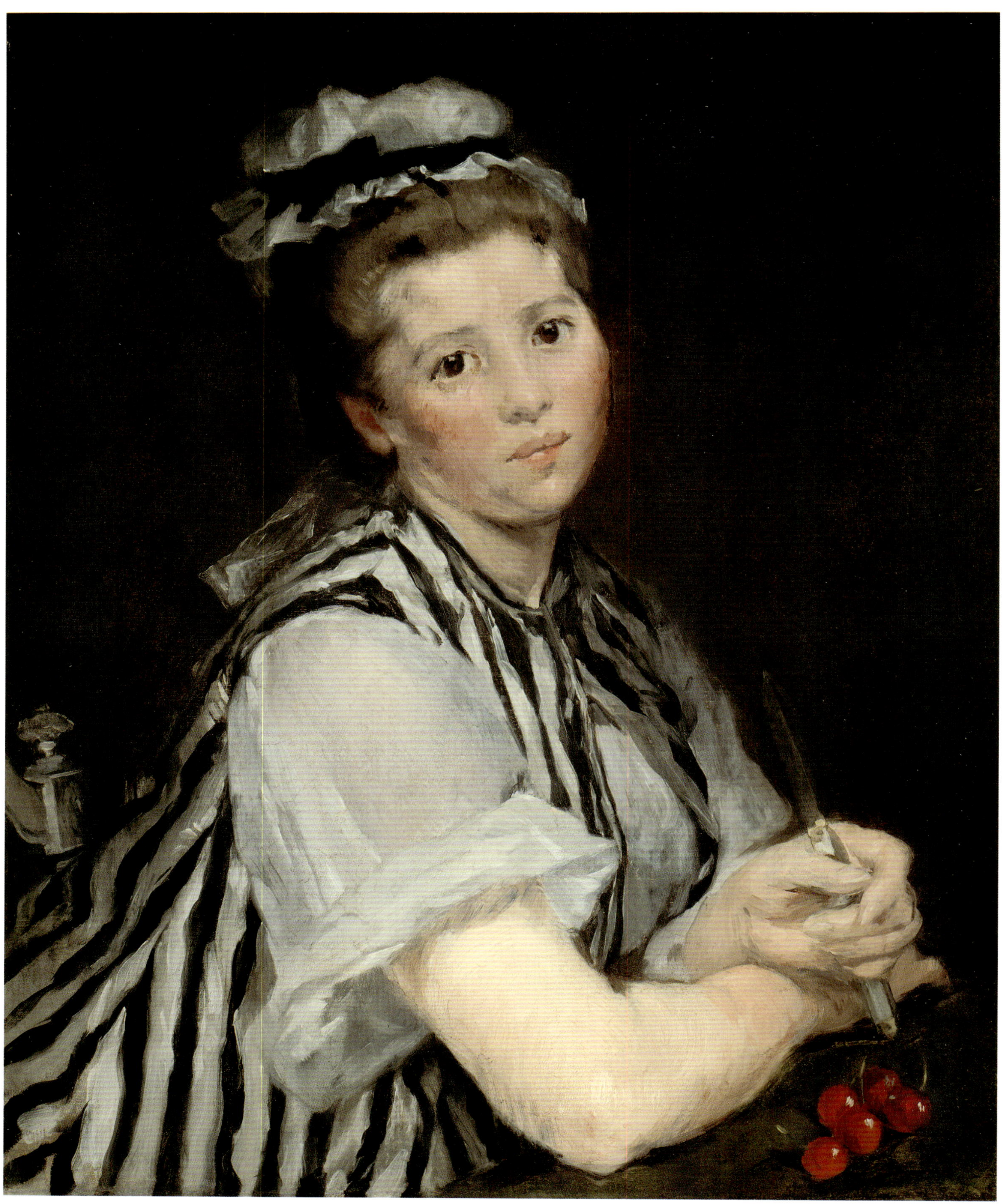

EVA GONZALÈS French, 1849–1883

5

Girl with Cherries, c. 1870

Oil on canvas; 56.2 x 47.4 cm (22 1/16 x 18 5/8 in.)
Mr. and Mrs. Lewis Larned Coburn Memorial Collection, 1940.32
Signed lower right: *Eva Gonzalès*

When Eva Gonzalès, the cultivated, beautiful, and affluent daughter of a celebrated novelist and an accomplished musician, began taking painting lessons in 1865, her choice of the fashionable society portraitist Charles Chaplin as a teacher was completely appropriate for a woman of her standing. Less acceptable was her decision four years later to leave Chaplin to study with Édouard Manet, becoming his first and only official pupil. For the painter Berthe Morisot, Manet's friend and sometime model, Gonzalès was a serious rival. Indeed, Morisot complained, "Manet lectures me, and holds up that eternal Mlle Gonzalès as an example: she has poise, perseverance, she is able to carry an undertaking to a successful issue, whereas I am not capable of anything." *Girl with Cherries*, painted shortly after Gonzalès signed on with Manet, is indebted to her teacher's Spanish-style works, such as *Beggar with Oysters* and *Beggar with a Duffle Coat* (cats. 2–3), which are characterized by dramatically lit figures set against dark backgrounds.

The model for this intimate portrait wears the frilled linen cap and loose striped gown (*robe à la française*) of an eighteenth-century servant—an occupation further hinted at by her rolled-up sleeve. Having adopted Manet's Realist subjects and painterly techniques (which are particularly visible in the long, loose peachy white strokes that describe the woman's foreshortened arm), Gonzalès softened the sense of confrontation between model and viewer that appears in many of her teacher's works. Although *Girl with Cherries* adheres to Manet's use of artifice and observation, the subject is far removed from his images of his favorite model, Victorine Meurent, whose immodest gaze so affronted the art establishment in *Déjeuner sur l'herbe* and *Olympia* (both 1863; Musée d'Orsay, Paris). Instead, Gonzalès's demure young servant girl returns the viewer's gaze with gentle candor, holding a fruit knife in mid-air as if caught unawares. In her choice of costume and pose, Gonzalès paid homage to the eighteenth-century artist Jean-Baptiste Chardin, who specialized in painting quiet domestic scenes of servants and children.

As model, muse, and pupil, Gonzalès is forever linked to Manet, who died in April 1883, just five days before her own premature death.

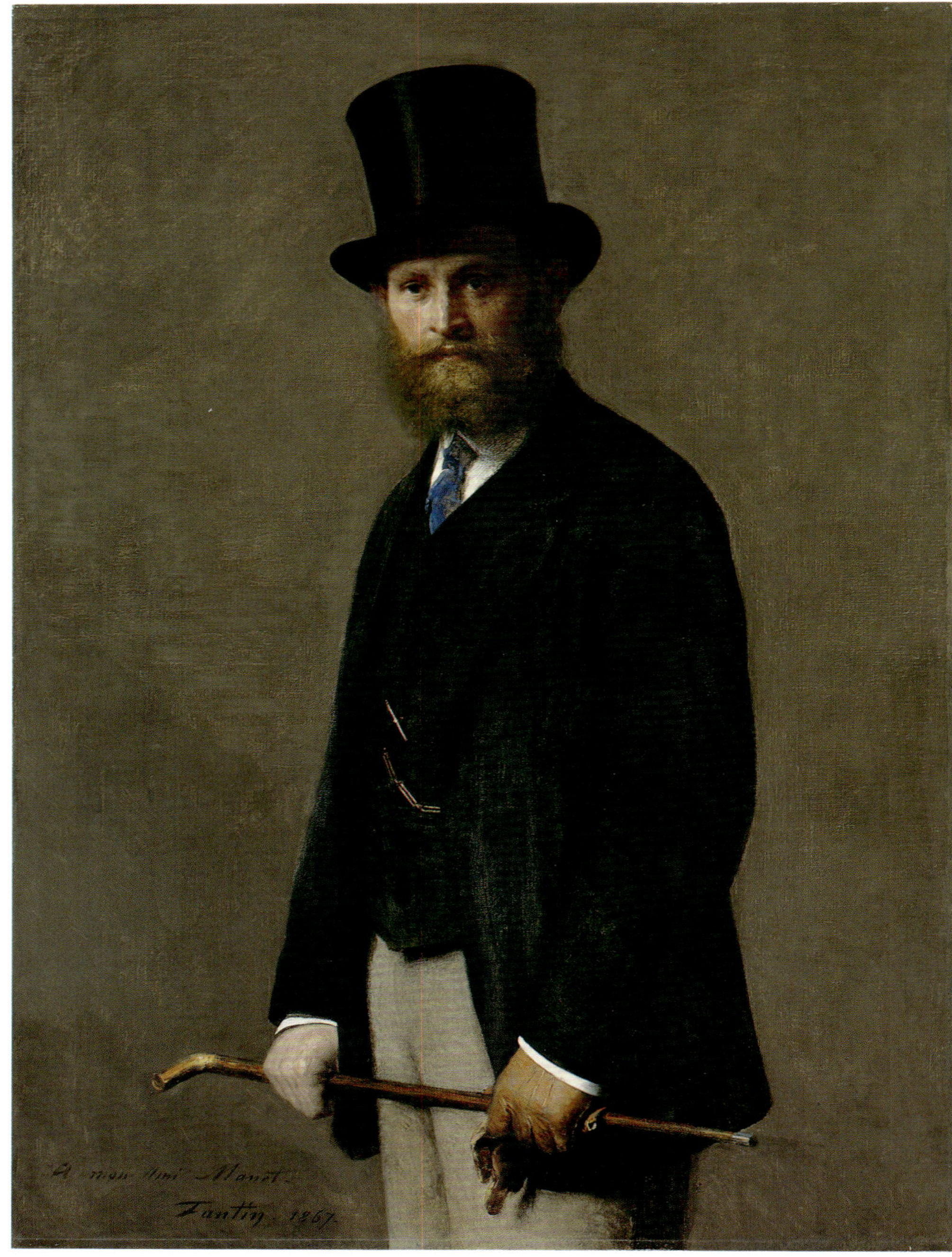

6

Édouard Manet, 1867

Oil on canvas; 117.5 x 90 cm (46 1/4 x 35 7/16 in.)
Stickney Fund, 1905.207
Signed lower left: *A mon ami Manet. / Fantin. 1867.*

Henri Fantin-Latour and Édouard Manet's friendship began sometime in 1857, while they were copying Old Master paintings at the Musée du Louvre, Paris, as part of their artistic training. Despite their increasing involvement in the early 1860s with the young artists who would come to be known as the Impressionists, both continued to look to the Salon for recognition and official approval. In 1867, after having been regularly rejected by that institution since his first submission in 1859, Manet decided not to exhibit there, instead paying for a private show of fifty-six of his works in an independent pavilion very near the Exposition Universelle. Fantin's decision to submit a portrait of his friend to the Salon that year may have been calculated to play off Manet's increasing notoriety. Inscribed in relatively large script in the lower-left corner, "To my friend Manet / Fantin 1867," the picture not only underscored his support for the embattled artist but also won Fantin a new level of critical respect.

Manet chose his own pose, which conveys decorous determination and alludes to the bourgeois social sphere in which both he and Fantin moved. The silver-tipped cane that he holds horizontally across his legs may hint at his readiness to fend off artistic attacks; however, it also suggests his preparedness for an urban outing in his role as artist-flaneur, a detached spectator of modern city life. The frank and easy confidence of this dignified gentleman both impressed and startled critics. As one of them admitted, he found it difficult to reconcile his preconceived image of Manet as a "long-haired art student"—as he had anticipated the author of the infamous *Olympia* (1863; Musée d'Orsay, Paris) to be—with the "well-gloved, well-dressed young man" who confronts the viewer in this canvas.

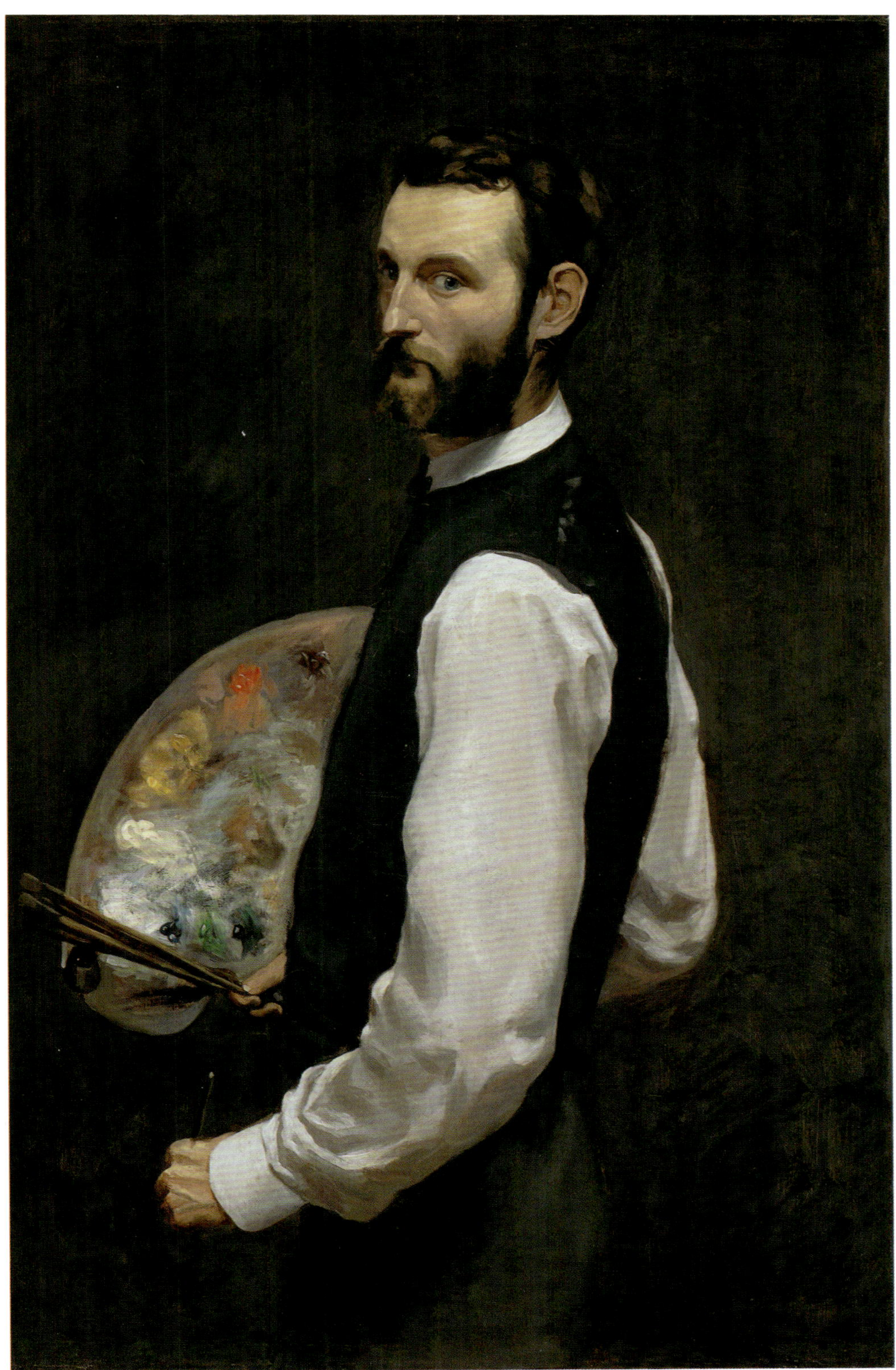

7

Self-Portrait, 1865/66

Oil on canvas; 108.9 x 71.1 cm (42 7/8 x 28 3/8 in.)
Restricted gift of Mr. and Mrs. Frank H. Woods in memory of Mrs. Edward Harris Brewer, 1962.336

During his brief career, which ended in 1870, when he was killed in the line of duty during the Franco-Prussian War, Frédéric Bazille produced about seventy paintings, four of which are self-portraits. Among these, the Art Institute's work is unique in the pose and scale of the figure. In fact, it could be the painting that Bazille began in 1865 and described as "a big portrait, life size," undertaken "especially to train myself." For the twenty-four-year-old artist, the portrait may have been both a practice piece (in which he observed and painted his reversed image as seen in a mirror) and a professional manifesto. Only a year earlier, he had failed his examinations for a medical career and received parental consent to rent an atelier. By December he was sharing an apartment-studio with Claude Monet and experimenting with new painting techniques that would be central to the Impressionist movement. Perhaps Bazille's exaggeration of the palette in this image, held vertically so that all eight pigments are visible, was intended to announce his commitment to a full-time artistic career.

In direct contrast to Henri Fantin-Latour's depiction of Édouard Manet as a poised and elegant boulevardier (cat. 6), Bazille presented himself as highly focused, an artist hard at work. His torso is angled away, but his head turns toward the viewer with a startled look, as if he wanted to catch his own image by surprise, or as if his portrait session had been unexpectedly interrupted. His strained neck muscles, the protruding veins of his left hand, and his short brush—snapped off at the handle so as to better render details—further convey the physical nature of the artist's craft. Recent conservation revealed that the background of the painting, formerly thought to be flatly monochromatic, is made up of sweeping brushstrokes of a dark brownish gray that complement the intense mood of the subject.

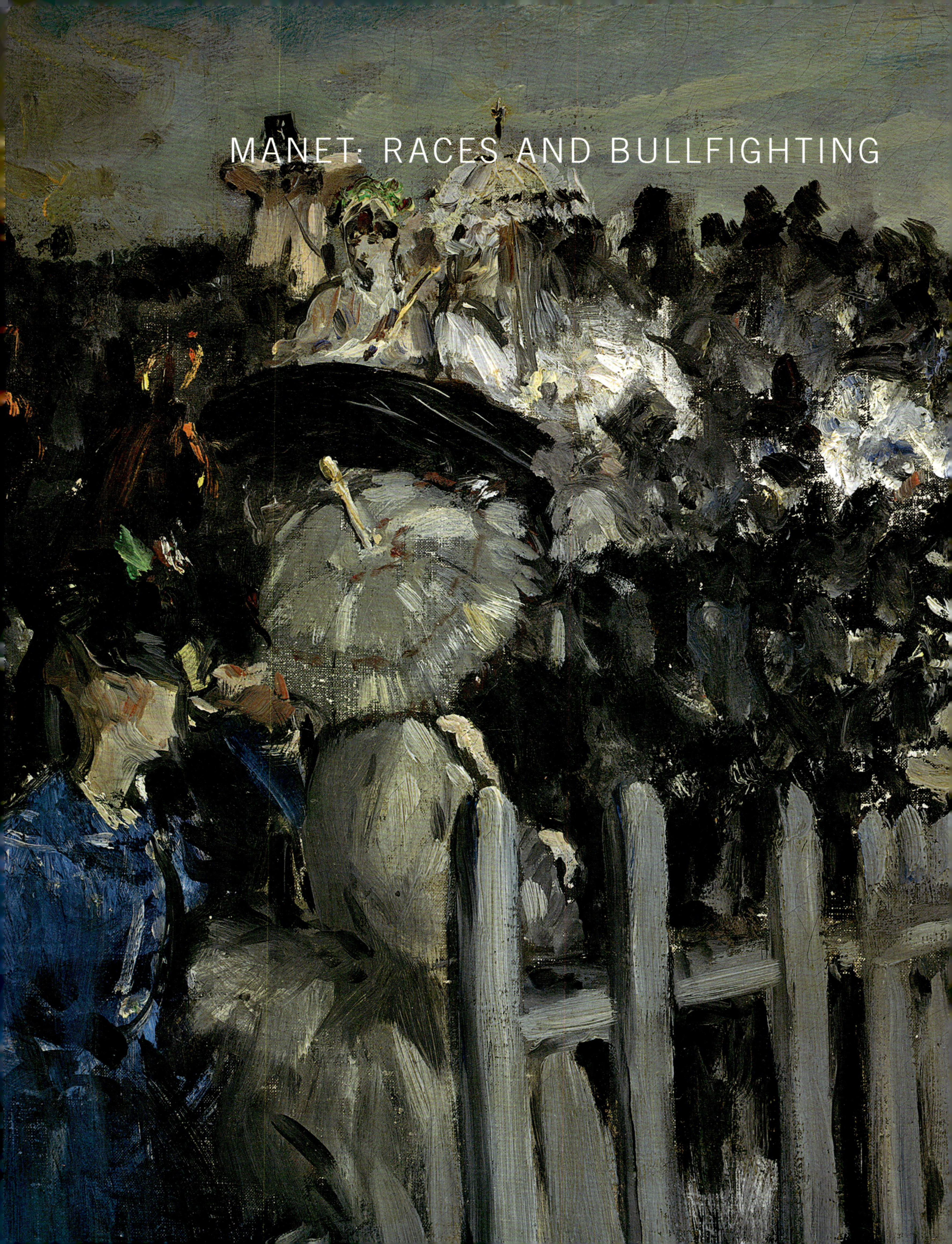

MANET: RACES AND BULLFIGHTING

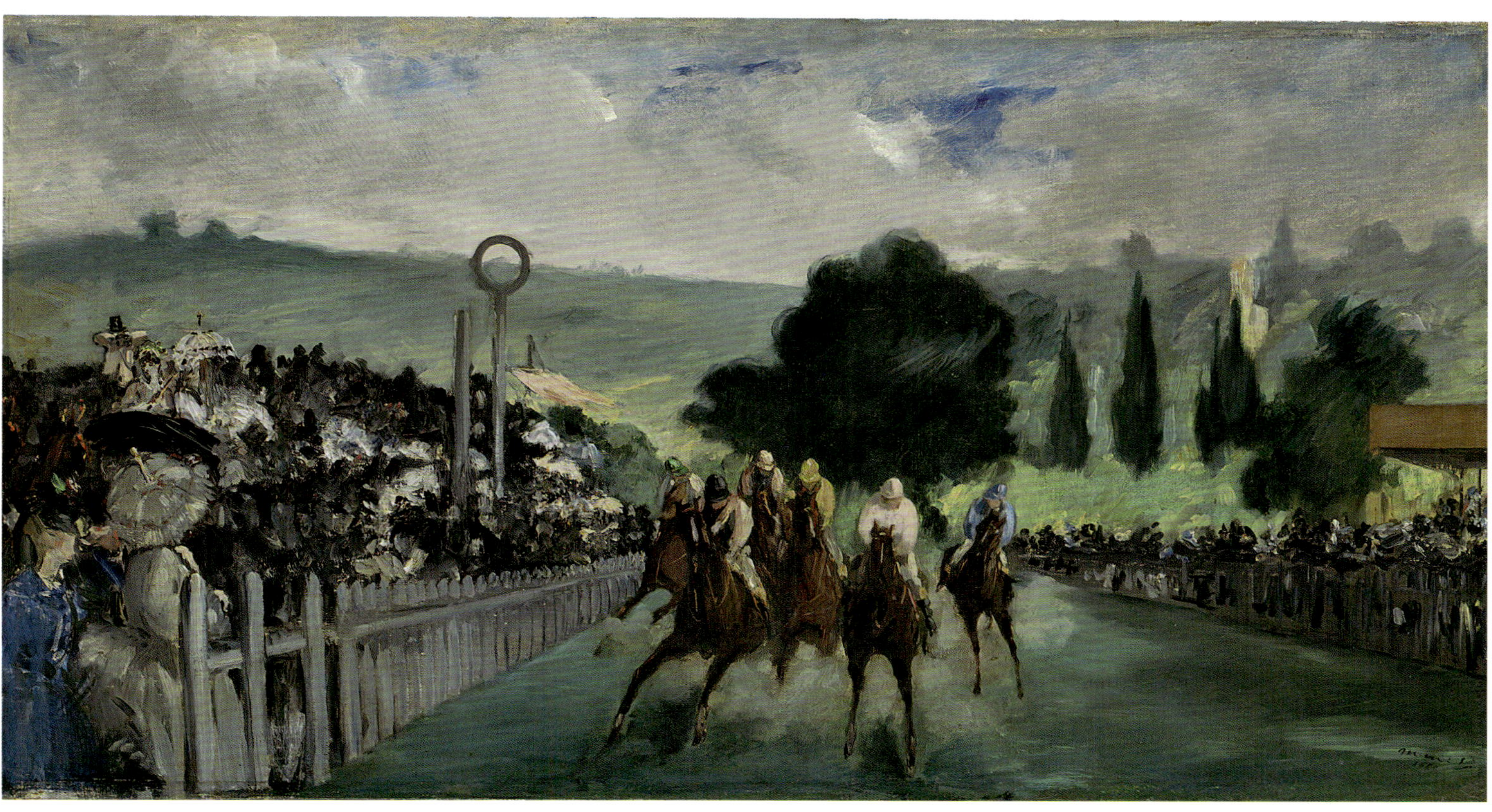

8

The Races at Longchamp, 1866

Oil on canvas; 43.9 x 84.5 cm (17 ¼ x 33 ¼ in.)
Potter Palmer Collection, 1922.424
Signed lower right: *Manet. / 1866*

The 1860s saw a growing trend among artists to paint ambitious canvases of the pleasures of modern life. Few are as savory as those by Édouard Manet, who introduced into the contemporary Realist project a deadpan irony, offhand elegance, and historical self-consciousness that utterly transformed it. In *The Races at Longchamp*, however, there is no sense of the classical or Old Master sources that inspired many of his early works. Instead, Manet suggested the explosive speed of the horses, the teeming crowds, and the masses of trees and hills in an exciting new pictorial language.

Manet's subject reflects the revival of horse racing during the Second Empire (1852–70), signaled by the opening in 1857 of the Longchamp track in the Bois de Boulogne, a park on the western outskirts of Paris. Although the artist took liberties with the surrounding landscape, he was specific when it came to the details of the track, from the viewing stands at left to the tribunal building at right. His faithful and innovative rendering of modern life was further exemplified by his depiction of the race itself. Manet chose to capture the last moments of the event, when the horses rush past the finish line, indicated by the pole with an open, circular disk on the left sideline. Revolutionizing the long tradition of pictures showing races from the side (clearly indicating which horse is in the lead), the artist dared to compose the scene so that the deafening and frantic throng of horses and satin-clad jockeys appears to thunder straight toward us. Rising above the flurry of horses and spectators is a man in a top hat looking at the finish through binoculars; he may be a stand-in for the artist himself.

When this painting was first shown at the artist's posthumous exhibition, one reviewer judged it "a pretty sketch that might have been a painting," but there is little doubt that this signed and dated composition represents the artist's full-fledged response to the attempts of other vanguardists to visually express motion and temporality.

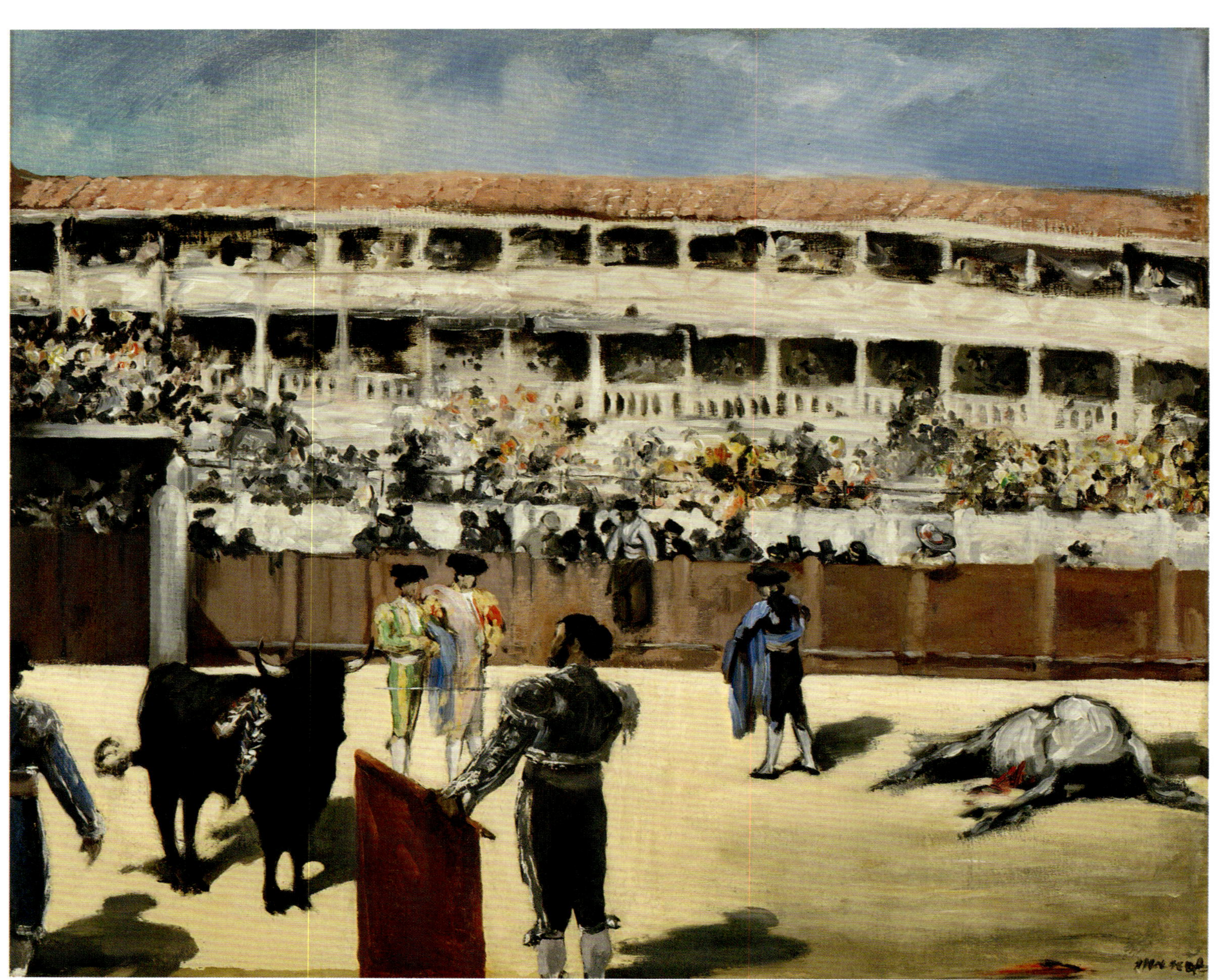

9

Bullfight, 1865/66

Oil on canvas; 48 x 60.4 cm (18⅞ x 23¾ in.)
Mr. and Mrs. Martin A. Ryerson Collection, 1937.1019
Signed lower right: *Manet*

Édouard Manet's trip to Spain in the fall of 1865 lasted only about ten days, but it had a profound impact on the artist. In addition to visits to the Museo del Prado, he attended a bullfight in Madrid, which he called "one of the finest, most curious and most terrifying sights to be seen" in a letter of September 14 to his friend the poet and critic Charles Baudelaire. To capture the excitement of the bullfight, he made quick sketches that informed several canvases. Of these, the Art Institute's *Bullfight* is both the smallest and the most carefully composed.

Although the fallen and bleeding horse on the right signals the aftermath of violence, the painting is devoid of the deadly combat (bull goring horse) or cruel actions (*banderillos* aggravating the bull to wear him out) of the two larger works (*Bullfight*, 1865; Musée d'Orsay, Paris; and *Bullfight*, 1865–66; formerly Matsukata Collection, present location unknown). Instead of showing the *espada* (bullfighter) in action, Manet presented the moment of truth, the confrontation between man and bull, as indicated by the bullfighter's *muleta* (a piece of red wool cloth hanging on a wood stick) and sword, which dramatically connect the two.

In this stop-action scene, Manet's primary actors and their shadows create decorative surface patterns. The focus, however, is on the silhouetted shape of the black bull, which joins with the flattened forms of the humans and their shadows in a triangular zone of danger and threat. As a backdrop for this mortal face-off, Manet painted the spectators with short, airy strokes, creating a blurred image of a crowd that mirrors his treatment of onlookers in a contemporaneous scene of modern entertainment, *The Races at Longchamp* (cat. 8).

The modernity of *Bullfight* was underscored by the fact that in 1913 its owner, Chicago collector Martin A. Ryerson, lent it to the controversial Armory Show, which introduced American audiences in Chicago, as well as New York and Boston, to many trends in avant-garde European and American art.

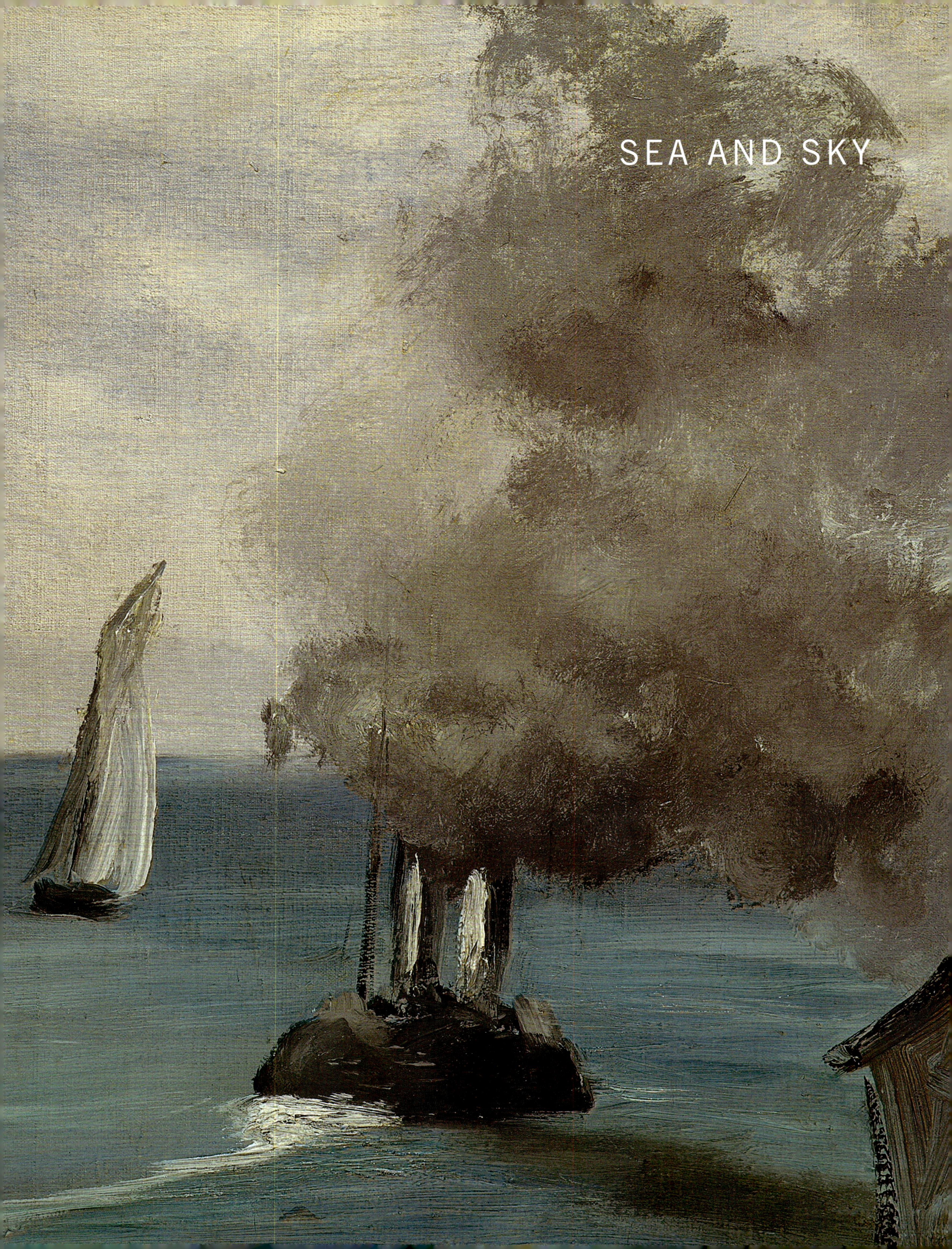

SEA AND SKY

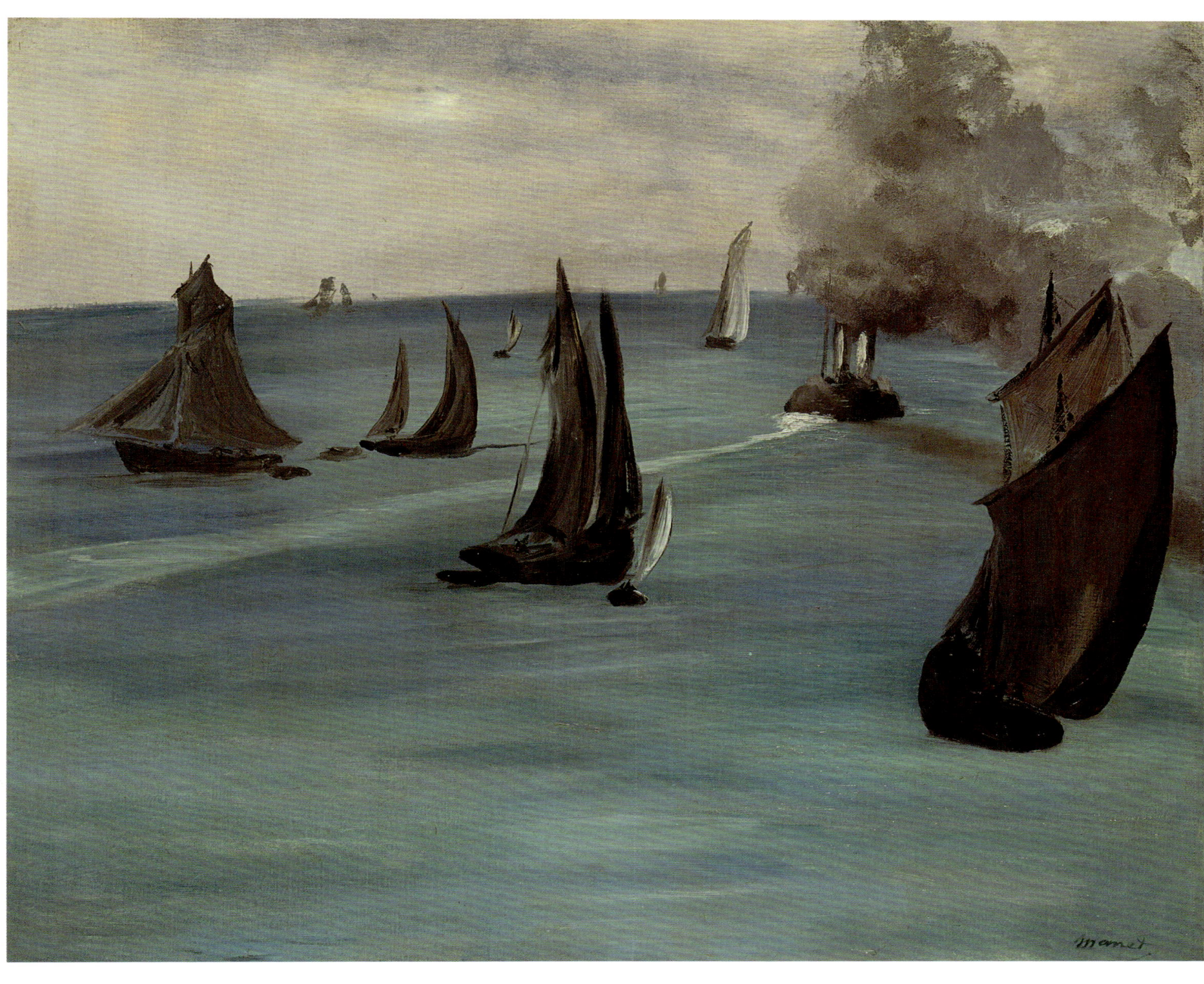

10

Steamboat Leaving Boulogne,

1864

Oil on canvas; 73.6 x 92.6 cm (29 x 36½ in.)
Potter Palmer Collection, 1922.425
Signed lower right: *Manet.*

Édouard Manet was thirty-two years old when he began painting the sea. Although they represent the least known aspect of his oeuvre, his marine pictures chart an artistic journey that lasted from 1864 until shortly before his death in 1883. During this time, Manet experimented relentlessly, pushing the boundaries of his craft and building on his own and others' achievements while responding to the emerging generation of avant-garde artists who would become known as the Impressionists. *Steamboat Leaving Boulogne* is one of three or four marines that Manet painted in Paris on the basis of sketches made on vacation with his family in the northern port town of Boulogne-sur-Mer. In stark contrast to the dark, solidly constructed and crowded still lifes from his Boulogne sojourn (see cat. 1), these seascapes are remarkable for their sense of light, wind, and water. Of the marines known to have been painted in 1864, this is the smallest and most formally audacious. X-ray examinations revealed that Manet painted the sea first, liquefying his pigments in order to apply them smoothly over a finely woven linen canvas that shows through the paint in places. Over this glossy blue-green expanse, which fills more than two-thirds of the canvas, creating a high horizon line, he added eleven boats, boldly brushed and almost calligraphic in form. Seemingly decorative and *japonisant* (influenced by the fashion for Japanese woodblock prints), these can be identified as specific boat types, including the side-wheel packet steamer heading up the Channel and leaving in its long wake the slower, sail-powered vessels. When Manet first showed this picture, in 1867, a caricaturist illustrated it in *Le Journal amusant* and titled it *Le Steam-Boat*, leaving no doubt as to its focus.

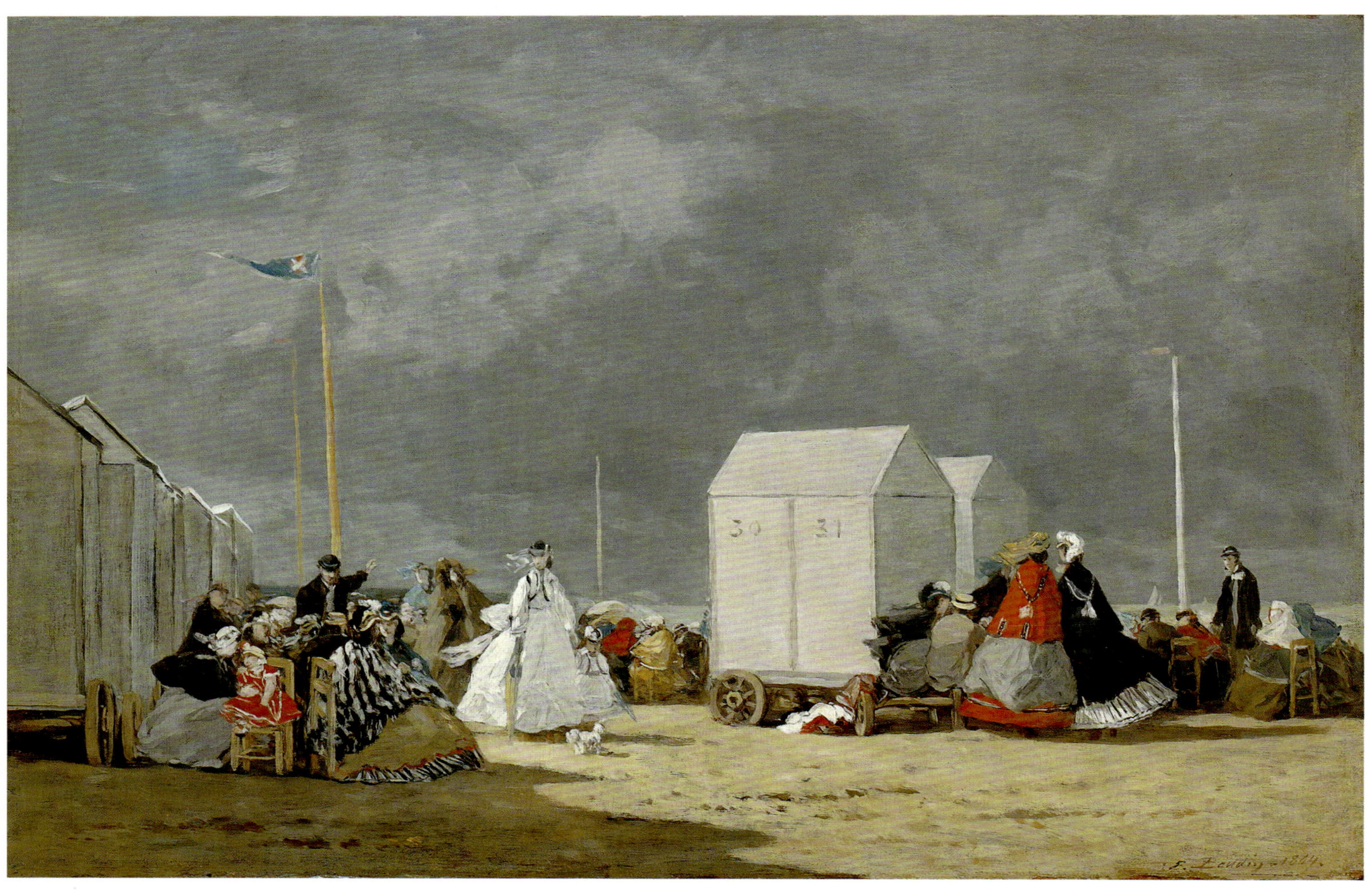

11

11

EUGÈNE-LOUIS BOUDIN

Approaching Storm, 1864

Oil on cradled panel; 36.3 x 57.9 cm (14⅜ x 22½ in.)
Mr. and Mrs. Lewis Larned Coburn Memorial Collection, 1938.1276
Signed lower right: *E. Boudin. 1864.*

12

JOHAN BARTHOLD JONGKIND

Entrance to the Port of Honfleur, 1863/64

Oil on canvas; 42.2 x 56.2 cm (16⅝ x 22¼ in.)
Louise B. and Frank H. Woods Purchase Fund in honor of The Art Institute of Chicago Diamond Jubilee, 1968.614
Signed lower right: *Jongkind 1864*

Eugène-Louis Boudin and Johan Barthold Jongkind changed the face of marine and seascape painting with works in which content, palette, and technical agility helped to develop plein-air (outdoor) painting. Claude Monet met Boudin in 1858 and adopted the artist as his principal mentor, but he claimed that it was Jongkind who "educated his eye." As they began to gain recognition from younger artists, Boudin and Jongkind also found admirers and buyers for their works. The rising popularity of their paintings relatively late in their careers coincided with a growing interest in the beach as a vacation spot. The Normandy coast in particular had become easily accessible for tourists and artists alike, thanks to the extension of the French railway system from Paris to the Atlantic.

Entrance to the Port of Honfleur is one of two seascapes that Jongkind showed at the Salon of 1864. At the same Salon, Boudin exhibited a work entitled *Beach near Trouville*, previously identified as the Art Institute's *Approaching Storm* but now thought to be a larger work (possibly *Vacationers on the Beach at Trouville*, 1864; Minneapolis Institute of Art). The majority of the beach scenes that Boudin painted in the fashionable tourist spots of Trouville and nearby Deauville date from 1864, his most intense period of work on the subject. These paintings usually feature the constantly changing Normandy skies over a beach populated by what the artist called his "little dolls." As he wrote to a friend in 1863, "People really like my ladies on beaches. Some claim that there is a gold mine there to be exploited."

Boudin's beach scenes translated the life of the Paris boulevards to the seashore. At a time when bathing costumes were a rarity, women, men, and children wore the same

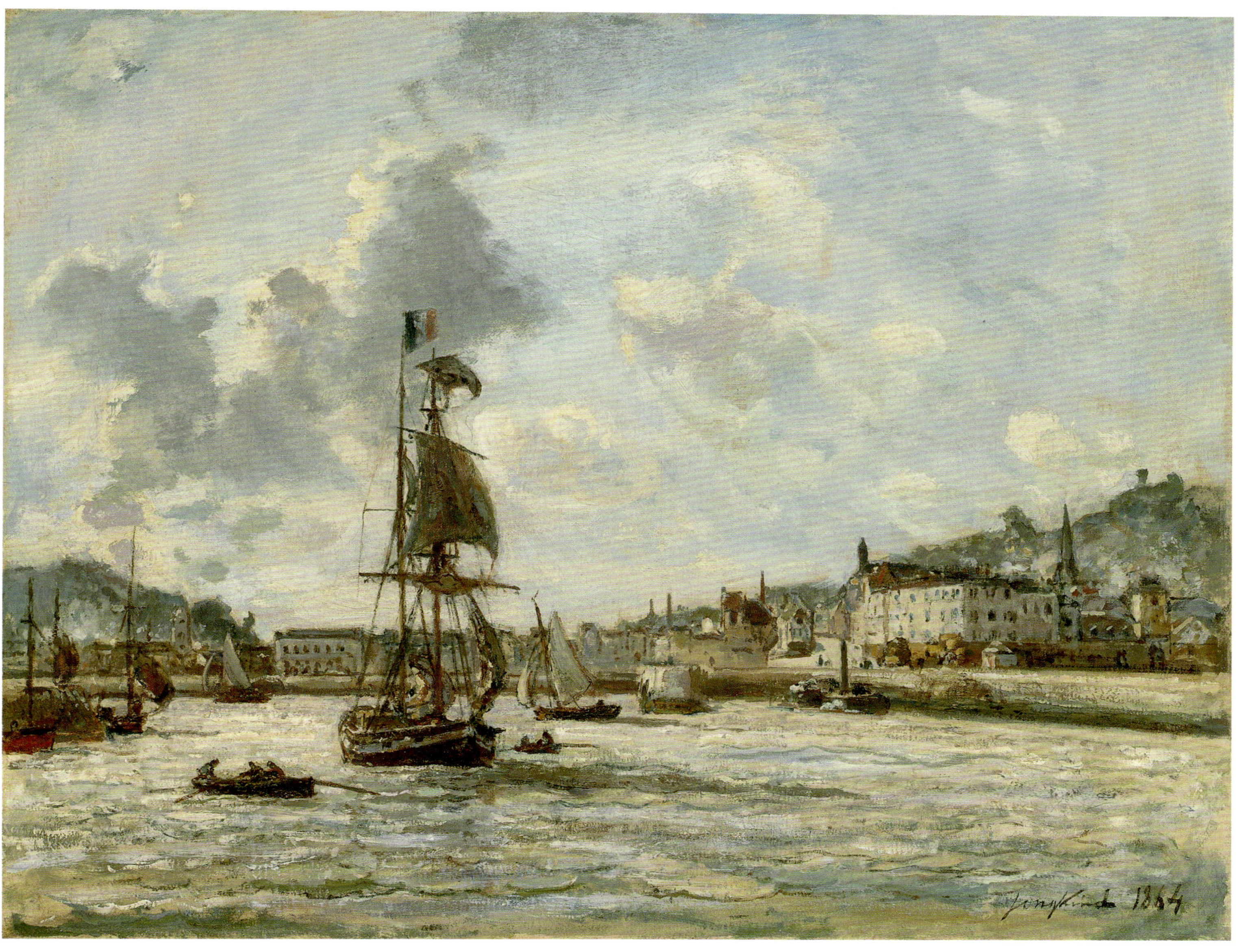

12

ponderous crinolines, frock coats, felted hats, and buckled shoes and participated in the same promenades, visits, and dinners at the beach as they did in their urban lives. Jongkind, on the other hand, focused on the sea rather than the crowds. During his early career in Paris, he was known as the "painter of the Seine," and on the Normandy coast, he continued to focus on waterways and ships entering and leaving the harbor, with only hints of the accompanying commercial activities.

Despite differences in the content of their paintings, both artists executed their final compositions in their studios, trying to retain the moist light and vivid spontaneity of the plein-air sketches from which they worked. They looked to the seventeenth-century Dutch marine tradition, and their compositions share a similar horizontal format and low horizon line. In each of the Art Institute's paintings, the eye travels from the lower-left corner to a central focal point—the woman and child in fluttering white crinolines in the Boudin, and the flapping sails of the wind-whipped ship in the Jongkind. Both artists included details that reveal an insider's knowledge of the scenes they depicted. At the right of *Port of Honfleur*, Jongkind showed the Hôtel Le Cheval Blanc in front of the hillside known as Côte de Grace. Equally precise (although not specifically identified) is the large sailing ship, with meticulously rendered masts punctuating the sky.

Boudin was no less exact in his representations of beach crowds. In *Approaching Storm*, he gave special emphasis to the portable changing machines (which were pulled into the water so that bathers could put on bathing suits without fear of being seen), whose silhouettes break up the frieze of figures and cast dramatic shadows. The darkening sky and high winds (indicated by snapping skirts and fluttering scarves) provide both entertainment for the seated figures at the shoreline and a sense of impending danger.

High Impressionism

CRADLE OF IMPRESSIONISM

CITIES AND SUBURBS

RENOIR'S TRANSFORMATIVE VISION

STILL LIFE

DEGAS: CLASSICAL TRADITION AND MODERN LIFE

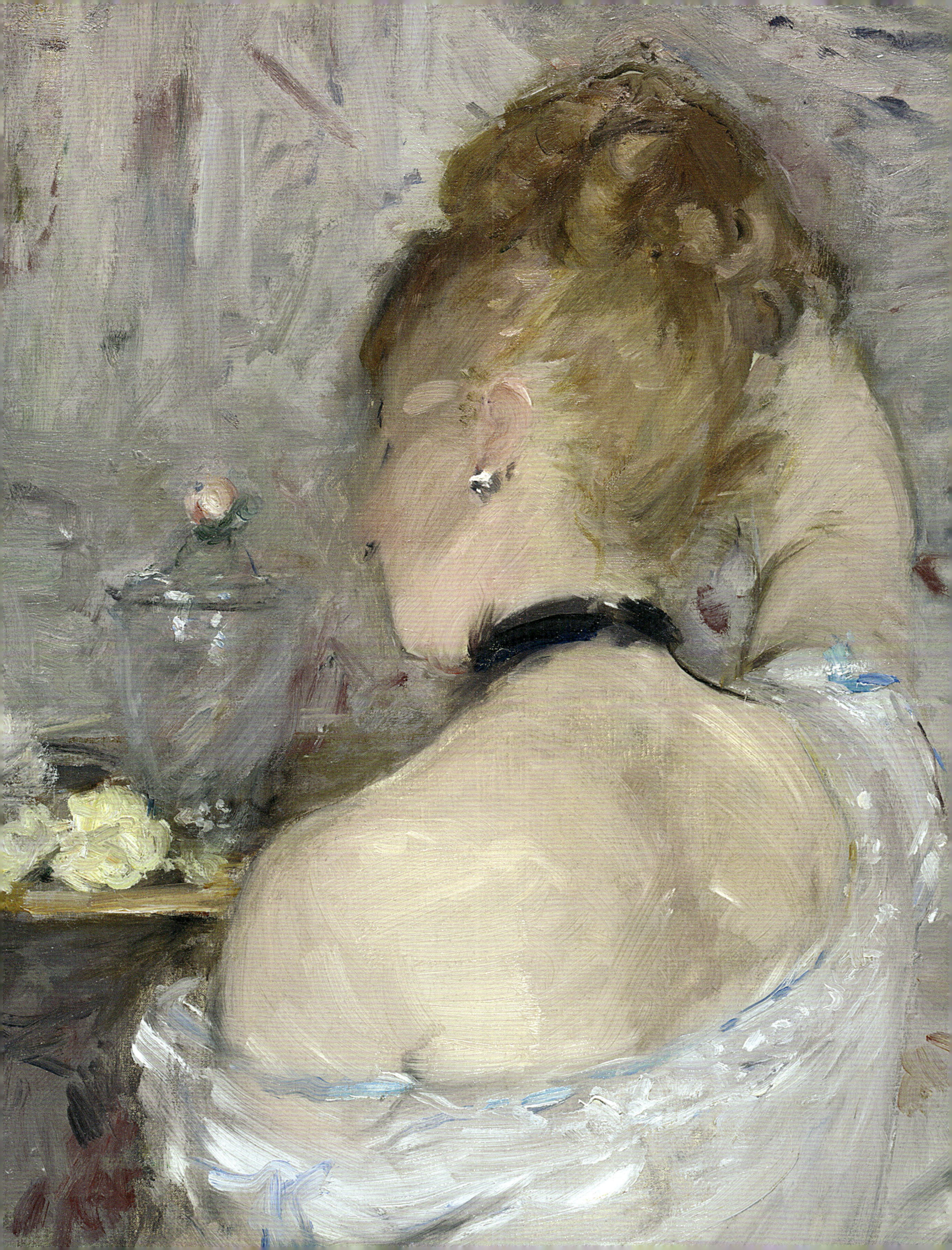

CRADLE OF IMPRESSIONISM

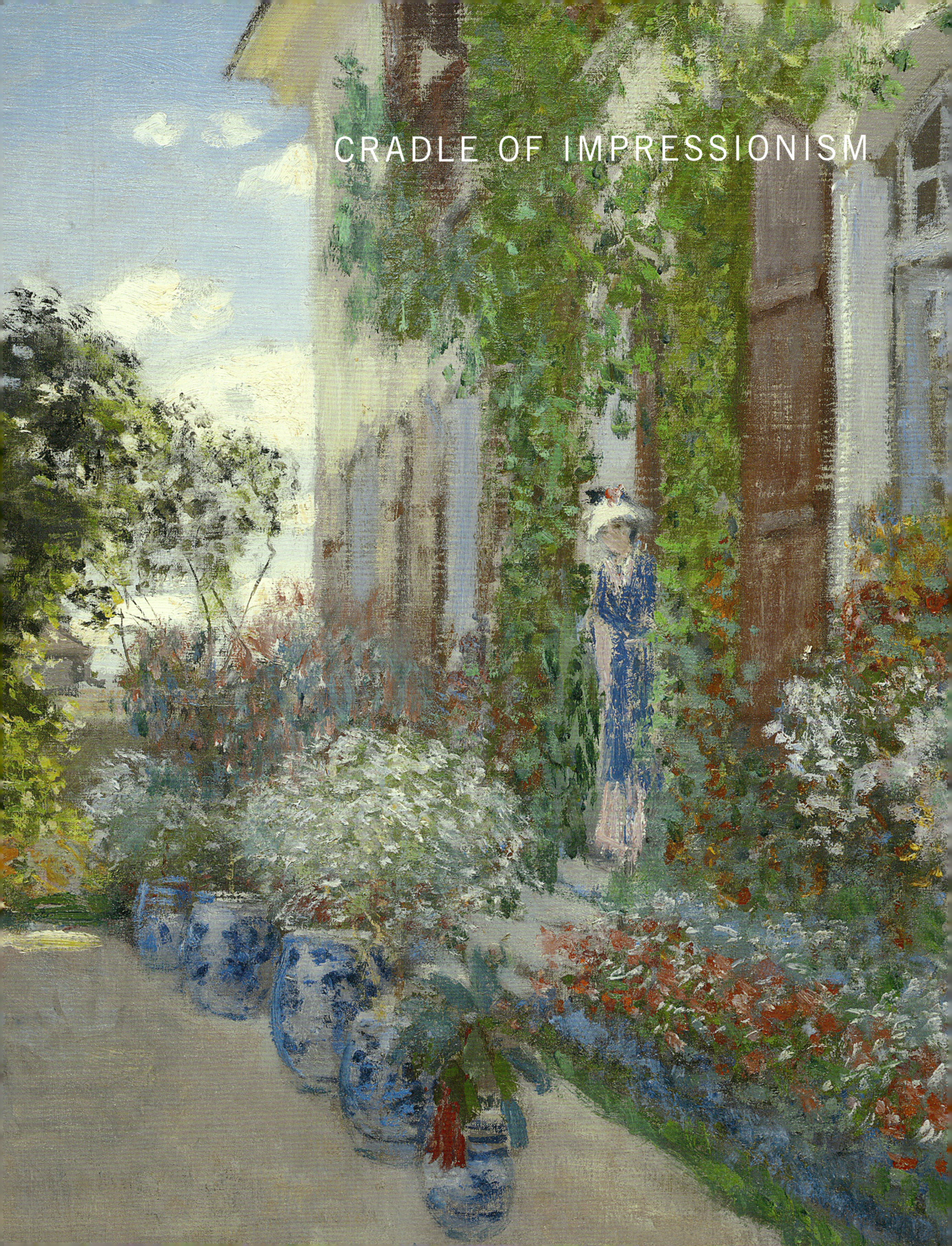

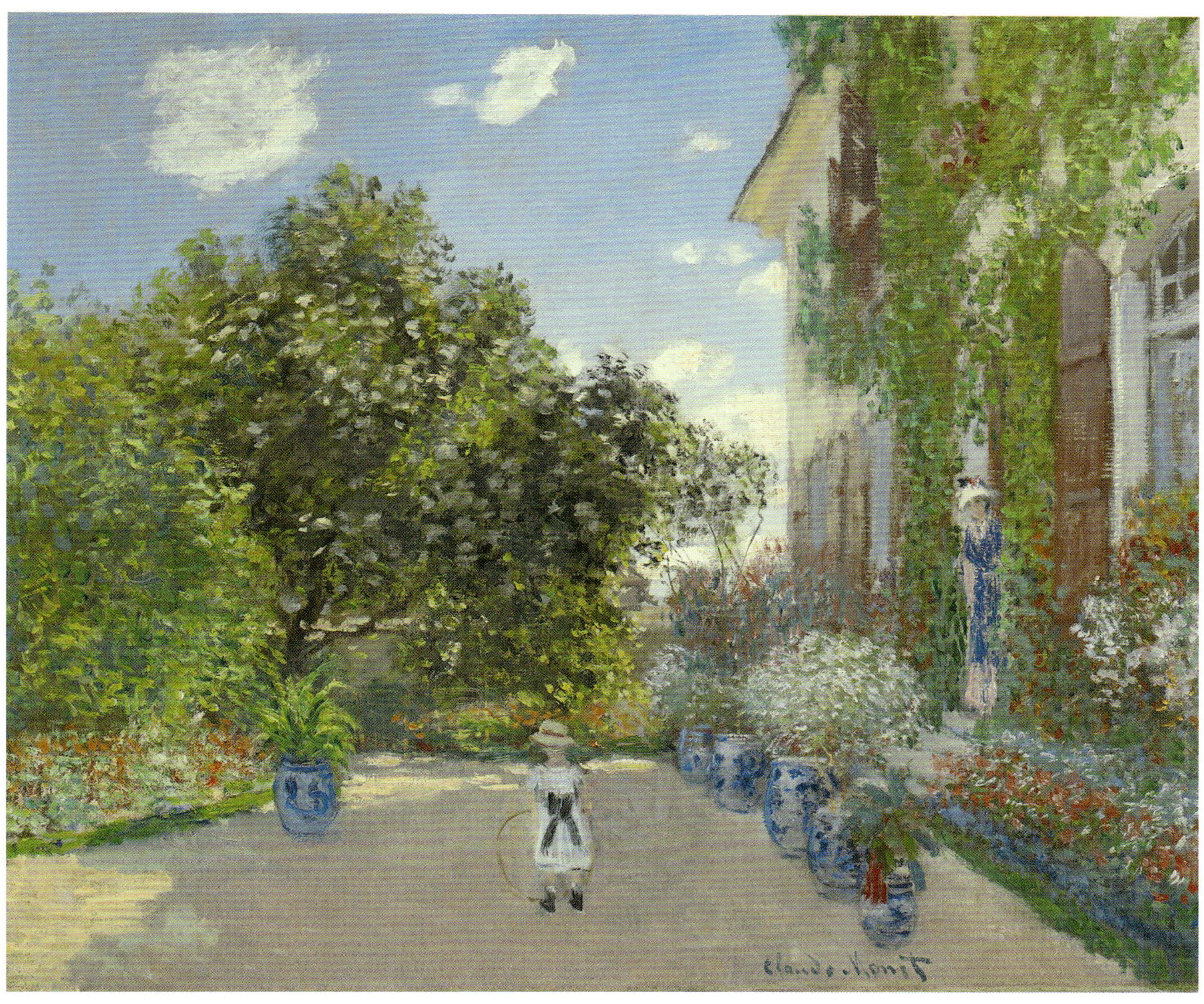

13

The Artist's House at Argenteuil, 1873

Oil on canvas; 60.2 x 73.3 cm (23 11/16 x 28 7/8 in.)
Mr. and Mrs. Martin A. Ryerson Collection, 1933.1153
Signed lower right: *Claude Monet*

This quintessentially Impressionist scene shows the garden of the house where Claude Monet and his family took up residence in late 1871. Its lush vegetation and sense of tranquility give visual testimony to the artist's material comfort at this time, thanks to recent sales of his work to the Paris dealer Paul Durand-Ruel.

The sun-dappled house, shaded gravel path, and circular flower beds form the stage on which Jean, the first of Monet's two sons (born in August 1867), plays with a wood hoop, while Camille Doncieux, whom Monet had married in 1870, watches from the open doorway. There are distinct similarities between Monet's famous final home in Giverny and this two-story, vine-covered house, whose back steps led to a profusion of multicolored flower beds and fruit trees. Over time Monet became exclusively a landscape painter; even in this candid familial scene, it is the garden setting and not the human activity that he chose to foreground. Unlike the many portraits that Monet made of his son, in this composition, Jean turns away from the viewer. Wearing a white linen frock over matching short pants tied with a blue sash (a popular outfit for boys because of its sailor connotations), he appears, like the blue-and-white glazed flowerpots, as a strategically placed decorative element.

Although Monet's financial security was short-lived and his relationship with Camille became increasingly fraught as a result of her deteriorating health (she would die in 1879), the seven years he spent at Argenteuil were significant. There he produced, in addition to numerous pictures of his home and its garden, some of his most celebrated landscapes and river views. Argenteuil was also close to Paris, where Monet and his colleagues planned a series of independent exhibitions, the first of which was held just one year after he executed this painting.

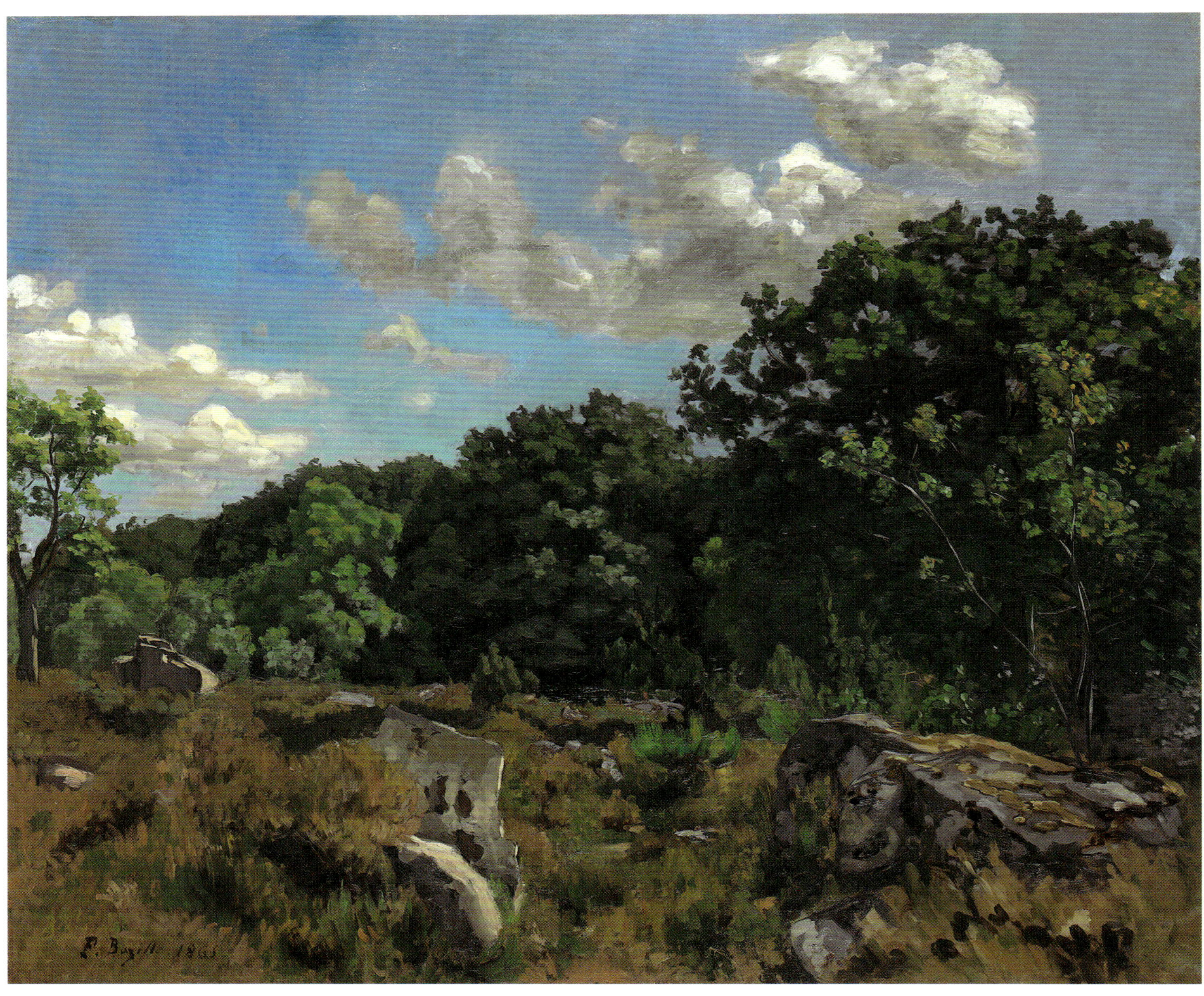

14

Landscape at Chailly, 1865

Oil on canvas; 81 x 100.3 cm (31 ⅞ x 39 ½ in.)
Charles H. and Mary F. S. Worcester Collection, 1973.64

Frédéric Bazille was an important figure during the formative decade of Impressionism. Born into a prosperous household in Montpellier, he started to paint early in his life but set out to become a doctor. Soon after arriving in Paris in 1862 to pursue his medical studies, he began to frequent the studio of Charles Gleyre, where he befriended Claude Monet, Pierre-Auguste Renoir, and Alfred Sisley. Bazille committed himself fully to art in 1864, and he produced an idiosyncratic body of work that, while closely related to his young colleagues' art, is more blunt in its handling and less overtly innovative in its ambitions. Tragically, just as Bazille was coming into his own artistically, he was killed in the Franco-Prussian War.

Late in 1865, Monet convinced Bazille to join him in the forest of Fontainebleau to pose for his projected composition *Déjeuner sur l'herbe* (1863; Musée d'Orsay, Paris). Executed during this sojourn, Bazille's *Landscape at Chailly* illustrates a site near the village of Barbizon. The overgrown boulders, flecked foliage, and jagged treetops bring to mind the work of Barbizon masters such as Théodore Rousseau and Jules Dupré, while the impenetrable blacks recollect similar passages in Gustave Courbet's landscapes. But the uninflected azure of the sky and the evocation of brilliant, almost merciless light strike an innovative note, as do the molten strokes on the rocks and the delicate white linear accents in the tree trunks at right.

Whether this landscape was intended for exhibition or as an experimental study is unclear and perhaps unimportant. For it was while elaborating their ambitious "sketches" in the late 1860s that Bazille, Monet, and Renoir began to question the viability of such a distinction, with results that would change the course of Western painting.

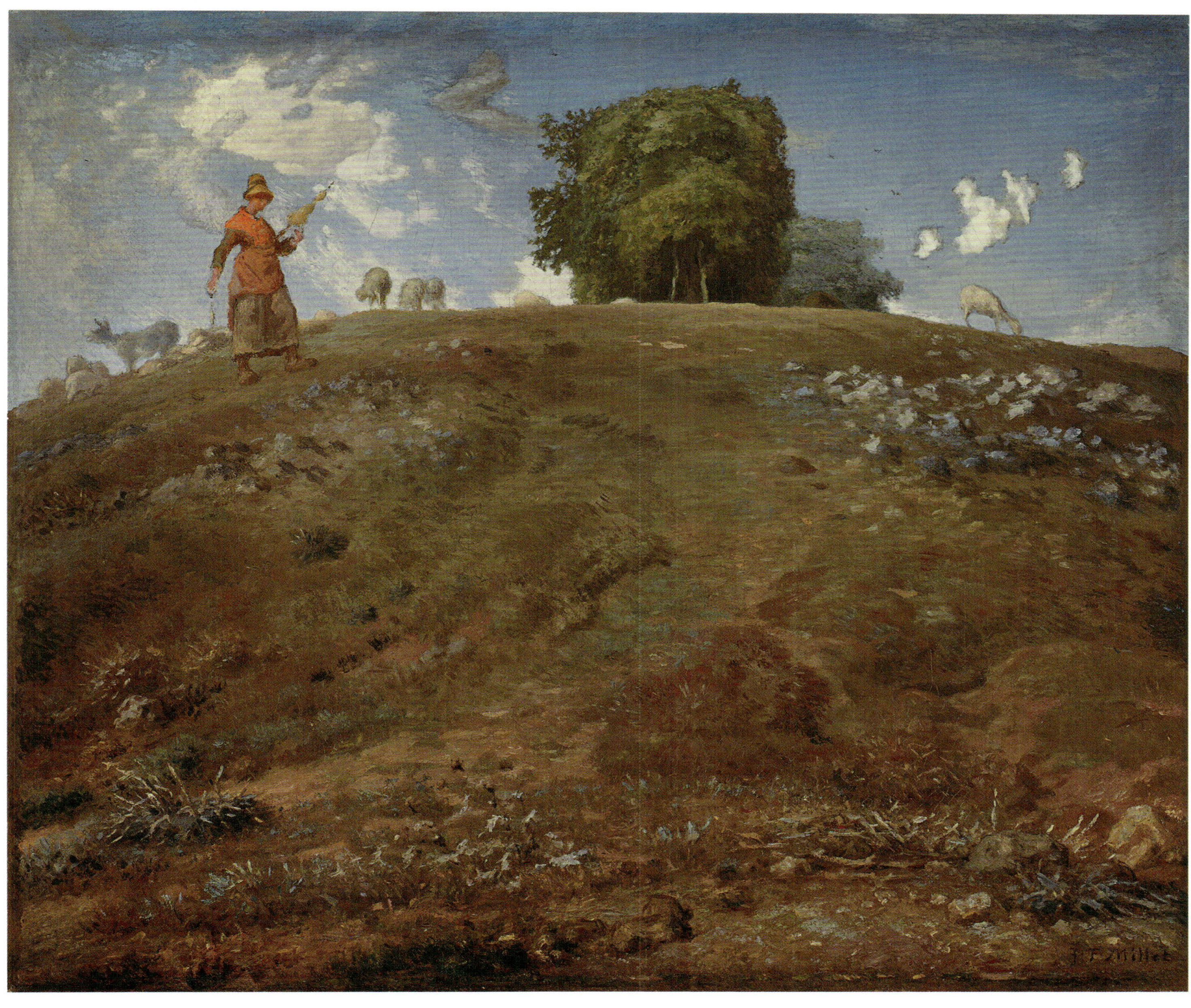

15

In the Auvergne, 1866/69

Oil on canvas; 81.5 x 99.9 cm (32 1/16 x 39 5/16 in.)
Potter Palmer Collection, 1922.414

The broad rise of a rock-strewn hill dominates the foreground of Jean-François Millet's *In the Auvergne.* The painting's low perspective forces a dramatically high horizon, marking a greater emphasis on landscape than that seen in Millet's previous rural genre scenes. During the 1850s, he had achieved critical acclaim with his portrayals of agricultural workers as iconic forms: monumental, anonymous, and innately dignified. Placing his figures close to the viewer, the artist anchored the compositions with their grand, solid silhouettes, stable and enduring as the earth itself. But in this work, the land assumes the primary position, and the figure of a young woman, spinning wool with a crude hand spindle as she tends her flock, appears almost as incidental detail.

Painted in the last decade of Millet's life, *In the Auvergne* represents his embrace of pure landscape. In the summers of 1866 and 1867, he accompanied his ailing wife to a spa in Vichy. To fill the long hours that she spent in the medicinal baths, Millet roamed the surrounding countryside. The rugged and unpredictable terrain, with its gullied slopes and rising cliffs, stirred the artist's memories of his native Normandy. He made rapid sketches of the region and, upon returning to his studio in Barbizon, used pastel and oil to record his memories of the textures and colors he had observed there. The thick brushstrokes and vivid tones of the grassy hillside in the foreground of *In the Auvergne* recall the calligraphic immediacy of drawing in pastel, and the work's bold composition reveals Millet's heightened response to a new and stimulating environment.

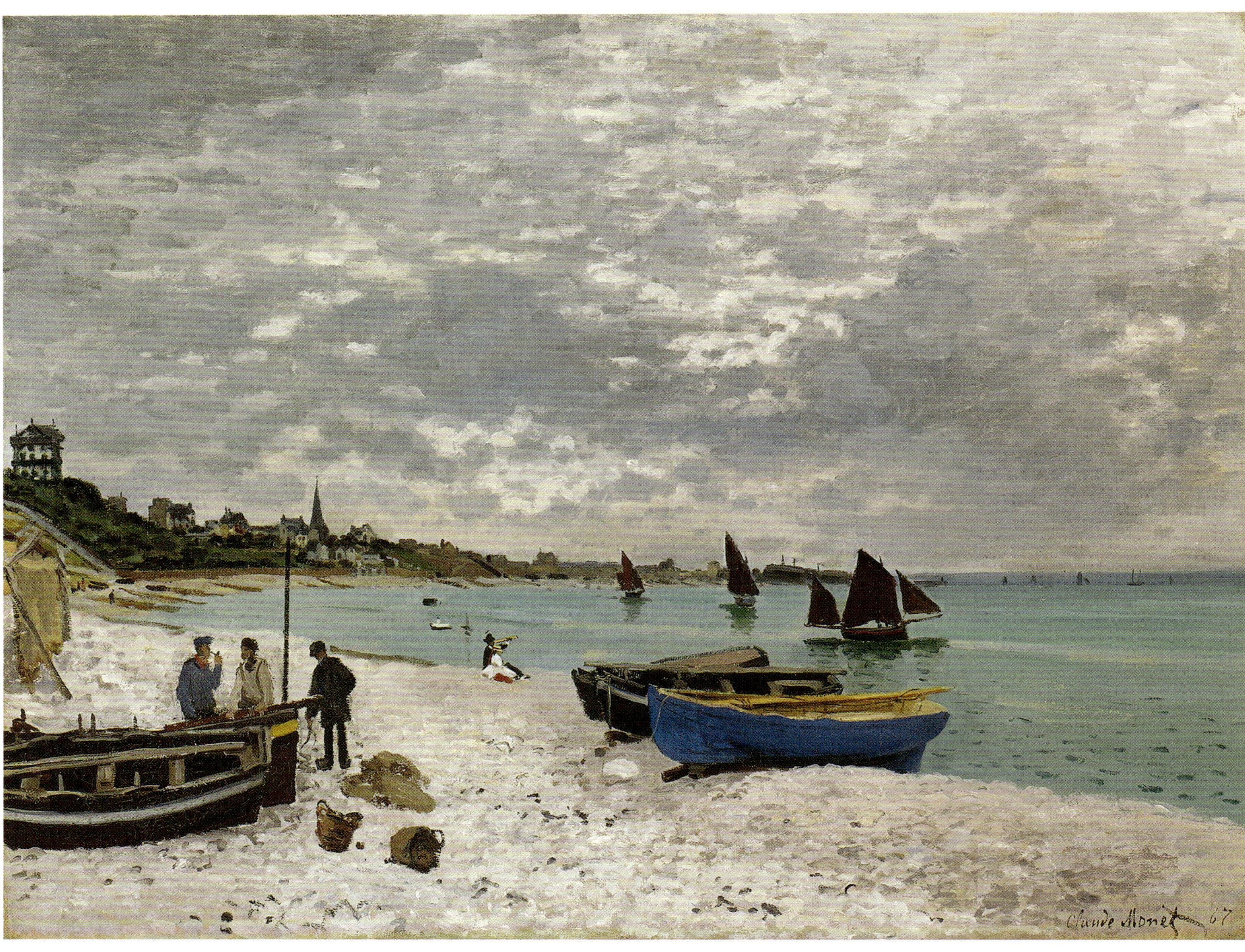

16

The Beach at Sainte-Adresse, 1867

Oil on canvas; 75.8 x 102.5 cm
(29 13/16 x 40 5/16 in.)
Mr. and Mrs. Lewis Larned Coburn Memorial Collection, 1933.439

Claude Monet spent most of his childhood and adolescent years in Normandy, absorbing its picturesque coastal sites, villages, and vantage points. The region changed dramatically over the course of the nineteenth century, due in large part to the expanded rail network and the proliferation of travel guidebooks. Waterfront locales like Sainte-Adresse, which were once small, rural fishing villages, rapidly became beach resorts for tourists and vacationers.

In the summer of 1867, Monet painted a number of works en plein air at Sainte-Adresse, including the Art Institute's *Beach at Sainte-Adresse* and its possible pendant, *Regatta at Sainte-Adresse* (1867; Metropolitan Museum of Art, New York). Although there is no evidence that he wanted to exhibit or sell these paintings as a pair, they are similar in size and depict the same stretch of beach from approximately the same viewpoint. Both reference the coexistence of local and tourist life at Sainte-Adresse; however, the Art Institute's overcast scene shows the beach at low tide, dominated by native fisherfolk and their dark-sailed working boats, while the Metropolitan Museum's features urban tourists and white-sailed leisure yachts on a sunny day at high tide.

Monet may not have originally intended to foreground local fishermen and their crafts in the Chicago painting. Infrared and X-ray images reveal that, in an earlier stage, he included three well-dressed tourists along the shoreline and a number of white-sailed pleasure boats in the water at right. Subsequently painting out these indicators of the leisure class and replacing them with three fishermen and their beached boats at left, the artist complicated the meaning of this work and, more significantly, the dialogue it shares with the New York picture. Though he may have begun these paintings as experiments in documenting the same subject under changing meteorological conditions, Monet deliberately revised the Art Institute's canvas, possibly in an attempt to speak to the complex social and physical transformations taking place in Sainte-Adresse at this time.

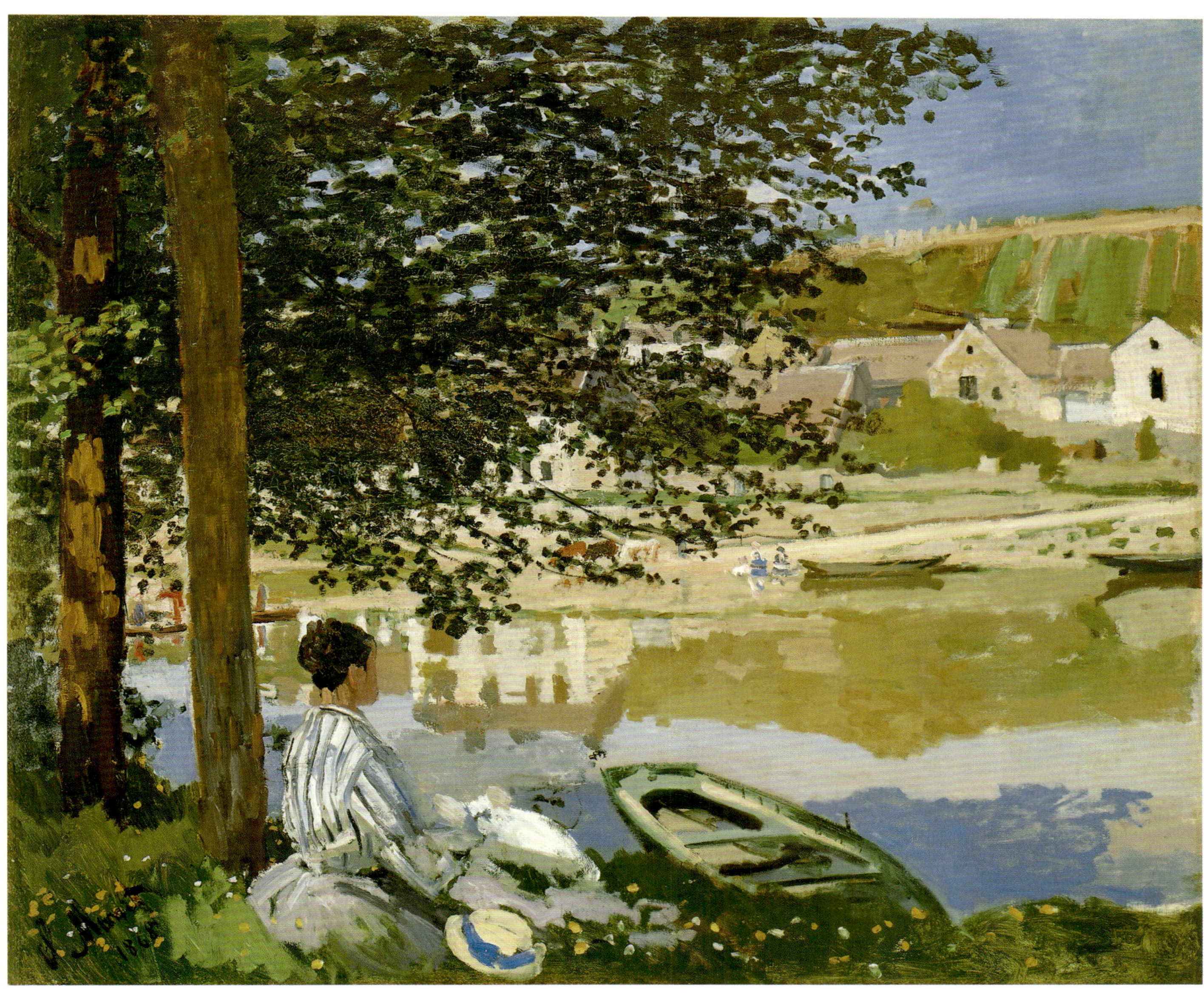

17

On the Bank of the Seine, Bennecourt, 1868

Oil on canvas; 81.5 x 100.7 cm (32 1/16 x 39 5/8 in.)
Potter Palmer Collection, 1922.427

In this nearly square canvas, Claude Monet depicted his future wife, Camille Doncieux, with whom he had only recently reunited after a separation of almost a year, seated on a riverbank on an island in the Seine River. Framed by trees on the left, she looks across the river to the hamlet of Gloton, next to the town of Bennecourt, from which she and Monet have just rowed. The writer Émile Zola recommended Gloton to Monet as a cheap rural retreat that was easily accessible from Paris. Perhaps acknowledging his friend's suggestion, Monet focused Camille's, and thus the viewer's, attention on the water's reflection of the hotel where Zola had stayed in 1866 and 1868.

Exhibited for the first time in 1889, this canvas—surprisingly experimental in both facture and coloration—is sometimes described as proto-Impressionist. Although the fluid blue and white stripes of Camille's dress appear to have been painted quickly over the green strokes that define the grass, there is evidence that Monet heavily reworked this area. Immediately to the right of Camille are vestiges of an earlier figure—perhaps a large, bonneted child (presumably the couple's nine- or ten-month-old son, Jean) standing on her lap with outstretched arms, or an adult female, who faces the viewer with what may be an infant child cradled in her arms. With its decorative, near-abstract brushwork, Monet's *On the Bank of the Seine, Bennecourt* has more in common with Paul Cézanne's structural facture (see cat. 18) or Paul Gauguin's zones of flat color (see cat. 84) than with the flickering brushstrokes that characterize the Impressionist touch.

Shortly after painting this image, Monet was forced to leave Bennecourt for nonpayment of his rent. The fact that this is the only work to survive from the artist's short but tumultuous stay suggests how highly he valued it.

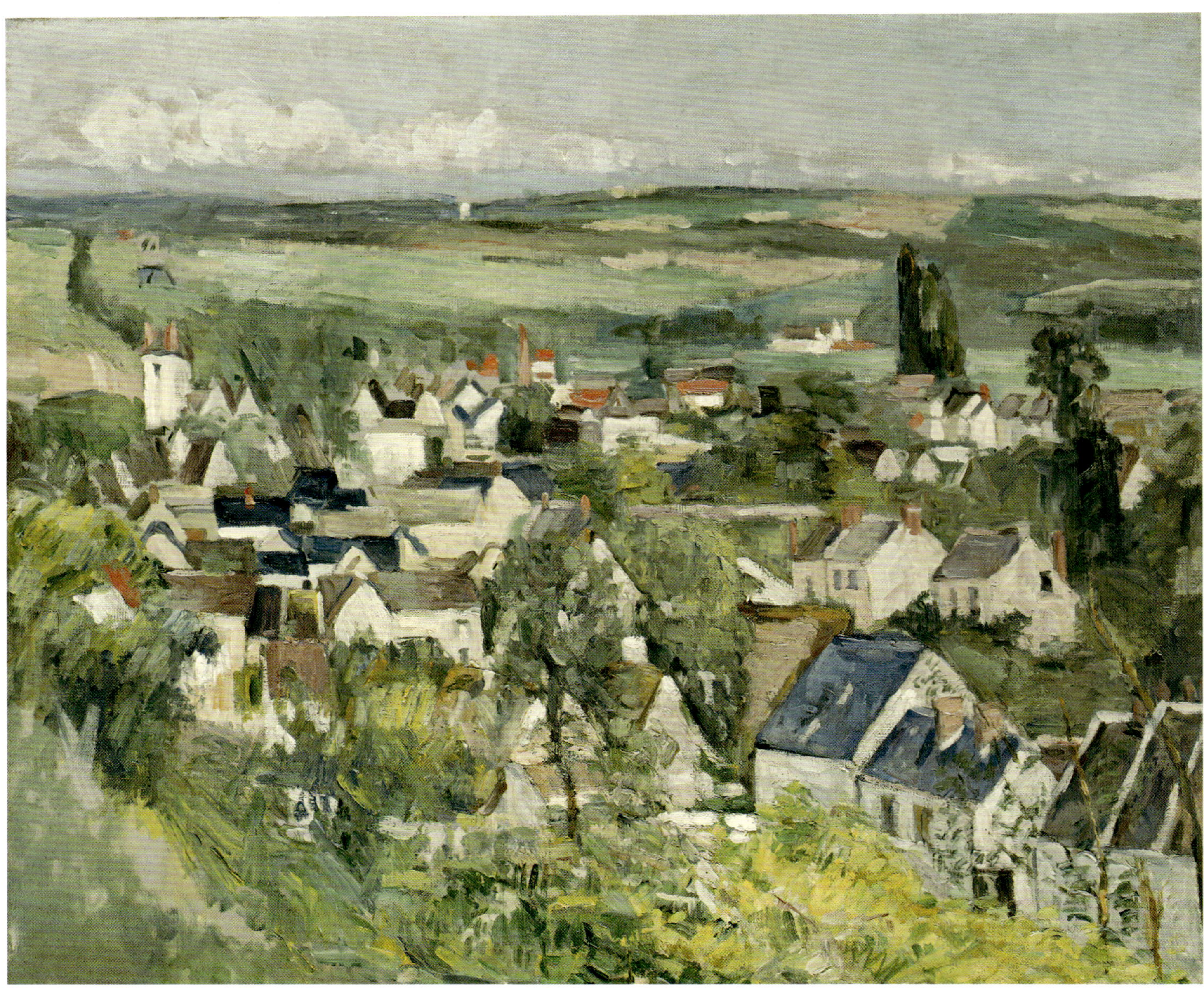

18

Auvers, Panoramic View, 1873/75

Oil on canvas; 65.2 x 81.3 cm (25⅝ x 32 in.)
Mr. and Mrs. Lewis Larned Coburn Memorial Collection, 1933.422

The title assigned to this panoramic depiction of Auvers-sur-Oise, a town about seventeen miles northwest of Paris, can be interpreted as a metaphoric allusion to Paul Cézanne's increasing openness to new modes of painting as he became involved with Camille Pissarro and the future Impressionists. Although he executed this work during his first prolonged stay at Auvers, with Pissarro as his mentor, its composition and facture are quite different from anything the older artist was working on at the time. They demonstrate that Cézanne was already well on his way to achieving a unique pictorial equivalent for the emotion he felt before a given motif, or what he called his "sensation."

In this view from a hill looking down on Auvers, Cézanne chose not to focus on a notable and picturesque site—the river Oise to the east of the city and the nearby medieval church of Notre-Dame—and concentrated instead on the crisp lozenges of rooftops, the cathedral-like trees, and the soft blanket of outlying fields. Most radical are the large, thinly applied, and choppy strokes in the lower-left corner, which he used to suggest the footpath that gave the villagers access to their fields on the plateau above, and that the artist himself used to approach the scene. The relative disorder of this patchy segment, the viewer's only entry into the landscape, suggests an unfinished, or at least unresolved, composition. On the other hand, emerging from the corner is an interlocking grid of carefully structured and progressively diminishing architectonic forms, representing the pitched-roof houses nestled at the bottom of the hill. Rising among these on the left is a vertical white rectangle with a single window—the house of Dr. Paul Gachet, a friend and patron of the Impressionists and the painting's first owner.

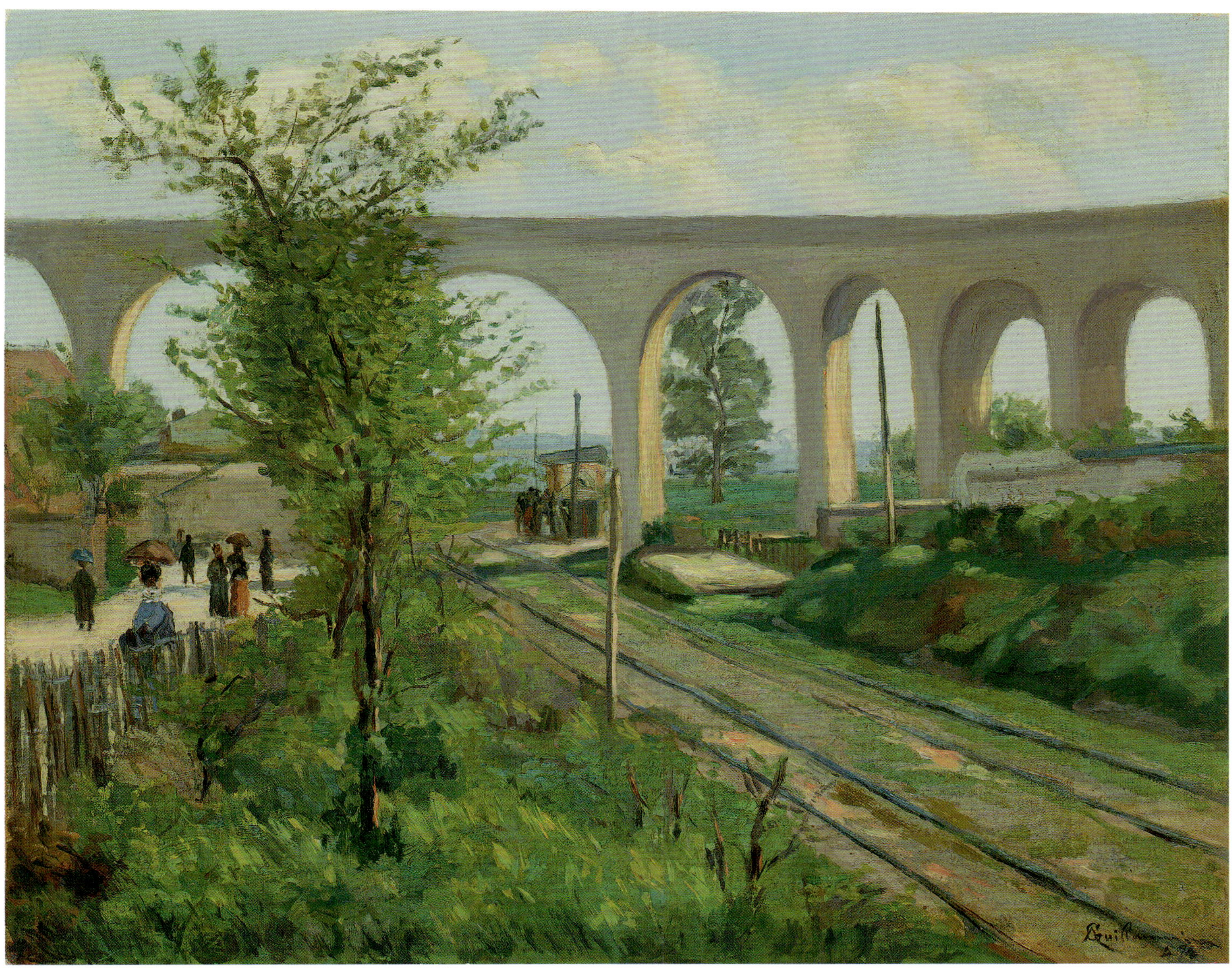

19

The Arcueil Aqueduct at Sceaux Railroad Crossing, 1874

Oil on canvas; 51.5 x 65 cm (20 1/4 x 25 9/16 in.)
Restricted gift of Mrs. Clive Runnells, 1970.95

During the early years of his career, Jean-Baptiste-Armand Guillaumin—whose working-class family did not support his ambition to become an artist—held a series of low-ranking administrative posts to make ends meet. While employed by the Paris-Orléans Railway, he began painting the countryside around the capital. The subject of this canvas is a new aqueduct, constructed in early 1874, that crosses over the tracks of the suburban Sceaux line in Arcueil, just south of Paris. Listed in contemporary guidebooks as a major tourist site, this was the latest in a series of regional water channels dating back to the Roman era.

In Guillaumin's painting, passengers await the train at a small, covered station just beyond the aqueduct, while pedestrians, including several well-dressed women with parasols, stroll along the road at the left. Between the tracks and the road lies a triangle of foliage, which Guillaumin sketched in thick, short strokes of brightly colored pigment that demonstrate his refined Impressionist technique.

The railroad symbolized modern technology for many of Guillaumin's contemporaries. It also played a crucial role in allowing the urban middle class (to which most of the Impressionists belonged) to make leisurely excursions to the suburbs and outlying villages. Around this time, Arcueil became an increasingly popular retreat, situated as it was in a picturesque valley only a short distance from Paris. *The Arcueil Aqueduct at Sceaux Railroad Crossing*, painted the year of the first Impressionist exhibition, may have been one of the dozen canvases Guillaumin contributed to the group's third show, held in Paris in 1877. There it would have joined Claude Monet's paintings of the Gare Saint-Lazare (see cat. 22).

ALFRED SISLEY French, 1839–1899

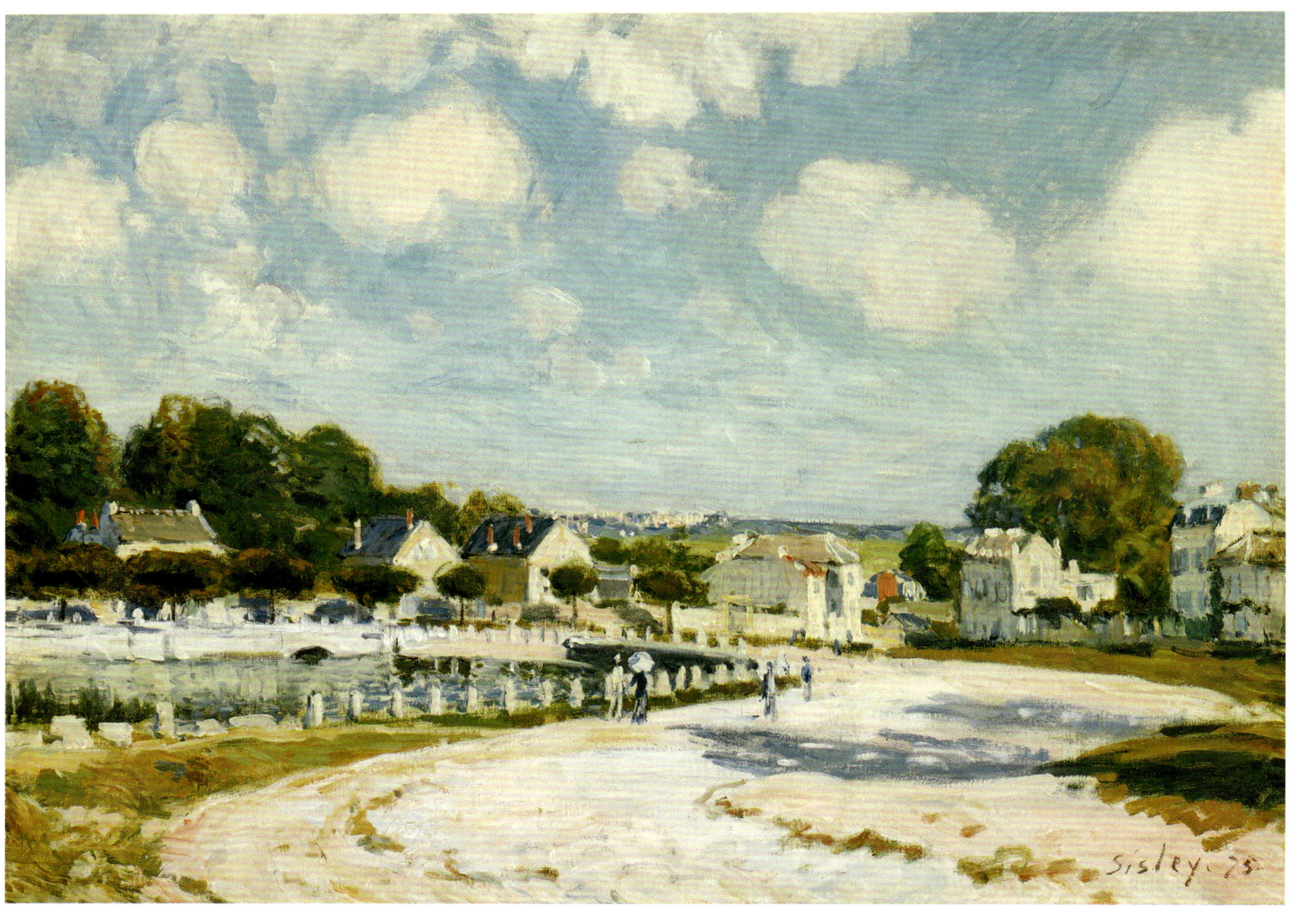

20

Watering Place at Marly, 1875

Oil on canvas; 39.5 x 56.2 cm (15 7/16 x 22 1/8 in.)
Gift of Mrs. Clive Runnells, 1971.875
Signed lower right: *Sisley. 75*

Of the original Impressionist group, Alfred Sisley remained most faithful to his early landscape subjects. Indeed, he spent most of his life painting in the villages dotting the Seine River—Argenteuil, Bennecourt, Bougival, and Louveciennes, among others—the region later called the "cradle of Impressionism."

At the beginning of 1875, Sisley moved from Louveciennes to the neighboring village of Marly-le-Roi, so named because of its original function as an elegant country retreat for Louis XIV. There the artist lived on the rue de l'Abreuvoir, or "street of the watering place," which flanked the shallow pool featured on the left of the canvas. This was all that remained of water gardens designed in the seventeenth century by André Le Nôtre; it served as an overflow basin on the edge of the adjacent former royal park, which is barely indicated by the trees at the extreme left.

Although Sisley depicted the watering place, with its low wall and bollards, at least a dozen times between 1875 and 1876, it was neither the once-royal connotations of the site, nor even its current use as a place for horses to drink and local laundresses to wash clothes, that attracted him to it. In this work, Sisley translated into paint a warm, blond light, which plays on the plaster surface of the houses and the wispy clouds that cast anemic shadows on the sun-bleached landscape. Examination of the canvas shows that, for all its immediacy and rapid execution, Sisley added small details in the studio after the original painting session. It is possible that these included the schematized figures, whose compositional role, like the bollards they pass by, is to provide necessary vertical elements to the exaggerated expanse of the serpentine road.

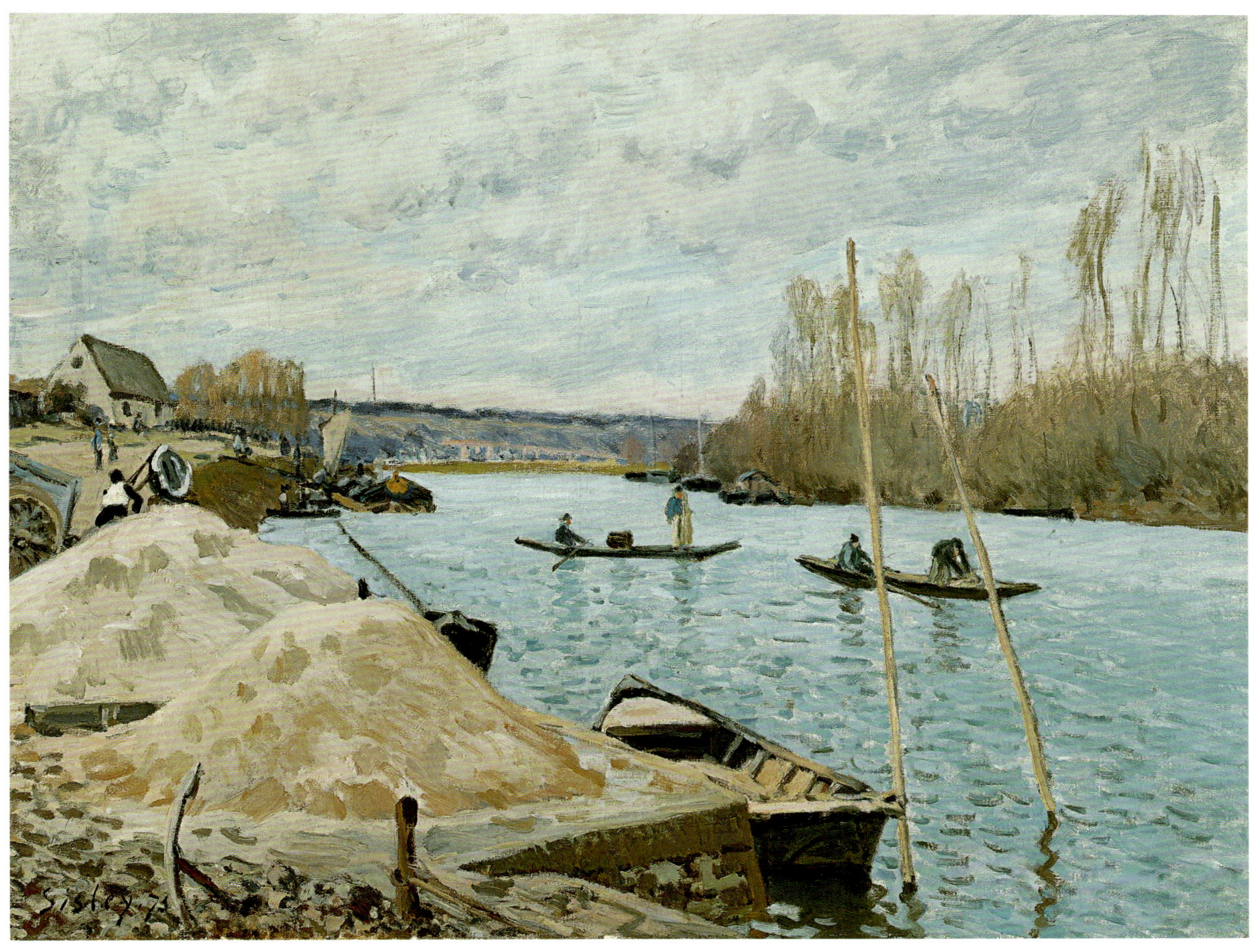

21

The Seine at Port-Marly, Piles of Sand, 1875

Oil on canvas; 54.5 x 73.7 cm (21 7/16 x 29 in.)
Mr. and Mrs. Martin A. Ryerson Collection, 1933.1177
Signed lower left: *Sisley. 75*

Of all Alfred Sisley's images depicting the landscape in and around Marly-Le-Roi, where he lived from 1875 to 1878, this scene of workers dredging sand from the river to facilitate barge traffic is the most unusual. In his choice of subject, Sisley underscored his singular response to the themes of modern life, which separated and, to some extent, isolated him from the marketplace and the notoriety gained by Gustave Caillebotte, Claude Monet, Pierre-Auguste Renoir, and his other artist friends. Although their river views celebrate leisure activities like row boating, yachting, and promenading, Sisley focused on what the river provided economically to the workers whose livelihoods depended on it. Unlike Renoir's riverside restaurant scenes (see cat. 29), this painting provides a glimpse of the Seine River during the workweek, focusing on a section that is devoid of the pavilions, kiosks, and paths that enticed Parisians to its shores.

Instead of walkways, the embankments are filled with sand, which has been dredged in buckets hoisted by the men in the low boats to be sold to contractors and gardeners. The workers themselves are, as is typical of Sisley's figures, summarily described and toylike, although their bending and rowing movements are readily discernible. The mundane nature of their activity belies the carefully and elegantly balanced composition, in which every vertical—figures, mooring poles at right, bollard, anchor, and roofline at left—finds a horizontal complement. Despite the work's highly calculated geometry, Sisley applied the pigments lightly to its surface. In the water, the aquamarine horizontals used to suggest the choppy surface are painted so loosely that they reveal the primed canvas beneath.

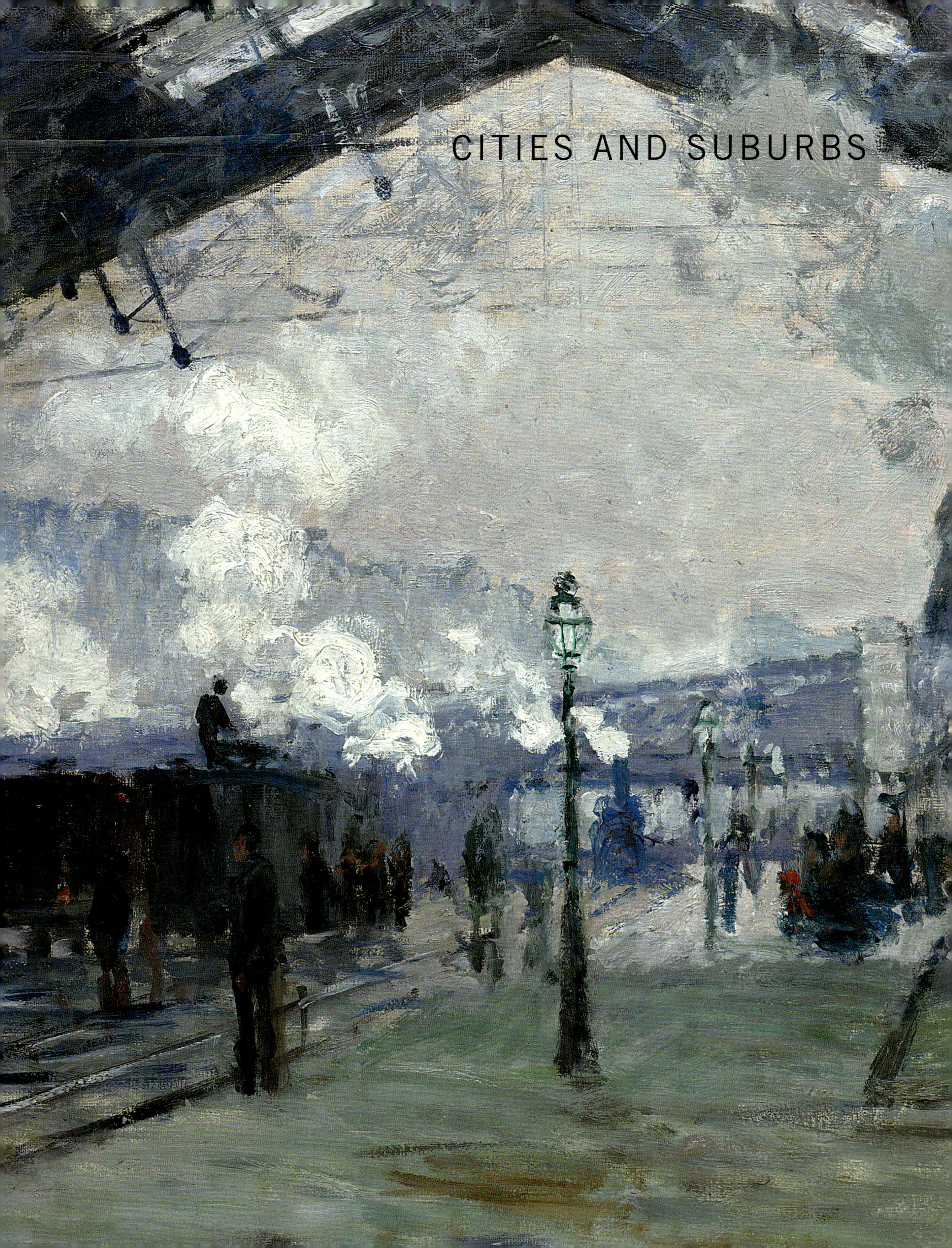

CITIES AND SUBURBS

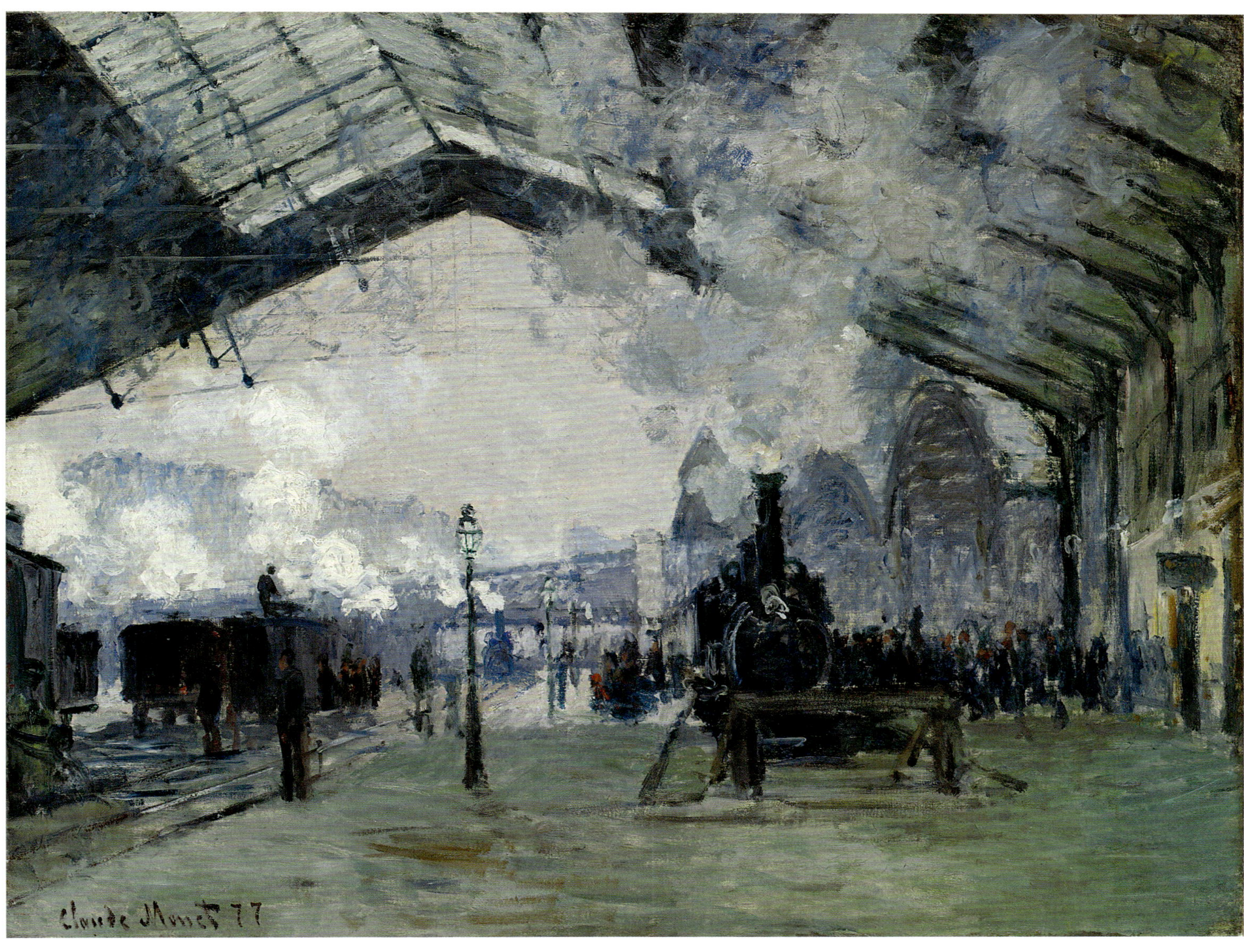

22

Arrival of the Normandy Train, Gare Saint-Lazare, 1877

Oil on canvas; 59.6 x 80.2 cm (23 ½ x 31 ½ in.)
Mr. and Mrs. Martin A. Ryerson Collection, 1933.1158
Signed lower left: *Claude Monet 77*

The Gare Saint-Lazare, which opened in 1837, quickly became the largest and busiest train station in Paris, attracting painters and printmakers who were interested in creating views of the modern city. But when, in early 1877, Claude Monet (financed by the artist Gustave Caillebotte) rented an apartment in the nearby rue Moncey and began the first of twelve canvases relating to the station, his aims, technique, and focus were quite different.

For Monet the train station represented the practical and critical link between his suburban home at Argenteuil and the business of art in Paris. In this particular canvas, one of four sold in March 1877 and included among seven shown at the third Impressionist exhibition the following month, the artist depicted the inside of the structure, whose lines serviced the villages along the route to Normandy that the Impressionists frequented. His use of the word *arrival* in the work's title signifies his desire to capture a specific moment—an intention reinforced by the use of dark strokes to show faceless workers and travelers, along with girders, signals, and engines. Legend has it that Monet even arranged for the stationmaster to add coal to the standing locomotives so that the painter could capture the effect of belching steam—dull gray when trapped inside the station, white and cloudlike when seen against the sky.

Despite its immediacy, the composition shows what a contemporary critic summarized as Monet's "skill in arrangement, that organization of the canvas"; at least one existing drawing (*Within the Gare Saint-Lazare: View of the Normandy Line*, 1877; Musée Marmottan, Paris) suggests a planned, rather than spontaneous, approach to the final composition. Its central lamppost aligns exactly with the apex of the glass canopy, bifurcating the work in much the same way as the lamppost in Caillebotte's *Paris Street; Rainy Day* (cat. 24), with which Monet would almost certainly have been familiar.

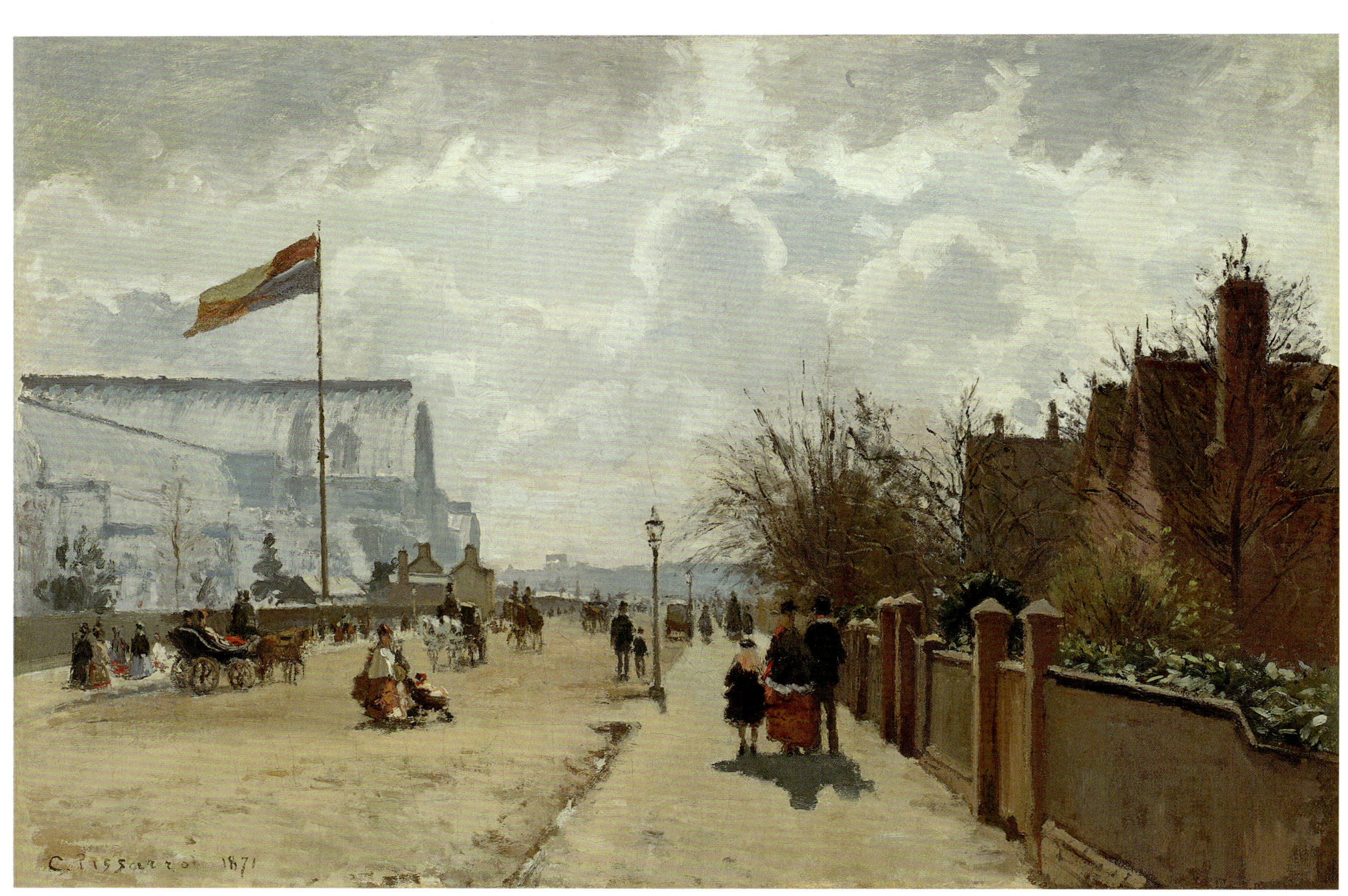
C. Pissarro 1871

23

The Crystal Palace, 1871

Oil on canvas; 47.2 x 73.5 cm (18 9/16 x 28 15/16 in.)
Gift of Mr. and Mrs. B. E. Bensinger, 1972.1164

Camille Pissarro painted nearly a dozen works, including *The Crystal Palace*, during his brief, self-imposed exile in England at the time of the Franco-Prussian War and the Paris Commune (1870–71). Fleeing his home in Louveciennes, near Paris, to avoid the Prussian invasion of France, he moved his family first to Brittany, on the coast of the English Channel, and then to Lower Norwood, outside of London. In the neighboring suburb of Sydenham, he encountered the soaring glass-and-iron Crystal Palace. Originally designed by Joseph Paxton in 1851 to house Prince Albert's *Great Exhibition of the Works of Industry of All Nations* in London's Hyde Park, the structure—immediately acknowledged as a landmark of modern architecture—was dismantled and reassembled in Sydenham in 1853 (it was destroyed by fire in 1936).

Pissarro's compositional strategy in *The Crystal Palace* recalls one he frequently used in his depictions of rural landscapes, in which he foregrounded a road or path that dramatically recedes into the distance. Surprisingly, now faced with a semiurban subject, Pissarro chose to relegate what had been labeled the world's largest building to the left side of this composition, while giving equal space to the recently constructed middle-class homes at the right and to the families and carriages parading down the street in the center. Within this space stroll fashionably dressed individuals; though they are English, they are no doubt wearing styles that originated in the French fashion industry.

Perhaps the artist, who typically depicted rural settings, was initially captivated by the play of sunlight across two very different forms of contemporary construction; he established a striking juxtaposition between Paxton's impressive edifice and the ordinary row houses across the way by focusing on atmosphere rather than disparity of scale. Rendering the Crystal Palace in a range of translucent aqua-blues that blend into the swirling sky beyond, Pissarro lent the spectacular exhibition hall a light airiness that contrasts with the solidity of the brick residences. Yet the painting accommodates both, presenting a balanced view of a unique, suburban landscape.

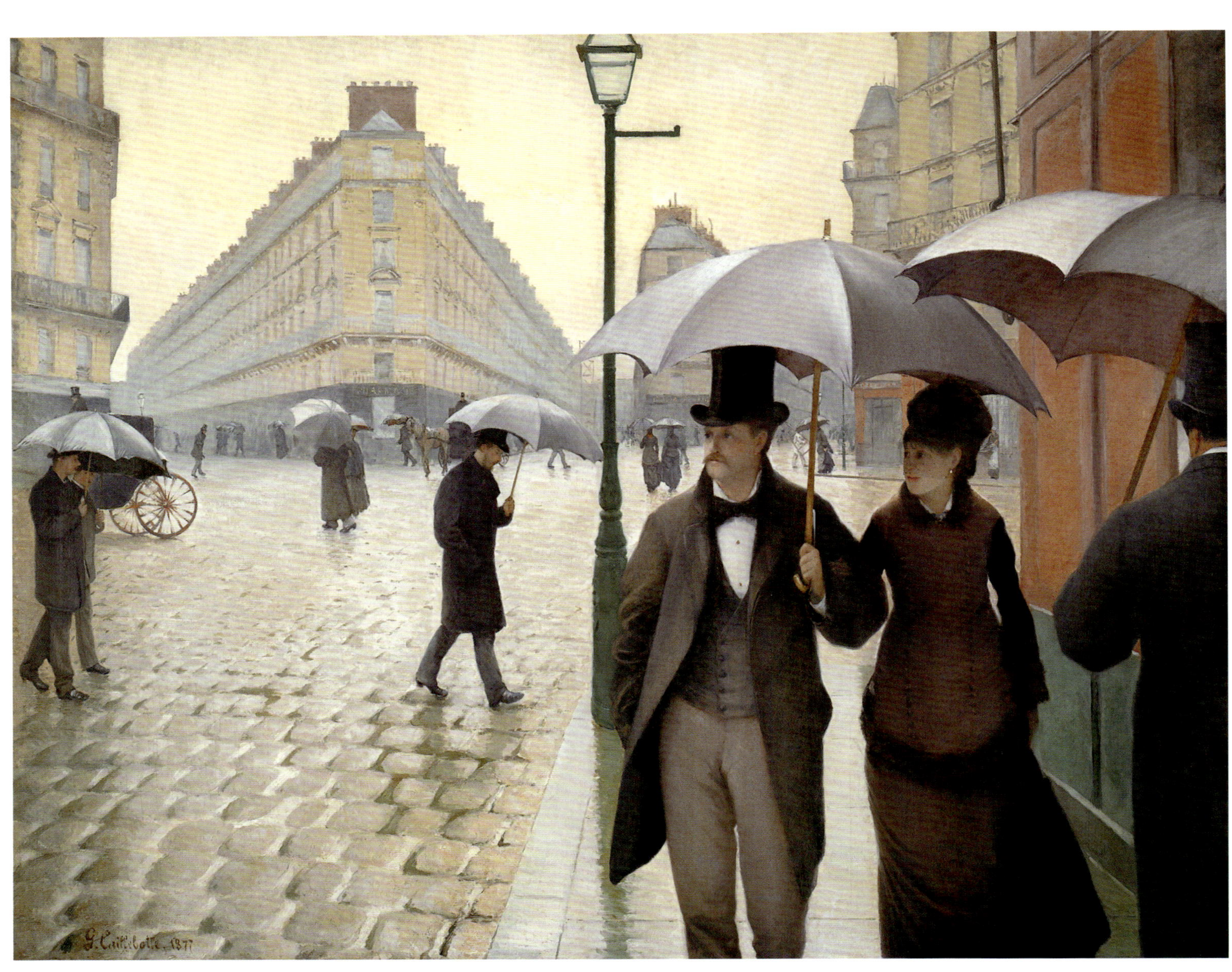
G. Caillebotte 1877

24

Paris Street; Rainy Day, 1877

Oil on canvas; 212.2 x 276.2 cm
(83½ x 108¾ in.)
Charles H. and Mary F. S. Worcester Collection, 1964.336
Signed lower left: *G. Caillebotte. 1877*

Paris Street; Rainy Day was, as one French anglophile reviewer said, "la masterpiece" of the third Impressionist exhibition, held in April 1877. Just four years earlier, the painting's creator, Gustave Caillebotte, had enrolled at the prestigious École des Beaux-Arts, Paris, where he received the technical grounding in painting and composition that would feature importantly in his future works. By 1877 the twenty-nine-year-old artist, a man of considerable wealth, was the youngest and most active member of the Impressionist group. He not only contributed six of his own canvases to the exhibition, but he also organized, financed, advertised, installed, and even lent works by Edgar Degas, Claude Monet, Camille Pissarro, and Pierre-Auguste Renoir from his personal collection. Upon his death at age forty-six, his collection was bequeathed to the state (only two-thirds of it was actually accepted), and it now forms the core of the Impressionist holdings of the Musée d'Orsay, Paris.

In this nearly ten-foot-wide canvas, Caillebotte took on a quintessentially Impressionist urban subject in a completely anti-Impressionist manner. Unlike Monet, who blurred architectural elements and abbreviated figures in his canvases of the Gare Saint-Lazare in order to express motion and immediacy (see cat. 22), Caillebotte here presented a frozen moment—one made permanent by his crisp technique and rigorously structured spatial composition. What makes the canvas so compelling is that it is both an irresistibly realistic depiction of life and a highly choreographed fiction. To achieve this balance, Caillebotte contrasted the minutely detailed cobblestones and two strolling city dwellers in the foreground with the smaller, less distinct figures in the background, who occupy the expansive spaces of the star-shaped intersection of the streets Saint-Pétersbourg, Turin, and Moscou. With their umbrellas providing visual links, these figures form rhythmic patterns while remaining firmly locked in the giant plus-sign structure of the composition, which is created by the vertical lamppost and its reflection, and by the imaginary horizontal axis connecting the bases of the buildings.

The pewter tones of the painting reinforce a sense of wetness that is both palpable and permanent, yet differs considerably from the Impressionists' depictions of atmospheric conditions. Indeed, the scene is not a captured impression, but a preconceived scenario based on a calculated perspective, into which Caillebotte added figures as both aesthetic and psychological elements. The sideways gaze of the nearly life-size woman at the right draws attention to the gleam of her pearl earring—a subtle reference to her bourgeois elegance. Behind her, framed by the umbrella handle and top hat of her male companion, the glint of a housepainter's ladder alerts the viewer to the presence of men and women of other social classes cohabiting the same urban space.

Although Caillebotte's title suggests a single street on a generically wet day, *Paris Street; Rainy Day* encapsulates both the monotony and the poetry of the boulevards designed by Baron Georges-Eugène Haussmann as part of his new Parisian city plan. The detached, noncommunicative character of the figures occupying the intersection may indicate Caillebotte's disdain for the anonymous and anti-picturesque nature of Haussmann's boulevards, which the novelist Edmond de Goncourt described as "without turnings, without chance perspectives, implacable in their straight lines." Although certainly different from Monet's and Renoir's lively views of the boulevards, which celebrate the spectacle of the capital, this work nonetheless pays homage to the quiet magic of the city, and more specifically to this intersection—topographically unremarkable from the many similar crossings of modern Paris, yet personally significant for the artist. Caillebotte's family residence was just a few blocks away, and in 1874 it had been expanded to include a studio space with a separate entrance, thus allowing him ready access to the streets he would immortalize.

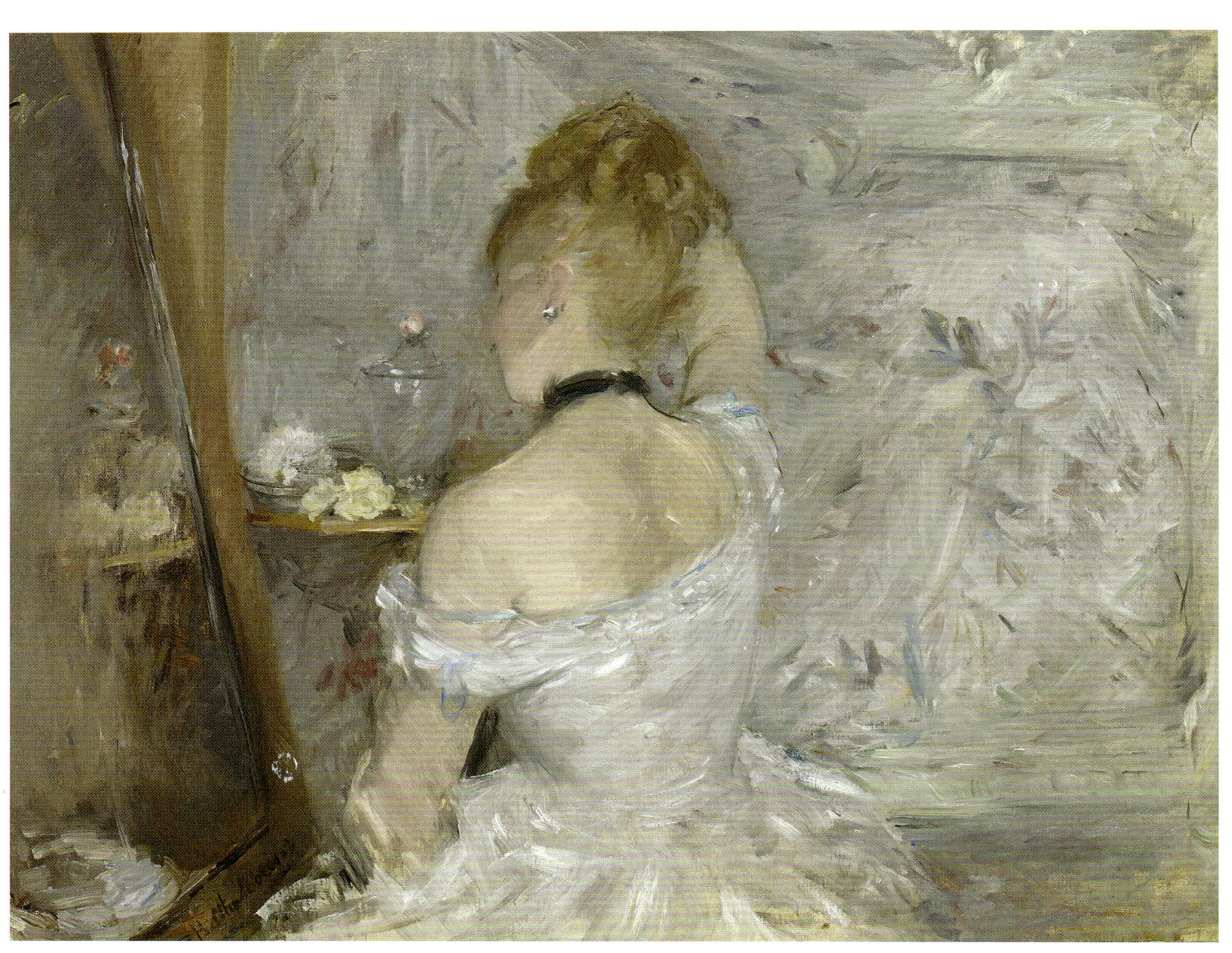

25

Woman at Her Toilette, 1875/80

Oil on canvas; 60.3 x 80.4 cm (23¾ x 31⅝ in.)
Stickney Fund, 1924.127
Signed lower left: *Berthe Morisot*

Berthe Morisot was, with Mary Cassatt, part of the small female contingent of the group of artists that came to be known as the Impressionists. In 1868, after studying with Camille Corot and showing her works at the official Salon, Morisot met Édouard Manet, who gave her entrée into the Impressionist circle. Although Manet (whose brother she later married) never felt entirely comfortable with the Impressionist style, Morisot became an enthusiastic and faithful adherent, exhibiting in all but one of the group's eight shows.

Woman at Her Toilette, presented at the fifth Impressionist exhibition, in 1880, is one of numerous canvases Morisot painted in the mid-1870s and early 1880s that depict the successive phases of well-to-do women dressing and readying themselves to appear in public. Although her brother-in-law often took on similar subjects, he eroticized his women—sometimes through the addition of a male admirer, other times by the attention given to undergarments or the model's state of undress. The sensuality of Morisot's boudoir scenes, on the contrary, results as much from her feathery soft, yet boldly free brushwork as from the pictures' narratives. Gustave Geffroy, a critic sympathetic to the Impressionists, admired the evanescent quality of Morisot's paintings and her ability to "fix the play of colors, the quivering between things, and the air that envelops them." In his view, "No one represents Impressionism with more refined talent or with more authority than Morisot." Geffroy applauded the balance that the artist established between her audacious painting style and her discretion in approaching her subjects, which allowed her to express a modernist vision of a private sphere without overstepping the limitations of what a respectable woman might paint.

In the rarified and perfumed realm of *Woman at Her Toilette*, Morisot's model starts the process of undoing the elaborate preparations made for her appearance at a society ball. Turned so that only her neck and the back of her head are visible, she has inclined the cheval glass toward her, effectively denying the viewer the pleasure of observing her or her reflection. Only the objects she used to create her public persona—the powder puff, crystal jar, and flowers—can be seen, indirectly, in the mirror. Morisot's virtuoso brushwork and pale color harmonies merge her model's pinkish white flesh and the light muslin or linen of her chemise or underdress with the floral background, from which emerges, as if floating, the headboard of an Empire bed. Probably Morisot's own bed (based on its appearance in other interior scenes by the artist), it is barely distinguishable, dissolved through her handling of paint, which one critic described as akin to spreading ground-up flower petals onto her surfaces "with airy, witty touches, thrown down almost haphazardly."

In fact, Morisot's technique was highly calculated to suggest the contours of the model, whose nuanced delicacy contrasts with the relative legibility of her toilette. Though she still wears her sparkling white earrings and navy blue velvet neckband, Morisot's young model has probably just removed the yellow and white roses from her chignon. The silvery palette, delicate brushwork, and carefully composed, discreet view of a private moment result in an image celebrating femininity and artifice. The presence of Morisot's signature on the lower edge of the mirror underscores the association between the artist's creation and that of her model, achieved with makeup and clothing rather than paint.

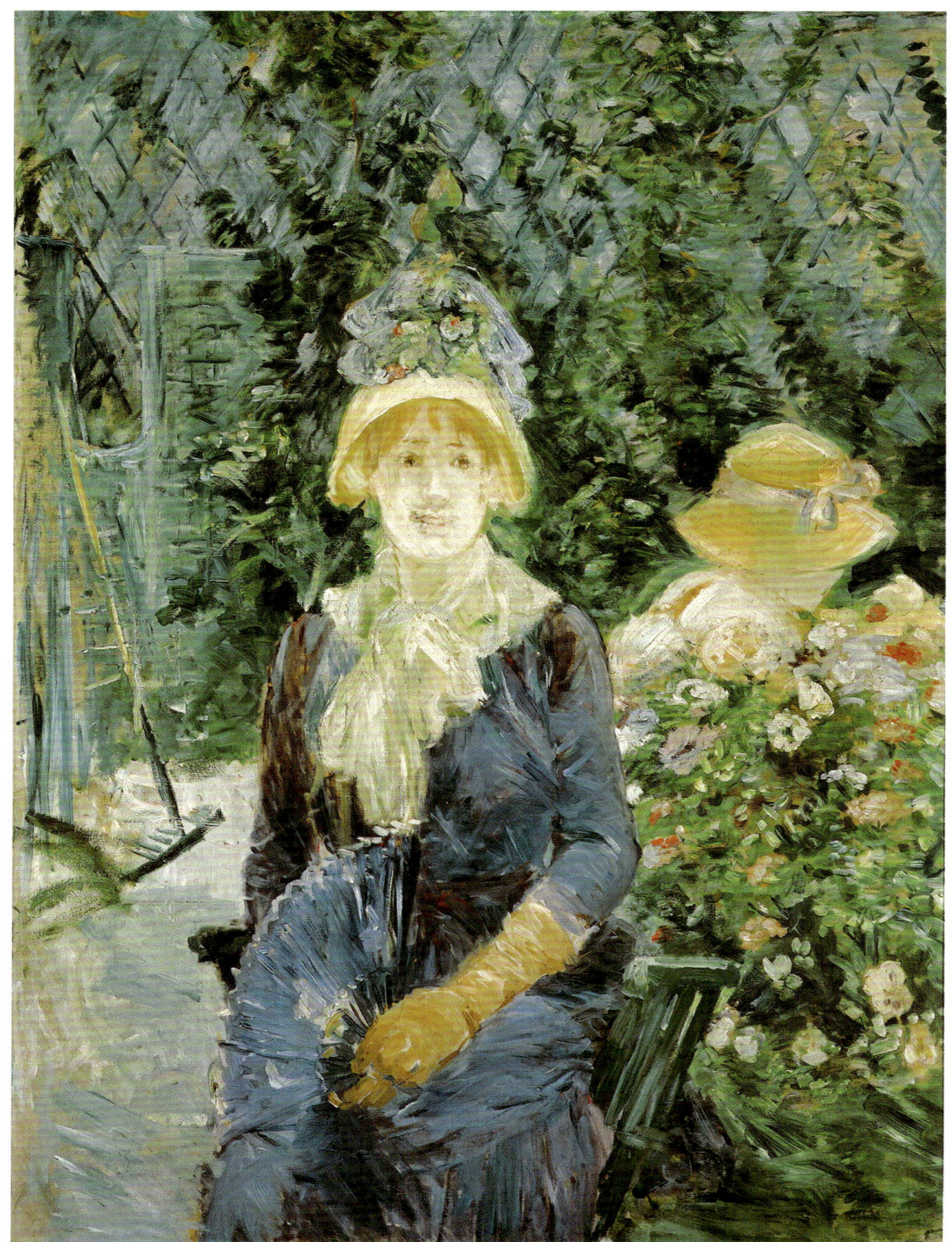

26

Woman in a Garden, 1882/83

Oil on canvas; 123 x 94 cm (48½ x 37 in.)
A Millennium Gift of Sara Lee Corporation, 1999.363

This ambitious canvas challenges the conventions of portraiture both compositionally and technically. Instead of flattering the sitter and making her the object of visual interest, Berthe Morisot deliberately treated the young woman as one of several focal points that serve to move the viewer's eye around the freely painted, yet highly structured composition.

Although undated, the work was probably begun in the summer of 1882, when Morisot—along with her husband, Eugène Manet; and their daughter, Julie—rented a house in Bougival, a picturesque village along the Seine River. The child wearing a straw hat and pinafore, who plays alone just behind the sitter, is undoubtedly the nearly four-year-old Julie. Both figures are surrounded by a profusion of flowers (some of which seem to have taken root atop the young model's hat) in a densely vegetated garden punctuated by the geometries of the trellis, the chair in the lower right, and the rake placed casually against the fence at the left. Far from creating a portrait likeness, Morisot applied paint as if she was making an Impressionist landscape, slashing acid green pigments and bluish ochers across the canvas to transcribe the effects of dappled sunlight without differentiating between the strokes used for the figure and setting. The resulting composition is both jarring—because it thwarts the anticipated treatment of the female as a beautiful complement to the natural setting—and captivating. Its rigorous and seemingly spontaneous brushwork unifies and electrifies the surface.

Although it was not exhibited at any of the Impressionist exhibitions, Morisot allowed the Paris dealer Paul Durand-Ruel to send the painting to London for an exhibition at a commercial gallery in April 1883. The fact that it remained in the artist's family for sixty years following her death may indicate that it was not marketable or, conversely, that it had been particularly important to her.

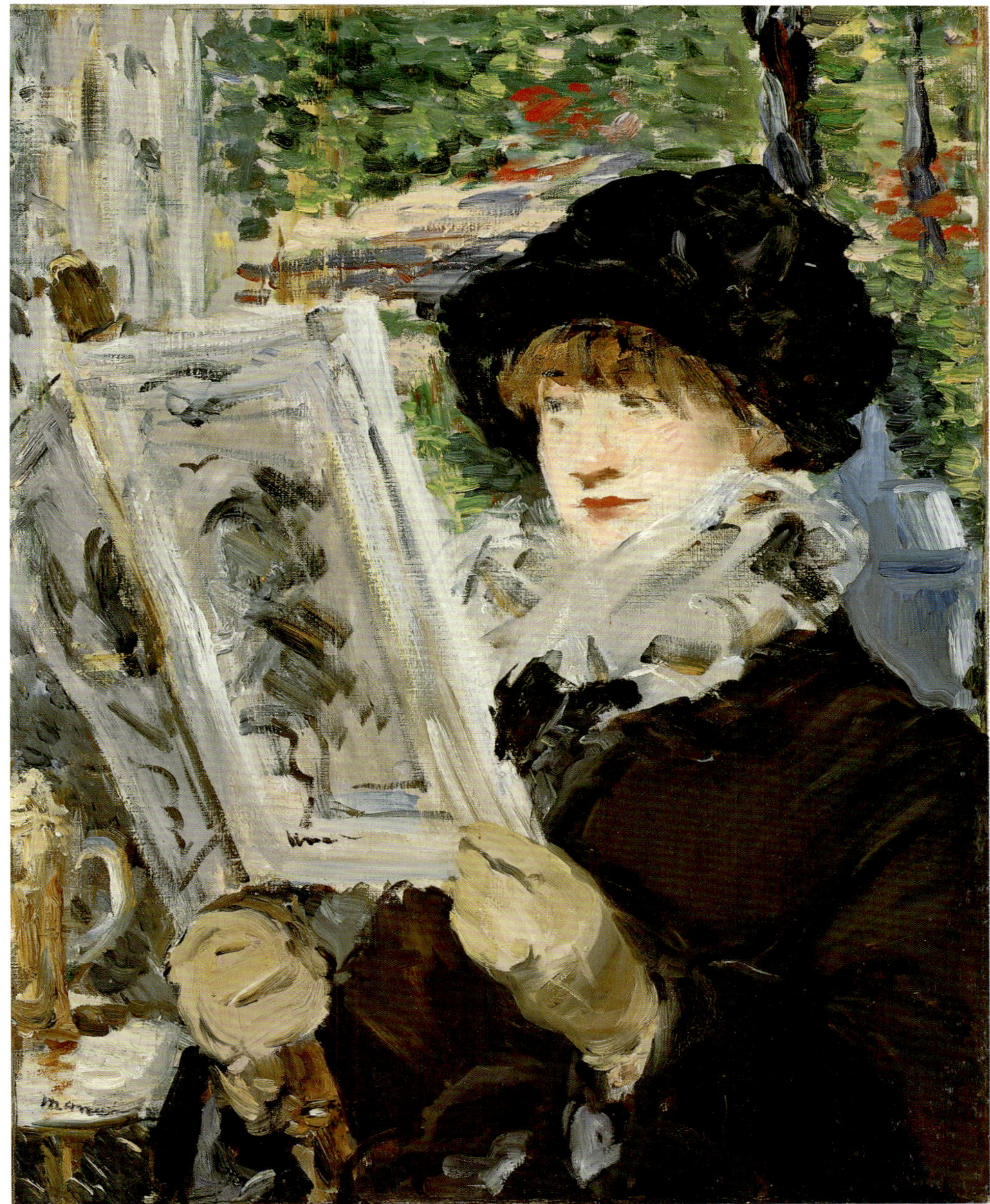

27

Woman Reading, 1879/80

Oil on canvas; 61.2 x 50.7 cm (24 1/16 x 19 7/8 in.)
Mr. and Mrs. Lewis Larned Coburn Memorial Collection, 1933.435
Signed lower left: *Manet*

Woman Reading may be Édouard Manet's most "impressionist" canvas. Although traces of a drawing visible beneath certain areas of the paint speak to a more deliberate execution in the studio, the canvas conveys just the sort of quick impression that a passerby might have had of a young and unaccompanied Parisienne in a café (or brasserie, since beer is being served).

The staccato reds, greens, and blues in the background—which has been variously described as a garden, a mirror, or a painting—intensify the sense of flux, as does the beer, whose frothy head indicates it has just been served. Even the woman's features consist of a few quick strokes, thinly painted on a white-primed canvas, as if Manet was applying makeup (kohl, lipstick, and rouge) to his model, rather than painting a flesh-and-blood woman.

The paper in her hands has a wooden rod holder, suggesting that she took it from the café's magazine rack. Its small format implies that it is an illustrated magazine, possibly *La Vie moderne*, a recently inaugurated journal with advertisements and short articles on literature, art, fashion, and society that appealed to men and women alike. Not only did Manet contribute drawings to this publication, but he also exhibited works in the magazine's offices, including this painting in April 1880. In *Woman Reading*, the journal's text is articulated with vigorous black and gray strokes that are teasingly illegible. These appear to fuse with the tulle collar of the stylish young woman, further connecting her to notions of modernity and consumerism in café life, advertising, and fashion. Perhaps the journal itself, with its schematic short texts and sketches, can be seen as a metaphor for the spirited painterly shorthand with which Manet treated his subject, just as the artist's flickering brushwork hints at her vivacious character.

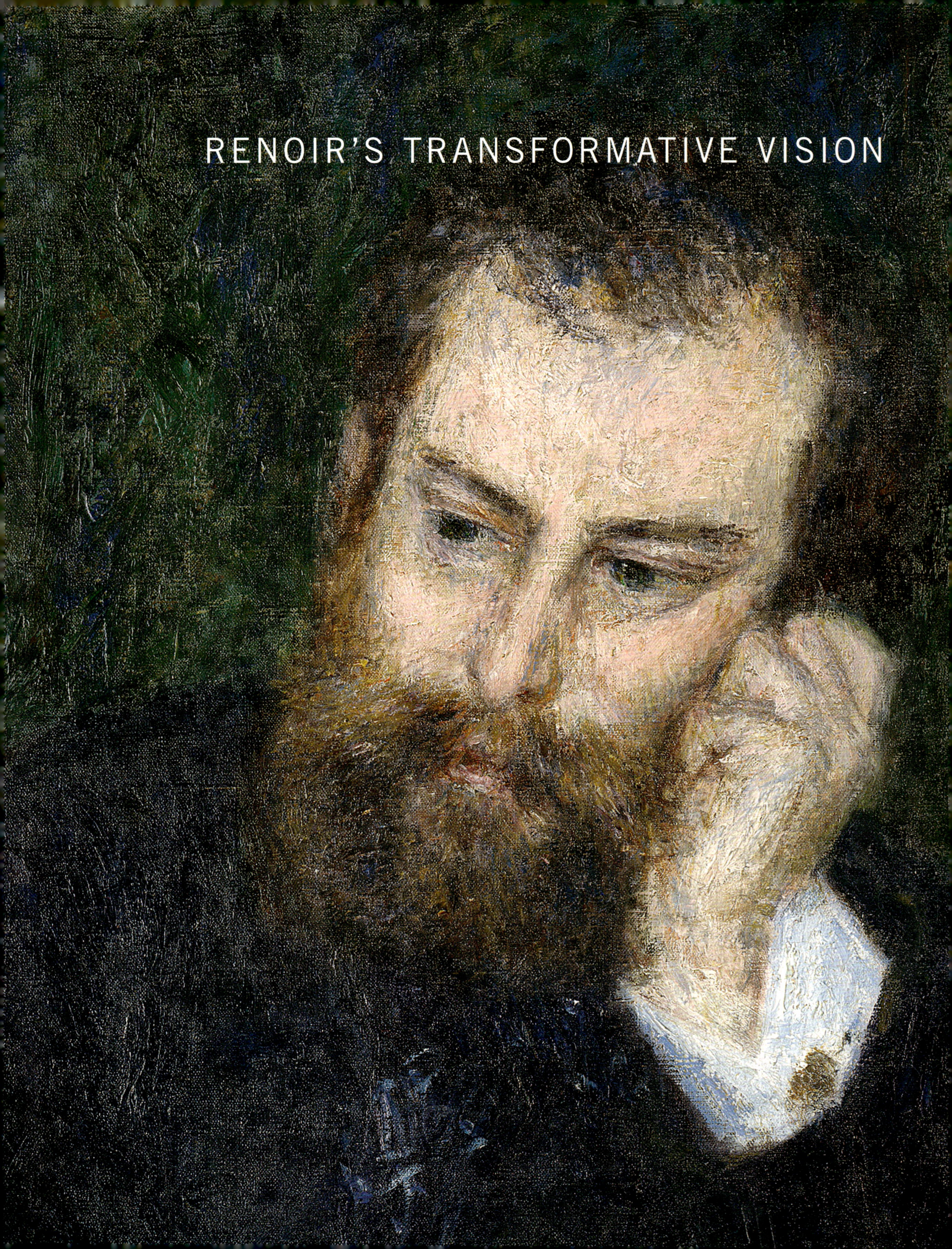
RENOIR'S TRANSFORMATIVE VISION

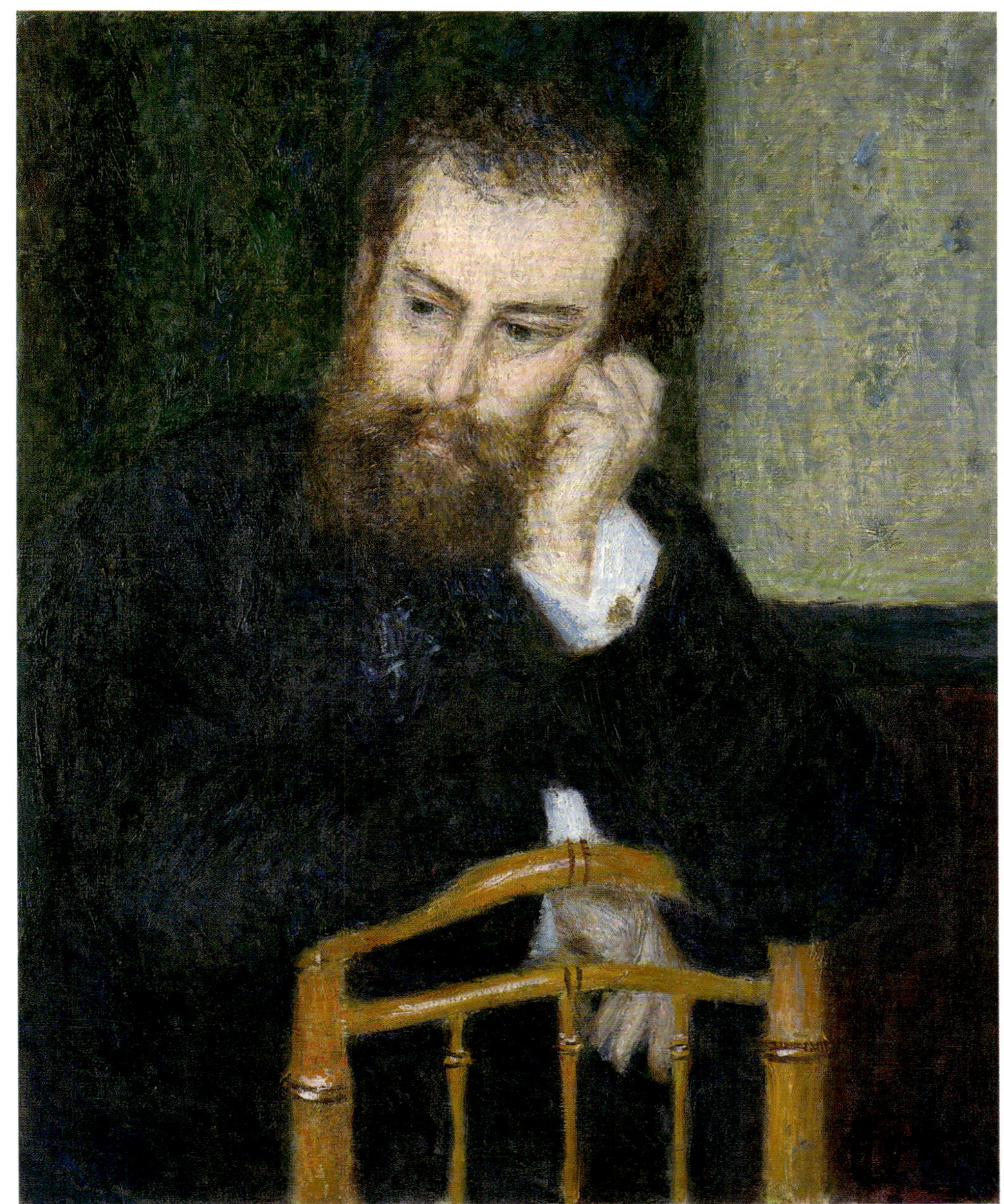

28

Alfred Sisley, 1876

Oil on canvas, mounted on composition board; 66.4 x 54.8 cm (26 1/8 x 21 9/16 in.)
Mr. and Mrs. Lewis Larned Coburn Memorial Collection, 1933.453
Signed lower right: *Renoir.*

Late in life, Claude Monet would recall that Pierre-Auguste Renoir painted this portrait of fellow Impressionist Alfred Sisley at the second house that Monet rented in Argenteuil, which was also the site of Renoir's portrait of Monet, executed in the summer of 1875 (Musée d'Orsay, Paris). Although Renoir exhibited both his depiction of Monet and a self-portrait at the second Impressionist exhibition, in April 1876, it was not until the third group exhibition, held the following year, that his portrait of Sisley was displayed. This suggests that the Art Institute's painting was finished too late in 1876 to be included in the second exhibition.

Sitting casually astride a bamboo-style chair, the handsome and well-groomed Sisley rests his head on his left hand, his eyes lowered and gently averted. It is a pensive and intimate portrayal. Set within a shallow, dark room, illuminated only by a window at the upper right, the sitter appears close to the viewer, his chair pressed against the plane marking the boundary between the viewer's space and the fictive space of the image. Although the composition's dominant tonality is blue, its mood is not one of melancholy; rather, Sisley appears thoughtful and serene, maybe even something of a dreamer. Unlike Renoir's 1875 depiction of Monet holding a palette and brushes, here there are no clues to the subject's vocation. Renoir's rather romantic characterization suggests the gentleness and elegance that impressed Sisley's friends, and speaks less to shared professional goals than to the artists' friendship. Two paintings of Sisley's children that Renoir made in 1875 also testify to this relationship.

One of seven portraits Renoir exhibited in 1877, and the only one fully identified in the catalogue that accompanied the show, *Alfred Sisley* was praised by one critic, who knew the sitter, for being an "extraordinary likeness and [for its] great value as a work of art."

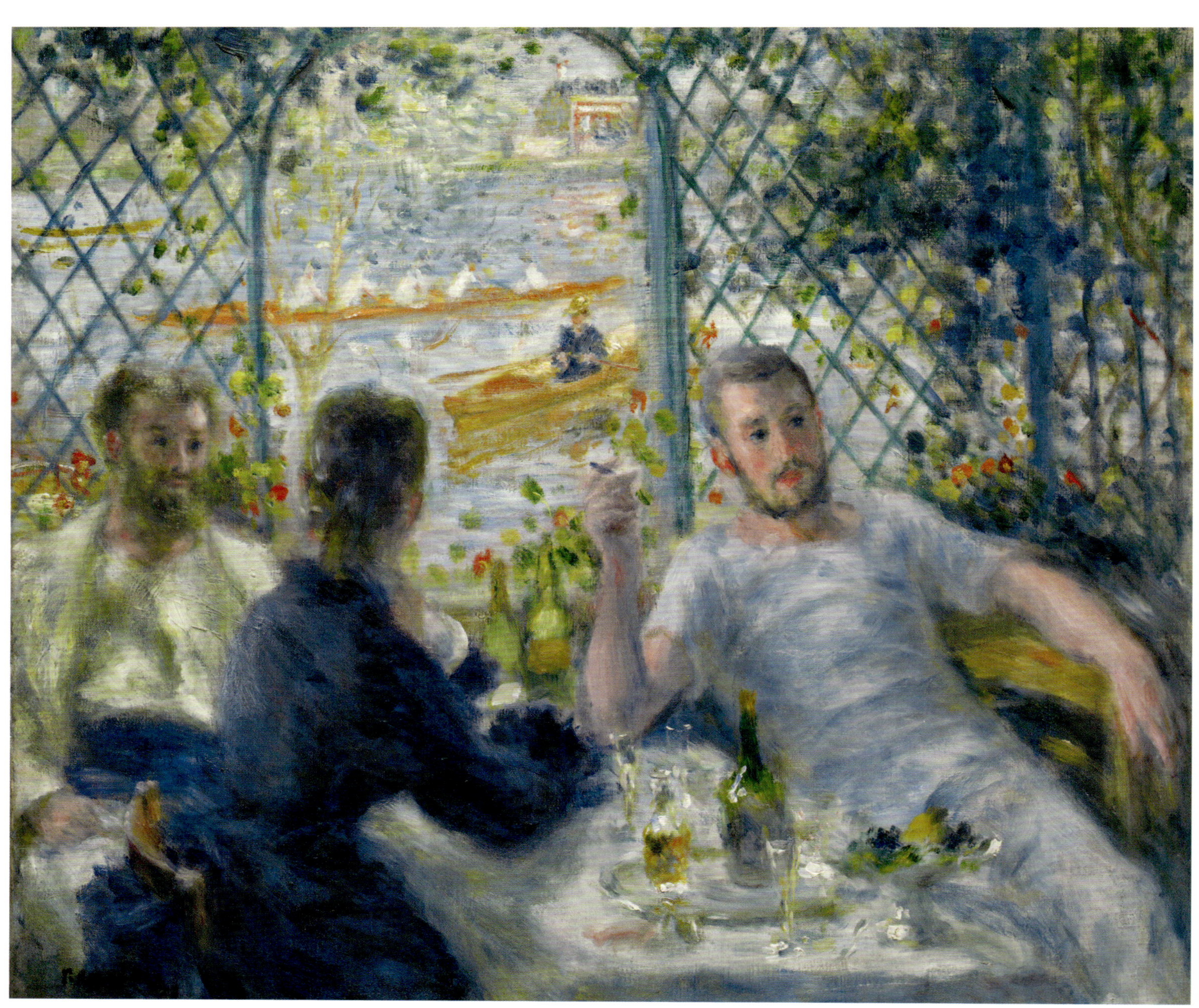

29

Lunch at the Restaurant Fournaise (The Rowers' Lunch), 1875

Oil on canvas; 55.1 x 65.9 cm (21 11/16 x 25 15/16 in.)
Potter Palmer Collection, 1922.437
Signed lower left: *Renoir.*

Pierre-Auguste Renoir painted this canvas—which he first showed at the second Impressionist exhibition, in April 1876, under the title *Déjeuner chez Fournaise*—during the summer of 1875 in Chatou, west of Paris on the Seine River. The town was near Bougival, where in 1869, in Claude Monet's company, he had painted his first pictures celebrating modern bourgeois leisure in the countryside. At Chatou, a popular spot for rowers, the artist befriended the Fournaise family, who owned a restaurant on an island upstream that was a well-known meeting place for oarsmen. Working on one of the terraces of that establishment, Renoir created a vision of middle-class relaxation that fulfills the promise of his earlier work painted alongside Monet.

Lunch at the Restaurant Fournaise is a paean to the joys of youth and summer, a celebration of the rituals of friendship and the bounties of nature, the seasonal rhythms of rest and play. Of the three figures around the table, only one, the young man in a white jacket at left, has been identified. He is M. de Lauradour, a habitué of the restaurant and the nearby bathing resort La Grenouillère. The sunburnt male at right wears white pants and a short-sleeved, collarless shirt—like those of the rowers in the racing boat on the river—which identify him as a boating-club member. Between the two men is a young woman seen from the back, her attention engaged by either the man to her left or the oarswoman near the shore, who is similarly costumed in the blue flannel favored by female boaters. If the interchange between the figures seems unclear, it is because Renoir avoided making the picture overly legible in narrative terms. Rather than recording a specific interaction, he evoked a mood of conviviality. The fruit, wine, and wineglasses on the table, and the way the boater languidly reclines in his chair, casually holding a cigarette, indicate that lunch is over. Pictorially, Renoir's loose brushwork succeeds at banishing narrative specificity and suggests the slightly fuzzy state of torpor that accompanies satiety. Contours blur, merging into one another and the surrounding atmosphere, and immersing the whole scene in soft, shifting light, with whites tinted by reflections and bluish shadows. The resulting dappled effect is echoed in the stricter rhythms of the trellis, which serves as a permeable barrier between the terrace and the river.

Suffused with a warmth that is both social and physical, *Lunch at the Restaurant Fournaise* is a picture of perfect harmony, a vision of a golden age located not in the ancient past but in the present. The focus on people and the lively delicacy with which the softly flickering light is conjured mark Renoir's unique contribution to what we might term classic Impressionism. Indeed, while Monet and Alfred Sisley concentrated almost exclusively on plein-air landscape painting, Renoir remained committed to the human figure, especially to representations of women. He executed several important pictures on the theme of rowing between 1875 and 1881, culminating in the famous *Luncheon of the Boating Party* (1880–81; Phillips Collection, Washington, D.C.; see p. 16). But despite the fact that he frequently worked in the country, Renoir was, unlike his two friends, a visitor there, remaining essentially a city artist until his definitive move from Paris to Cagnes-sur-Mer in 1907.

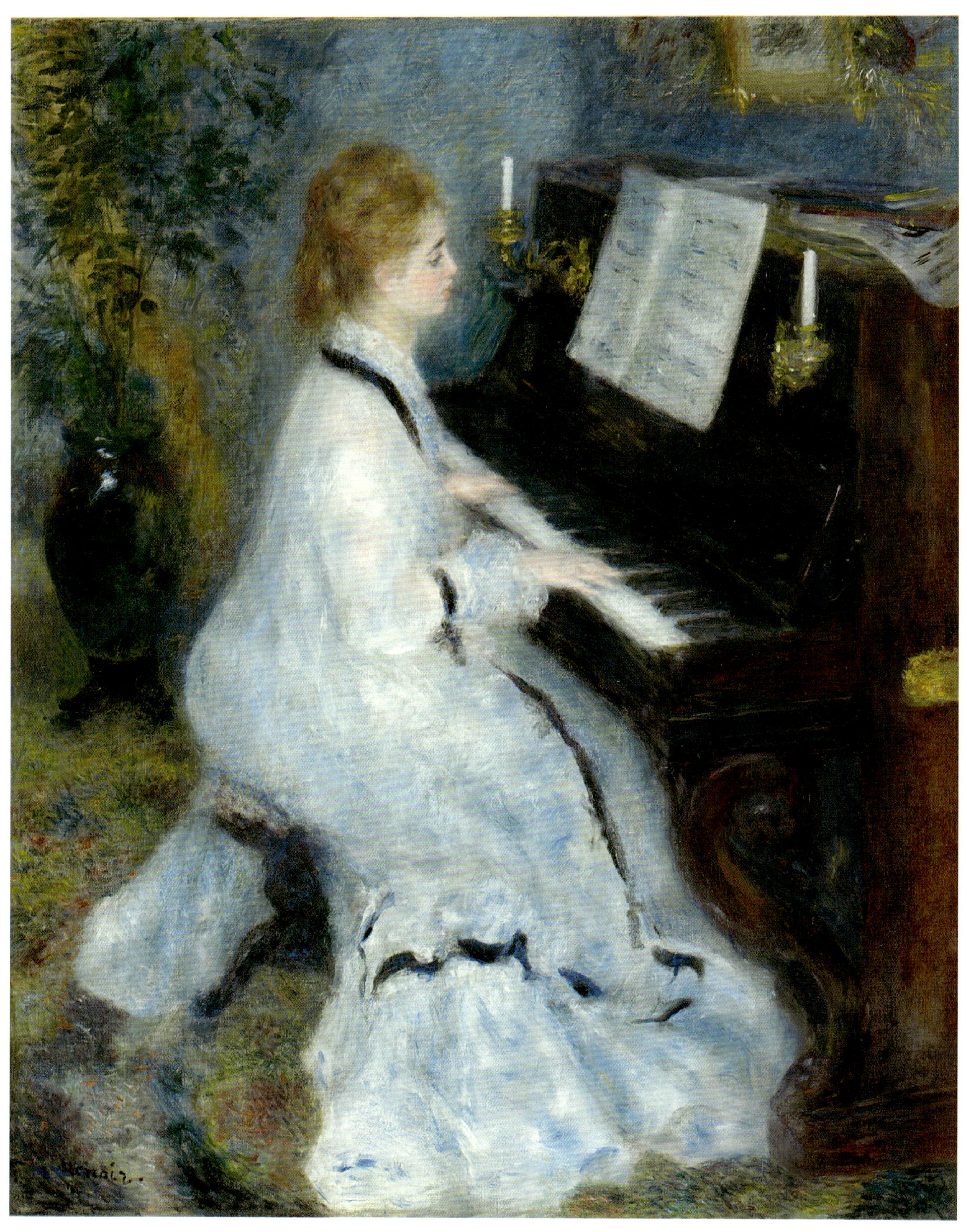

30

Woman at the Piano, 1875/76

Oil on canvas; 93.2 x 74.2 cm (36 5/8 x 29 1/2 in.)
Mr. and Mrs. Martin A. Ryerson Collection, 1937.1025
Signed lower left: *Renoir.*

Along with *Lunch at the Restaurant Fournaise* (cat. 29), Pierre-Auguste Renoir showed this canvas at the 1876 Impressionist exhibition. Featuring a woman at a piano, it represents the distillation of the artist's quintessentially Parisian brand of Impressionism, as well as a subject to which he would return frequently in later life. He was not the first of his circle to explore this theme: in the previous decade, Paul Cézanne, Edgar Degas, and Édouard Manet had each treated it, though in ways that were consonant with their own pictorial and expressive aims and thus quite different from Renoir's.

Here the scene is a richly appointed interior with a patterned carpet on the floor; a potted plant placed before a curtain that seems to mark the opening to an adjoining space; and a picture hung on a fabric-covered wall, above a dark, gleaming upright piano, its top piled casually with music. A remarkably pretty young woman, her luminous pink hands caressing the bluish white keyboard, is reading the sheet music open on the stand before her. Her performance seems as effortless as her beauty, as if we are witnessing a totally natural musical extension of the ravishing visual harmony the player embodies. Judging from her at-home dress (*robe d'intérieur*), one might assume her to be alone or in the company of an intimate. A confection of diaphanous white fabric over a bluish underdress, offset by a winding, dark band, it takes on, through the wizardry of Renoir's brush, a life of its own: its brilliant play of chromatic harmonies and counterpoint of sinuous and cascading rhythms provides more than a match for the sounds produced by the piano's black-and-white keys. Designed to conceal, the garment also reveals, as we see glints of pink flesh, which are picked out on the young woman's shoulder and arm by the light that seems to fall softly over her upper body. Renoir presented the scene from a rather odd vantage point: looking down on the pianist from above, a location coincident not only with the painter's but also with the source of the light that pierces the cool darkness of the interior. Yet neither viewer nor artist obstructs the light, casting a shadow. Are we then meant to be looking in through a window? To ask such a question is to take the picture as a representation of fact, when in fact it is a fantasy.

As the almost insistently striking color harmonies, based on blue, remind us, Renoir is the artist and the performer: the palette is his keyboard, and the woman at the piano is wholly his creation. This is not a portrait of an individual, or even a study of a social type, the skilled bourgeoise; instead it is the depiction of ideal womanhood, uncomplicated by any of the contingencies of the real world. Renoir was in fact uncomfortable with intellectual and educated women, particularly those who nourished professional ambitions. He did not intend, as did Manet, to use the theme of a female pianist to suggest such attributes. His woman at the piano represents the performance of her "natural" function, not the exercise of musical abilities. As Renoir would later write, "In antiquity and among simple peoples, the woman sings and dances.... Gracefulness is her domain and even her duty." Eighteenth-century artists might have pictured this ideal as one of the legendary Three Graces, or perhaps as a goddess amid a froth of clouds; Renoir also enveloped his ideal in gossamer, but he transported her from the heavens to a piano stool, from the realm of the gods to the modern drawing room.

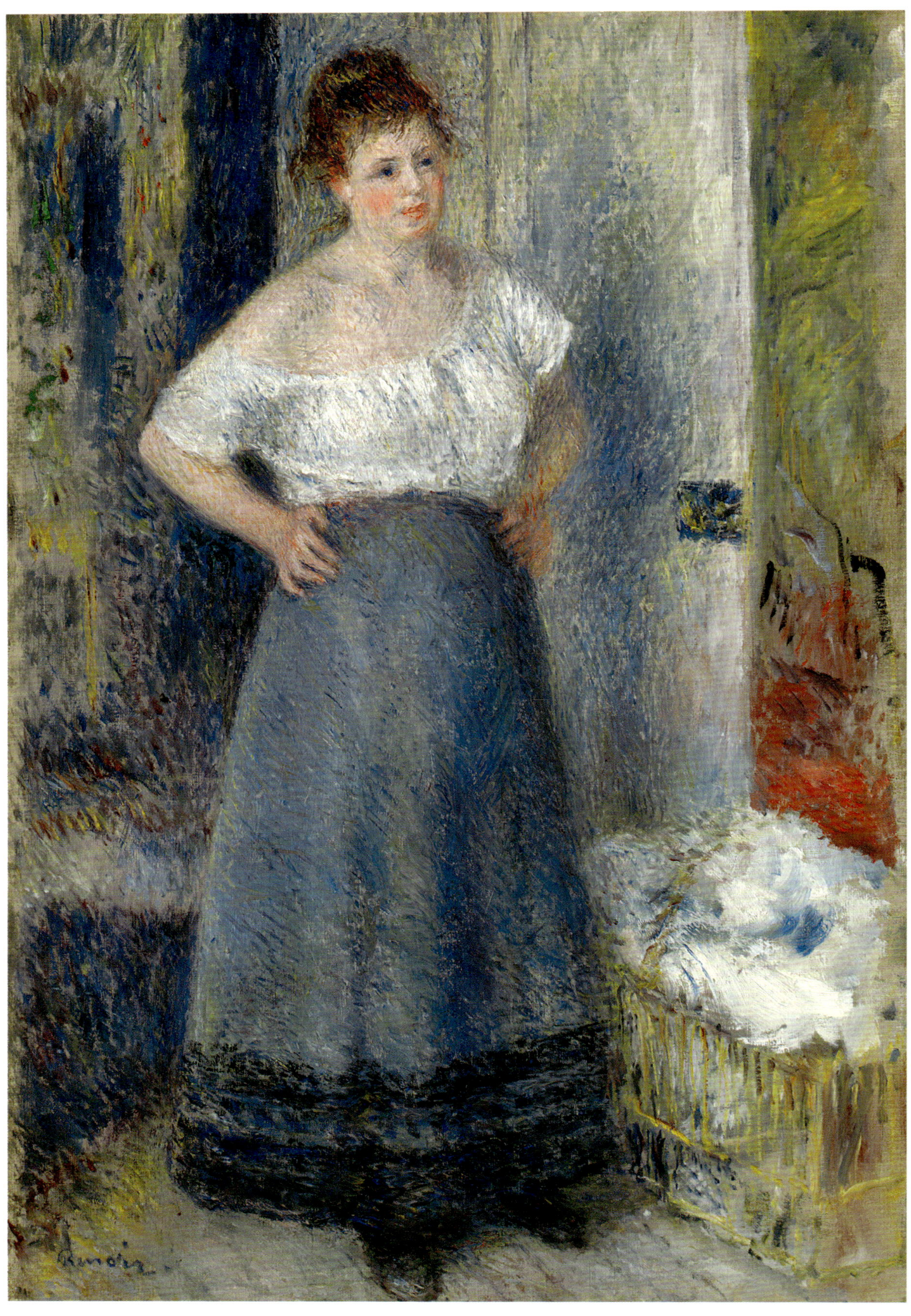

31

The Laundress, 1877/79

Oil on canvas; 81.4 x 56.5 cm (32 1/16 x 22 1/4 in.)
Charles H. and Mary F. S. Worcester Collection, 1947.102
Signed lower left: *Renoir.*

The model for Pierre-Auguste Renoir's *The Laundress* was Nini Lopez, a pretty blonde whom the artist employed regularly between 1874 and 1880 for images of modern life; she may also have posed for *Woman at the Piano* (cat. 30). Artists' models usually came from tough, working-class backgrounds, and assigning these street-smart young women roles, like actresses in a play, was commonplace. Renoir, whose background as the son of a tailor was not so different from that of his models, seems to have enjoyed using his art to transform these Eliza Doolittles, occasionally situating them in rich surroundings, like those of the Parisian elite to which his art had provided him entrée.

The Laundress can be related to Renoir's association in the late 1870s with the publishing giant and art collector Georges Charpentier and his wife, whose glittering literary salon the artist attended in the company of the stable of Realist writers then making Charpentier's fortune. These included Renoir's old acquaintance Émile Zola, who was enjoying celebrity thanks to the incredible success of *L'Assommoir* (published in 1877), his gritty novel detailing the downfall of a laundress in the brutal and degrading urban environment that was working-class Paris. Despite the fact that he was born considerably closer to the experience of poverty than the author of *L'Assommoir*, Renoir did not see the moral potential of ugliness key to Zola's Naturalist program; he preferred to create beauty in its place. This made Zola's request of him to make drawings for *L'Assommoir* problematic.

Undertaken not long after Renoir completed the illustrations for the book, *The Laundress* casts the theme in a more sanguine light than had the novelist or Renoir's fellow Impressionist Edgar Degas. The latter's representations of the subject in the 1870s and early 1880s stress the backbreaking nature of the work, the poses of his figures eloquently conveying the profession's strenuous physical demands and stultifying boredom. Renoir avoided these concerns, situating his laundress in a location that is difficult to pinpoint. Given the suggestion of an elegant yellow table set in front of a richly patterned background at the left, it appears that the setting is the private residence of a client. The ruddy young laundress stands, hands on her hips, beside a half-open door. She glances to the right, apparently engaged by someone or something outside the picture space, and so she is caught unaware, in this moment of apparent repose, by the viewer's gaze. The large basket on the floor beside her is filled with unfolded, and therefore probably unwashed, laundry, which the artist nonetheless rendered in white. Although Renoir included signs of the woman's toil—the heavy basket and her reddened hands—he did not show her hard at work, as Degas's laundresses usually are. There is thus no pretext for her blouse to have provocatively slipped from her shoulder.

Renoir's audience would have been sensitive to the innuendos in this scene in ways that we cannot be today, since laundresses and working women like them were known to be sexually available, occasionally supplementing their meager incomes with prostitution. Zola's protagonist, Gervaise, attempts this near the end of *L'Assommoir*, as she sinks deeper and deeper into poverty. One wonders if more can be read into the frank stance and thick waist of Renoir's laundress, although such an allusion to social problems is not consistent with his general artistic aims. If there are notes of social discord, he chose to resolve them chromatically, employing dominant strokes of blue and white, accented with yellows and reds. *The Laundress* signals both his interest in pursuing the modern-life themes favored by the writers and artists who espoused the Naturalist aesthetic and his desire to temper its cutting edge.

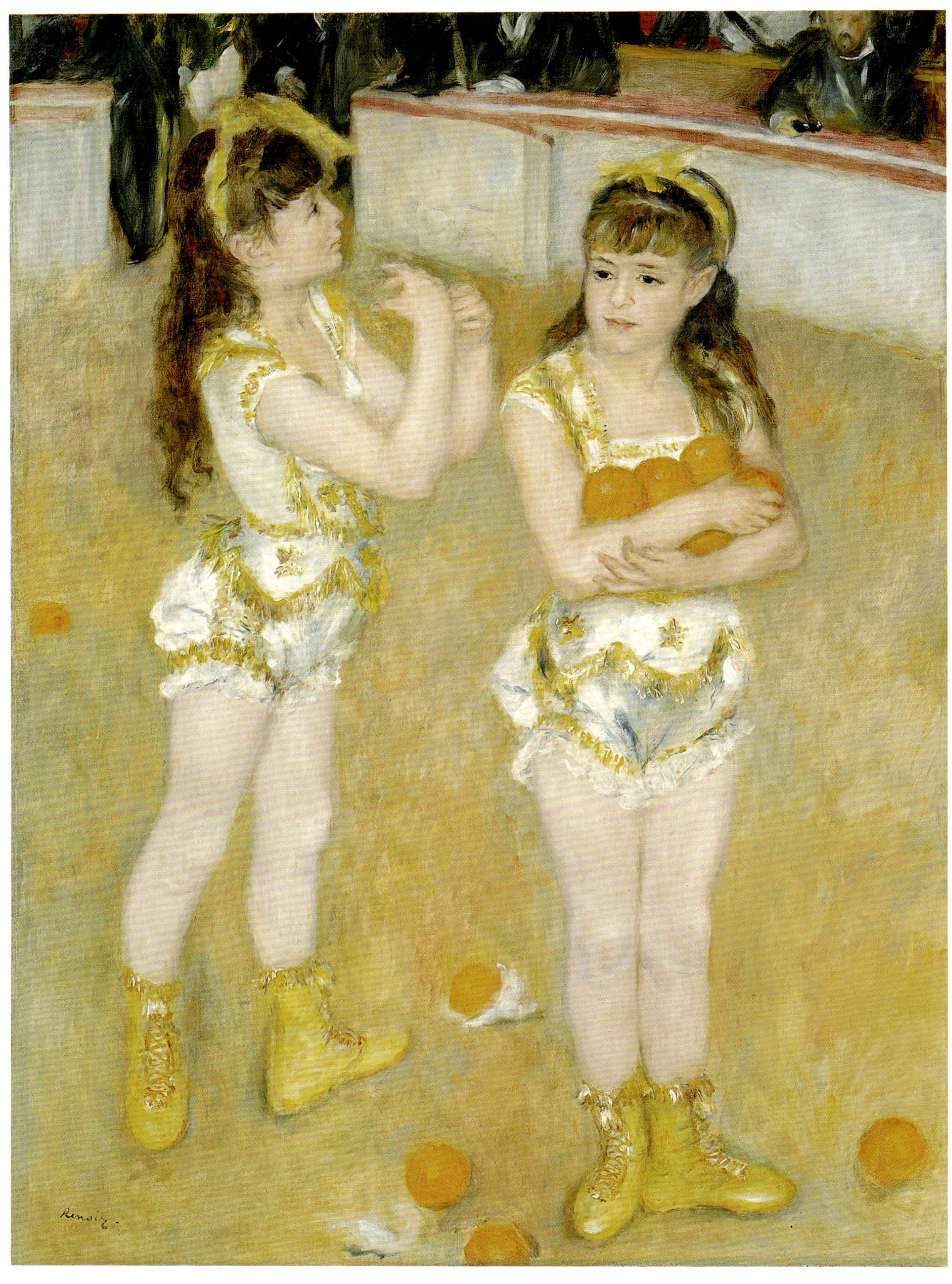

32

Acrobats at the Cirque Fernando (Francisca and Angelina Wartenberg), 1879

Oil on canvas; 131.5 x 99.5 cm (51 ¾ x 39 ⅛ in.)
Potter Palmer Collection, 1922.440
Signed lower left: *Renoir.*

One of four permanent circuses in Paris, the Cirque Fernando opened its new circular, brick-and-iron building in Montmartre in June 1875, attracting an enthusiastic following that included Édouard Manet and his friends. Soon the popularity of this entertainment also began to influence the work of the painters and writers who frequented the salon of the publisher and art collector Georges Charpentier. In March 1879, Charpentier published Edmond de Goncourt's *Frères Zemganno*, a novel about two brothers who are circus performers. Just two months earlier, Edgar Degas had attended the Cirque Fernando to make sketches for a painting of the gymnast Miss La La suspended from the ceiling by a rope clenched between her teeth (*Miss La La at the Cirque Fernando*; National Gallery, London).

By this time, Pierre-Auguste Renoir had probably begun his own painting of the Cirque Fernando, featuring Francisca and Angelina Wartenberg, members of an itinerant German acrobatic troupe. The sisters take their bow and gather tributes to their just-completed performance—tissue-wrapped oranges, tossed to them by affluent members of the audience, who are visible at the top of the canvas, seated at ringside in formal attire. Like Degas often did, Renoir represented his subject close-up, as if seen through opera glasses, though in this case from above rather than from below. In part, the foreshortening produced by this viewpoint makes Francisca, who gracefully raises her arms, and Angelina, her arms filled with oranges, appear smaller and younger than their actual ages—seventeen and fourteen, respectively.

Renoir might have conceived this composition for an exhibition of his work held in June 1879 at the spacious offices of the fashionable periodical *La Vie moderne*, which the Charpentiers had launched in April. The fifth in a series held there, Renoir's show, including this work complemented by pastels, occasioned a feature article in the magazine written by the artist's younger brother, Edmond:

> In *Acrobats*, there is really no sense of arrangement. [Renoir] has captured the two children's movements with unbelievable subtlety and immediacy. This is exactly how they walked, bowed, and smiled in the circus ring.... [W]hat we have here is real life with all its poetry and all its savor. This absence of the "conventional"... gives the impression of nature with all its unexpectedness and its intense harmony; it is nature speaking to me.

Yet Renoir's supposedly natural depiction is, in truth, a fiction. Unlike Degas, Renoir banished from his representation the harsh effects of the gaslight that was used during evening performances, believing, as he stated, that it "turns faces into grimaces." Rather, he painted the sisters as if en plein air, eliminating shadows and building up his forms with thin, diaphanous washes of color, and using delicate, multi-directional brushwork that extends the color of the figures into the space around them and vice versa. To increase this visual harmony, the artist employed a highly arbitrary palette that emphasizes chromatic resonance: the yellows and oranges of the circus floor echo in the girls' costumes, as well as in the delicate reflections on their skin, most apparent in the area of Angelina's neck. Nor do awkward or unseemly poses, like that of Miss La La in Degas's painting of the circus, mar this scene. Renoir captured not the sometimes antic postures that were depicted in a poster advertising the sisters' act, but rather, in the performance's aftermath, a moment of almost balletic grace and dignity.

It has been suggested that in the 1879 *La Vie moderne* article, Renoir, with his brother as his mouthpiece, was claiming for himself the mantle of the alternate Realism that Edmond de Goncourt—like Renoir, a passionate devotee of the art of the eighteenth century—had called for in his preface to *Les Frères Zemganno*: a vision of modern life that emphasizes its poetry rather than its sordidness.

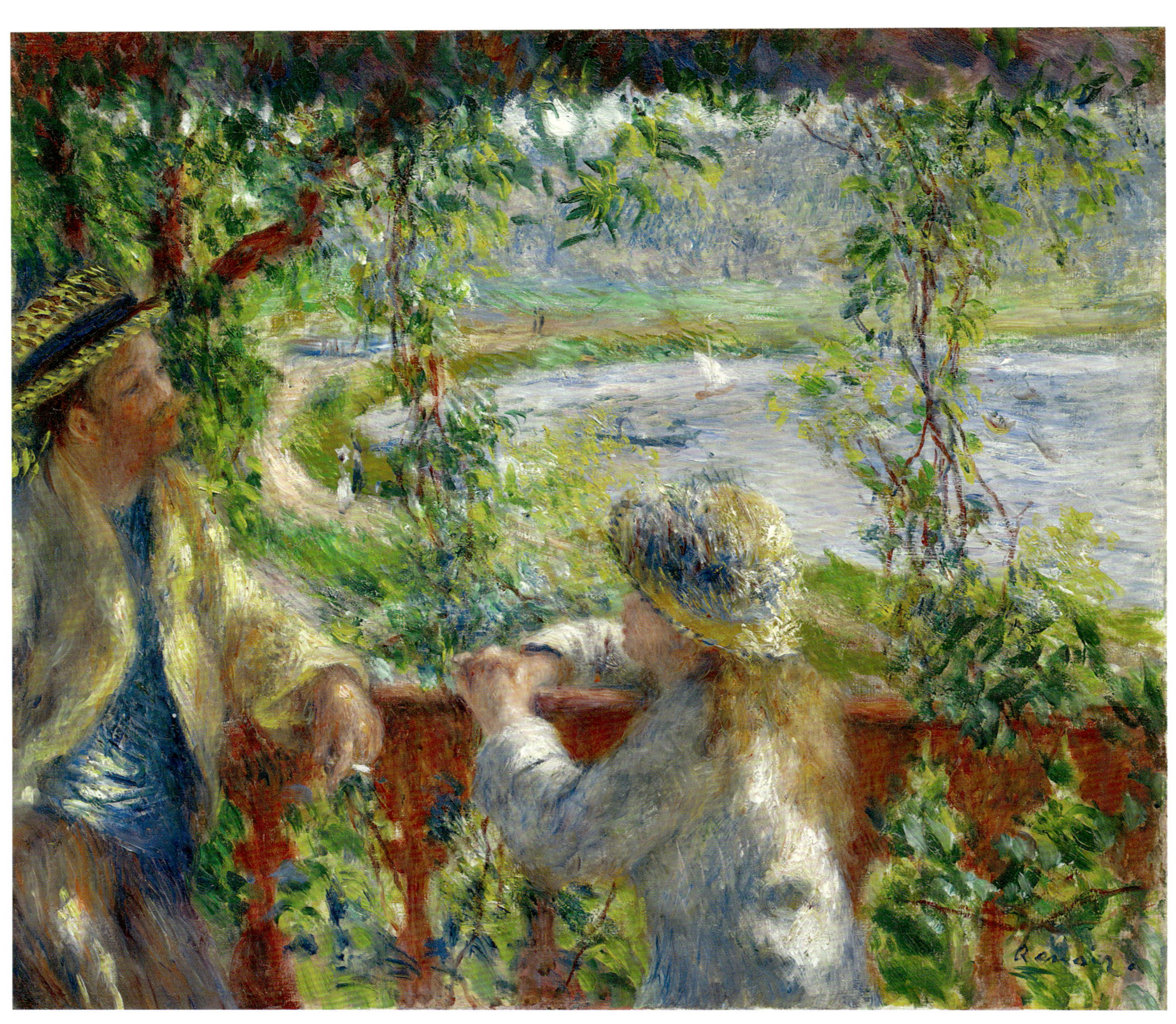

33

Near the Lake, 1879/80

Oil on canvas; 47.5 x 56.3 cm (18 x 22 in.)
Potter Palmer Collection, 1922.439
Signed lower right: *Renoir.*

In the fall of 1879, Pierre-Auguste Renoir returned to Chatou, where he revisited his earlier themes of recreation and leisure (see cat. 29). It may have been at this time that he painted *Near the Lake*, a canvas whose title (which it has carried since at least 1887) makes it difficult to specify its subject and date. There is no record of Renoir visiting a body of water other than the Seine River or the Atlantic Ocean during the years to which, stylistically, this painting must date. Is the setting in fact a bend in the Seine; or did the painter make an undocumented visit to a site such as Lac Enghien, a popular vacation spot fifty minutes by train from Paris via Argenteuil?

Whatever the circumstances of the painting's creation, Renoir here represented a youngish man casually leaning on a balustrade, cigarette in hand, engaged in conversation with a girl depicted in profile, her eyes hidden by the wide brim of a flower-bedecked straw hat. *Near the Lake* hearkens back to the Art Institute's earlier *Lunch at the Restaurant Fournaise* and, like it, can be seen to anticipate the ambitious work that Renoir would begin in the summer of 1880, when, following a second stay at the vacation estate of the diplomat and banker Paul-Antoine Berard at Wargemont, near Dieppe on the Normandy coast, he wrote to his erstwhile host: "I am at Chatou.... I'm doing a painting of oarsmen which I've been itching to do for a long time." The result was Renoir's masterpiece, *Luncheon of the Boating Party* (1880–81; Phillips Collection, Washington, D.C.).

In *Near the Lake*, we see two figural types that Renoir would recast in this large, multi-figured composition of the following summer. The man in the Chicago painting wears the banded straw hat of a boater, as well as the casual jacket and blue collarless shirt that complete the costume. His companion's pose, as well as her hat, invite comparison with the woman at the left of the large canvas. The model for this figure was Aline Charigot, a twenty-one-year-old seamstress who would soon become the artist's mistress and eventually his wife.

Although there is an obvious thematic continuity from *Lunch at the Restaurant Fournaise* through *Near the Lake* to *Luncheon of the Boating Party*, the three works represent different points in the evolution of Renoir's style. We have only to compare *Near the Lake* with *Lunch at the Restaurant Fournaise* to recognize differences between the two in both touch and palette. Instead of the freely brushed surface and unified atmosphere of the earlier work, Renoir here employed more varied brushwork to differentiate the components of the scene: for example, he used longer, horizontal strokes for the water; shorter, more vertical ones for the hanging vines; and still thinner and more abbreviated hatching marks for parts of the clothing. While the artist again suggested the effects of outdoor sunlight, entering obliquely below the scalloped awning that protects the terrace, he made less of an attempt to absorb everything into an overriding harmony of colored light. Rather, the play of tinted reflections seems confined to individual forms, and the palette itself is more saturated with deeper accents, as in the rich, dark blue of the boater's shirt.

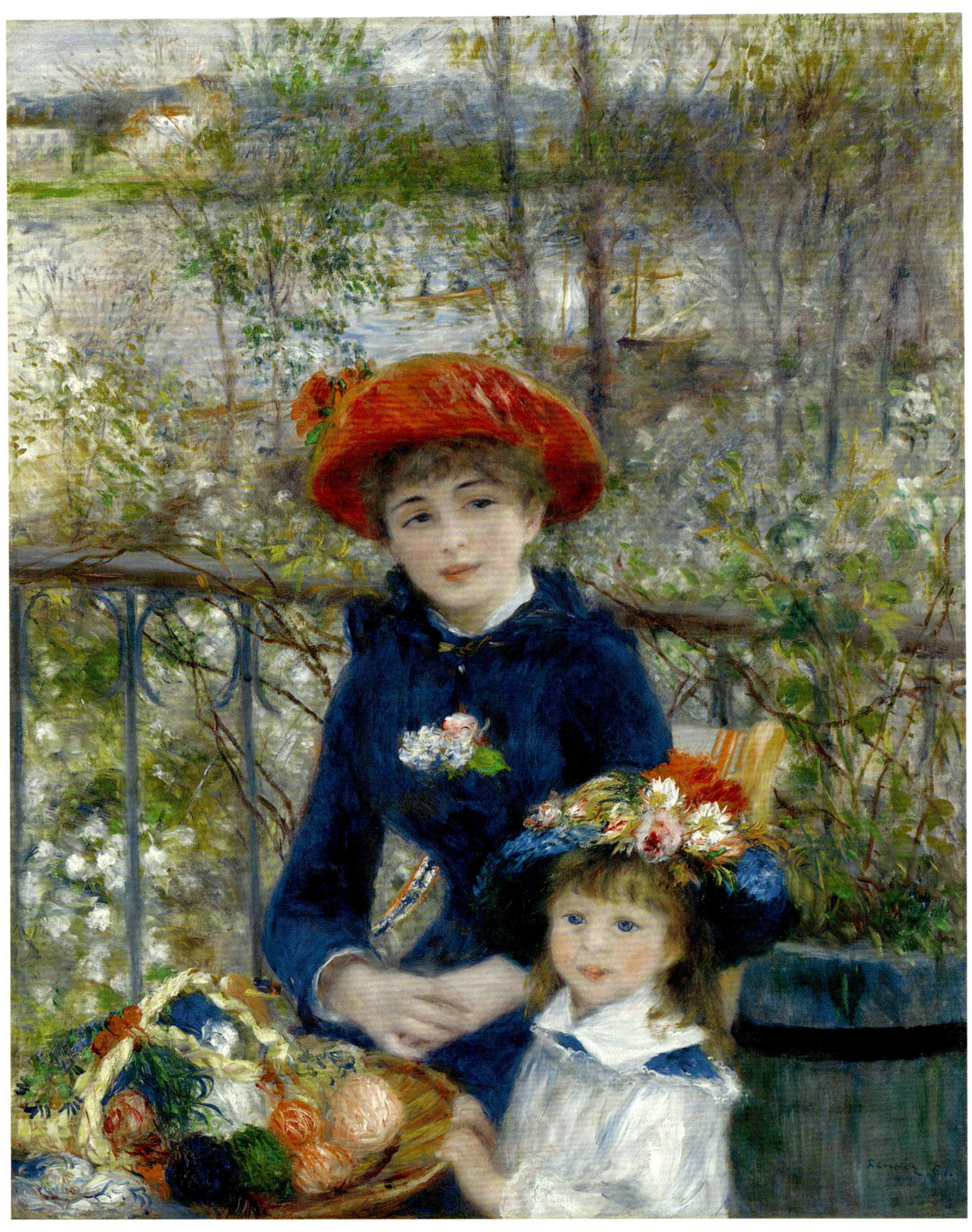

34

Two Sisters (On the Terrace), 1881

Oil on canvas; 100.5 x 81 cm (39 9/16 x 37 7/8 in.)
Mr. and Mrs. Lewis Larned Coburn Memorial Collection, 1933.455
Signed lower right: *Renoir. 81.*

Two Sisters (On the Terrace) was already under way by April 19, 1881, when, at lunch in Chatou with the expatriate American painter James McNeill Whistler, Pierre-Auguste Renoir shared his reason for postponing a planned trip to London. He explained, "I am engaged in a struggle with trees in bloom and women and children and can see no further than that at the moment. . . . The weather is fine and I have my models; that's my only excuse." Close study of this painting reveals little in the way of struggle, however. The work is a technical and compositional tour de force, in which the artist crystallized the stylistic shift signaled in his 1880–81 *Luncheon of the Boating Party* (Phillips Collection, Washington, D.C.) and informed it with the vibrant palette inspired by his spring 1881 trip to Algeria. *Two Sisters* celebrates both his recent artistic gains and the promise of beauty inherent in spring and youth.

Situated on yet another terrace of the Restaurant Fournaise, the two figures in this painting—unrelated models—occupy a shallow area that is a provocative extension of the viewer's space. The table supporting a pannier of brightly colored yarn inhabits a zone that both the figures and the spectator share. And yet the two girls seem oblivious to the artist and viewer standing directly before and above them; otherwise distracted, they glance in different directions. This allows us the freedom to stare, to take in the beauty of the scene without the risk of having our gaze returned.

Renoir ensured that the figures hold the viewer's attention. The foliage and river behind them, freely painted, are softer in focus and chromatically more muted than the tightly delineated figures of the young woman wearing the female boater's blue flannel and the little girl in white beside her. Renoir, displaying extraordinary refinement in blending the continuous tones that build up the faces, endowed each with a delicate porcelain complexion. This is set off by a brightly colored hat, enhanced, especially in the case of the child, by vivid decorations of flowers executed in rich, luxuriant impasto. The effect of the intense, saturated blues, reds, and pinks is not, as it would have been in the artist's earlier work, compromised by colored reflections; these, like shadows, have been largely banished. The result is an almost startling luminosity.

Looking at the picture, especially for the first time, is something of a revelation, as if cataracts have been removed and we are able to see the world afresh, recapturing the sense of wonder that we attribute to children. Indeed, as has been observed, Renoir's fascination with childhood led him, in his paintings of children, to attempt "to recreate his idea of the child's immediate response to visual experience, unconditioned by the knowledge of good and evil." He achieved this here by endowing the wide-eyed little girl with irises of an almost startlingly clear, translucent blue. On the other hand, those of her sloe-eyed, older companion are notably darker, less penetrable, and more knowing. These distinctions, as well as the contrasts in color and value of the costumes, the number of flowers decorating the hats, and the evident (though undisclosed) differences between what attracts the two girls' attention, suggest successive moments in the evolution from innocence to experience, from a state of nature to one in society. It may have been this sense of the stages of growth or development that prompted the dealer Paul Durand-Ruel, who purchased the picture from Renoir in July 1881, to give it the title *Two Sisters*.

This canvas brought down the curtain on Renoir's remarkable series of paintings dealing with the theme of Parisians relaxing in the countryside. Exhibited by Durand-Ruel against the artist's wishes at the 1882 Impressionist exhibition, along with *Luncheon of the Boating Party* and others, *Two Sisters* also announced Renoir's departure from "classic" Impressionism's preoccupation with rendering transient effects of light by means of flickering brushwork.

35

Young Woman Sewing, 1879

Oil on canvas; 61.5 x 50.3 cm (24 3/16 x 19 13/16 in.)
Mr. and Mrs. Lewis Larned Coburn Memorial Collection, 1933.452
Signed upper left: *Renoir 79.*

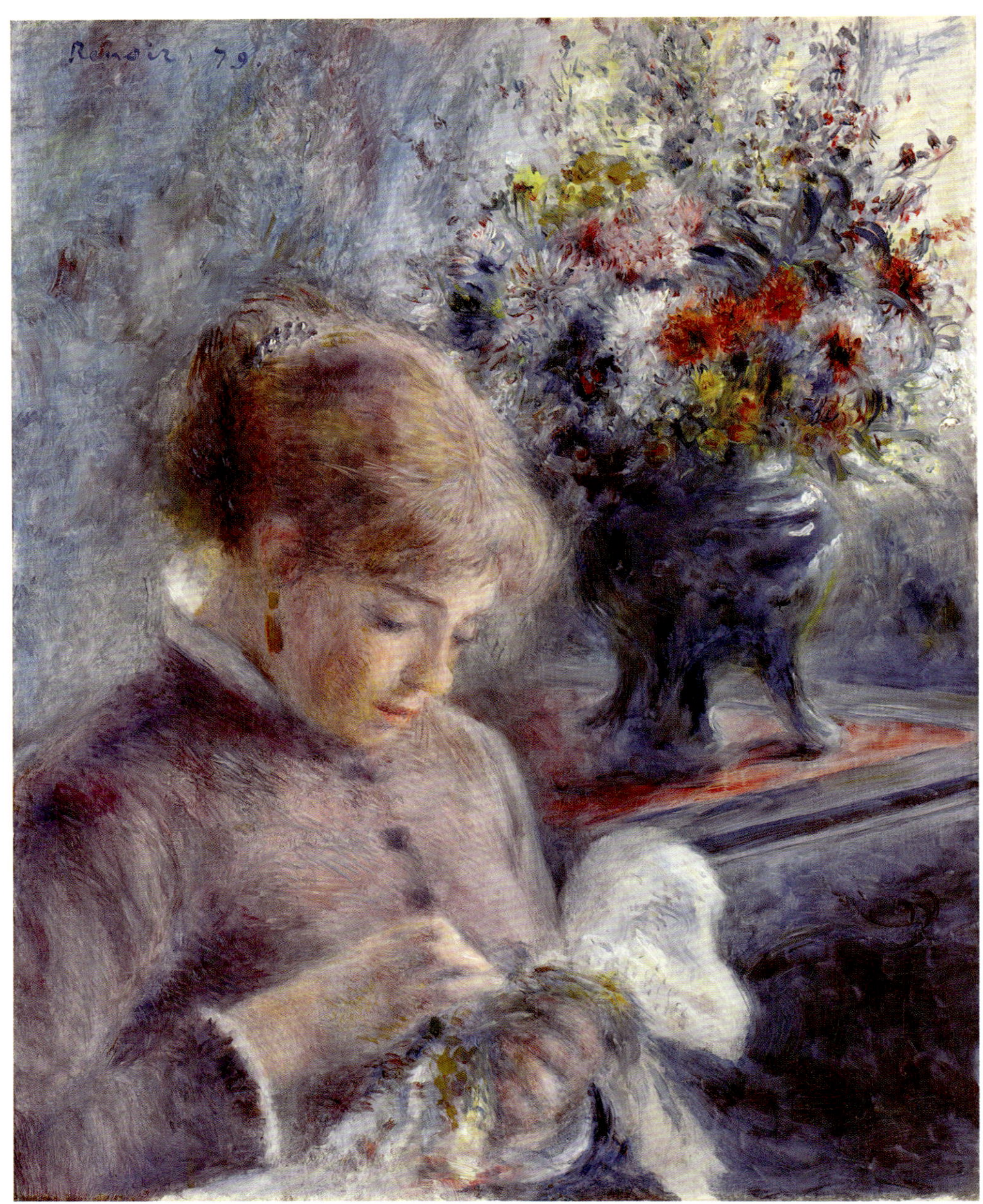

Pierre-Auguste Renoir painted this canvas on his first visit to the estate of Paul-Antoine Berard at Wargemont. The artist had met Berard and his wife at the Charpentier salon. During his stay, he painted a series of individual portraits of Mme Berard and her children, as well as decorations for the château: still lifes of game for the dining room and of flowers for both the library and drawing room. Still-life and figure painting come together in *Young Woman Sewing*, probably one of a number of non-commissioned canvases Renoir painted there.

The flowers—apparently asters and chrysanthemums—suggest that Renoir executed the composition in late summer. His decision to depict the young woman close-up and slightly from above, as if she were unaware of his proximity, results in a sense of informality and ease that the social distance between the painter and the members of the Berard family would not have allowed. However, this is not a portrait but a genre scene; the unidentified young woman—simply dressed but wearing jewelry—assumes the role of model rather than sitter. Giving almost equal visual emphasis to the still life and the figure, Renoir joined two representational traditions, establishing a type of equivalence between the transient beauty of flowers in bloom and that of the young female in her physical prime, and thus expressing his unquestioning belief in the traditional gender distinctions that identified women with nature and men with culture.

The young woman's activity underscores this identity. She is engaged in the virtuous pastime of needlework. It seems that she is embroidering, adding colors to the white material she holds in her hands. Her creative efforts offer parallels to those of the painter, who applies color to white prepared canvas; yet her work, unlike his, is confined to the domestic sphere, where, Renoir believed, a woman's true role lay.

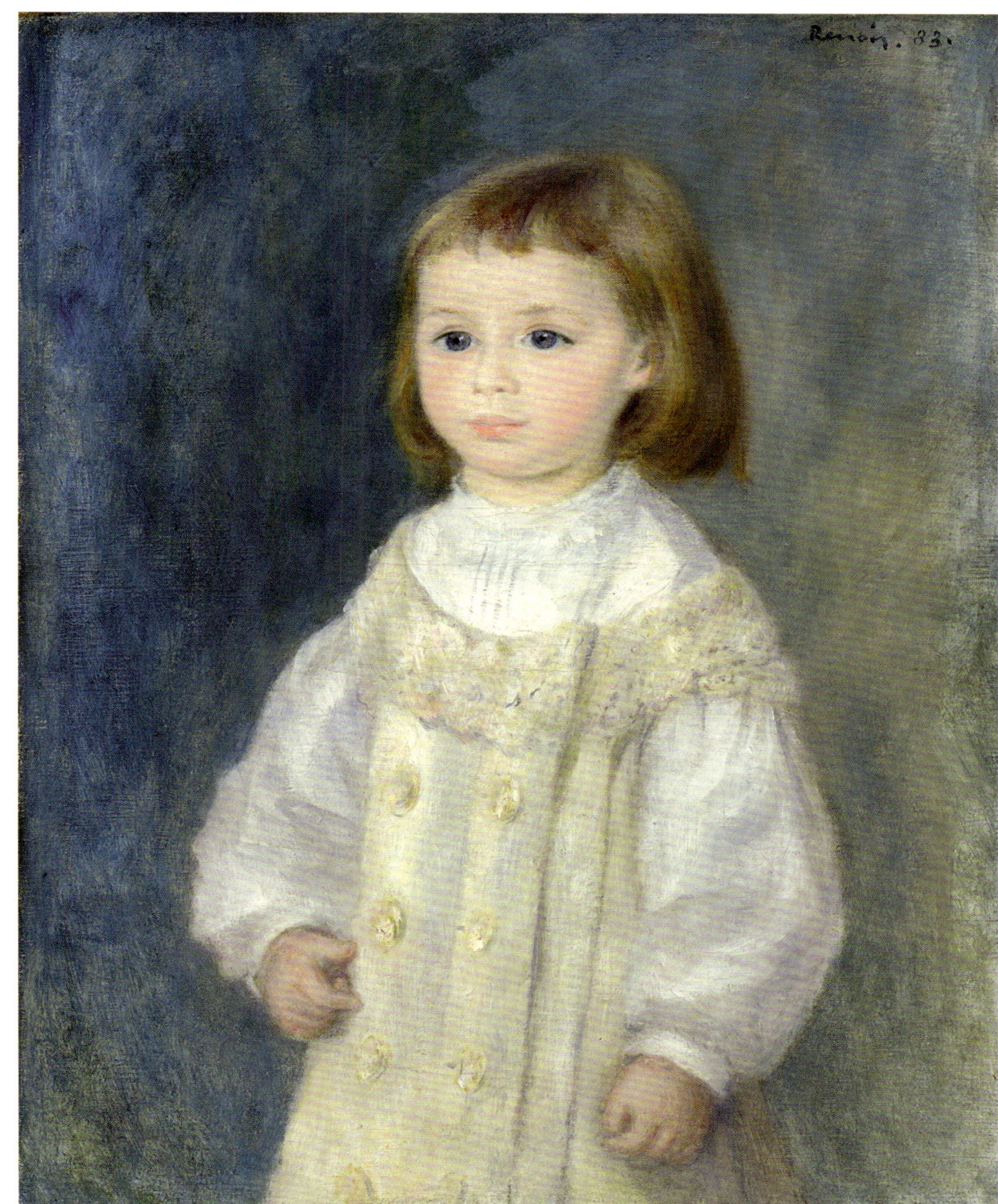

36

Lucie Berard (Child in White), 1883

Oil on canvas; 61.7 x 50.4 cm (24 ¼ x 19¾ in.)
Mr. and Mrs. Martin A. Ryerson Collection, 1933.1172
Signed upper right: *Renoir. 83.*

By the summer of 1883, Pierre-Auguste Renoir had produced a number of likenesses of Paul-Antoine Berard's four children. The youngest, Lucie, had thus far figured only in a single canvas, an intimate "study sheet" in oil featuring all of the children (Sterling and Francine Clark Art Institute, Williamstown, Massachusetts). In this work, painted in the summer of 1881, the artist showed the one-year-old child asleep as well as awake and a picture of alertness. In the Art Institute's portrait, the three-year-old Lucie is a personification of attentive innocence: dressed in white—with her small, soft hands positioned rather helplessly at her sides and her clear blue eyes unclouded—she looks out past the viewer, as if toward her future. As in his portrait of Mme Clapisson (cat. 37), Renoir apparently fashioned a picture that suited his sitter, but here it was his own vision that dictated its form. For although in conception and handling *Lucie Berard* recalls the portrait of the older woman, Renoir's treatment of the young girl is softer. Setting the little girl against a background of violet-blues with touches of yellow that envelops her white smock, he portrayed his sitter with a delicacy that preserves her tentativeness.

Viewers today often find Renoir's depictions of children almost too appealing, but this was not the case at the time they were painted. Lucie's father wrote that although he and his wife "swoon with pleasure in front of [the portrait] . . . unfortunately for Renoir, we cannot get others to derive the pleasure that we do from his work, and this portrait, so different from the type that [is currently fashionable], simply frightens people away." Over the next few years, the artist's aggressive pursuit of a new, linear manner so discouraged potential patrons that, by the mid-1880s, portraiture had ceased to be a major source of his income.

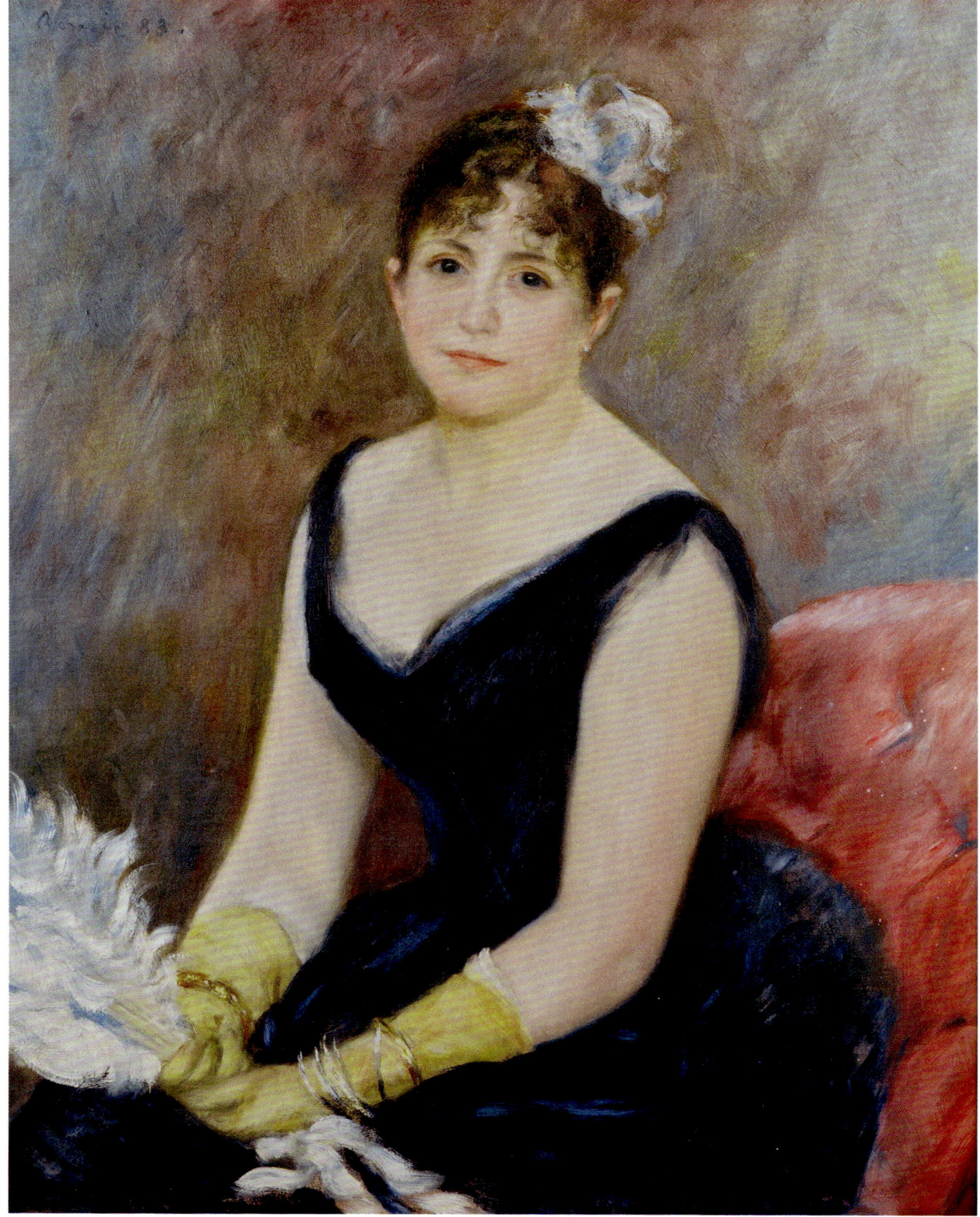

37

Madame Léon Clapisson, 1883

Oil on canvas; 81.8 x 65.2 cm (32 5/8 x 25 5/8 in.)
Mr. and Mrs. Martin A. Ryerson Collection, 1933.1174
Signed upper left: *Renoir 83.*

This picture, completed early in 1883, is Pierre-Auguste Renoir's second attempt to satisfy a commission from Léon Clapisson to paint his thirty-four-year-old wife, Valentine. Clapisson, a stockbroker, had recently begun collecting the work of the Impressionists, including several of the Algerian paintings that Renoir had just deposited with the dealer Paul Durand-Ruel. Perhaps this is the reason that the artist initially decided to paint Mme Clapisson out of doors, taking tea in a rose garden. But despite his sitter's compliance, the sessions did not go well, and Renoir complained of having difficulty completing the "wretched portrait, which will not work." When, after many sittings and much frustration, he finally finished the canvas, M. Clapisson found it "too audacious." He returned the picture to the painter, who agreed to undertake a more acceptable likeness.

Renoir executed his second portrait very differently from the first, using less diluted, stiffer paint. Representing Valentine indoors, in an evening dress that shows off her shoulders and arms, this portrait found favor with his clients. A fashionable image of a woman sufficiently à la mode to have had her white sauce discussed in the society pages of *La Vie moderne*, it was tailored to satisfy the Clapissons' needs. Yet Renoir's recipe here is not that of the conventional society portraitist of the time. Although he had jokingly proclaimed that he intended to swear off doing "portraits in the sunlight" and instead to adopt the plain, dark backgrounds then in vogue, Renoir in fact set Valentine before a light-filled, abstract design in which he wove together the red, yellow, and blue that he employed with greater concentration in her chair, gloves, and dress.

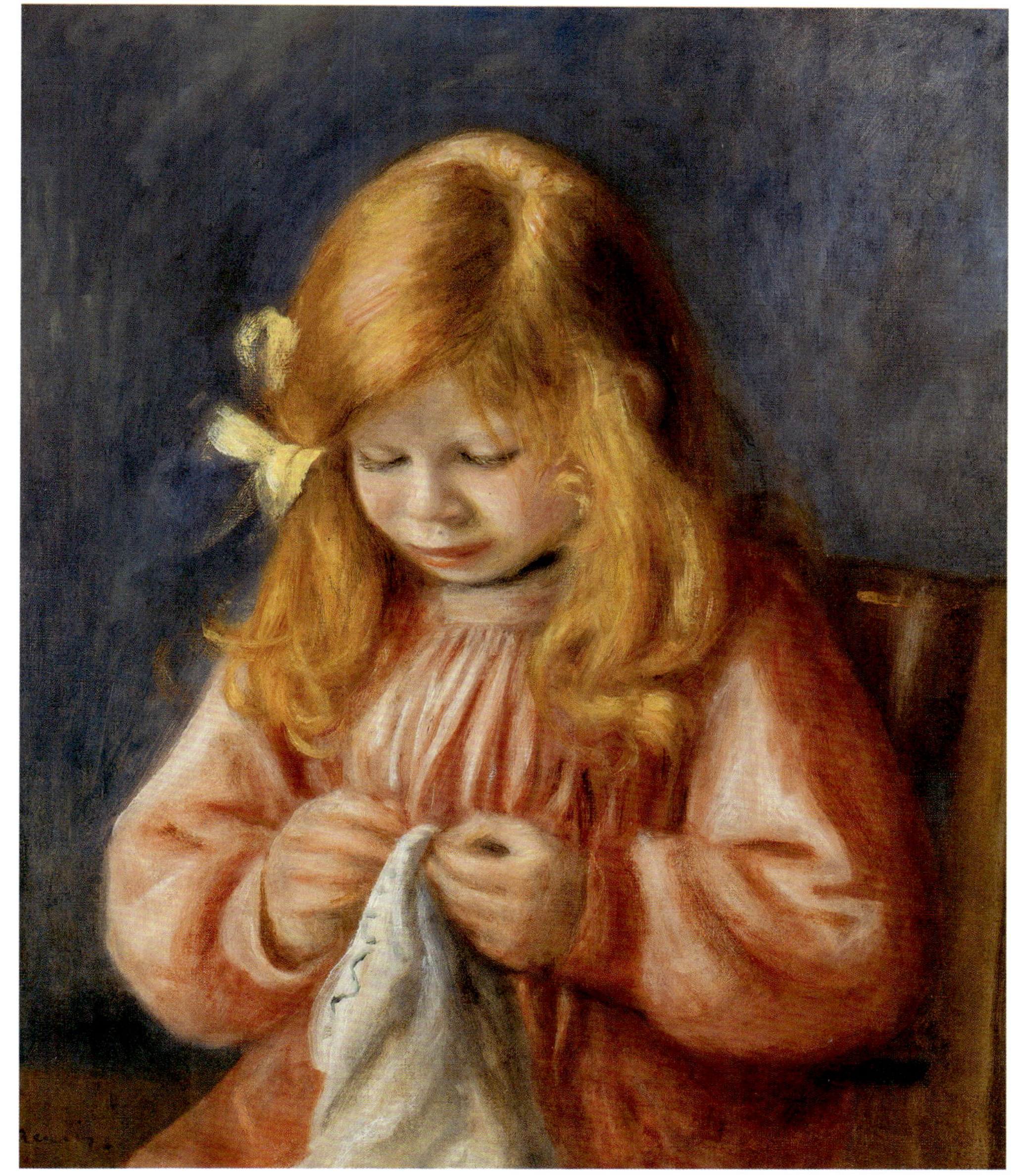

38

Jean Renoir Sewing, 1898/99

Oil on canvas; 55.4 x 46.5 cm (21 3/4 x 18 1/4 in.)
Mr. and Mrs. Martin A. Ryerson Collection, 1937.1027
Signed lower left: *Renoir.*

Like Edgar Degas, Pierre-Auguste Renoir had the Old Masters very much in mind during the 1890s. Although he shared Degas's reverence for the great practitioners of the classical tradition of line, notably Andrea Mantegna and Nicolas Poussin, he was now more focused on the masters of color and broad handling—Rembrandt van Rijn, Peter Paul Rubens, Titian, and Diego Velázquez—and, as he declared, on the art of the eighteenth century in particular.

Renoir's passion for the eighteenth century is reflected in the new importance he gave to the theme of youth, especially after the birth of his second son, Jean, in 1894. "One must be personally involved in what one does," Renoir wrote to a friend when Jean was just seventeen months old. "At the moment, I'm painting Jean pouting. It's no easy thing, but it's such a lovely subject, and I assure you that I'm working for myself and myself alone." Jean later claimed to "remember quite clearly all the preparations for the picture now in the Art Institute of Chicago, showing me sewing." However, although he maintained that he was over five years old at the time, other dated pictures suggest that *Jean Renoir Sewing* actually portrays him about a year younger. The length of his hair is of little help in dating works like this. For while long tresses were in fashion for infant boys, Jean, to his great embarrassment, was forced to wear his hair this way for an unusually long time—until the autumn of 1901, when, at age seven, he went to a school whose regulations required that it be cut. Renoir's love of the "pure gold" of Jean's silken hair, as well as his desire to preserve this attribute of innocence in his paintings of his son, overrode any concern for the relentless taunts that Jean had to endure from other boys.

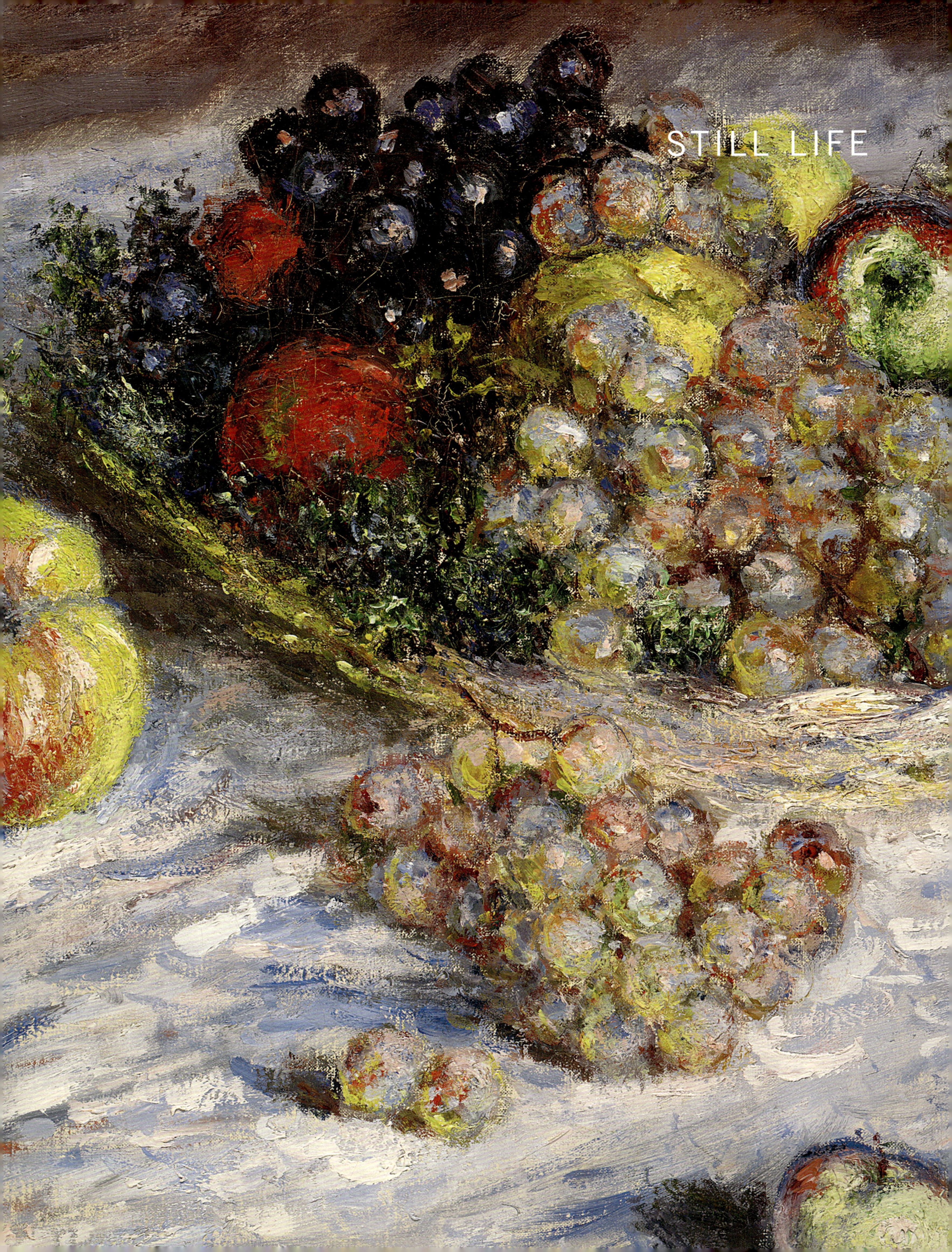

STILL LIFE

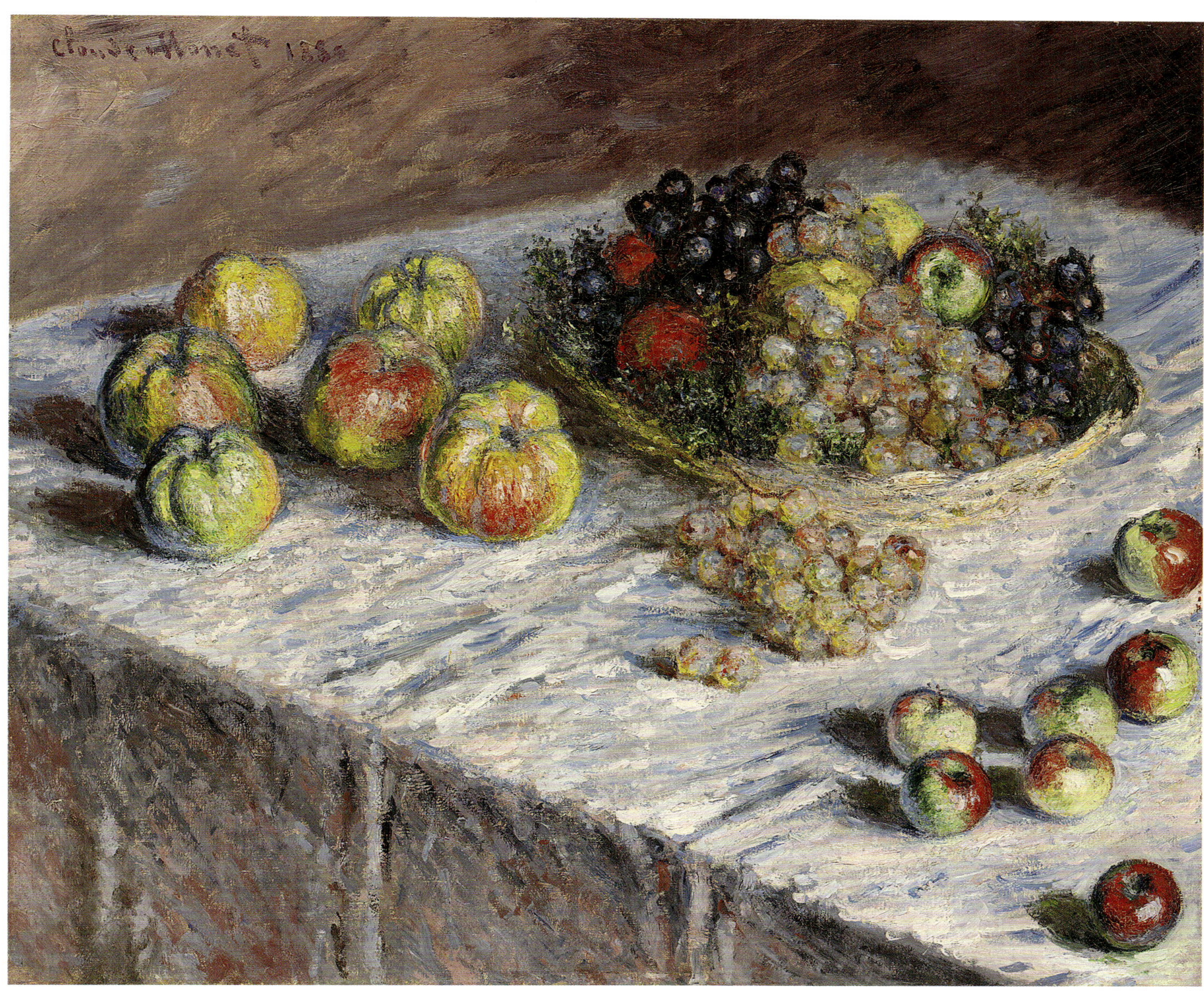

39

Apples and Grapes, 1880

Oil on canvas; 66.2 x 82.3 cm (26 1⁄16 x 32 3⁄8 in.)
Mr. and Mrs. Martin A. Ryerson Collection, 1933.1152
Signed upper left: *Claude Monet 1880*

Although he is primarily known as a landscape painter, Claude Monet periodically painted still lifes, which generally found a ready market. In contrast to his earlier still-life compositions, reminiscent of those by Édouard Manet, which showed objects set on gleaming white tablecloths against dark backgrounds (see cat. 1), *Apples and Grapes* embodies the Impressionists' aim to express the textures, colors, and vibrancy found in nature. Monet had several reasons for returning to still-life painting in 1879–80. Having received a mixed response to the twenty-nine works he showed at the fourth Impressionist exhibition, in April 1879, he may have wanted to engage with a theme that was less fraught and more readily accessible. Sales of these images of fruit helped the artist during a time of great financial difficulty following the death of his wife, Camille, in September 1879. Instead of the shortages and strains that he was personally experiencing, Monet's depiction of plump, juicy grapes and shiny red and green apples displayed on a freshly laundered tablecloth conveys a sense of plenitude and well-being. Only the grapes have a translucent fragility (achieved with dabs of white pigment), which the artist used to emphasize the solidity of the apples. They provide a counterweight to the slanting table that fills more than three-fourths of the space, thus eliminating any sense of interior setting or décor. Monet's own viewpoint, looking down at the tabletop from a high, steep angle, anticipates the radical cropping he would use for his later views of Normandy cliffs. Indeed, he treated the extensive cloth surface like a landscape; the play of light on the horizontal brushstrokes, indicating the folds in the tablecloth, recalls other works in which the artist employed similar short, horizontal marks to suggest various terrains or water rippling in sunlight (see cat. 59).

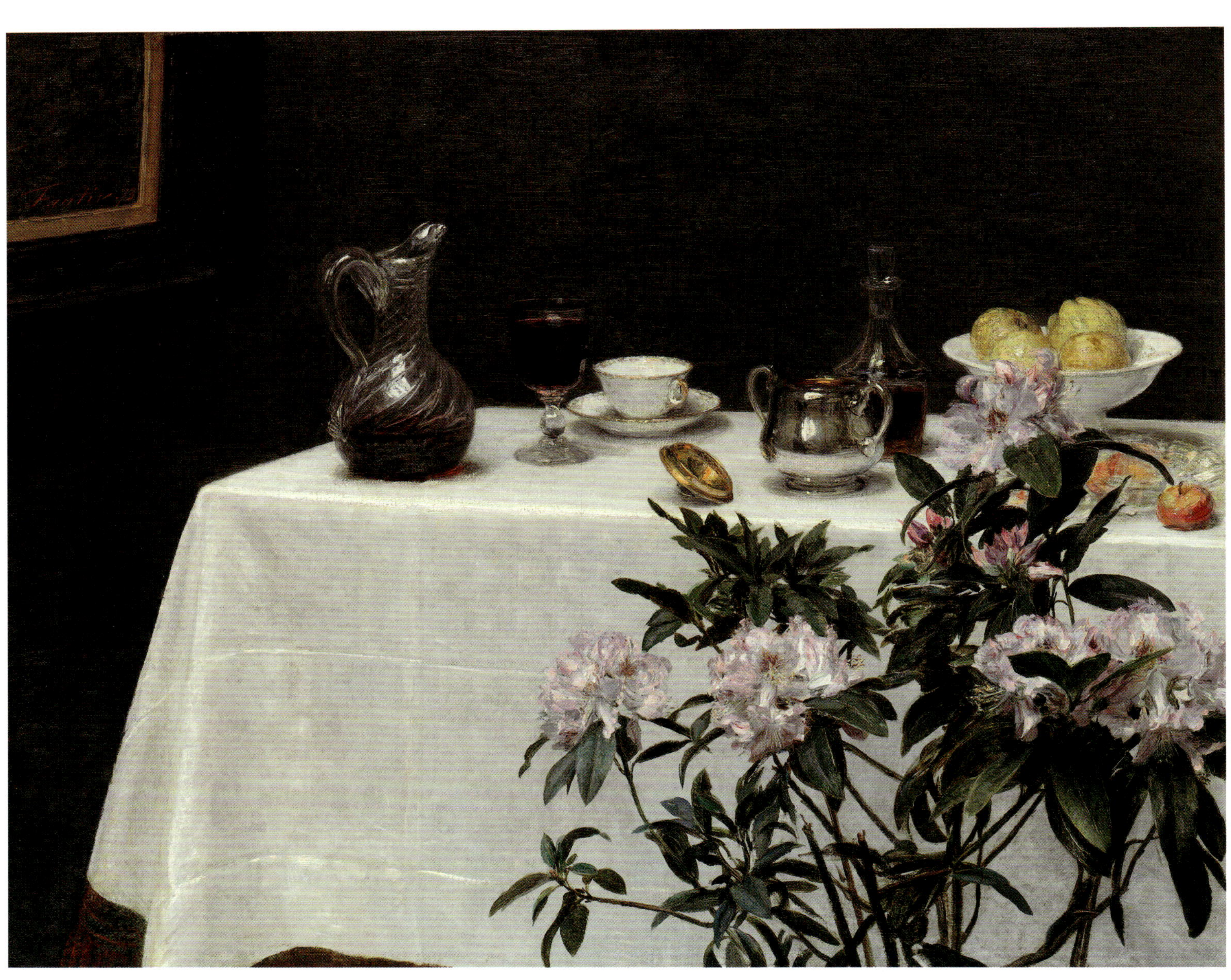

HENRI FANTIN-LATOUR French, 1836–1904

40

Still Life: Corner of a Table, 1873

Oil on canvas; 96.4 x 125 cm (37 15/16 x 49 3/16 in.)
Ada Turnbull Hertle Endowment, 1951.226

Henri Fantin-Latour's view of Realism was so strict that he felt it was impossible to represent what he could not study closely over time. As a result, he would not consider painting out of doors, where he would be beset by changing light and atmospheric conditions. Instead, he limited his study of the world around him to acutely observed and precisely rendered portraits and still lifes, maintaining a parallel career painting subjects from his imagination, in which he could attempt to represent movement. A similar compartmentalization characterized his marketing strategy as well as his reputation. In France it was the single and group portraits of family and artist friends that Fantin sent to the annual state-sponsored Salons that secured his reputation and brought him, in 1870, official recognition. But the praise he received for his portraiture did not translate into sales. Rather it was the floral still lifes marketed by friends in England that secured his livelihood from the 1860s on.

In 1872 the dealer Paul Durand-Ruel's purchase of twenty-two still lifes emboldened Fantin to hope that the flower pieces hitherto sold only to English collectors might now find buyers in France and fuel his career. To this end, he embarked on *Still Life: Corner of a Table*, an uncommonly large and ambitious still life that he would send to the Salon of 1873. The subject—"the same table and the same objects as in . . . *A Corner of the Table*," his group portrait of the previous year—was treated in a way he described as "an attempt to realize the natural": "I tried to make a painting representing things as they are found in nature; I put a great deal of thought into that arrangement, but with the idea of making it look like a natural arrangement of random objects . . . giving the appearance of a total lack of artistry."

To achieve his aim and heighten the sense of the haphazard, Fantin adopted a low viewpoint and framed his subject so that forms are cropped by the edges of the composition on all sides. Both the arbitrary cropping and the dramatic, prominent placement of the rhododendrons silhouetted against the white tablecloth at the picture plane reveal the influence of the compositional strategies found in the Japanese prints that so captivated the artists in Fantin's circle. Exquisitely rendered and subtly differentiated, the objects on the table, a number of which had appeared in the group portrait, are disposed in a zigzag arrangement that, in fact, is considerably less random than the still-life arrangement in the earlier picture, in which the composition was structured by the positioning of the figures. Fantin could not resist giving some order to the haphazard.

Still Life: Corner of a Table did not find favor at the Salon. Nor did another ambitious, though slightly smaller still life that Fantin exhibited there the following year. Thereafter, the artist abandoned his hopes to engage a French audience with his work in this genre and returned to painting smaller-scale flower pictures almost exclusively for the English market.

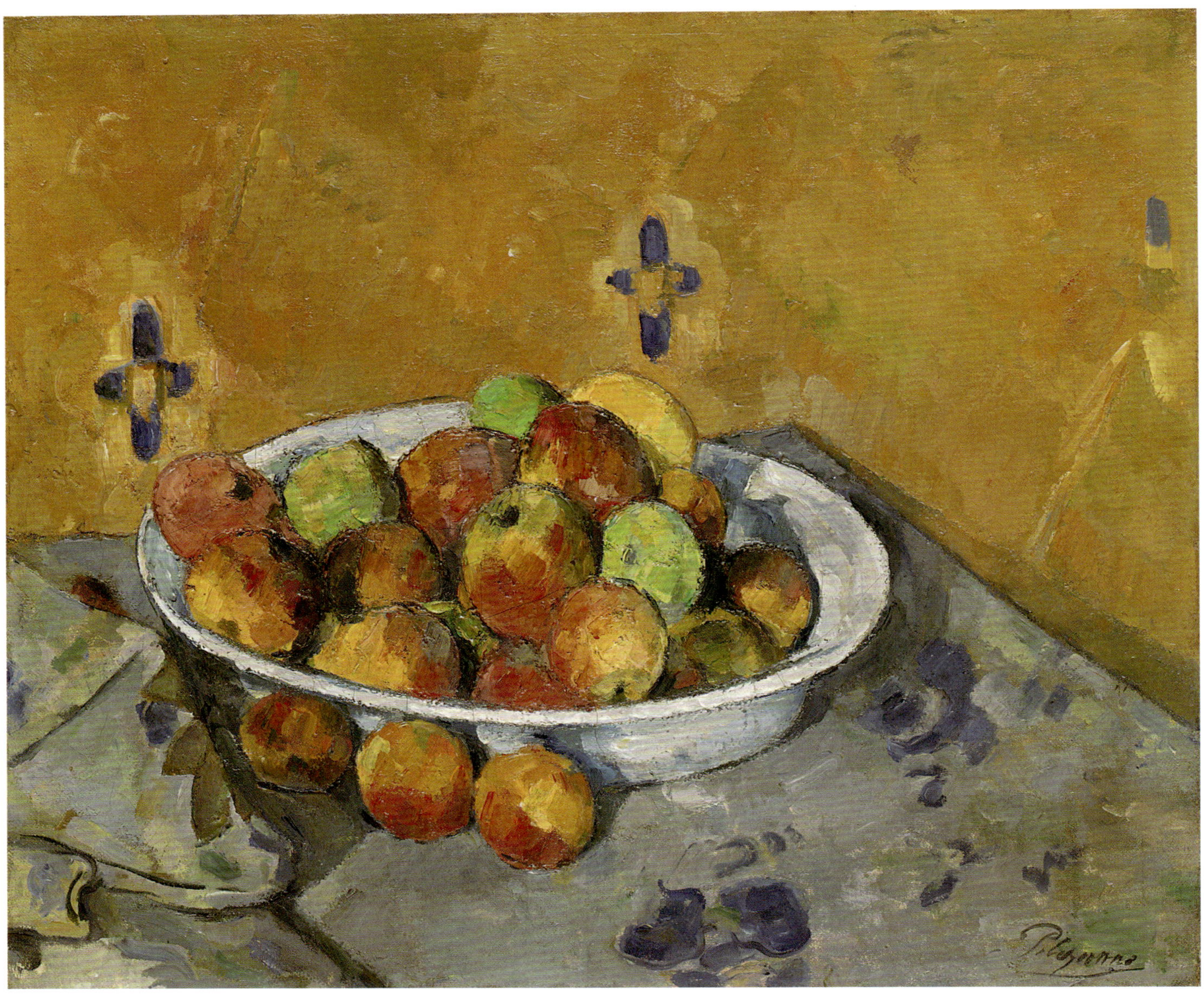

41

The Plate of Apples, c. 1877

Oil on canvas; 45.8 x 54.7 cm (18 ⅛ x 21 ½ in.)
Gift of Kate L. Brewster, 1949.512
Signed lower right: *P. Cezanne*

Paul Cézanne was thirty-eight years old when he executed this modest still life, one of several works featuring the ocher wallpaper with blue lozenge-shaped motifs that probably covered the walls of his Paris apartment on the rue de l'Ouest. Although his experience with Camille Pissarro in Auvers and Pontoise in 1872–74 (see cat. 18) had motivated him to paint directly from nature and eliminate the heavy light-dark oppositions that characterize his studio works from the 1860s, Cézanne's approach to still lifes remained very much his own. With its densely pigmented brushstrokes and heavy contours, *The Plate of Apples* is a transitional work—between the thickly "troweled" surfaces of his early paintings and the late compositions in which he applied transparent tones in parallel or blocky strokes. While avoiding the illusionism, modeling, and dramatic chiaroscuro so antithetical to the Impressionist idiom, Cézanne nonetheless sculpted, as much as painted, the surface of this work. His use of a limited range of hues—ocher, blue, and grayish white—underscores the painting's sense of solidity. In some places, the artist employed a palette knife or the end of his brush to incise contours and emphasize dimensionality (around the apples, for example); in others, he created edges by allowing the primed canvas to show between zones of paint, as if he were working from a template that he filled in with color. The diagonal pattern of the decorative wallpaper has been largely painted over; indeed, its encrusted, stuccolike surface may cover an earlier composition. Cézanne's signature, which is stylistically quite different than the painting, is thought to have been added by the artist at a later date. He may have decided not to include this work among the three still lifes he showed in the third Impressionist exhibition, in April 1877, as a result of its reworked and experimental nature.

PIERRE-AUGUSTE RENOIR French, 1841–1919

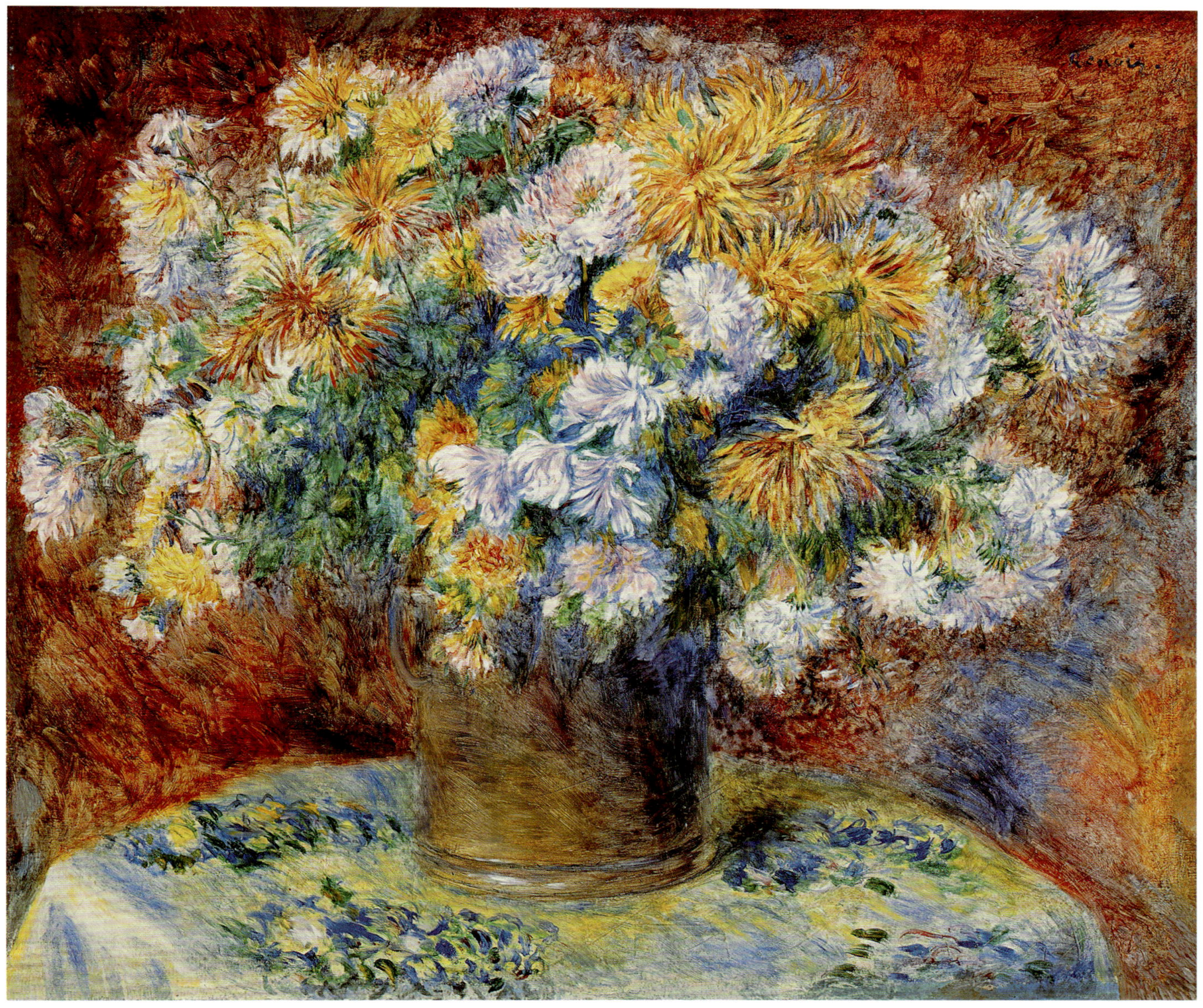

42

Chrysanthemums, 1881/82

Oil on canvas; 54.7 x 65.9 cm (21 ½ x 25 15/16 in.)
Mr. and Mrs. Martin A. Ryerson Collection, 1933.1173
Signed upper right: *Renoir.*

It was around the time that Pierre-Auguste Renoir was working on his problematic portrait of Valentine Clapisson (see cat. 37) that he painted the glorious still life *Chrysanthemums*, featuring flowers in a simple brown earthenware kitchen crock set on a floral-patterned tablecloth. Renoir had recently produced a number of elaborate flower pieces. Sensitive, like Claude Monet, to the market potential of such works, he also took personal satisfaction in making them. Renoir would later say:

> I just let my brain rest when I paint flowers. I don't experience the same tension as I do when confronted by the model. When I am painting flowers, I establish the tones, I study the values carefully without worrying about losing the picture. I don't dare do this with a figure piece for fear of ruining it. The experience I gain from these works, I eventually apply to my [figure] paintings.

In *Chrysanthemums* Renoir explored effects of transparency and luminosity. Taking an unprimed canvas, he used a palette knife to lay in a ground of lead-white paint. Although this layer was thick and took time to dry, Renoir may have thought it would offer particular advantages. Obscuring the grain of the canvas, it resulted in a surface that was arguably smoother and more capable of reflecting light than one that had not been prepared in this way. Exploiting this technique to maximum effect, Renoir worked very quickly, building up the image with freely applied, thin layers of washlike paint. The remarkable transparency he achieved invites comparison with watercolor—a medium that had not yet attracted Renoir's attention—as well as with the art of overglaze porcelain painting. The artist's early grounding in this craft must have helped to fuel experimentation.

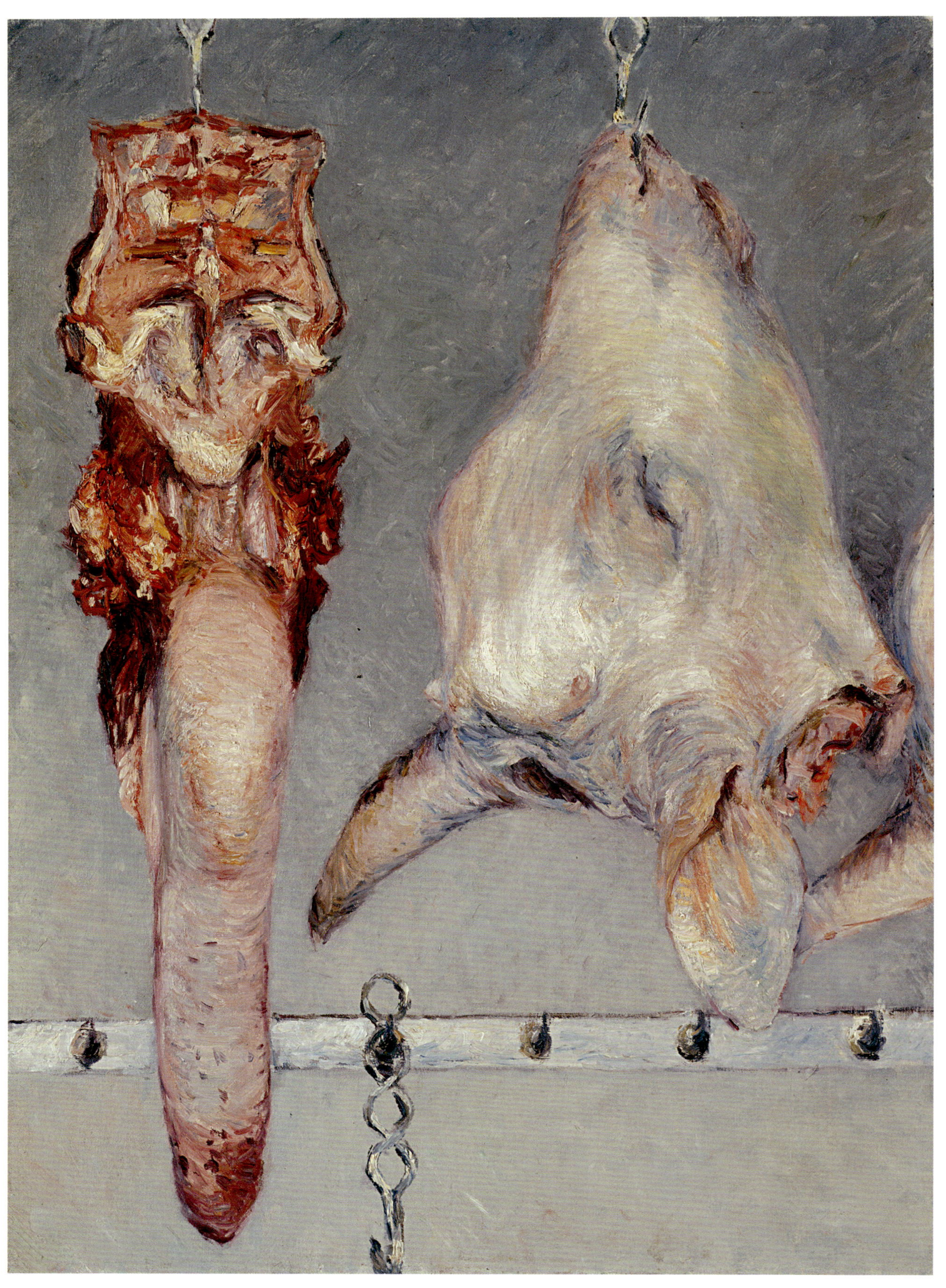

43

Calf's Head and Ox Tongue, c. 1882

Oil on canvas; 73 x 54 cm (29 x 21 in.)
Major Acquisitions Centennial Endowment, 1999.561

Gustave Caillebotte had made only a handful of still lifes—and relatively insignificant ones at that—prior to 1879, when he took up the subject more seriously. The resulting works constitute some of the most provocative and original compositions in his oeuvre, as potent and charged as his most ambitious domestic interiors or representations of street life. Within this series, *Calf's Head and Ox Tongue* is among the most subversive in its challenge not only to the historical tradition of still-life painting but also to the ways his contemporaries approached the genre. With the exception of Paul Cézanne (for whom still lifes played an important role in the development of technique), the Impressionists considered still-life painting to be commercially appealing as well as a kind of artistic "time-out"—a non-demanding break from the exploration of themes of modern life.

Caillebotte's inspiration and intentions were quite different, however. Independently wealthy, he did not need to sell his work. His choice of subject for this painting was not his own creation but an arrangement he came upon in a shop window, similar to the kinds of displays he saw in the butcher and tripe shop below his family home near the Gare Saint-Lazare in Paris. In many ways, *Calf's Head and Ox Tongue* is even more resolutely modern than the street views for which Caillebotte is best known (see cat. 24). This unexpectedly stark composition confronts issues of modern production, marketing, and consumerism. Disassociated from their original sources, isolated, dismembered animal parts are suspended in a kind of commercial purgatory, between death and consumption—dead matter cut off from life and not yet transformed and revalidated as food.

Although he was inspired by the still lifes of seventeenth-century Dutch masters like Rembrandt van Rijn, as well as by the works of nineteenth-century Realist artists such as François Bonvin (who painted bloody slabs of beef hanging in modest interiors), Caillebotte's choices of color and composition distance the raw meat from the brutal reality of its production. In place of the somber chiaroscuro that both Rembrandt and the Realists used to set the stage for such themes, Caillebotte adopted a lively and insouciant near-pastel palette. The fiery red and orange tongue and soft bluish mauve head set against pale blue-gray lend an oddly festive, even seductive, quality to the motif. While the hooks at the top underscore the fact that the meat is lifeless flesh set out for purchase, Caillebotte's decorative palette, soft, caressing brushwork, and elegantly structured composition give new life to "dead nature" and imbue it with a disconcerting ambiguity that invites comparison with works by twentieth-century and contemporary artists such as Chaïm Soutine and Lucien Freud.

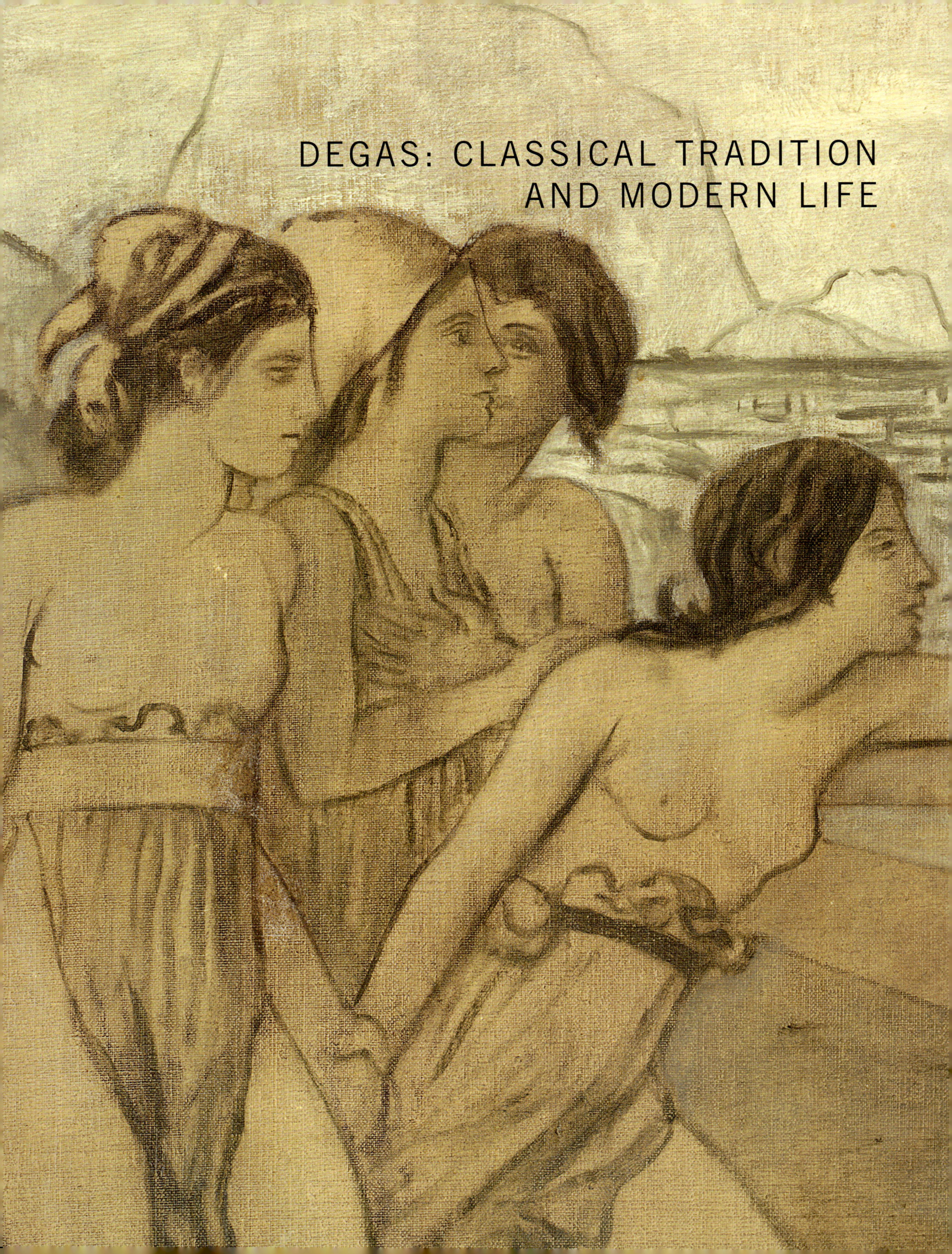
DEGAS: CLASSICAL TRADITION
AND MODERN LIFE

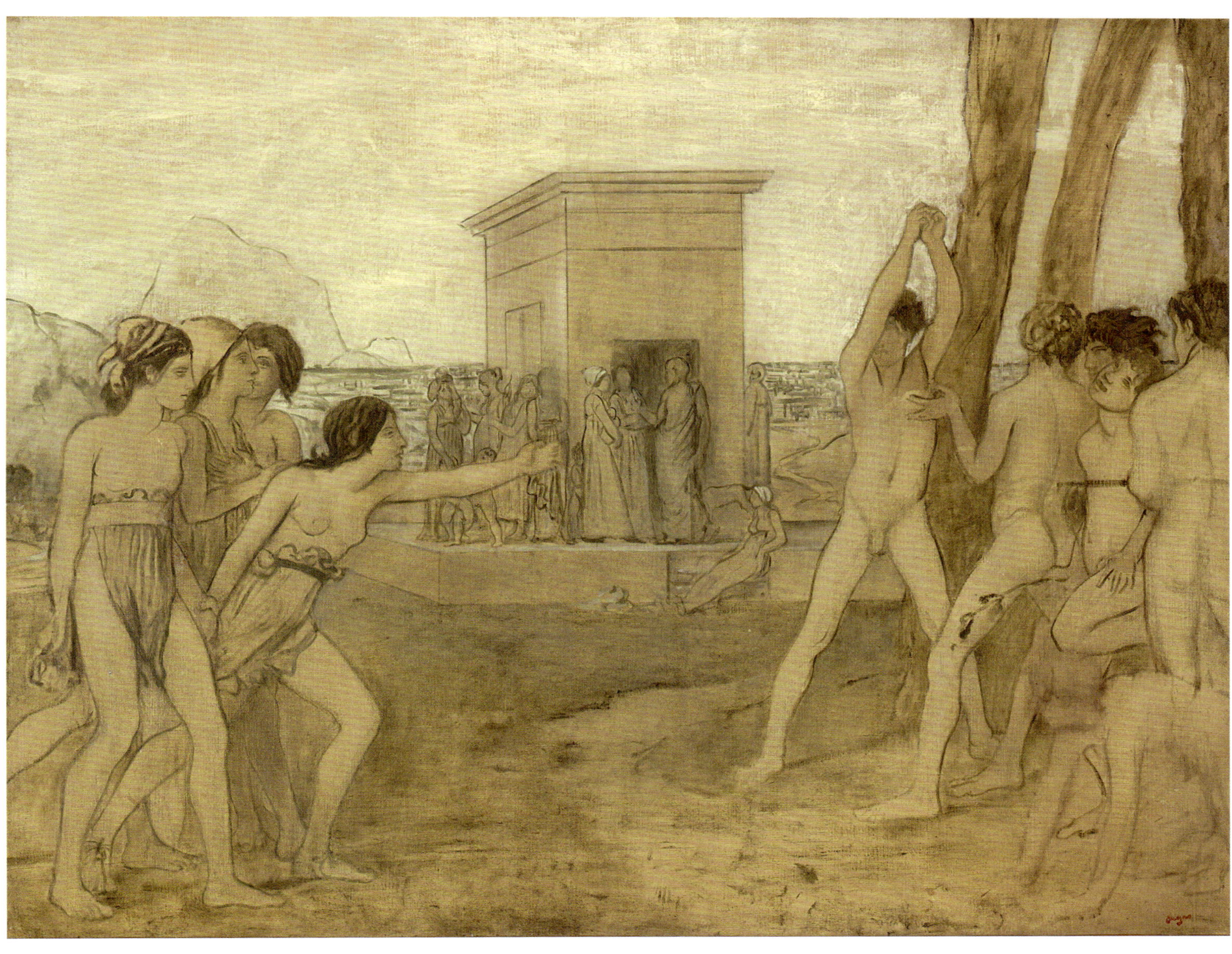

44

Young Spartan Girls Challenging Boys, c. 1860

Oil on canvas; 97.4 x 140 cm (38 5/16 x 55 1/8 in.)
Charles H. and Mary F. S. Worcester Collection, 1961.334
Signed lower right: *Degas*

In 1859 Edgar Degas returned to Paris following a prolonged stay in Italy, where he had visited relatives in Naples and Florence and attended life classes at the Académie Française, Rome. This picture, undertaken around 1860, speaks to the artist's early ambition to realize canvases featuring scenes from the Bible, as well as ancient and more recent history, and thus to compete in the official forum for artistic achievement provided by the state-sponsored Salons. An entry in a contemporary notebook that Degas kept indicates the subject: "young girls and boys fighting in the Plane-tree grove, watched by the elderly Lycurgus and the mothers." His inspiration was the Roman historian Plutarch's account of the life of Lycurgus, a legendary ninth-century B.C. Spartan lawgiver. Lycurgus's social reforms included an unusual egalitarian training whereby female adolescents competed on equal ground with males, exercising publicly in a state of nudity that signified "complete probity, without any . . . corruption whatsoever." Having first explored the idea in both compositional and figure drawings, Degas embarked on this canvas, delineating his composition with considerable detail using brush and diluted oil over charcoal. This initial monochrome stage, resembling a large drawing on canvas, would have been further developed with color layers had Degas continued. But he did not; instead, he started another related painting, removing both the trees and the architecture (National Gallery, London). In the late 1870s, he reworked this second canvas with an eye to showing it in the fifth Impressionist exhibition as *Young Spartan Girls Challenging Boys.* He recast the physiognomies of the youths so that they appear more like contemporary Parisians than do the classicized heads of the figures in the Chicago painting. Although the artist clearly found contemporary resonance in the subject of adolescent sexuality, he never exhibited either picture.

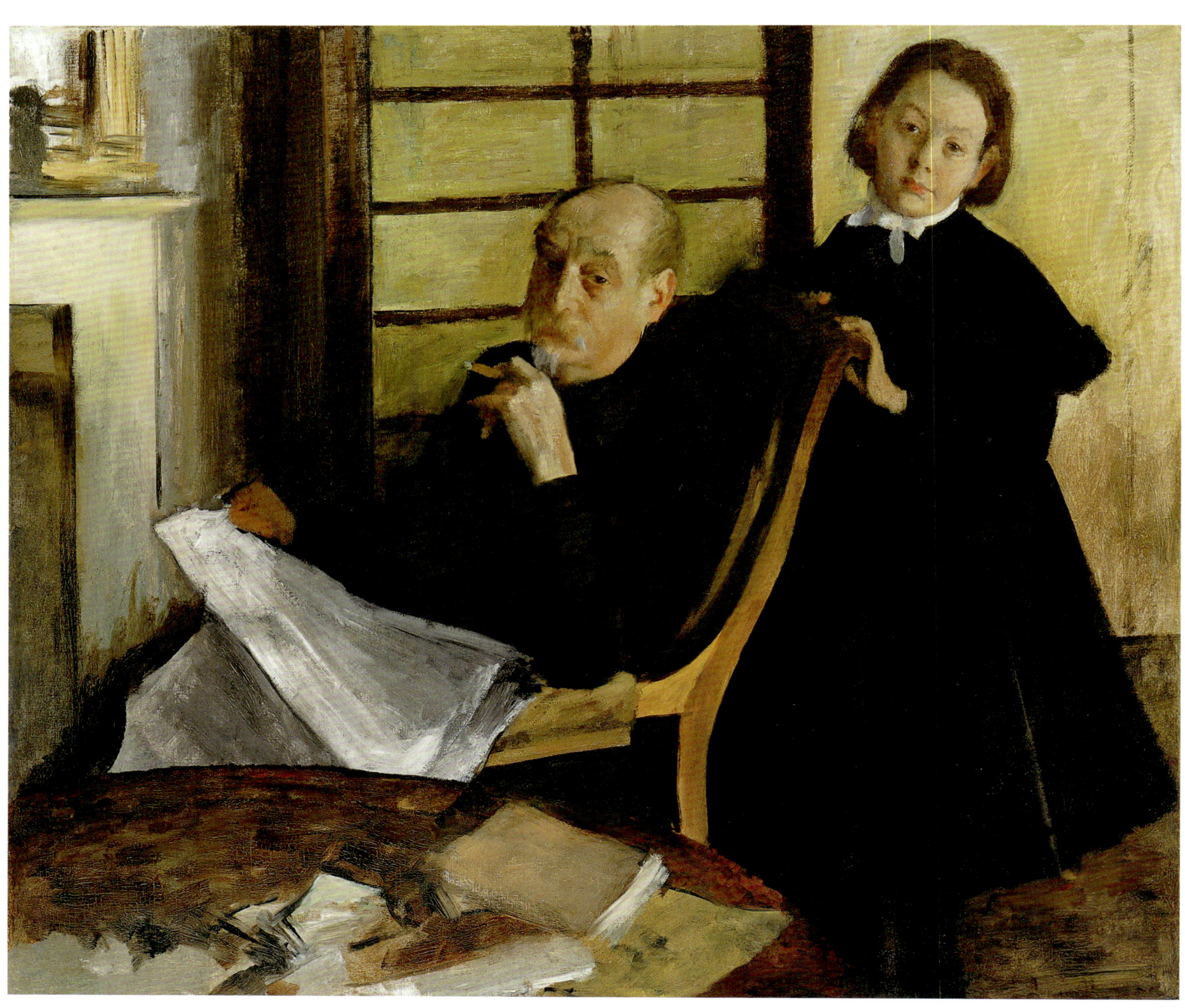

45

Henri Degas and His Niece Lucie Degas (The Artist's Uncle and Cousin), 1875/76

Oil on canvas; 99.8 x 119.9 cm (39 1/4 x 47 3/16 in.)
Mr. and Mrs. Lewis L. Coburn Memorial Collection, 1933.429

A great portraitist, Edgar Degas seldom took commissions, largely restricting his subjects to family members and friends whom he knew intimately and often depicted with keen psychological acuity. He painted this double portrait in Naples, most likely during his four-month stay there in early 1875, but possibly on his brief return visit in June 1876.

The city was home to the artist's paternal family, and during and following his first Italian trip of the 1850s, Degas depicted many of his relatives, including his grandfather Hilaire (1857; Musée d'Orsay, Paris), who had established the family banking fortunes. Hilaire's sons Édouard, Henri, and Achille had remained in Naples, although their elder brother, Auguste, the artist's father, moved to Paris to open a branch of the family firm, changing the spelling of his name to the seemingly more aristocratic de Gas. Degas's father had traveled to Naples in 1873 and died there early the following year. It was this and subsequent family losses that necessitated the artist's trips to Naples in 1875 and 1876 and illuminate the melancholy that informs this portrait of his uncle Henri and first cousin Lucie.

Born in 1867, the little girl had lost her mother in 1869 and was orphaned with her older brother, Georges, the following year, on the death of their father, Édouard. The children became the wards of their bachelor uncle Achille. Thereafter, Lucie lived in the vast, underfurnished Palazzo Degas with Achille and his brother Henri. When Achille died in 1875, Lucie became Henri's ward. The next year, her thirteen-year-old brother died; his funeral may have been the occasion for the artist's June visit.

Degas depicted his uncle and cousin as if they have been interrupted in their solitary pastimes by his presence. Henri looks up from his newspaper and cigar, raising his head somewhat quizzically. Standing behind him, Lucie responds likewise. Her body is enveloped by heavy black mourning clothes, and the tilt of her head and her becalmed expression convey a resigned sadness that scholars have likened to that of Italian Renaissance Madonnas and saints. Degas presented her as a child in an environment that contains no signs of childhood pastimes but is rather centered on an old man. This idea is compositionally reinforced by Henri's position on the central axis, which is emphasized by the mullion of the screen behind his head. Similarly, the child's isolation is suggested by her position in the right third of the picture space, contained in a zone of yellow. Although Henri pursues his interests, Lucie apparently has none of her own; rather, it seems she reads the newspaper over his shoulder. The lonely girl touches the back of her uncle's chair with an affecting tentativeness, as if her connections to her family are fragile. In fact, they were; Henri died in 1879, at which point the young heiress changed guardians for the third time in three years. Degas left this picture in Naples, where it remained in Lucie's possession until her death in 1909.

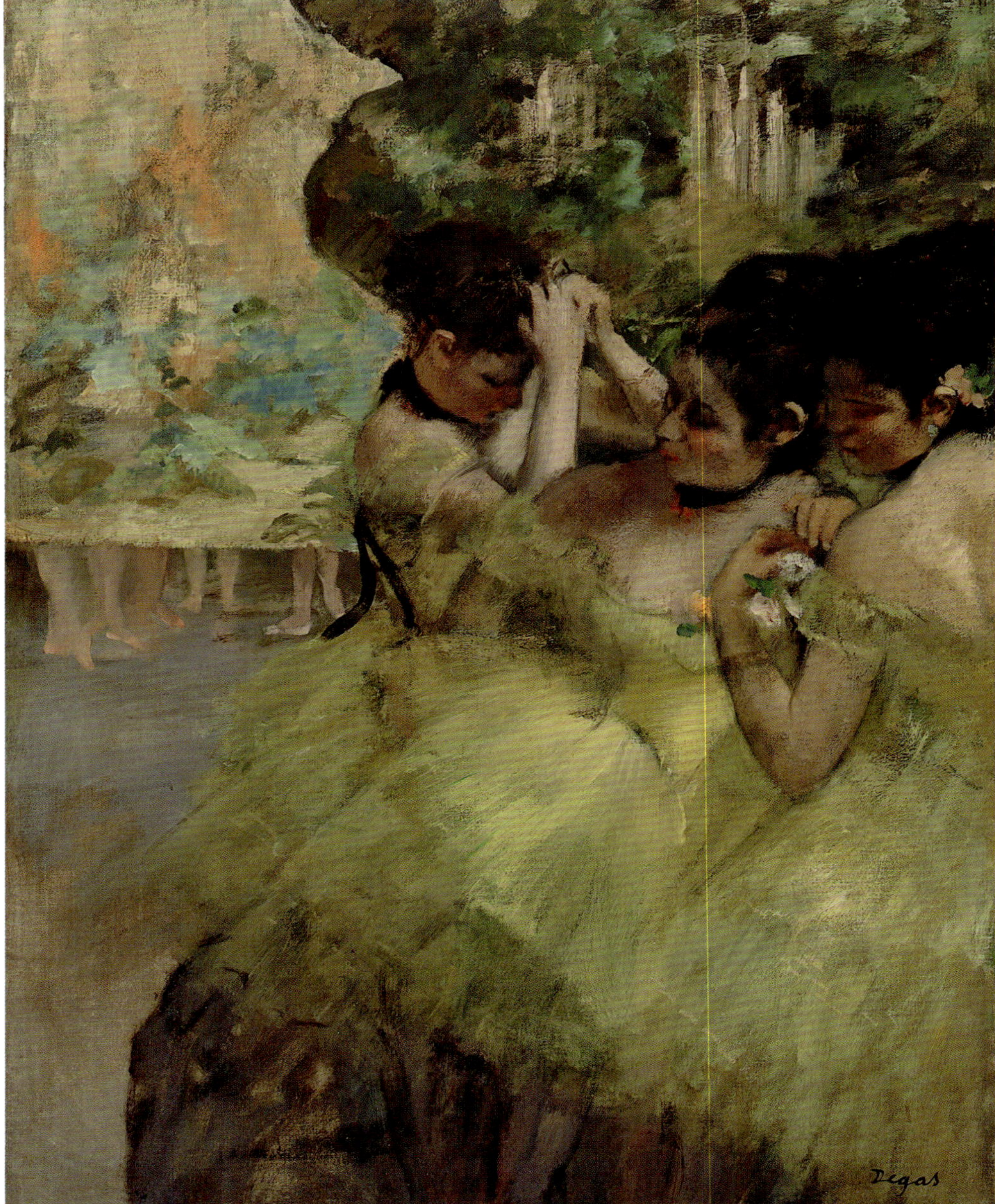

46

Yellow Dancers (In the Wings), 1874/76

Oil on canvas; 73.5 x 59.5 cm (28 15⁄16 x 23 7⁄16 in.)
Gift of Mr. and Mrs. Gordon Palmer, Mrs. Bertha P. Thorne, Mr. and Mrs. Arthur M. Wood, and Mrs. Rose M. Palmer, 1963.923
Signed lower right: *Degas*

During the 1860s, the racecourse was the one contemporary subject that Edgar Degas, the future painter of modern life, treated regularly. Dancers first appear in his work at the end of the decade as secondary figures in paintings of orchestra pits, then as an independent subject in 1871. Nearly half the artist's total output, in a variety of media, was devoted to depictions of dancers. His engagement with the subject can be related to his attendance of performances and rehearsals onstage and in special rooms at the Paris Opéra, often in the company of his friend the writer Ludovic Halévy, who is celebrated for his short stories recounting the backstage adventures of two young dancers. Ballets usually accompanied the operas, but they were also performed independently. The viewer's position in this painting, in the wings near the dancers about to go onstage, is, in fact, that which was afforded to elite Opéra subscribers, who were allowed to roam and socialize backstage. Importantly, dance subjects allowed Degas to pursue and contemporize his interest in representing the human body in complex movements and postures, shifting his focus from the pages of ancient history (see cat. 44) to the stage of modern Paris.

The artist apparently began this picture in 1874, the year of the first Impressionist group exhibition, and continued reworking it extensively, adjusting the postures of the yellow-costumed dancers. He finished and signed the canvas in time for the second Impressionist show, in April 1876. One of several dance subjects exhibited there, it was curtly listed in the catalogue as *Coulisses*, rather than more idiomatically as *Dans les coulisses* (*In the Wings*), and was favorably remarked upon by several reviewers. In May Degas sent the picture he now referred to as "my Yellow Dancers" to the London dealer Charles Deschamps.

47

The Star, 1879/81

Pastel on cream wove paper, edge mounted on board; 733 x 574 mm (28 7/8 x 22 5/8 in.)
Bequest of Mrs. Diego Suarez, 1980.414

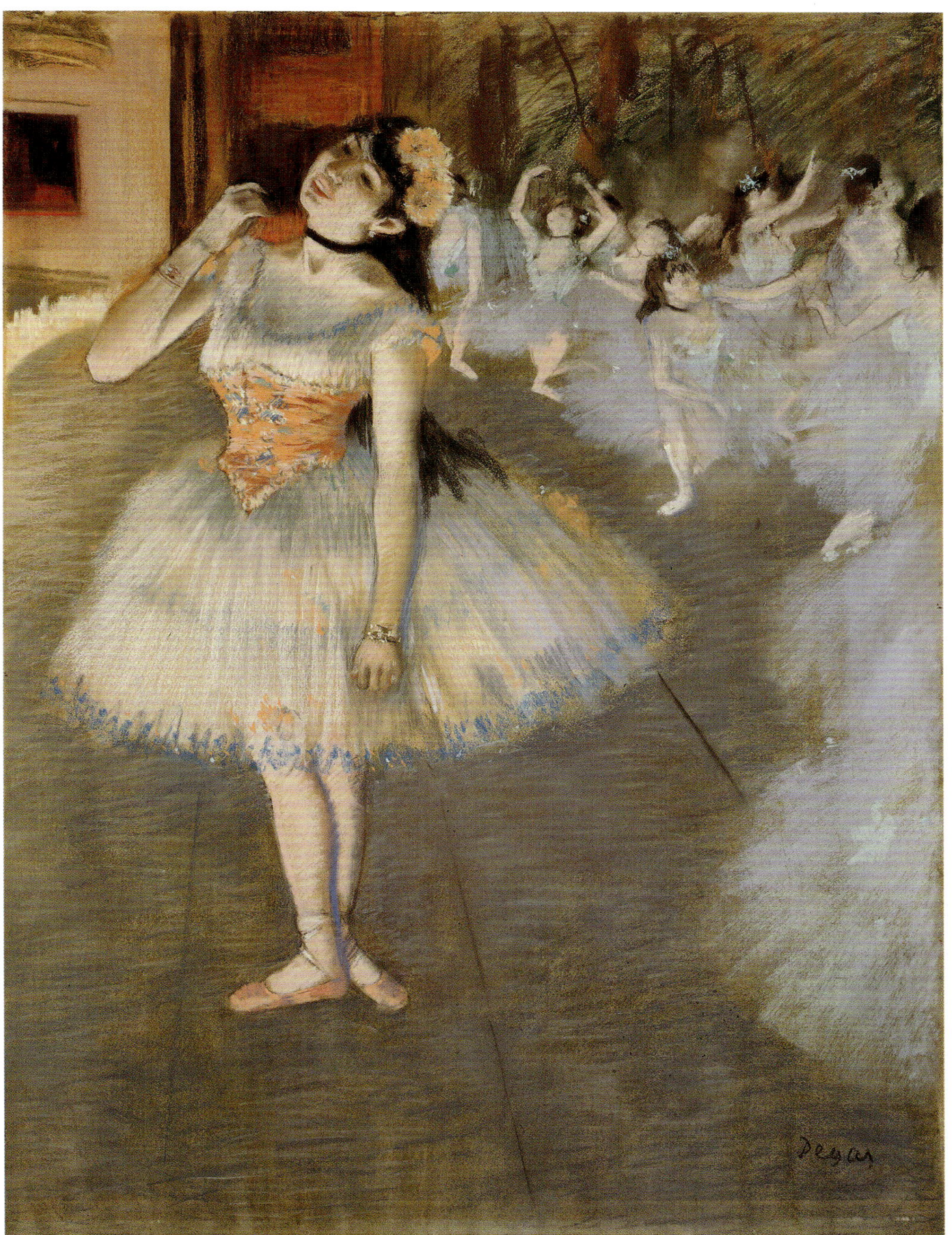

Edgar Degas portrayed dancers throughout his career (see cats. 46, 48, and 51), most often as types rather than individuals. In this glowing pastel, however, he described the model's features sufficiently to allow us to identify her as Rosita Mauri, a popular young ballerina who made her debut at the Paris Opéra in 1878 and had become a star by 1880, when she took the lead in *La Korrigane*, a ballet in two acts that became her most popular role. One of the dancer's most distinctive features—in addition to her wide-set, almond-shaped eyes and eyebrows—was her long black hair, the "magnificent black tresses flowing over her shoulders" extolled by reviewers and very much present in Degas's portrayal.

This composition serves to reinforce Mauri's star status: the receding lines of the floorboards, the curve of the stage at the upper left, and the halo of tutus along the right all focus attention on the dancer, who stands in third position and looks up toward the balconies. Describing her features and costume in considerable detail, the artist further underscored her prominence by only sketchily rendering the faces and costumes of the members of the corps de ballet who surround her.

The contrast between the solidity of the star and the insubstantiality of the other dancers points to a shift in Degas's interests. While the artist's subjects remained, in part, constant, he would increasingly simplify his compositions and concentrate on a single figure or figural group. Indeed, as the human form loomed larger, humor and anecdote would disappear from his work.

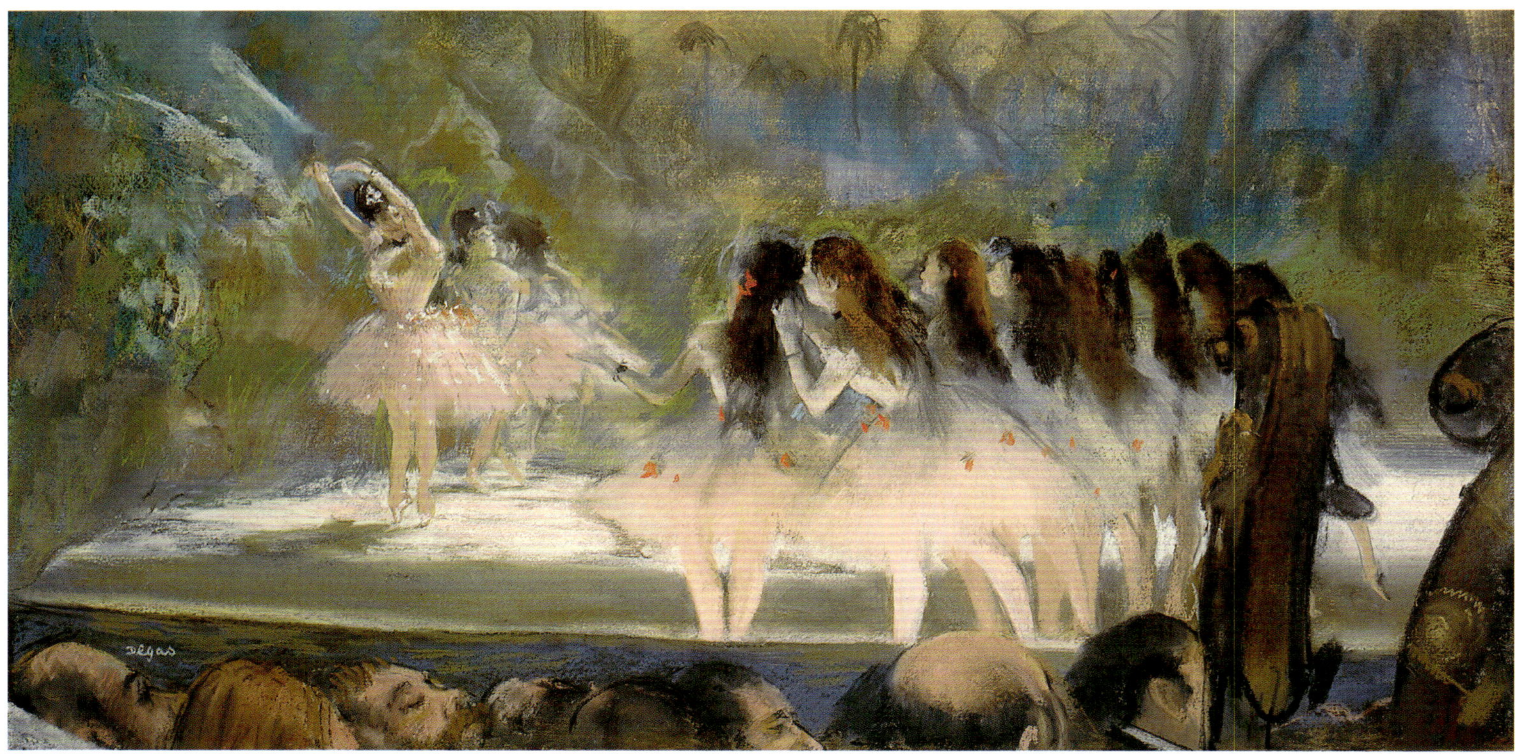

48

Ballet at the Paris Opéra, 1877

Pastel over monotype on cream laid paper; plate: 352 x 706 mm (13⅞ x 27 13/16 in.); sheet: 359 x 719 mm (14⅛ x 28 5/16 in.)
Gift of Mary and Leigh Block, 1981.12
Signed lower left: *Degas*

Edgar Degas may have exhibited this luminous depiction of a ballet performance at the Paris Opéra at the third Impressionist exhibition, held in the spring of 1877. He certainly displayed other work made in the medium that serves as the basis for this picture, what he described in the catalogue as "drawings made with greasy ink and printed." This process, monotype, was a little-used but centuries-old technique wherein an artist makes a design with ink on a metal plate that is subsequently printed, the composition thereby transferred to paper. Degas had begun working in monotype in 1876, sometimes using it—as he did here—as the foundation for a composition developed in pastel. As recent scholarship on Degas's involvement with the Paris Opéra underscores, this work—with its low vantage point and juxtaposition of a partial view of the musicians in the pit with a panorama of the performance above—places the viewer in the position of the *abonnés*, or subscribers who sat nearest the stage. The background of lush vegetation and silhouettes of tropical palms has also been connected with an 1877 production of Giacomo Meyerbeer's popular *L'Africaine* (first performed in 1865), staged in the new Opéra building designed by Charles Garnier. Degas greatly enjoyed *L'Africaine*—he saw it at least nine times in the 1880s. Similarities between the setting he evoked and an existing maquette in the Bibliothèque Nationale, Paris, for the tropical garden scenery of the fifth act of the Opéra production suggest that the artist drew directly upon his own experience of the performance.

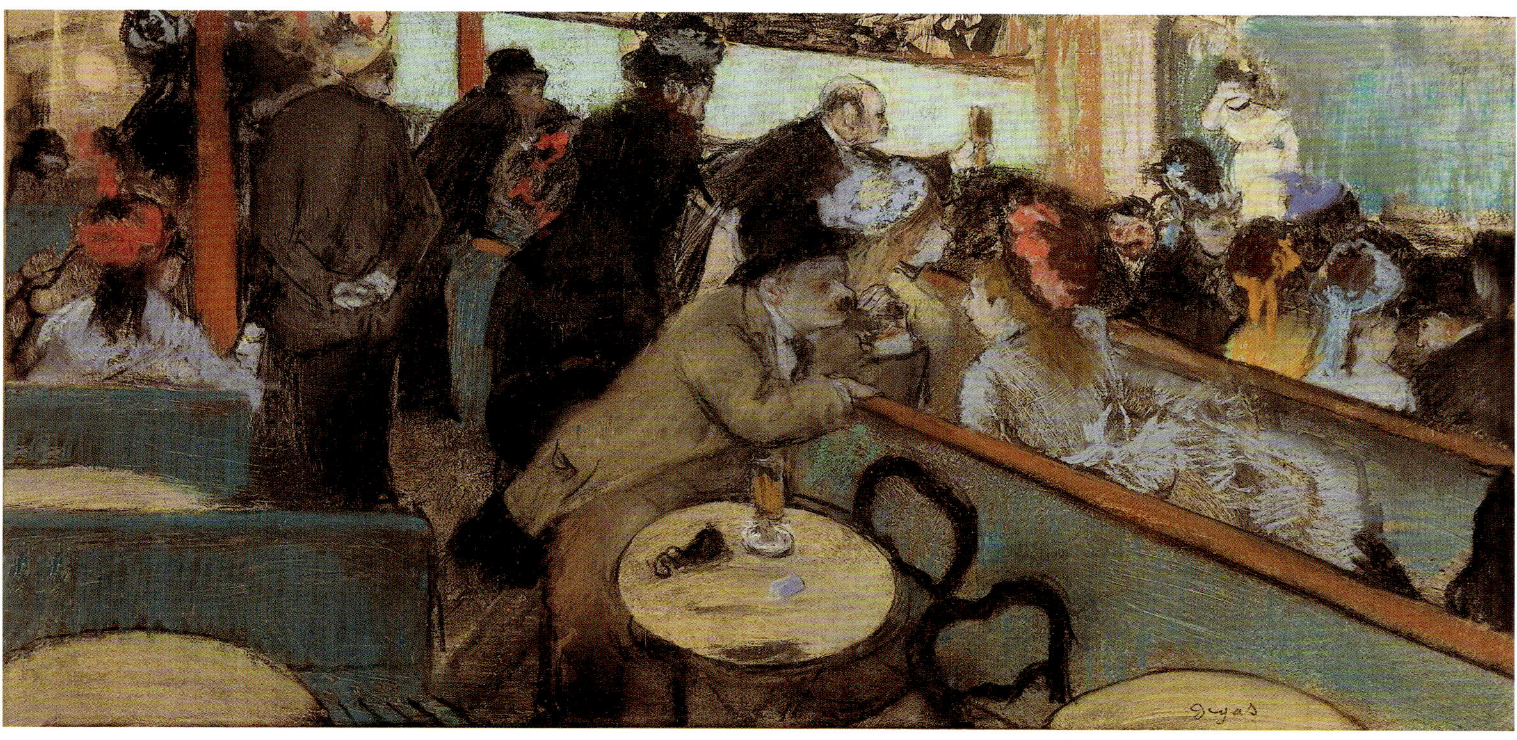

49

Café concert, 1876/77

Pastel over monotype on buff wove paper, laid down on tan card; image: 20.1 x 41.5 cm (7 15/16 x 16 5/16 in.)
Bequest of Brooks McCormick, 2007.286

By the summer of 1876, Edgar Degas's friends reported that he had immersed himself in the process of creating monotypes (see cat. 48). Although the first impression of such a print is usually the clearest (hence the term *monotype*), the ink residue on the plate's surface allows for subsequent cognate impressions, which are increasingly ghostlike in appearance. Degas usually printed two impressions, often using the paler second image as the monochrome foundation for a composition that he developed with colorful pastels. His practice was inconsistent, however, and he evidently executed several of his early pastel over monotype works—including this one—over impressions for which no cognates are known.

The artist reinvented and reenergized this medium in over two hundred examples; in 1877, at the third Impressionist exhibition, he showed both pure monotypes and those enhanced with pastel. This work was likely one of two that the catalogue listed simply as *Café concert*, as distinct from a third, *Chanteuse de café concert*. The latter title describes the majority of Degas's images of these popular entertainments, in which he focused on the performances of the star vocalists, both up close and within the outdoor settings of the fashionable establishments along the Champs Elysées. What makes this work so distinctive in Degas's oeuvre is that the performer plays a notably subordinate role in the composition. Concentrating instead on interior space, the artist took as his subject the audience, including the more attentive members seated closer to the stage and those stationed at the tables and banquettes further back, who are more involved in the dubious socializing for which *café concerts* were famous.

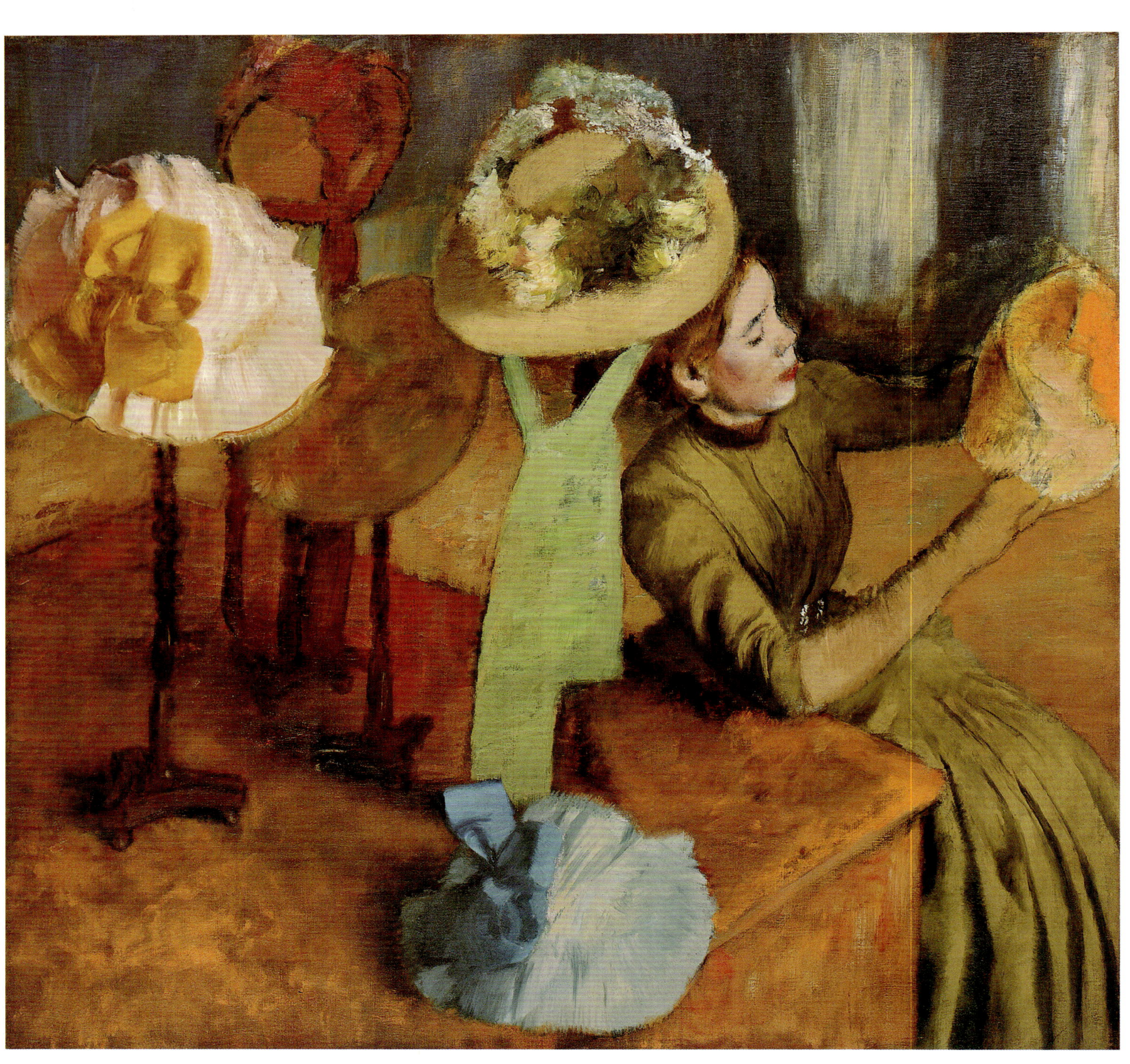

HILAIRE-GERMAIN-EDGAR DEGAS French, 1834–1917

50

The Millinery Shop, 1879/86

Oil on canvas; 100 x 110.7 cm (39⅜ x 43⁹⁄₁₆ in.)
Mr. and Mrs. Lewis Larned Coburn Memorial Collection, 1933.428

Edgar Degas's most ambitious statement on the theme of millinery shops, with which he had first engaged in the early 1880s, remained in his studio until 1913, when he left it with Paul Durand-Ruel. Despite its scale and resolution, the painting was not exhibited until 1932, shortly before it entered the Art Institute's collection. It has traditionally been presumed to represent a young hatmaker seated next to a colorful still-life arrangement of hats on decorative wood stands. We see her as if in passing, catching sight of her as she examines her handiwork with lips pursed, perhaps around an invisible pin.

Just as the hat the woman holds is unfinished, the paint used to describe it is also thinner and more sketchily applied than that of the surrounding scene. Other hats in progress and lacking the milliner's decorative garnishes are equally sketchy, in contrast to the richly decorated and thickly painted trio at the center. Degas's expression of spontaneity results from a highly calculated and carefully constructed composition, worked on over a protracted period of time and preceded by three pastel studies showing a woman examining a hat. In the studies, however, the woman wears an imposing toque, a hat with a narrow brim, that nearly covers her face. X-radiographs of the painting show that the figure of this milliner began her pictorial life as a client, similar in pose, angle, and gesture to the figure in the studies. In the final oil painting, the hat she holds has been adjusted so that the pentimenti from the original hat being admired show through just to the left of the apricot toque. At the same time, the centermost hat, floating above her head with light green baize ribbons, seems to have been made to match her own olive brown outfit and ocher kid gloves.

In fact, Degas made few changes to the woman's attire between the initial and final stages of the painting, causing speculation as to whether she is indeed a milliner or rather a customer surveying a potential purchase. Her wool dress with fur-trimmed collar is similar to those worn by the fashionably dressed clients in other Degas works on the subject, just as her soft gloves are traditional signifiers of a bourgeois woman. Only her gesture and the fact that she is without a hat—the totemic emblem of social rank and wealth—suggest a different status. Perhaps Degas's fashionable milliner was intended to be ambiguous, mirroring the uncertainties in fashion brought on by mass manufacturing and large department stores, which, in direct conflict with the tradition of millinery shops, offered cheaper versions of apparel formerly reserved for wealthy customers.

Why and when Degas decided to scrape out and repaint this canvas is not known. By the early 1890s, he had moved away from depicting clients trying on hats assisted by milliners (*essayage*) to focus on the *garnisseuses*, or the milliners who decorated the hats for display and sale. Just as the work's only known title, *The Millinery Shop*, offers no further identification of the subject, it remains unclear whether the picture shows an *essayage* or *garnisseuse*. What is apparent is that Degas presented his customer-cum-milliner alone—not as (or with) a sales girl, but carefully scrutinizing one of the hats. Whether she is a consumer or creator, the woman's intense focus on the handcrafted goods may well have resonated with Degas's own identity as an artist working in solitude to create a unique product for display and subsequent consumption.

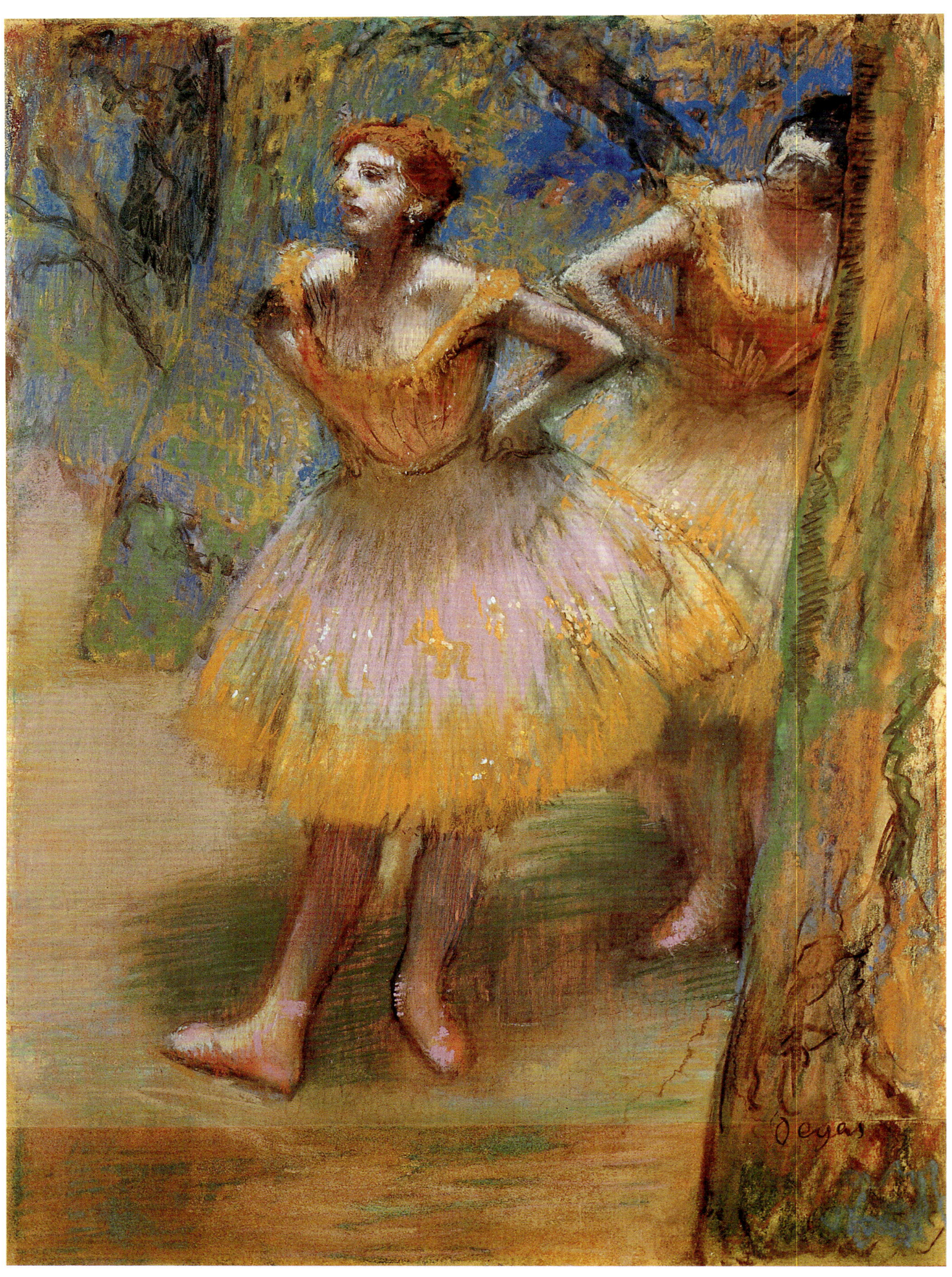
Degas

HILAIRE-GERMAIN-EDGAR DEGAS French, 1834–1917

51

Two Dancers, c. 1893/98

Pastel and charcoal, with stumping and burnishing, on tracing paper, pieced and laid down on cardboard; 705 x 536 mm (27¾ x 21⅛ in.)
Gift of Col. Robert R. McCormick to the Amy McCormick Memorial Collection, 1942.458
Signed lower right: *Degas*

Beginning in the early 1880s, Edgar Degas's attention gradually shifted away from the observation of Parisian life toward a vision rooted in classical tradition. Although the artist's subjects remained more or less constant, his focus changed: he simplified his compositions, depicted shallower spaces, and concentrated on a single figure or figural group. As the human form loomed larger in his later treatments of dancers, the narrative impetus found in his earlier realizations of the theme disappeared along with humorous and anecdotal details.
A fascination with process, replication, and variation characterizes the artist's late work. This is true of *Two Dancers*, from the mid-1890s, which features ballerinas clad in costumes of vivid violet-pink and orange, set against painted flats on the stage, and so harshly lit from above that their faces appear as masks. It is one of a family of related works that includes dozens of drawings of the foreground figure with hands on hips and right leg forward, rendered both nude and dressed, as well as richly colored pastel variants, most notably that in the Art Institute. Many, like this pastel, are on tracing paper, a support that allowed the artist to trace and make adjustments to earlier drawings in order to spawn a potentially endless series of elaborations of the same theme. The aim of such replication was not market-driven mass production but rather the desire to explore nuanced variations on the posture, weight, and torsion of the human body alone or in relationship to others.

All of the related works on paper began as charcoal drawings, some of which the artist continued developing with pastel to greater and lesser degrees. Often he pursued his search for that "balance" of pictorial forms that he described to contemporaries by adding peripheral strips of paper to the sheet on which he had begun working, thus modifying its compositional format. In *Two Dancers*, the strip attached to the bottom changes the relationship of the figures to the pictorial space in which they were originally conceived. The addition is far from seamless, the colors less than a perfect match. Indeed, it seems the artist liked revealing the process of his pictorial elaboration, signing the work at the lower right, just below the join, to which the signature draws attention.

The figure, with hands on hips and leg forward, appears in two of the artist's contemporary paintings (*Blue Dancers*; Musée d'Orsay, Paris; and *Dancers, Pink and Green*; Metropolitan Museum of Art, New York) and is the subject of two of his contemporary wax sculptures—one depicting the figure nude, the other dressed—that were posthumously cast in bronze. It is thought that Degas, who had made sculpture throughout his career, created these three-dimensional works to assist him in realizing the figure in pastel and oil. Not long after he finished them, he observed, "The only reason I made wax figures of animals and humans was for my own satisfaction, not to take time off from painting or drawing but in order to give my paintings and drawings greater expression, greater ardor and more life." Clearly the figure of the ballerina with hands on hips and right leg forward was of particular interest to Degas in his late career. He explored the assertive yet awkward posture in almost every medium in which he worked, analyzing the figural mechanics with a persistence that borders on the obsessive.

Post-Impressionism

PISSARRO AND MONET:
NEW DIRECTIONS

NEO-IMPRESSIONISM

VAN GOGH AND GAUGUIN

TOULOUSE-LAUTREC AND
MONTMARTRE

CÉZANNE'S CLASSICISM

GAUGUIN AND THE SOUTH SEAS

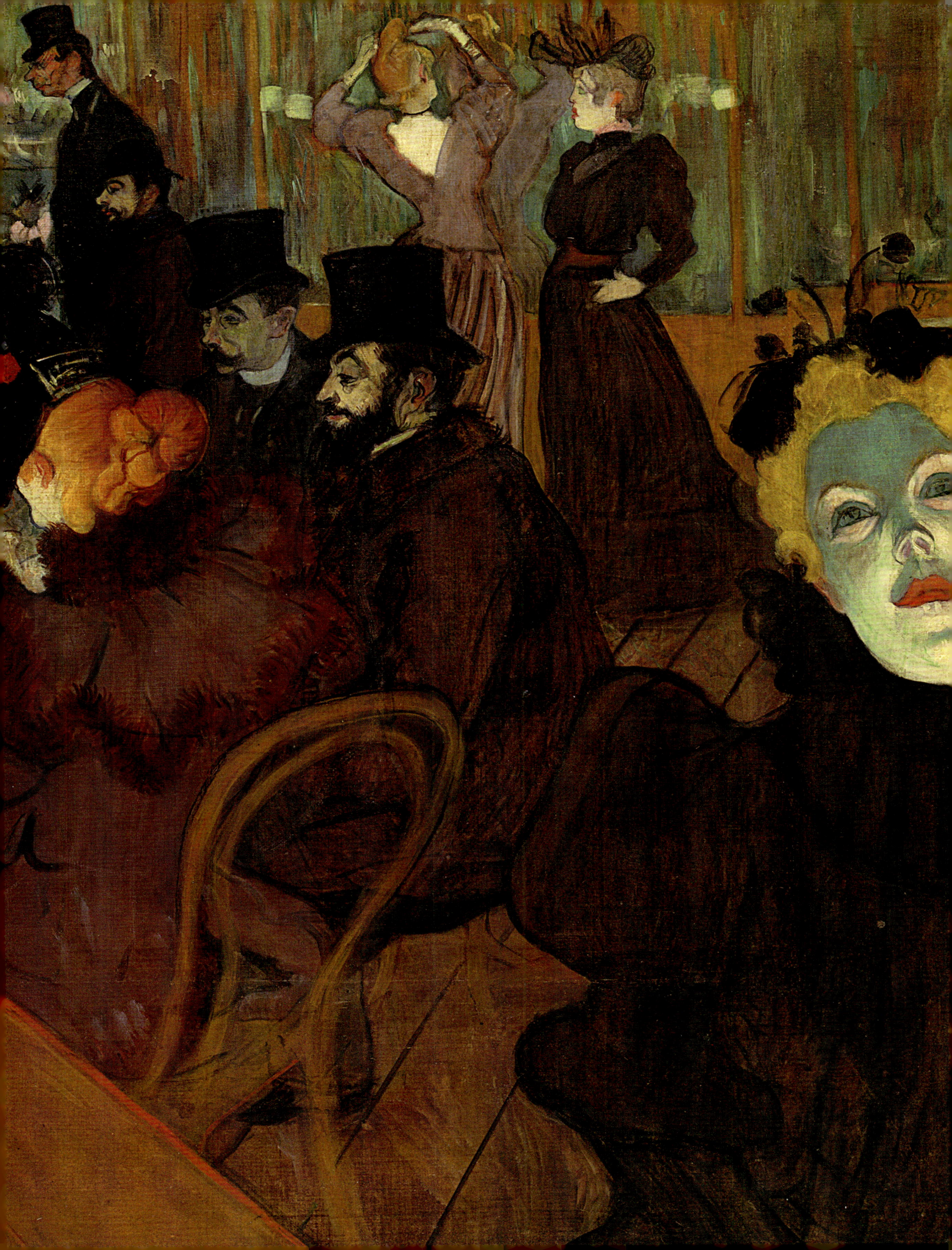

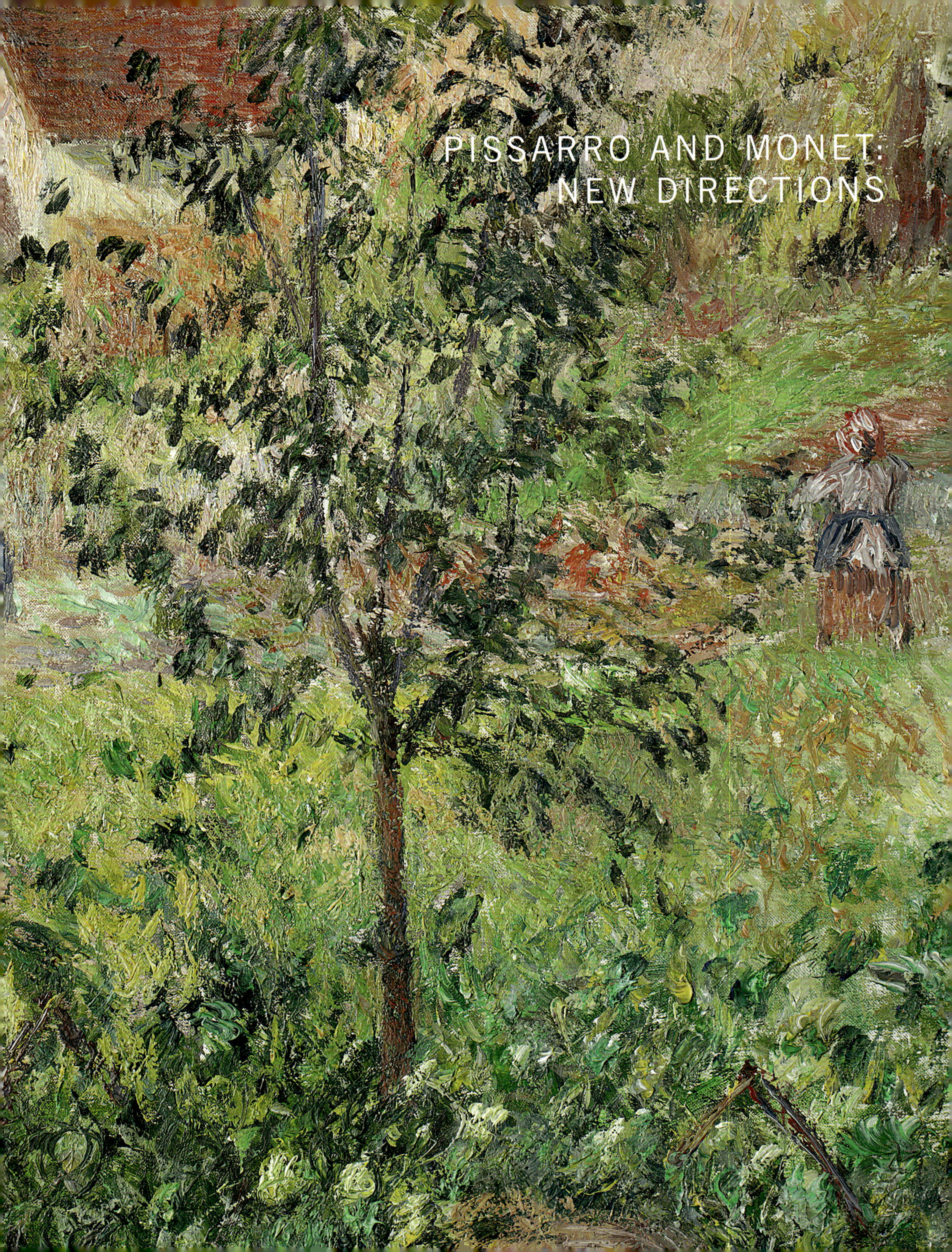
PISSARRO AND MONET:
NEW DIRECTIONS

52

Woman and Child at the Well, 1882

Oil on canvas; 81.5 x 66.4 cm (32 ⅛ x 26 ⅛ in.)
Potter Palmer Collection, 1922.436
Signed lower left: *C. Pissarro / 82*

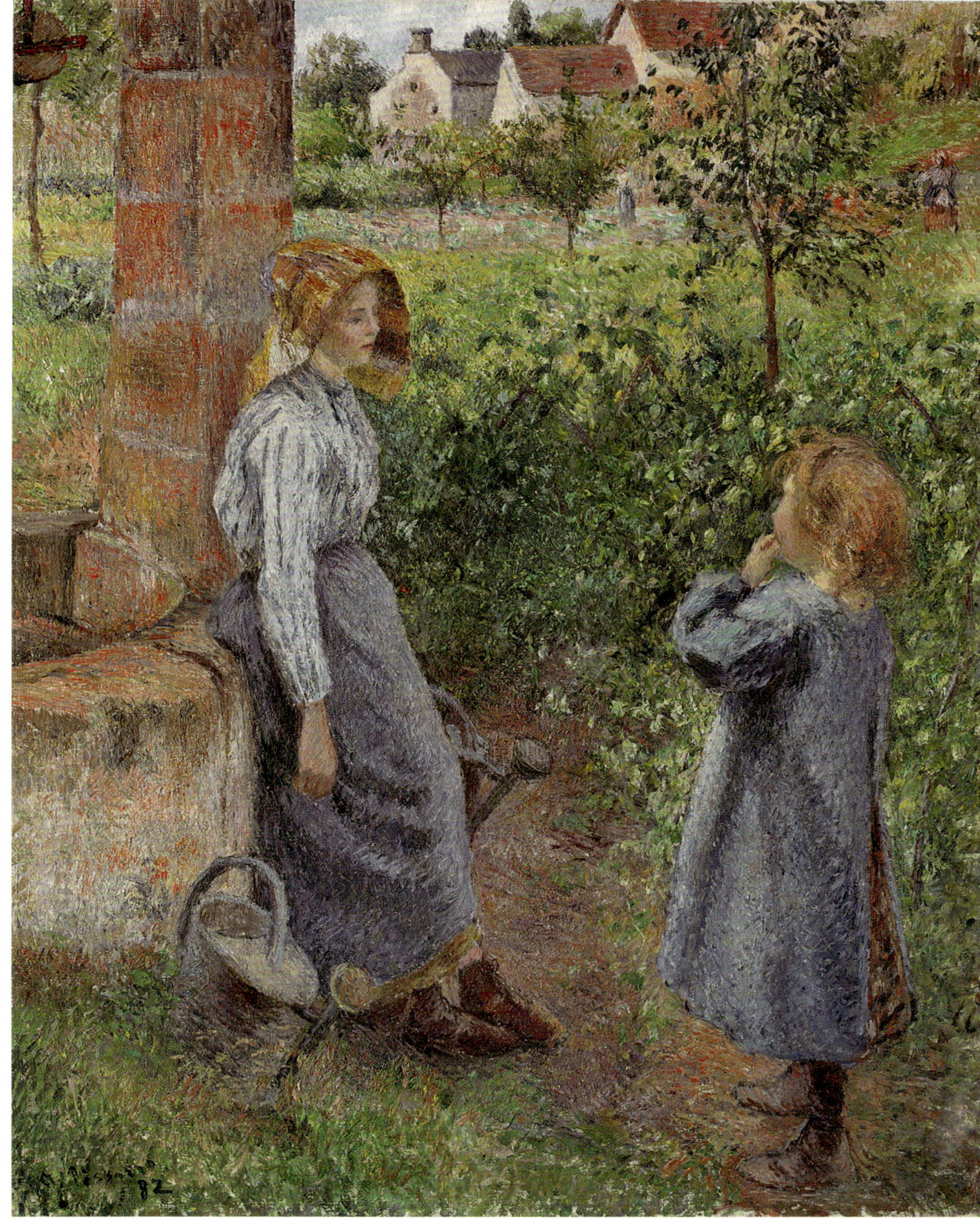

By the 1880s, Camille Pissarro, like most of his Impressionist colleagues, sought an alternative to the style he had employed over the previous decade. He decided to depict figures rather than landscapes; of the thirty-six paintings he showed at the seventh Impressionist exhibition, in the spring of 1882, twenty-seven were figurative. He probably executed *Woman and Child at the Well* later that summer, since the dealer Paul Durand-Ruel purchased it from him in August. Its format, scale, and technique relate it to a series of paintings showing young peasant girls taking a break from chores, their poses and gestures suggesting narratives that remain ambiguous.

The young girl with a striped blouse in this painting, for example, appears as a domestic servant in other works from the period, including *The Young Country Servant* (1882; Tate Gallery, London). In the Art Institute's canvas, she leans against a well and looks distractedly in the direction of a child identified as Pissarro's fourth son, Ludovic-Rodolphe, who would have been four years old at the time. Raising one hand to his face, which is seen in *profil perdu* (lost profile), Ludovic conveys as little information as the servant girl he confronts.

In many of his compositions of peasant girls from this time, Pissarro set his figures in grassy, horizonless landscapes composed of densely interlocked strokes. Here, however, he included details that recall his earlier landscape imagery: farmhouses, vegetable gardens, and women who diligently irrigate the young sprouts. Many critics saw in Pissarro's works of this period a direct connection to the art of Jean-François Millet, the Barbizon artist who lived like the peasants that he painted. Pissarro never considered himself a man of the soil. Although he felt strongly that "one must be committed to one's subject to represent it well," he asked, "Is it necessary to be a peasant? Let's be artists above all."

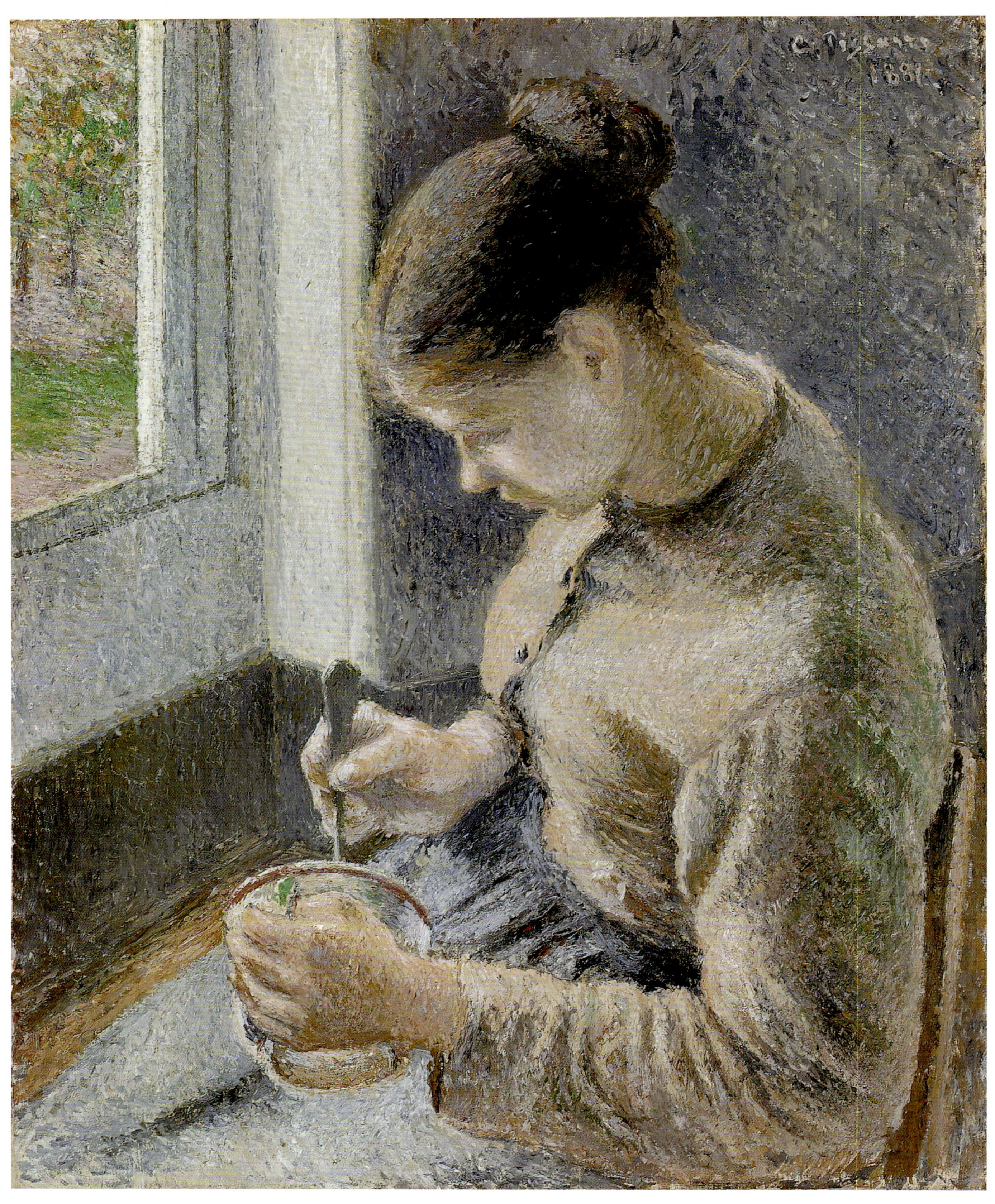
1881

53

Young Peasant Woman Drinking Her Café au Lait, 1881

Oil on canvas; 65.3 x 54.8 cm (25 11/16 x 21 9/16 in.)
Potter Palmer Collection, 1922.433
Signed upper right: *C. Pissarro / 1881*

In the 1880s, at a time when many of the original Impressionist painters had begun to pursue independent styles, Camille Pissarro remained an active proponent of the group. He persuaded Gustave Caillebotte and Claude Monet to take part in the seventh Impressionist exhibition, in 1882, and was himself particularly visible that year with a number of works showing female peasants—washing, harvesting, weeding, chatting, or sitting, as in this image of a young girl by a window, who tilts her bowl to get the last drops of coffee out of it. Parisian critics admired *Young Peasant Girl Drinking Her Café au Lait*, although many of them were generally unhappy with Pissarro's turn to figure painting.

In this work, the model is bathed in a diffused gray light, her intense focus elevating her action from a morning routine to a quasi-ritual event. Pissarro showed his subject from above and at an oblique angle, so that the large curve of her body dominates the compressed space, while the green tint of her face reflects the grass and trees beyond the window. The small brushstrokes applied one next to the other and sometimes overlaid with dabs of thicker paint result in an irregularly built-up surface, which serves to integrate figure and setting and to evoke the textures of the model's wool clothing. It was this rough, woven paint surface that London critics, who viewed this and other paintings by the artist at an Impressionist exhibition held there from April to July 1883, found objectionable. As Pissarro wrote to his son Lucien, they considered his works offensive to English taste, deeming them "uncouth." Although Pissarro was proud of this work, describing it as among his most "careful" and "finished" paintings, his dealer, Paul Durand-Ruel, may have taken these criticisms to heart. A year later, he urged Pissarro to abandon figure painting and return to "attractive landscapes."

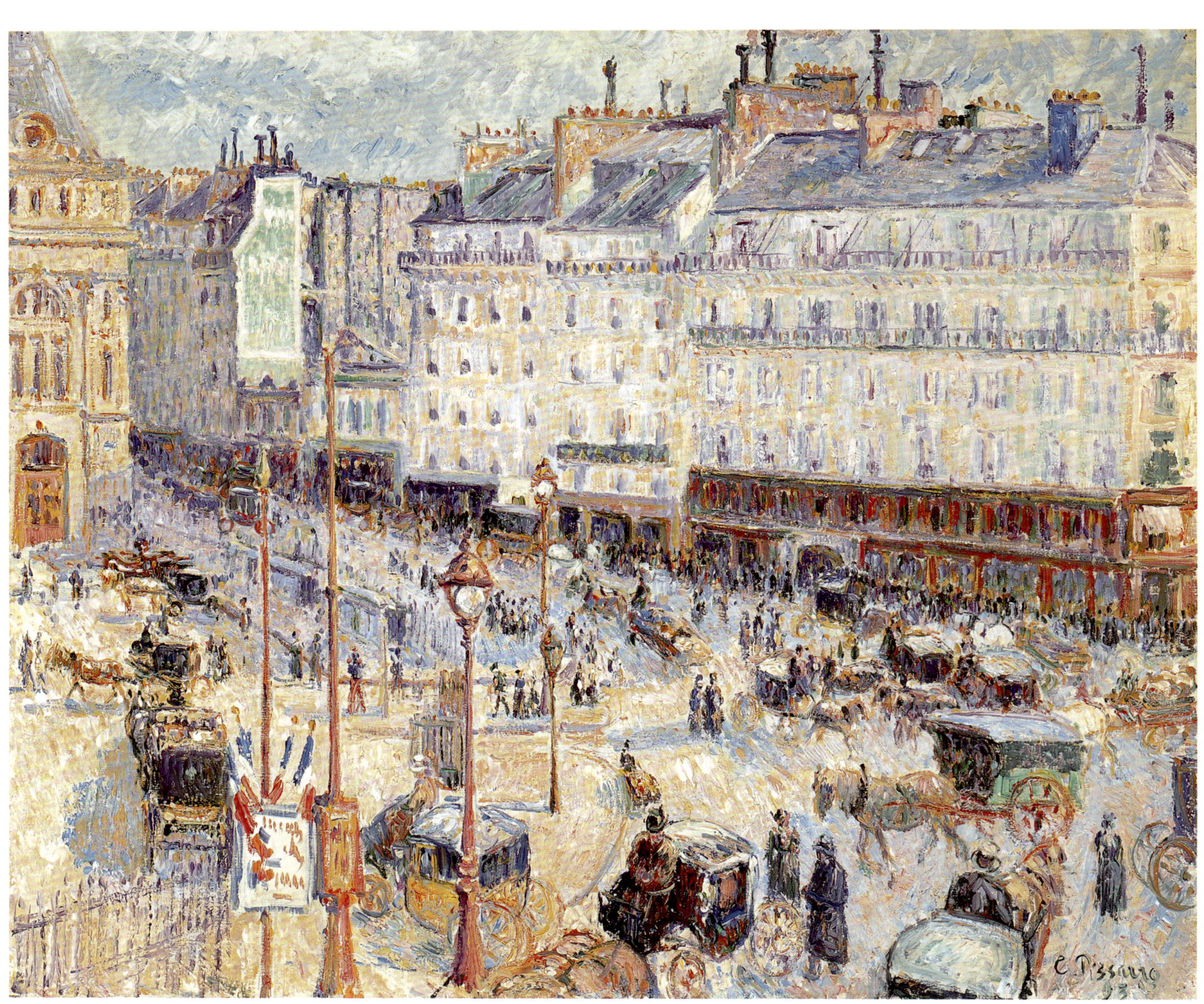
C. Pissarro

54

The Place du Havre, Paris, 1893

Oil on canvas; 60.1 x 73.5 cm (23⅝ x 28 13/16 in.)
Potter Palmer Collection, 1922.434
Signed lower right: *C. Pissarro / 93*

After a brief experimentation with the Neo-Impressionist style developed by Georges Seurat, Camille Pissarro returned to the loose, multi-directional brushstrokes that he had used in his earlier Impressionist works. He also reconsidered a quintessentially Impressionist subject—the modern city—which, by the 1890s, his colleagues had all but abandoned. The artist painted this bustling scene, alive with the noise and movement of trams, carts, and pedestrians, from his window at the Hôtel Garnier, Paris. Although he did not begin the series of cityscapes including *The Place du Havre* until he arrived at the hotel on February 27, the sixty-three-year-old artist started to think about the project even before leaving for Paris from his home in Eragny. In the relatively short interval between his arrival and the opening of an exhibition of his work at the Durand-Ruel Gallery on March 15, he completed at least two large paintings from his window—the Art Institute's and another vertical canvas of the same scale with a similar subject (private collection, Philadelphia).

Part of the reason for Pissarro's intense artistic activity was his confinement indoors due to an eye infection that was exacerbated by exposure to cold and wind. Without making series in the more formal sense of Claude Monet's 1890–91 *Stacks of Wheat* (see cats. 88–93), which share the same scale, subject, and technique, he clearly explored the serial nature of urban life, as framed by his window, through which he could see the newly expanded Gare Saint-Lazare. Just as he viewed the country with the detachment of a bourgeois, through his elevated viewpoint, he distanced himself from the activities on the streets of the city. *The Place du Havre, Paris* shows the intersection of two streets—rue d'Amsterdam and rue Saint-Lazare—at the place du Havre. The painting reads from the lower edge up, following the flow of traffic on the rue d'Amsterdam as it angles north around the east side of the train station. The buildings form a weightless decorative curtain below which curlique-like dabs of thick paint applied over the background color suggest figures in action. Although they appear as seemingly random marks, Pissarro picked out certain details—bowler hats, the red pants of a military cadet, shawls, and muffs—to suggest the social class and profession of the figures. Instead of the calm harmony of his rural compositions, in this and his other cityscapes from 1893, he captured the jarring irregularity of the capital, in which the calligraphically described people, carts, and trams disrupt easy legibility while creating a decorative unity and rhythm. Pissarro never lived in Paris, but he had no difficulty moving physically or artistically from country to city and seeing each as an extension of the other; when he exhibited the Chicago and Philadelphia canvases in March 1893, he grouped them with paintings executed at Eragny under the same rubric of "landscapes."

In 1897 and 1898, Pissarro was in Paris and again painted its streets, squares, and architecture. As one critic put it in an article that appeared shortly after the artist's death in 1903, he had become "what he had been only intermittently: a landscape painter of towns."

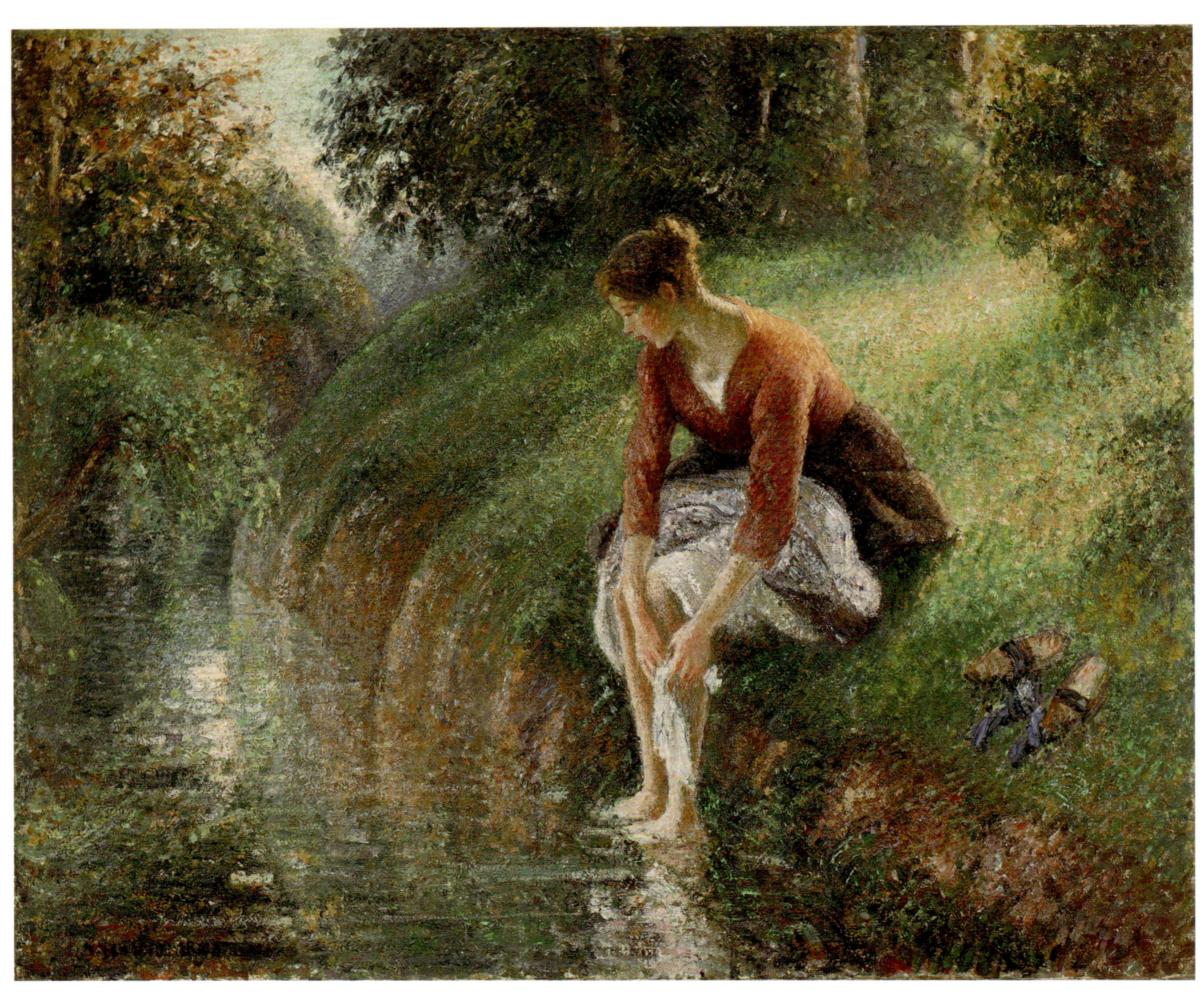

CAMILLE PISSARRO French, 1830–1903

55

Woman Bathing Her Feet in a Brook, 1894/95

Oil on canvas; 73 x 92 cm (28½ x 36 in.)
A Millennium Gift of Sara Lee Corporation, 1999.364
Signed lower left: *C. Pissarro 1895*

During the last decade of his life, Camille Pissarro painted mostly cityscapes and landscapes, often in extended series. His images of bathers, nude and clothed, executed between 1894 and 1896, are exceptions; *Woman Bathing Her Feet in a Brook* is the most ambitious and diligently worked of this group. Pissarro referred to the painting in November 1894, when he wrote to his son Lucien that he wanted to send him a picture of "a little peasant girl dipping her feet in the water, canvas size 30." At the time, Pissarro considered the work finished but still lacking "that little something," although he exclaimed optimistically, "I think I will get it, I feel it!"

His continued ruminations on the composition may explain its heavily encrusted surface and the numerous pentimenti to the model's arms and legs. Pissarro completed the painting by February 1895, when, obviously proud of the picture, he sent it along with three other recent works to be shown at a gallery in Dresden and, a few weeks later, at the Fritz Gurlitt Gallery in Berlin. That same year, he painted *Bather in the Woods* (Metropolitan Museum of Art, New York), a variation of the Art Institute's canvas showing an identically posed nude (a rarity in his oeuvre) in the same setting. Pissarro's interest in this classical theme brings to mind Rembrandt van Rijn's images of Susanna at the bath and the long tradition of representations of bathers by French artists, from François Boucher in the eighteenth century to Pissarro's contemporaries Édouard Manet and Pierre-Auguste Renoir.

In this canvas, and in a smaller one painted in 1894 (*Woman Washing Her Feet in a Brook*; Indianapolis Museum of Art), which may well be a study for *Woman Bathing Her Feet*, however, the model is neither fully dressed nor undressed. She has taken off her wood clogs and cobalt blue stockings and raised her skirt, revealing a cotton underskirt.

For Pissarro this series was a new direction and one that was complicated by the difficulty of engaging models in rural Eragny. Given the even greater challenge of finding women willing to pose in the nude, it seems likely that Pissarro used a fully realized drawing of a seated peasant (*Study of a Young Woman Bathing Her Legs*, c. 1895; Ashmolean Museum, Oxford) for the Art Institute's painting and for the unclothed model in the Metropolitan Museum's version. In both pictures, the surface is thickly textured with a dense overlayer of staccato strokes. These raised dabs catch the light and move the eye around the composition; they also unite the various elements—skin, fabric, water, and vegetation—into a coarse, tapestry-like surface. Although he claimed to have abandoned the Neo-Impressionist style, Pissarro retained the use of complementary colors, as well as the technique of applying pigments in small strokes to achieve maximum luminosity. In this work, he employed variegated, acidic yellows and greens to suggest sunlight striking a patch of grass just beyond the figure and to highlight the back of her neck and the neckline of her bodice. Likewise, in the brook, pinkish yellow dabs applied next to dark moss greens suggest the play of light on the rippling water, which seems momentarily to distract the model from her washing. Despite the outdoor setting, the composition's densely patterned surface creates a sense of airlessness and flattens and distorts the woman's physiognomy. In the end, the painting has less to do with Impressionism than with the tighter, more decorative style of younger avant-garde artists such as Pierre Bonnard and Édouard Vuillard.

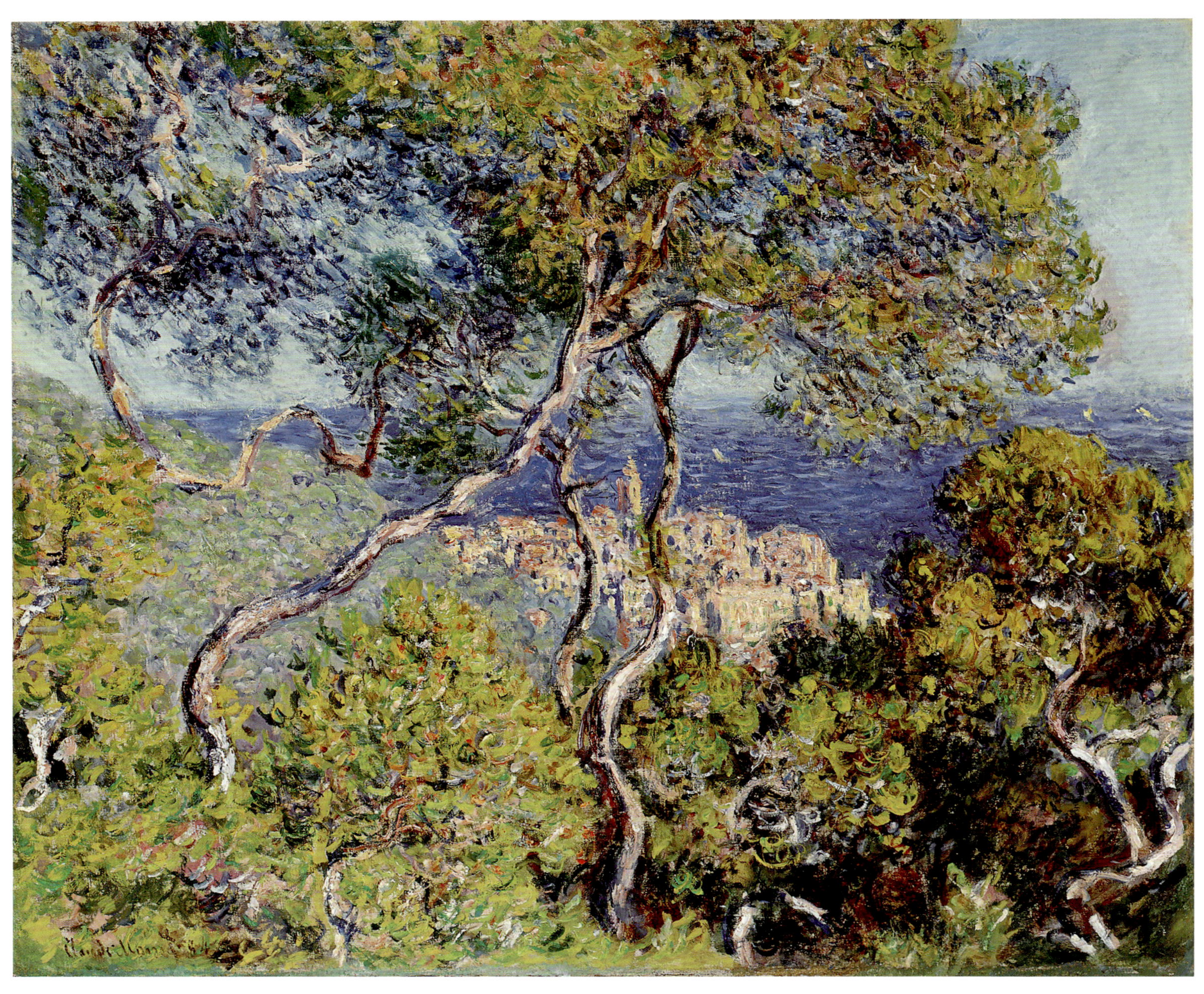

56

Bordighera, 1884

Oil on canvas; 64.8 x 81.3 cm (25½ x 32 in.)
Potter Palmer Collection, 1922.426
Signed lower left: *Claude Monet 84*

After renting a house at Giverny (a village northwest of Paris) in 1883, which he would inhabit for the rest of his life, Claude Monet spent most of the next ten years away from it—traveling to, among other destinations, the Normandy coast in 1883 and, in the first months of 1884, Bordighera, a town on the Italian Riviera just across the French border. Monet had already visited this picturesque village as a tourist with Pierre-Auguste Renoir in December 1883. Writing to his dealer, Paul Durand-Ruel, he described it as "one of the most beautiful places" that he and Renoir had seen, one he intended to return to alone in order "to bring back a series of new things."

A month later, on January 18, Monet arrived in Bordighera, where he began to work intensely for what he thought would be a period of three weeks, but instead lasted for nearly three months. In a letter to the sculptor Auguste Rodin, Monet declared that he was "fencing, wrestling with the sun" in order to translate into paint the seductive but blinding light that played tricks on the eye. The artist also equated painting with battle in his near-daily correspondence with Alice Hoschedé, who would become his companion and second wife, as he tried to "rediscover each new day the light and . . . to fight to capture its effect."

The diverse topography and exuberant vegetation of the region also challenged Monet: the artist, who described himself as a "man of isolated trees and large spaces," was frustrated by the difficulty of finding self-contained subjects to paint. Even so important a motif as the Mediterranean seemed impossibly hidden by dense vegetation. In the Art Institute's painting, undoubtedly among the six canvases that he worked on feverishly in the first two weeks of his stay in Bordighera, Monet's solution to these challenges was to set his easel on a hillside, near the Mostaccini Tower on the outskirts of the city, so that he could look down on the village and sea.

The real subject of this composition, however, is not that vista, but rather the lush growth that both thrilled and thwarted the artist. Here the interlaced trunks of local pines (interestingly, not the olive and palm trees for which Bordighera is known) create a decorative screen that displays the same mosaic-like touches of pinks, blues, and whites as the houses, church, and bell tower that appear half-concealed in the background. Brilliant blue water cuts across the horizon, creating an exaggerated contrast that Monet worried would upset the "enemies of blue and pink" and would only partially express the sensation of the light, which he termed "fairylike."

Bordighera was one of three paintings of the same subject that Monet showed along with other works at the *International Exhibition of Painting* held at the Georges Petit Gallery, Paris, in May–June 1887. Although not listed in the catalogue, the Art Institute's canvas can be identified as the picture that Gustave Geffroy, Monet's future biographer, singled out for special commendation. In his 1922 biography of the artist, Geffroy was even more effusive in his praise of *Bordighera*, calling it the work that best summarized the visual experience of this Italo-Franco coastal town and an "extraordinary canvas, crammed with an eruption of unimaginable vegetation ablaze with light that bursts forth like the sudden appearance of the sun, making everything around it fade."

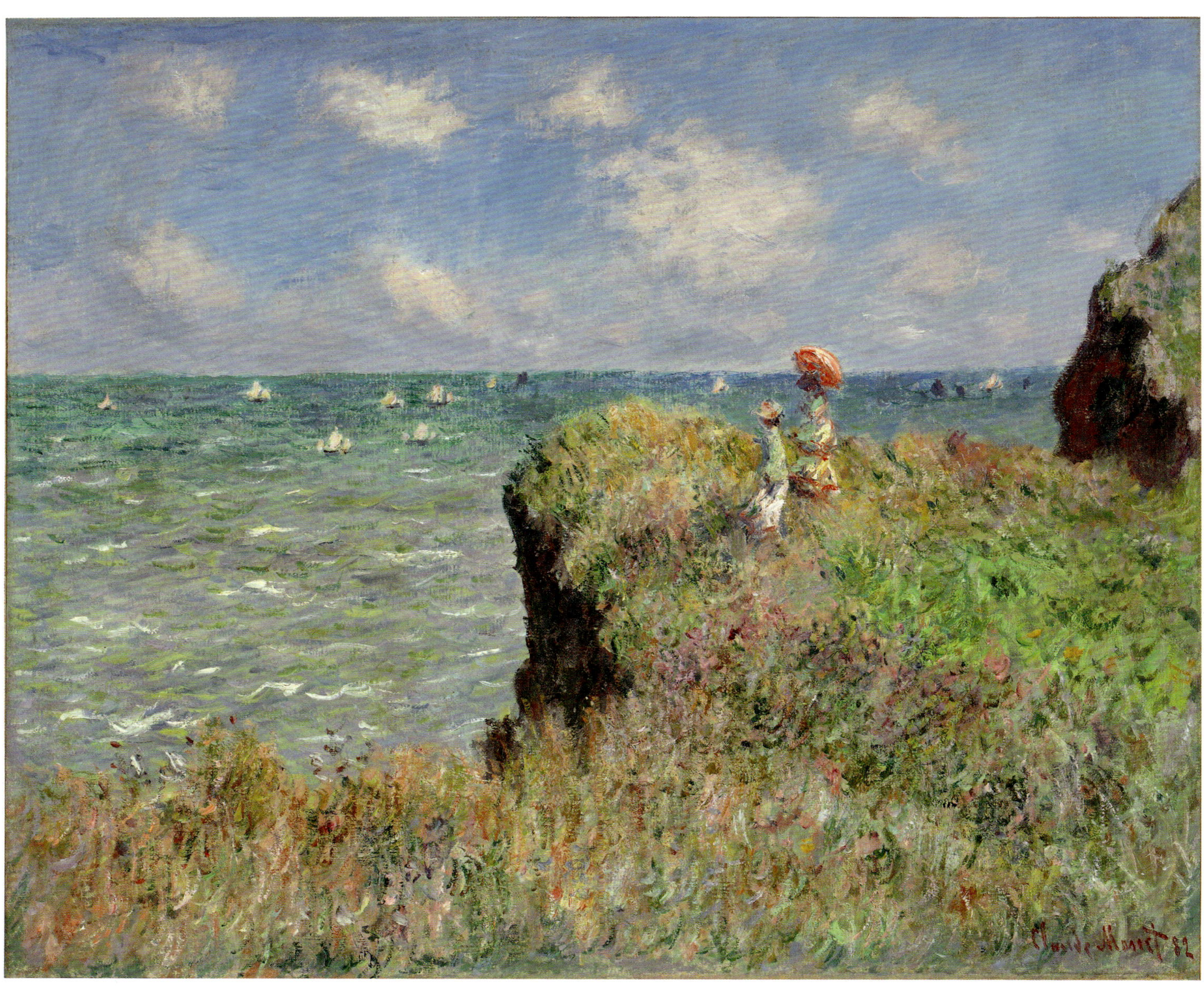

57

Cliff Walk at Pourville, 1882

Oil on canvas; 66.5 x 82.3 cm (26 3⁄16 x 32 7⁄16 in.)
Mr. and Mrs. Lewis Larned Coburn Memorial Collection, 1933.443

In February 1882, Claude Monet went to Normandy to paint, one of many such expeditions that he made in the 1880s. This was also a retreat from personal and professional pressures. His wife, Camille, had died three years earlier, and Monet had entered into a domestic arrangement with Alice Hoschedé (whom he would marry in 1892, after her husband's death). France was in the midst of a lengthy economic recession that affected Monet's sales. In addition, the artist was unenthusiastic about the upcoming seventh Impressionist exhibition—divisions within the group had become pronounced by this time—and he delegated the responsibility for his contribution to his dealer, Paul Durand-Ruel.

Disappointed in the area around the harbor city of Dieppe, which he found too urban, Monet settled in Pourville and remained in this fishing village until mid-April. He became increasingly enamored of his surroundings, writing to Hoschedé and her children: "How beautiful the countryside is becoming, and what joy it would be for me to show you all its delightful nooks and crannies!" He was able to do so in June, when they joined him in Pourville.

The two young women strolling in *Cliff Walk at Pourville* are probably Marthe and Blanche, the eldest Hoschedé daughters. In this work, Monet addressed the problem of inserting figures into a landscape without disrupting the unity of its painterly surface. He integrated these elements with one another through texture and color. The grass—composed of short, brisk, curved brushstrokes—appears to quiver in the breeze, and subtly modified versions of the same strokes and hues suggest the women's wind-whipped dresses and shawls and the undulation of the sea. X-radiographs show that Monet reduced the rocky outcropping at the far right to balance the proportions of sea and sky.

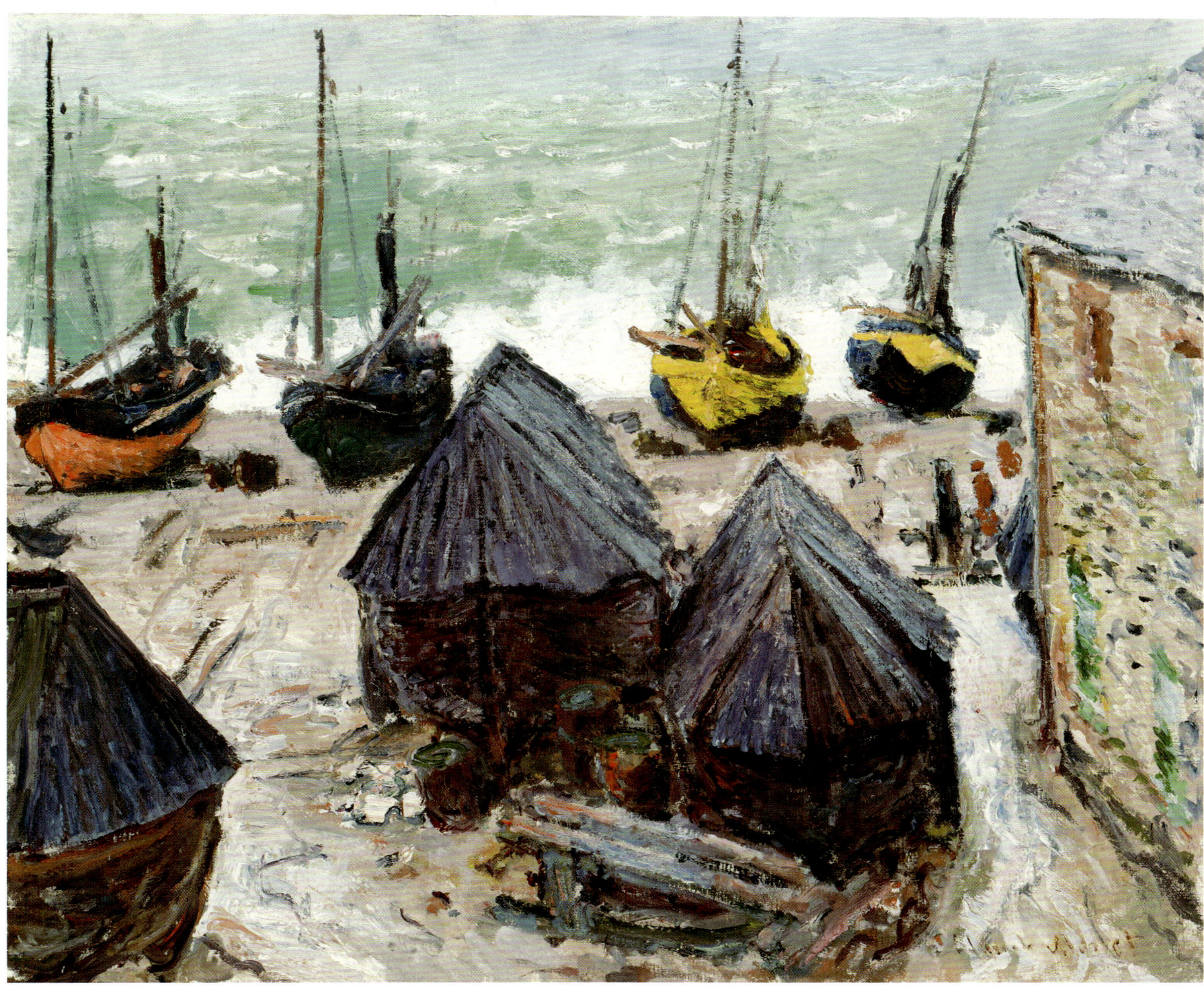

58

Boats on the Beach at Étretat, 1885

Oil on canvas; 65.5 x 81.3 cm (25 ¾ x 32 in.)
Charles H. and Mary F. S. Worcester Collection, 1947.95
Signed lower right: *Claude Monet*

By the mid-1880s, Claude Monet had distanced himself from the modern city, seeking challenging, inaccessible landscapes to paint. One of these sites was the Norman town of Étretat, famous for its monumental cliffs, dramatic coastal rock formations, and fashionable summer homes. *Boats on the Beach at Étretat* depicts none of these familiar views, however, focusing instead on a narrow patch of beach devoid of holiday travelers, below a stormy sky. Forced indoors by inclement fall weather, Monet framed his subject from the window of his room in the Hôtel Blanquet, where he stayed from mid-October to mid-December 1885. In one of his daily letters to Alice Hoschédé, dated November 24, he noted that he spent the afternoon in his room, "painting the *caloges* [retired fishing boats covered with tarred planks and used for storage] in the rain, and then still at my window I tried to paint the departure of the boats." Both of the works he described are in the Art Institute's collection: in *Boats on the Beach*, despite the rough seas, the masts of the boats are raised, ready to sail; in the other, slightly larger canvas, *Departure of the Boats from Étretat*, the masts are lowered, though the weather has improved. In each painting, Monet contrasted the dark, massive forms of the *caloges* with the orange and yellow fishing vessels on the shore, underscoring their lowly status and the increasingly obsolete role of fishing in coastal villages that were being transformed by tourism. However, Monet was undoubtedly also interested in the *caloges* as forms that evoke solidity and shelter, a theme to which he would return in his series *Stacks of Wheat* (see cats. 88–93).

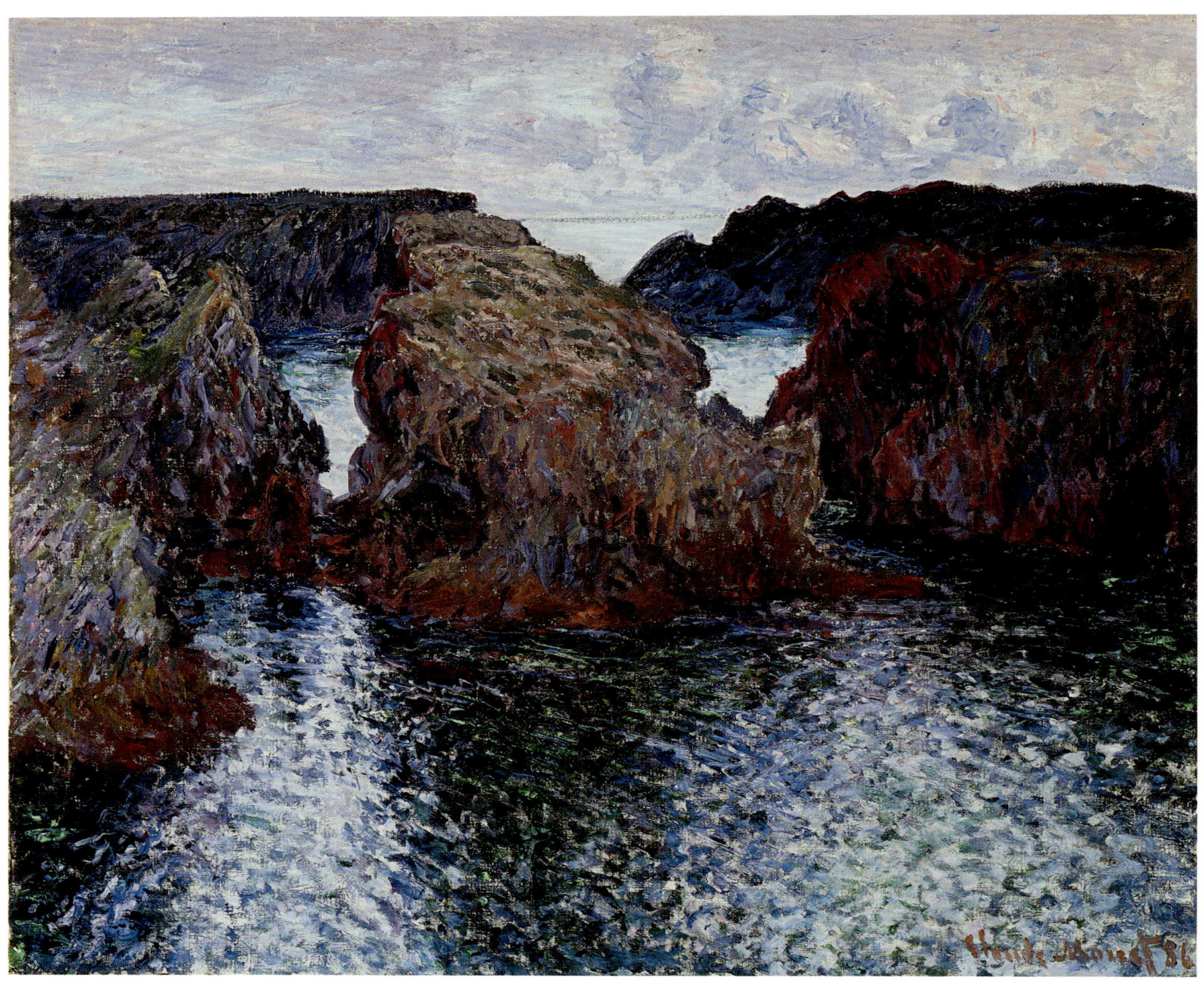

59

Rocks at Port-Goulphar, Belle-Ile, 1886

Oil on canvas; 66 x 81.8 cm (26 x 32 3/16 in.)
Gift of Mr. and Mrs. Chauncey B. Borland, 1964.210
Signed lower right: *Claude Monet 86*

Claude Monet's quest for unknown and compelling landscapes led him to Belle-Ile-en-Mer, a small island off the southern shore of Brittany known for its "savage coast" of fantastic grottoes, needles (sharp rocks), reefs, and cliffs. As he often did, the artist misjudged the time he would need to explore and capture the beauty of the place, which he called "lugubrious," "terrifying," and "very beautiful"; he stayed for more than two months, rather than the two weeks he had initially planned.

This canvas is one of a group depicting the frieze of rock configurations known as Port-Goulphar. It may have been among the first works that Monet executed after arriving at Kervilahouen, the village nearest to Port-Goulphar, on September 15, 1886. Since the painting clearly depicts fair weather, he may have made it before the tempest that overtook the island from October 9 to 15. Monet painted *Rocks at Port-Goulphar* from a cliff top, providing no indication of the ground on which he stood; instead, the triangular patterns of light on the rippling water pull the viewer vertiginously up and down. Anchoring the composition are the firm silhouettes of massive, dolmenlike rock formations, described with dense brushwork and kaleidoscopic colors that suggest their craggy surfaces. Throughout his Belle-Ile campaign, Monet continually reworked his compositions. For this reason, he refused to send any of the works to his dealer, claiming that he needed to reassess the effect of the group back in his Giverny studio. Less than a month later, however, he was still working on nearly forty canvases, a number of which were not shown until the following spring at the Georges Petit Gallery, Paris. Despite their apparently direct touch, the Belle-Ile paintings mark the beginning of Monet's move to pure landscape painting, and to a more deliberate technique, palette, and concern for decorative unity, which he would develop further in his series.

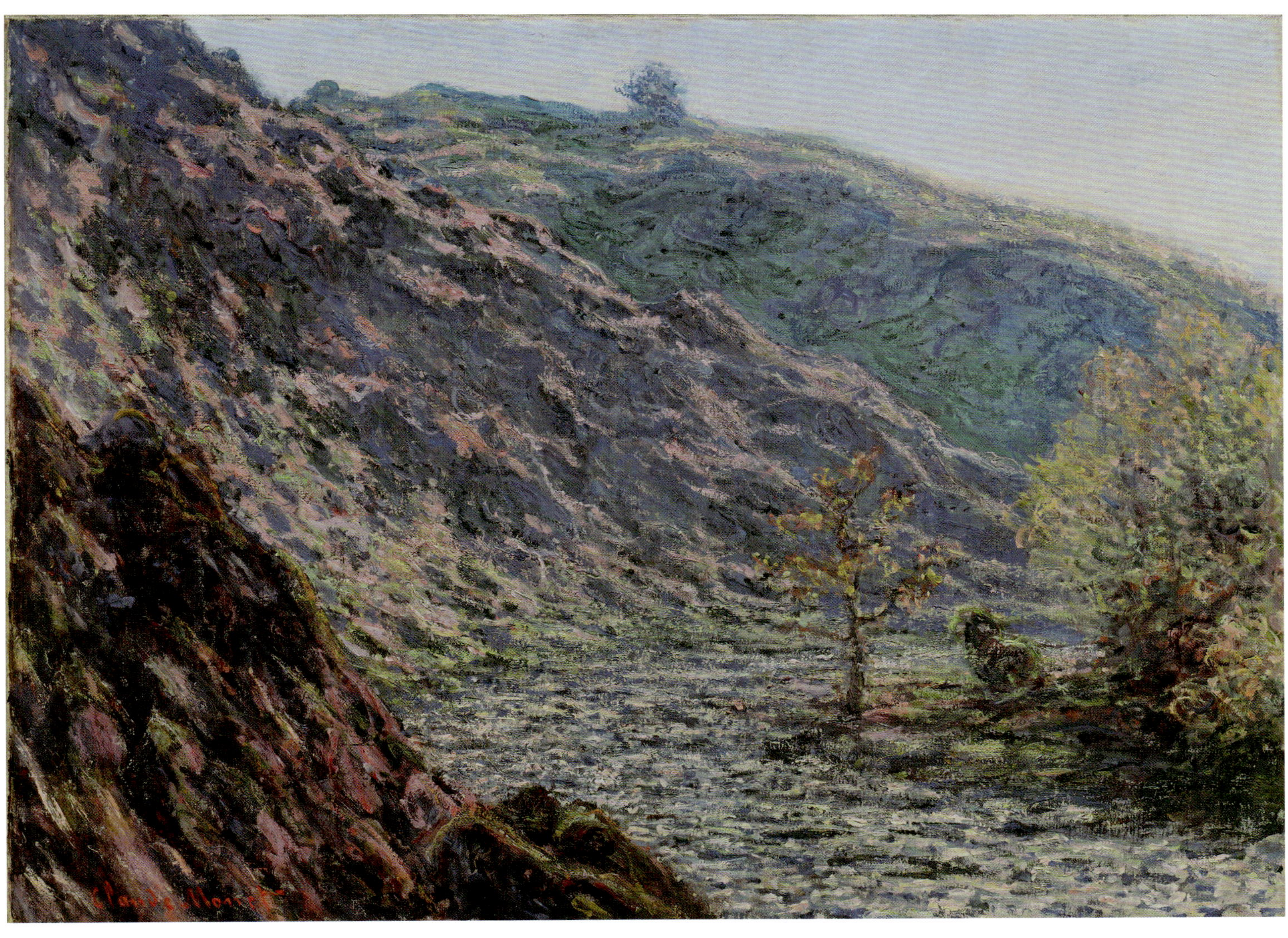

60

The Petite Creuse River, 1889

Oil on canvas; 65.9 x 93.1 cm (25 15⁄16 x 36 5⁄8 in.)
Potter Palmer Collection, 1922.432

Claude Monet undertook one of his most arduous painting campaigns in the spring of 1889, spending three months working near the remote village of Fresselines, in central France, where the Grande Creuse and the Petite Creuse rivers converge. The area is rugged and rocky, with deep valleys, steep hillsides, and a harsh climate.

Monet completed twenty-four canvases at Fresselines, each one a struggle against the elements and his own growing sense of physical vulnerability. He simplified the forms that he observed day after day, rendering the hills as monumental, almost primeval. At the same time, he allowed strong, brooding colors to express not only what he observed but also something of the complex feelings of exhilaration and frustration that this challenging site aroused in him. Although the sky in this painting is a cold white, strokes of bright blue, yellow-green, and even lavender animate the craggy slopes; only the outcropping in the left foreground consists of conventional browns and mossy greens. Even the trees seem overwhelmed by the strong shapes and colors of the landscape.

The Creuse campaign was a turning point for Monet. His goal was to create a series of works representing a scene at different times of day, but when he returned to the same spot to resume work on a composition, he found the motif transformed by factors beyond his control, such as the river's changing levels. But despite the meteorological difficulties and physical suffering he experienced during the painting campaign, this project was critical to Monet, for it paved the way for the ambitious series *Stacks of Wheat,* which he would begin in Giverny the following year.

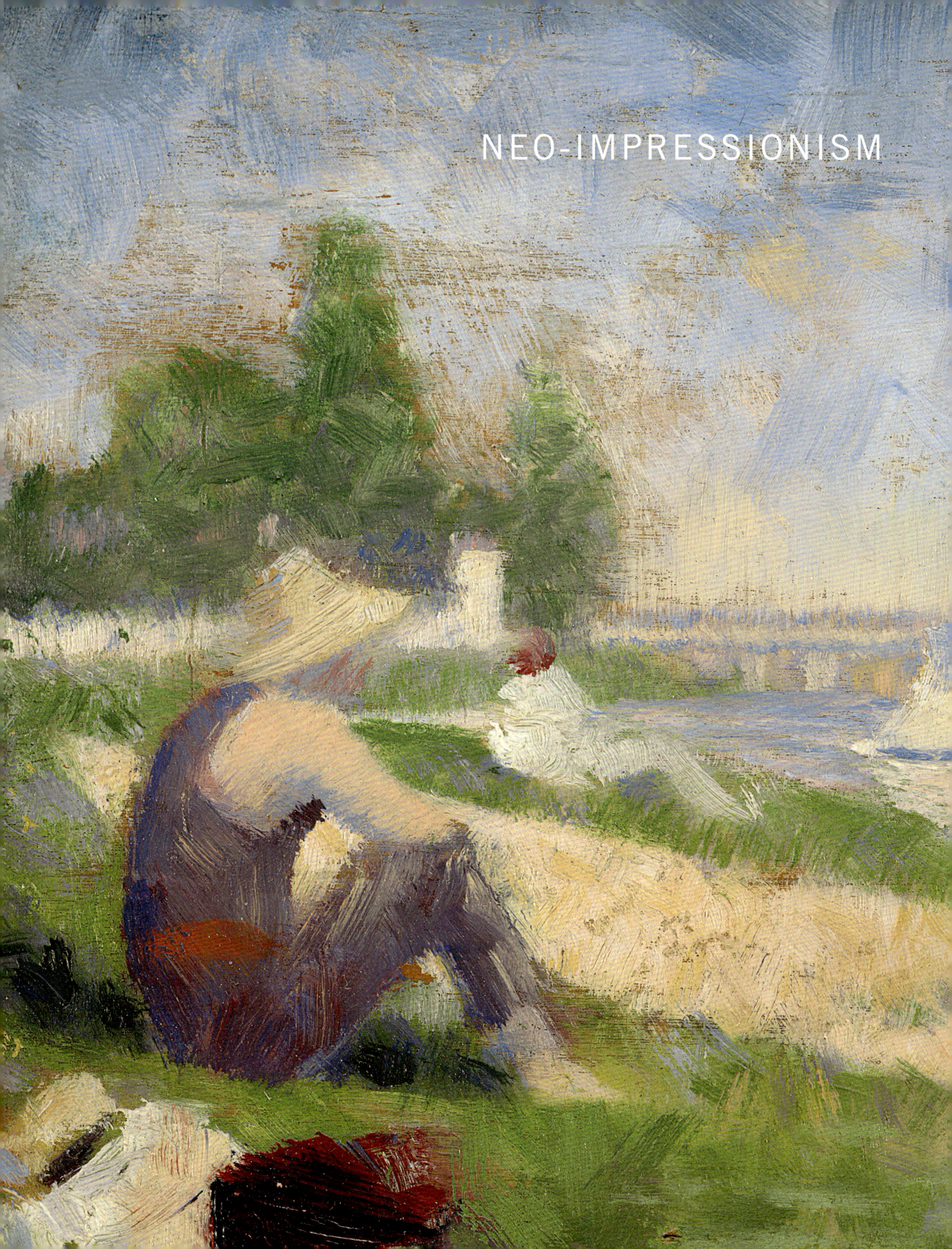

NEO-IMPRESSIONISM

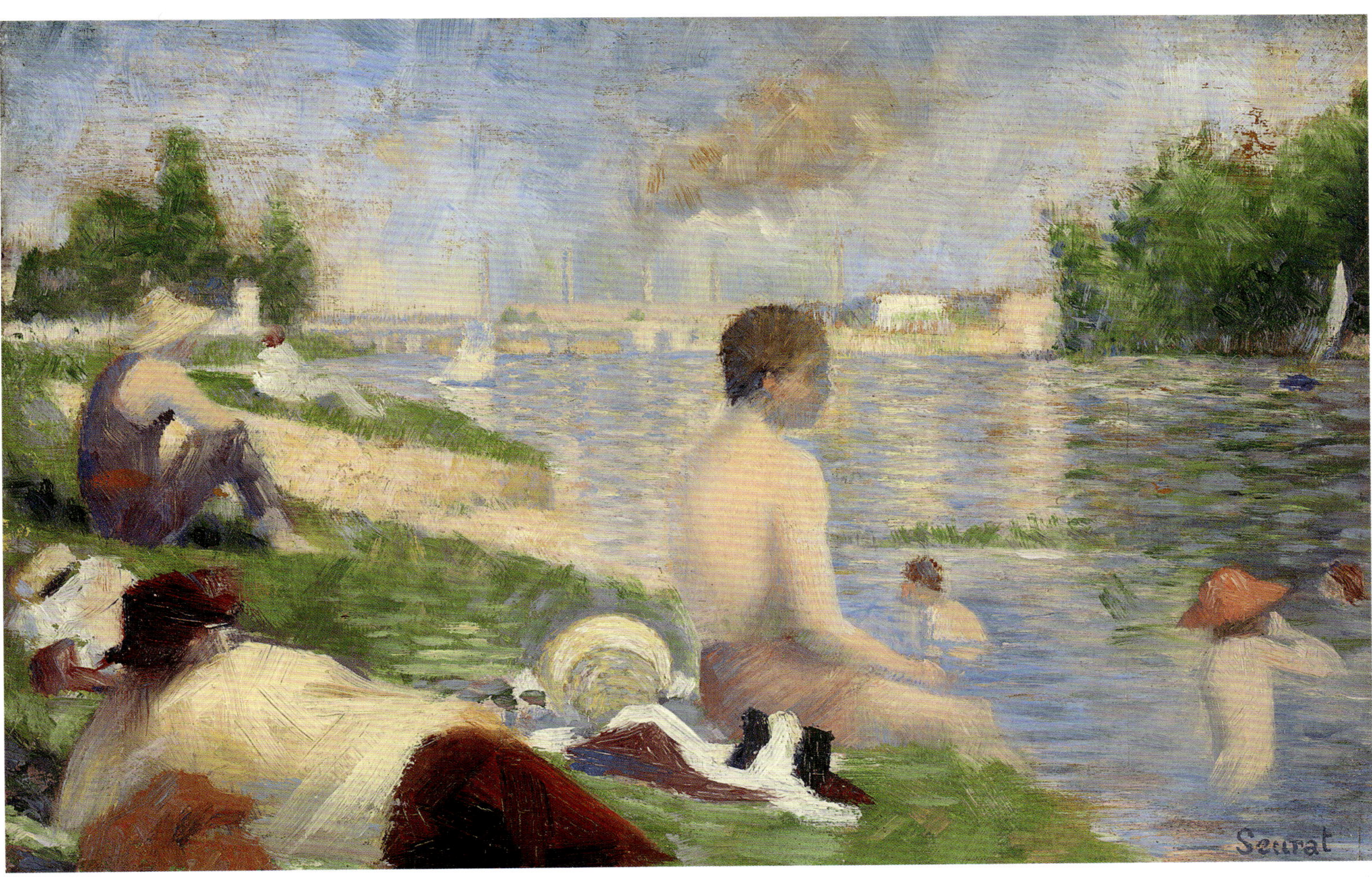

61

Final Study for "Bathers at Asnières," 1883

Oil on panel; 15.8 x 25.1 cm (6¼ x 9⅞ in.)
Gift of the Adele R. Levy Fund, Inc., 1962.578
Signed lower right: *Seurat*

Having received traditional instruction at the École des Beaux-Arts in Paris, Georges Seurat set himself the daunting task of creating a new classicism, one that employed forms that embody an art of enduring ideals, while preserving the vitality of the Impressionists' exploration of modern life. Seurat revealed the full extent of his ambition in *Bathers at Asnières* (1884; National Gallery, London), on which he began working in 1883. Monumental in scale, it exhibits affinities with the Impressionists' modern-life themes and lightened palette, although its subject—men and boys on the bank of the Seine River in the working-class suburb of Asnières—differs greatly from Claude Monet's and Pierre-Auguste Renoir's sparkling depictions of leisure activities in attractive outdoor settings (see cats. 17 and 29). In Seurat's compositions, Impressionist spontaneity yielded to a more academic approach; to prepare for this and other major projects, the artist made careful drawings of models in his studio, as well as numerous small oil-on-panel studies (*croquetons*) at the site. The Art Institute's oil sketch is considered closest to the final picture, but its multi-directional, free brushstrokes distinguish it from the larger canvas, with its meticulously worked surface. Seurat exhibited the nearly seven-by-ten-foot *Bathers* in May 1884 at the new artist-run, non-juried Salon des Indépendents in Paris; he must have been equally pleased with the Art Institute's final study, which he signed prominently and may have shown at a smaller exhibition that same year. In both canvas and panel, the firmly contoured and rhythmically balanced figures underscore the overall stillness and solemnity of a composition that was intended to bring together classical tradition and contemporary innovations. This synthesis would be fully realized in the artist's next project, *A Sunday on La Grande Jatte—1884* (see cats. 62–63), which is set across the river from Asnières, on the island just visible as a clump of green foliage in the upper right of *Bathers*.

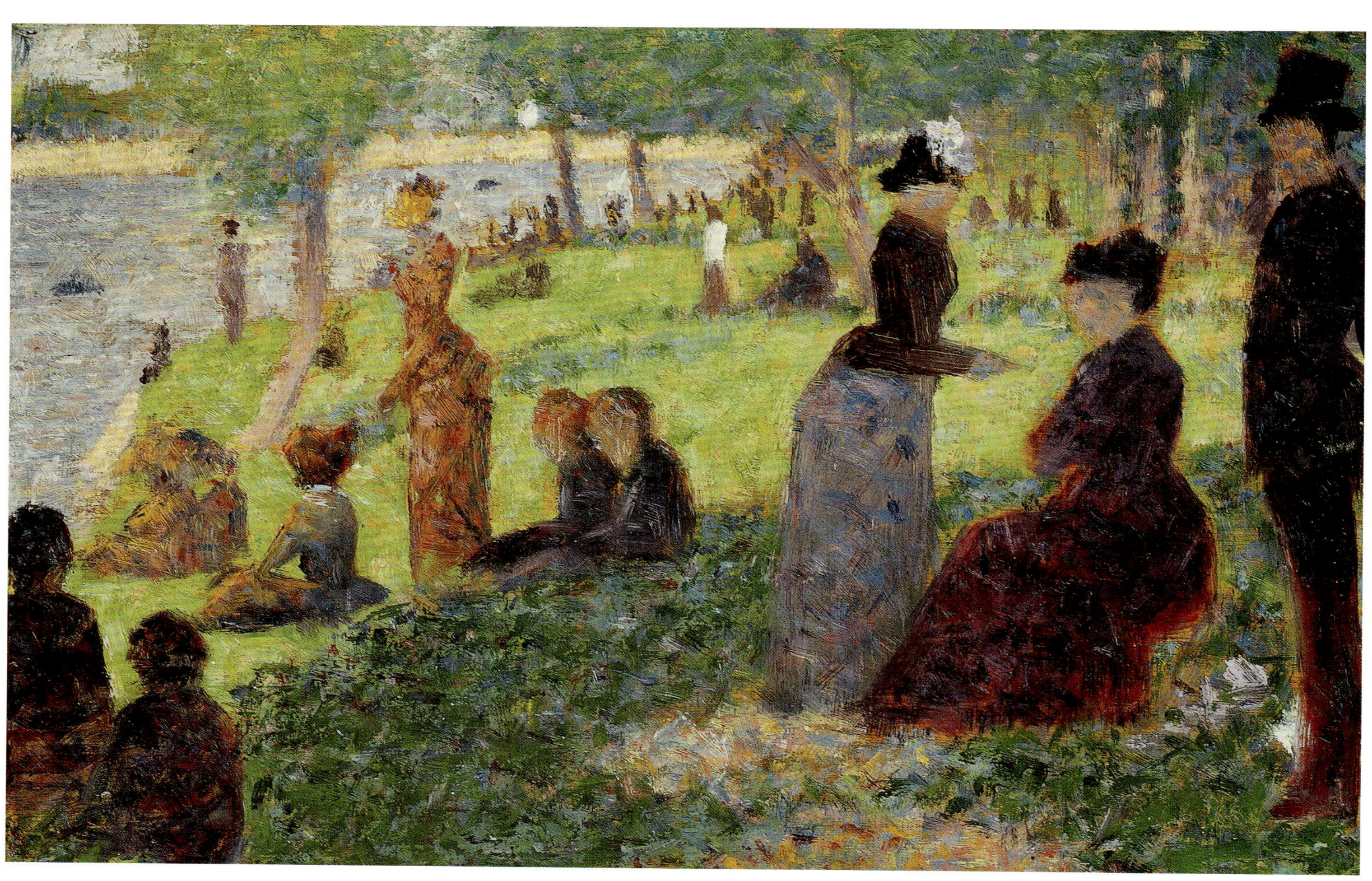

62

Oil Sketch for "La Grande Jatte,"

1884

Oil on panel; 15.5 x 24.3 cm (6⅛ x 9⁹⁄₁₆ in.)
Gift of Mary and Leigh Block, 1981.15

Just weeks after exhibiting *Bathers at Asnières* at the Salon des Indépendents, Georges Seurat began work on the painting that is considered the masterpiece of his career and a watershed in the history of modern art. This ambitious canvas took two years to execute; Seurat actually completed it in 1886, in time for the eighth Impressionist exhibition, but he included the year of its inception in the painting's title, *A Sunday on La Grande Jatte—1884* (cat. 63). In so doing, he probably hoped to underscore his primacy in the new movement that he called "chromo-luminism," now known as Divisionism or Pointillism. Inspired by research on optical and color theory, Seurat devised a technique in which he applied small dashes and dots of related or opposing tints to create gradated shades and blend tonalities into a decorative unity. He also sought to emphasize the long gestation period of this composition, which aimed to recast the Impressionists' concern for light, shadow, and color into an art of permanence firmly rooted in classical ideals.

The setting for this painting was a suburban park located on an elongated island across the Seine River from the suburb of Asnières. Begun on May 22, 1884, the undertaking involved approximately twenty-eight drawings, twenty-eight small oils on panel (*croquetons*), and three larger canvases. Seurat probably made the Art Institute's panel midway through the process, when, having laid in the general landscape and made studies of some of the figures, he developed the idea of spreading seated and standing men, women, and children, as well as animals, across the foreground and placing smaller figures along the bank and under the trees. Although, at first glance, the panel's composition seems close to that of the larger canvas, its twenty-plus figures have little to do with the final arrangement of some forty people, animals, and boats. For example, Seurat completely rethought the trio at right in the canvas, which shows a man in a top hat and a woman walking a monkey, rather than the elderly seated woman and her companions depicted in the oil sketch. The final group conveys a sense of grand solemnity but also a wry sense of humor—a sophisticated irony that is completely absent in the clumsily positioned figures of the Chicago panel.

Nonetheless, this study is highly complex in both its organization and surface treatment. Seurat used a divided brushstroke that is more Impressionist in character than the layer of dots and dashes he would employ in his second campaign on the final work, begun in October 1885. But even in this earlier study, he had already conceived of the landscape as zones of light and dark, with the beige and lavender patch in the foreground indicating sunlight in an otherwise shaded area. Although Seurat was criticized for what was deemed a mechanical and impersonal style, the genesis of *La Grande Jatte* not only involved a calculated and methodical preparatory process, but also intuition and trial and error. The Art Institute's panel demonstrates the artist's method of thinking and rethinking, altering, and at times rejecting each element before arriving at the final solution. Having chosen the stage—in this case, a well-known Impressionist site—Seurat took on the functions of both playwright and director, selecting the performers and their placement onstage in a number of rehearsals. Despite the Chicago panel's lively surface and compositional interest, the figures in *Oil Sketch for "La Grande Jatte"* failed their audition.

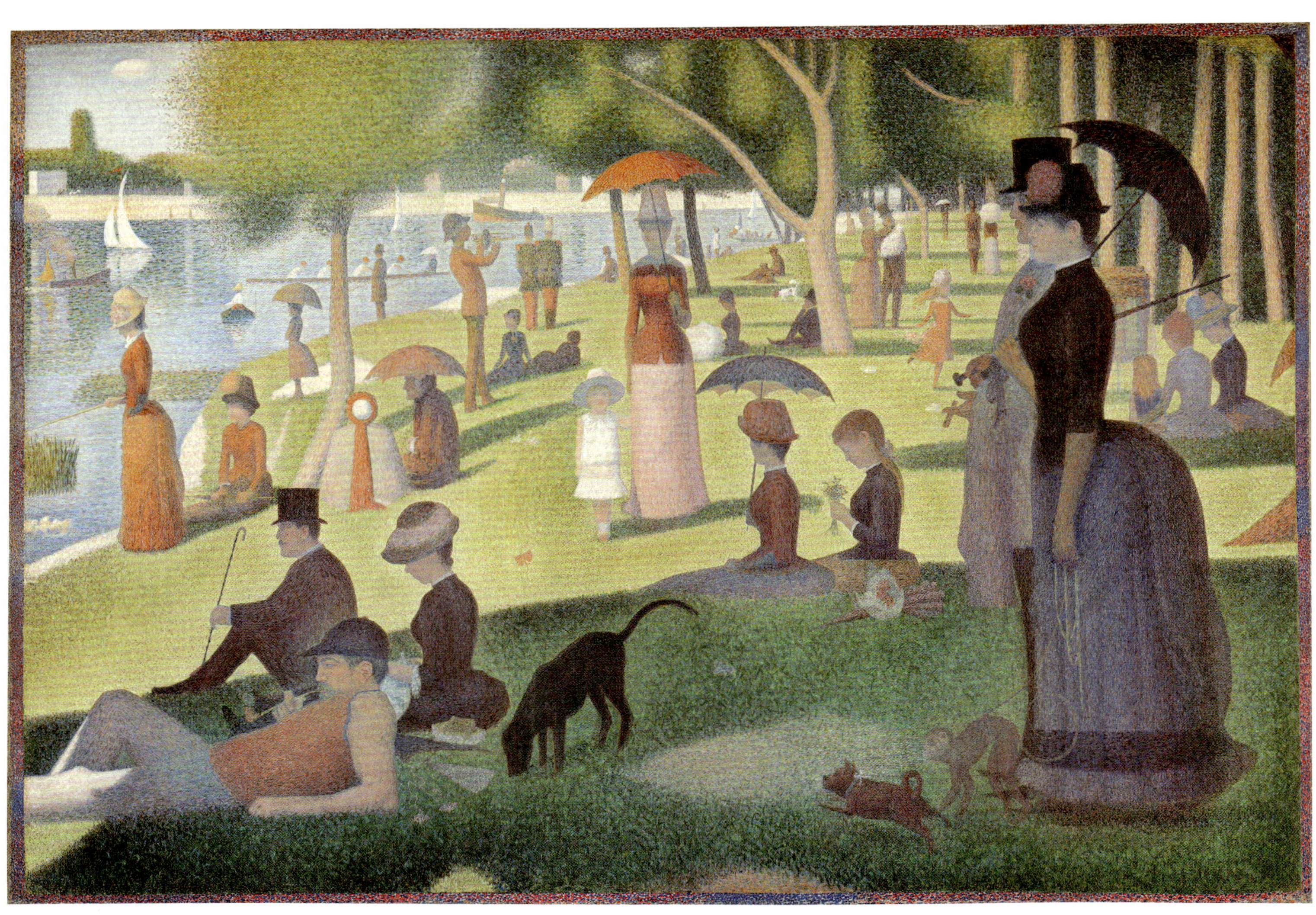

63

A Sunday on La Grande Jatte—1884, 1884–86

Oil on canvas; 207.5 x 308.1 cm (81 11/16 x 121 5/16 in.)
Helen Birch Bartlett Memorial Collection, 1926.224

In *A Sunday on La Grande Jatte—1884*, Georges Seurat recast Impressionism, using both optical theory and idealist aesthetics as his guides. When first shown in 1886, at the eighth and final Impressionist exhibition, this impressive painting of middle-class Parisians relaxing on an island in the Seine River just west of the city attracted considerable attention. Although many artists had portrayed similar subjects in recent years, none had used so rigorous and schematic a style. The hieratic figures, shown mostly in profile or from the front, recall ancient Egyptian reliefs, and the deliberate compositional rhythms amount to a pointed critique of Impressionist ephemerality. As if to dispel any lingering doubts on this point, Seurat also rejected free, sketchy handling, choosing instead to render the entire scene with meticulous, dotlike touches of paint, which were meant to be brilliantly luminous; one critic described a "vibration of light, a richness of color, [and] a sweet and poetic harmony."

Seurat arrived at *A Sunday on La Grande Jatte—1884* by way of a prolonged trial-and-error process, during which he produced many drawings and oil studies (see cat. 62). He was ready to show the painting for the first time in the spring of 1885. When the exhibition he had planned to include it in was canceled, he kept working and, from October 1885 to May 1886, added many small dots and dabs of paint to enhance the sunlit effect he strove to achieve. In the final canvas, the artist's grave stylization and playful irony are more prominent than in his earlier studies, and the resulting tone is complex. The distancing quality of Seurat's novel technique—further enhanced by his addition of the painted border between 1888 and 1889—made it an effective vehicle for his dry wit. This is evident in the occasional visual pun—note the wisps of cigar smoke that morph into a white dog near the man in a top hat at right—as well as in a remarkable gallery of contemporary social types, from the brooding rower reclining at the lower left to the gawky standing man playing a horn in the middle distance. But the pervasive self-absorption of the figures seems at odds with the integrative harmonies of the composition as a whole. The painting is rich in such enigmatic tensions, which are perhaps the secret of its enduring fascination.

La Grande Jatte brought Seurat fame and made him the leader of an artistic school; many painters, notably Camille Pissarro (see cat. 54) and Paul Signac (see cat. 64), chose to adopt Neo-Impressionism, as Seurat's style came to be known (it is also referred to as Pointillism or Divisionism). Although short-lived as a movement—largely due to Seurat's untimely death, at age thirty-one—the style is historically important for its introduction into avant-garde painting of new elements, such as the simplification of form, a classical mode of spatial organization, and a sophisticated sense of decorative unity.

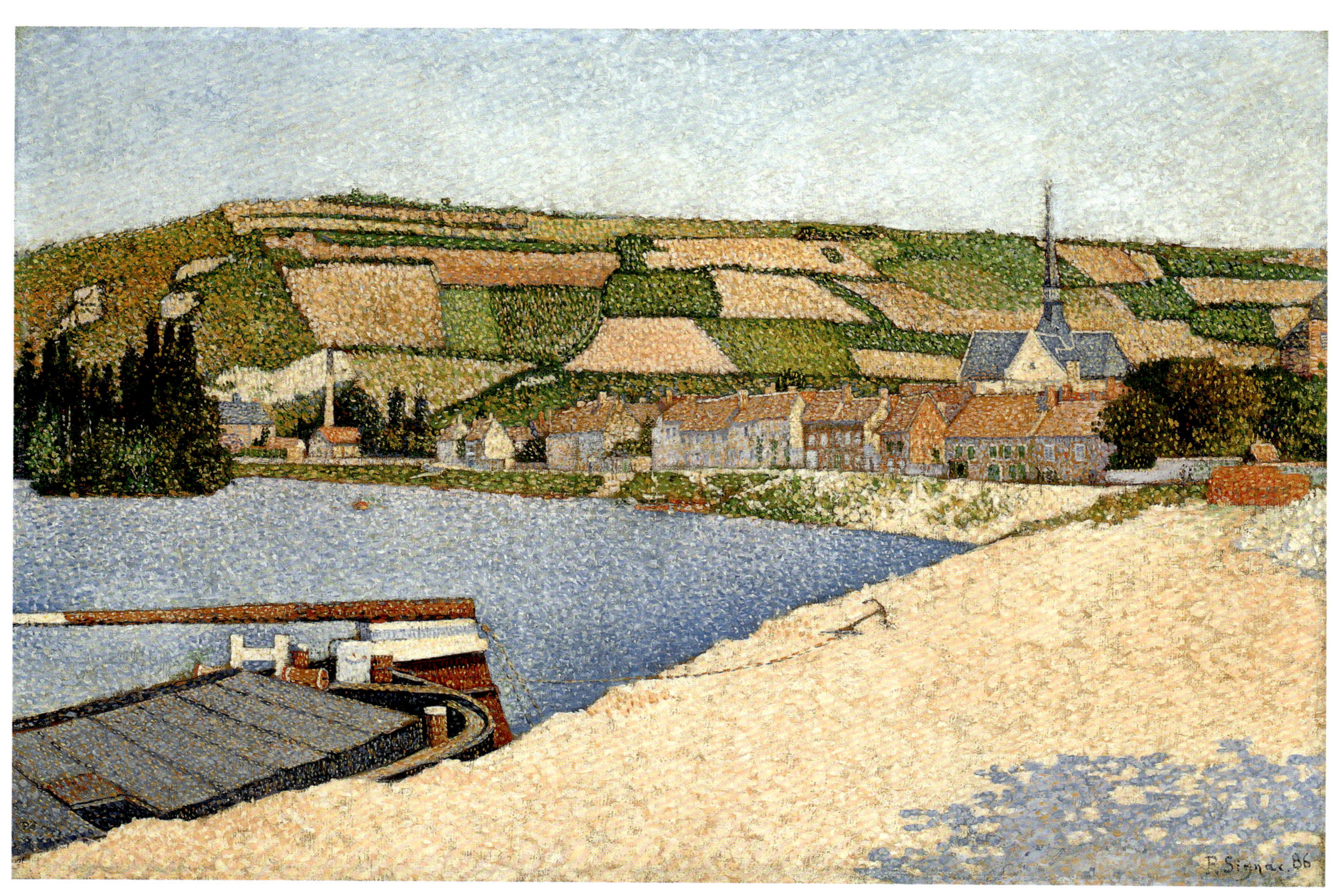
P. Signac 86

PAUL SIGNAC French, 1863–1935

64

Les Andelys, Côte d'Aval, 1886

Oil on canvas; 60 x 92 cm (23⅝ x 36¼ in.)
Through prior gift of William Wood Prince, 1993.208
Signed lower right: *P. Signac. 86*

This luminous image shows the harbor of Les Andelys, a village on the curve of the Seine River near Giverny, about sixty miles from Paris. It is one of a suite of ten works that Paul Signac made in the summer and early fall of 1886, and it marks the first time that he painted a series using Divisionist or Neo-Impressionist techniques. Signac chose Les Andelys as the setting for this composition not only because it was among the loveliest villages along the Seine, but also because of its relative proximity to Paris, where he was in charge of preparing for the August opening of the Salon des Indépendents. Two years earlier, at the inaugural exhibition of that group, he had met Georges Seurat. This encounter proved to be a turning point for Signac's art, which until then had consisted largely of landscapes painted in the Impressionist style and palette.

After meeting Seurat, Signac transformed his style from what Camille Pissarro (himself a recent convert to Divisionism) called "romantic Impressionism," an art associated with the spontaneous capturing of nature, to "scientific Impressionism," which was based on technical innovations grounded in optical and color theory. Although entirely different in temperament—Seurat was laconic and introverted, while Signac was jovial and sociable—the artists found their friendship to be mutually beneficial. As Signac adopted the Divisionist technique to obtain more luminous and vibrant color effects, he awakened Seurat to the Impressionists' use of pure colors. Unlike Seurat—whose stylistic innovations sprang from his training at the École des Beaux-Arts, Paris, and his deep-seated belief in classical structure—Signac, a basically self-taught artist, embraced Seurat's method as a refinement and modification of Impressionism, rather than a complete break with it.

Les Andelys, the largest and most radically synthesized of the series that Signac undertook, exhibits his mastery of the new style. A study for the same canvas (1886; Norton Simon Museum, Pasadena) displays more spontaneous Impressionistic brushwork and a greenish blue palette that captures the look of the small harbor and surrounding hills. From study to final canvas, the artist simplified forms and created a geometric structure of two triangles—one blue, one yellow—that intersect at the composition's center. In the distance can be seen farmland, or what one critic described as a "sparkling [patchwork] of cultivated fields." To the Art Institute's canvas, Signac added a small boat, its dropped mast perfectly aligned with the thicket of pines on the small island directly opposite it. Using these geometries, as well as zones of complementary colors, he played with notions of near and far, of surface and depth, emulating the spatial innovations that Seurat had used in his monumental painting *A Sunday on La Grande Jatte—1884*. The lacy blue pattern at the lower right, which evokes dappled sunlight appearing through overhead foliage, and the broadly brushed sky suggest that Signac had not yet fully relinquished the Impressionist focus on color and handling. In a few years, he would abandon these concerns for a consistently decorative style that relied increasingly on primary colors.

Signac showed *Les Andelys* and other canvases from the series within a year of their completion at the Salon des Indépendents and the avant-garde Théâtre Libre d'Antoine, Paris, before presenting this painting to Alexandre Charpentier, a sculptor friend also involved in the Théâtre Libre. The fact that Signac gave most of the works in the series to family and friends suggests that he wanted to keep these paintings—his first concerted effort in the Neo-Impressionist technique—close at hand, out of the marketplace, and perhaps among those who were favorably predisposed to his new style.

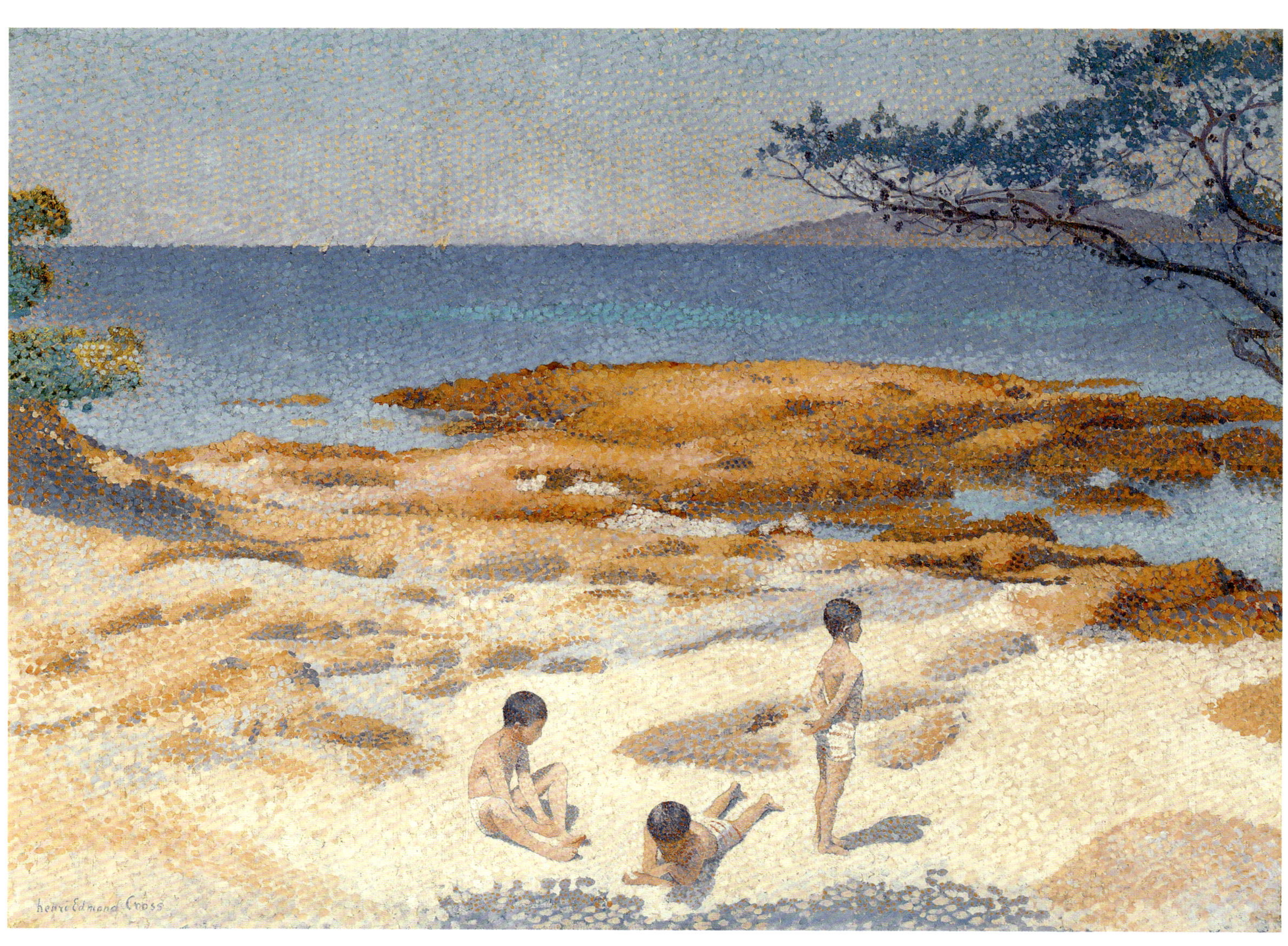
henri Edmond Cross

65

Beach at Cabasson (Baigne-Cul), 1891–92

Oil on canvas; 65.3 x 92.3 cm (25¾ x 36⅜ in.)
L. L. and A. S. Coburn, and Bette and Neison Harris funds; Charles H. and Mary F. S. Worcester Collection; through prior acquisition of Kate L. Brewster Collection, 1983.513
Signed lower left: *henri* [sic] *Edmond Cross*

In October 1891, Henri-Edmond Cross, seeking relief from his rheumatoid arthritis, moved to Cabasson, a small hamlet in the Var region on the Côte d'Azur. There he painted this sun-drenched beach scene, one of his first completely realized Neo-Impressionist works. Like Paul Signac, who introduced Cross to the region (and who would move a year later to nearby Saint-Tropez), Cross became acquainted with Georges Seurat and his innovative color theories in 1884, at the newly founded Salon des Indépendents.

Unlike Signac, however, Cross did not immediately assimilate the theories of complementary colors and optical mixture. In 1884, when Signac was still a fledgling painter working on the margins of the Impressionist movement, Cross was an established artist, known for the somber, sensuous portraits and still lifes he exhibited at the official Salon. Although he became friends with Charles Angrand, Camille Pissarro, Seurat, Signac, and other Neo-Impressionists, it was only after settling on the Mediterranean coast that he embraced the divided brushwork and color gradations of "scientific Impressionism" (see cat. 64) as a means to express the region's radiant heat and vibrant hues.

Despite his residency in Cabasson and the neighboring village of Saint-Clair, where he lived from 1892 until the end of his life, Cross continued to be involved with Signac's group and to exhibit with the Indépendents. In the spring of 1892, he showed *Beach at Cabasson* and *Coast near Antibes* (1891–92; National Gallery of Art, Washington, D.C.), the two important paintings he had begun in the fall of 1891 and finished in the winter of 1892. Although one reviewer of the exhibition felt that the artist's new style "irritates the eye," he singled out four works, including the Art Institute's, for their "luminous charm." Cross felt strongly about both the Cabasson and Antibes canvases, showing them in at least five different exhibitions between March 1892 and May 1893, including at the important venue for avant-garde art Les Vingt (The Twenty), Brussels.

Writing to Signac about *Beach at Cabasson* in particular, Cross noted that he had worked "in harmonies of oranges and blues." To achieve these colors, he added dotlike orange touches over blue in precise rows for the sky and used thick impasto strokes made with a small, flat brush for the beach. For the boys (whose close resemblance to one another suggests that the same model posed for all three), he employed a different technique entirely, outlining them in thin blue paint filled in with cream pigment. To punctuate the expanse of orange and yellow sand, Cross painted a blue and lavender patch over the orange that suggests the dappled shadow of a Mediterranean pine, recalling Signac's own decorative motif-cum-shadow in the river scene *Les Andelys*. But whereas Signac's canvas evokes a specific place and moment, only the title elucidates the setting for Cross's depiction of a timeless arcadia. Like Seurat, who wanted to make permanent expressions of modern-life subjects, Cross here conveyed a feeling of repose, mitigated only by the standing youth shown looking out to sea.

In his later Mediterranean visions, Cross would reject the soft palette and carefully determined structural zoning (sand, sea, and sky) of this and other early works made in the Neo-Impressionist style. By 1896 he had adopted more forceful compositions and a brilliant palette that would appeal to the future Fauves, especially Henri Matisse, who owned paintings by the older artist and worked closely with him in 1904.

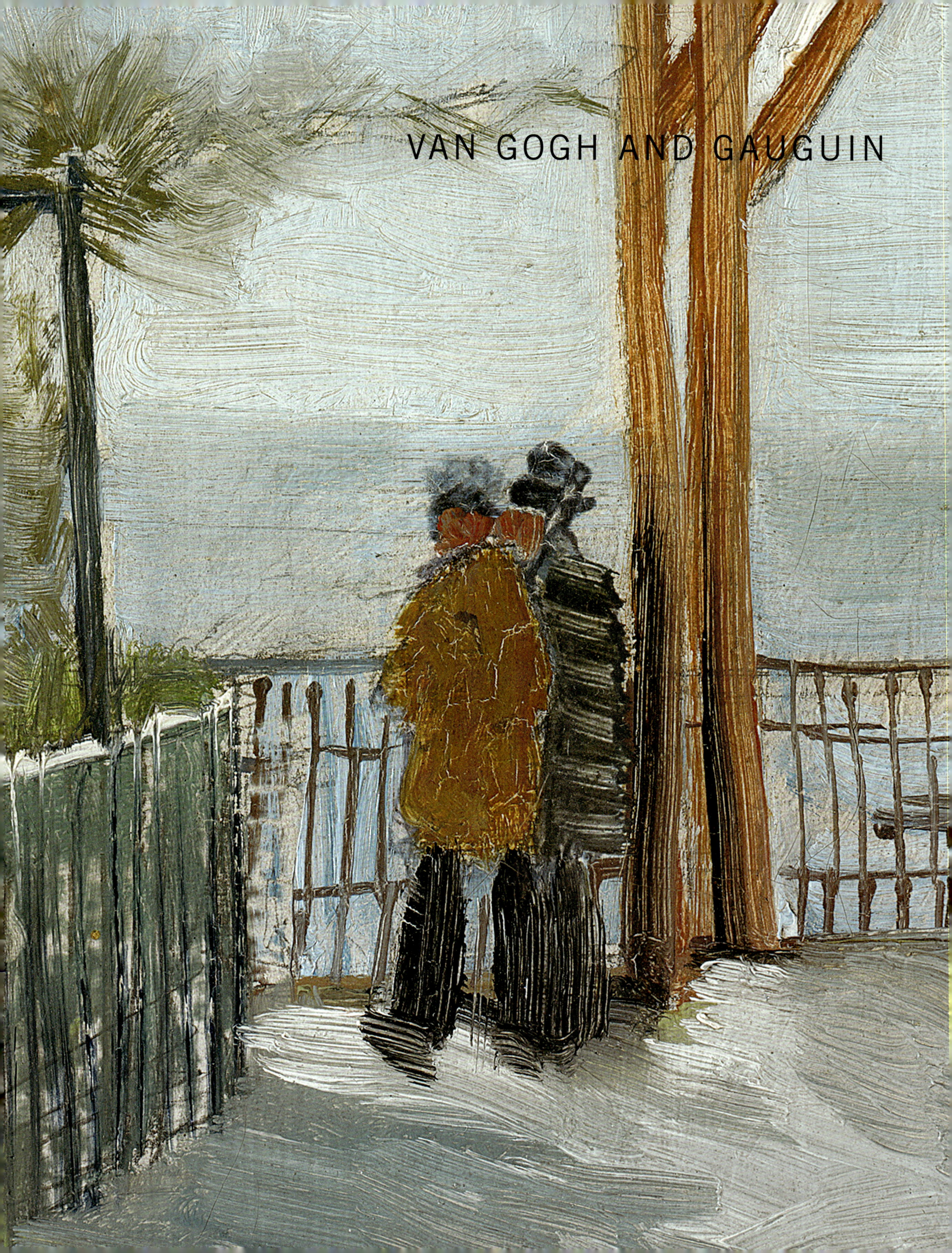

VAN GOGH AND GAUGUIN

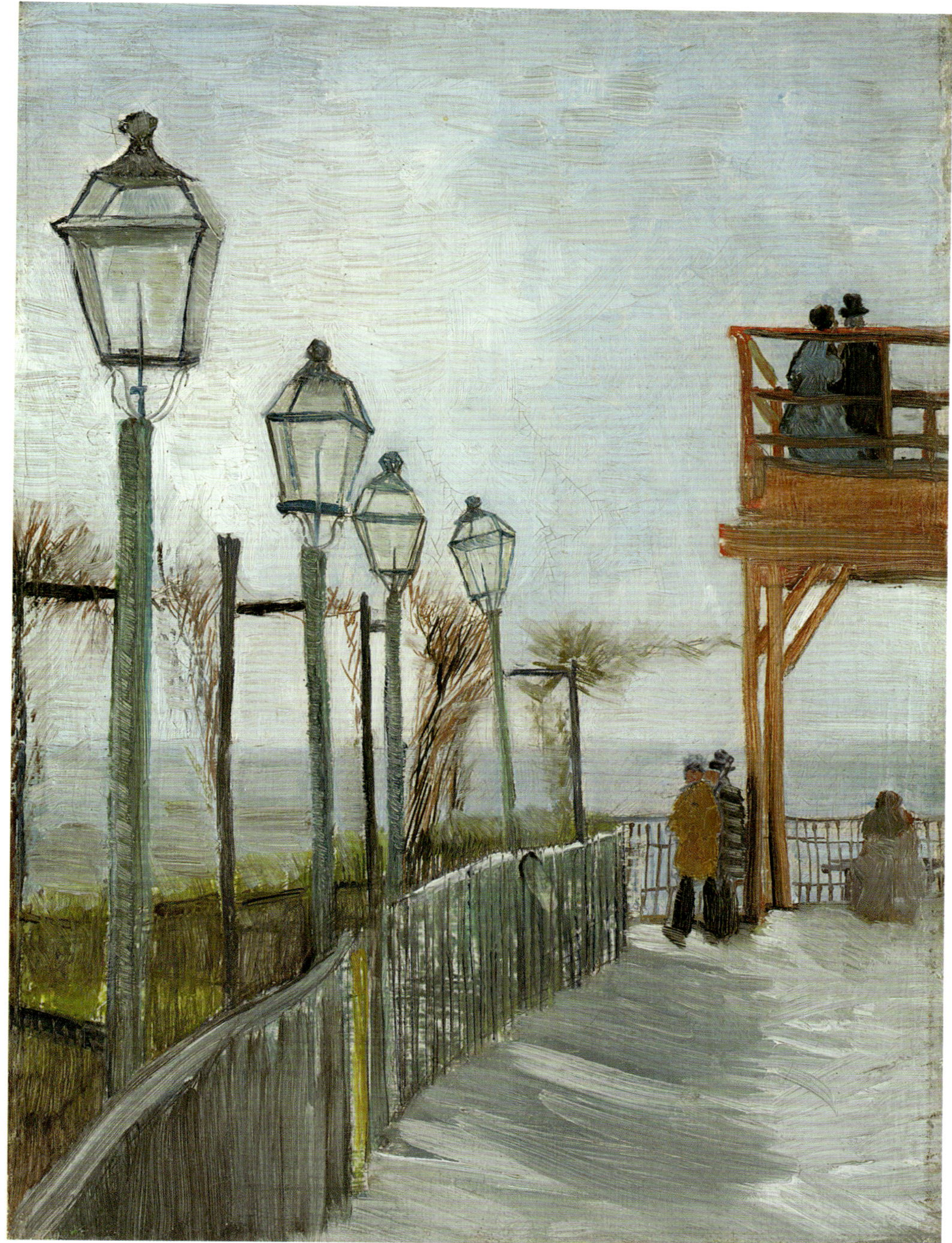

66

Terrace and Observation Deck at the Moulin de Blute-Fin, Montmartre, 1887

Oil on canvas, mounted on pressboard;
43.6 x 33 cm (17 1/8 x 13 in.)
Helen Birch Bartlett Memorial Collection, 1926.202

This picture dates to the winter of 1887, roughly one year after Vincent van Gogh arrived in Paris to join his brother the art dealer Theo van Gogh. He had traveled from Antwerp, where he worked for several months after leaving his native Holland in late 1885. An infrared reflectogram of the canvas revealed that the artist painted this Paris view over an earlier Antwerp study that he had described in a letter of December 1885 as "backs of old houses, seen from my window."

Reflecting his new Parisian neighborhood, *Terrace and Observation Deck* is one of a sizeable group of landscapes featuring the Butte Montmartre, a short climb from the apartment on the rue Lepic where Vincent and Theo had moved in June 1886. Situated on Paris's northern edge and rising high over the city, Montmartre was dotted by traces of its quickly receding rural past—abandoned quarries, kitchen gardens, and three surviving windmills, including the Moulin de Blute-Fin, virtually at the artist's doorstep. The nonfunctional mill had become a tourist attraction, affording spectacular panoramic views over Paris from the observation tower erected beside it. It was also part of the dance-hall complex known as the Moulin de la Galette. Although Henri de Toulouse-Lautrec would later treat the somewhat sordid goings-on of the dance hall (see cat. 74), Van Gogh focused on the exterior, here excluding the mill altogether in favor of the terrace and observation deck with visitors contemplating the haze-wrapped city below. The underlying charcoal drawing, also revealed by infrared reflectography, shows that the artist established the rapid spatial recession marked by the line of slightly tipsy lampposts by using the threaded perspective frame that he had had made in The Hague in 1882 to help him master relative proportions in his depictions of deep space.

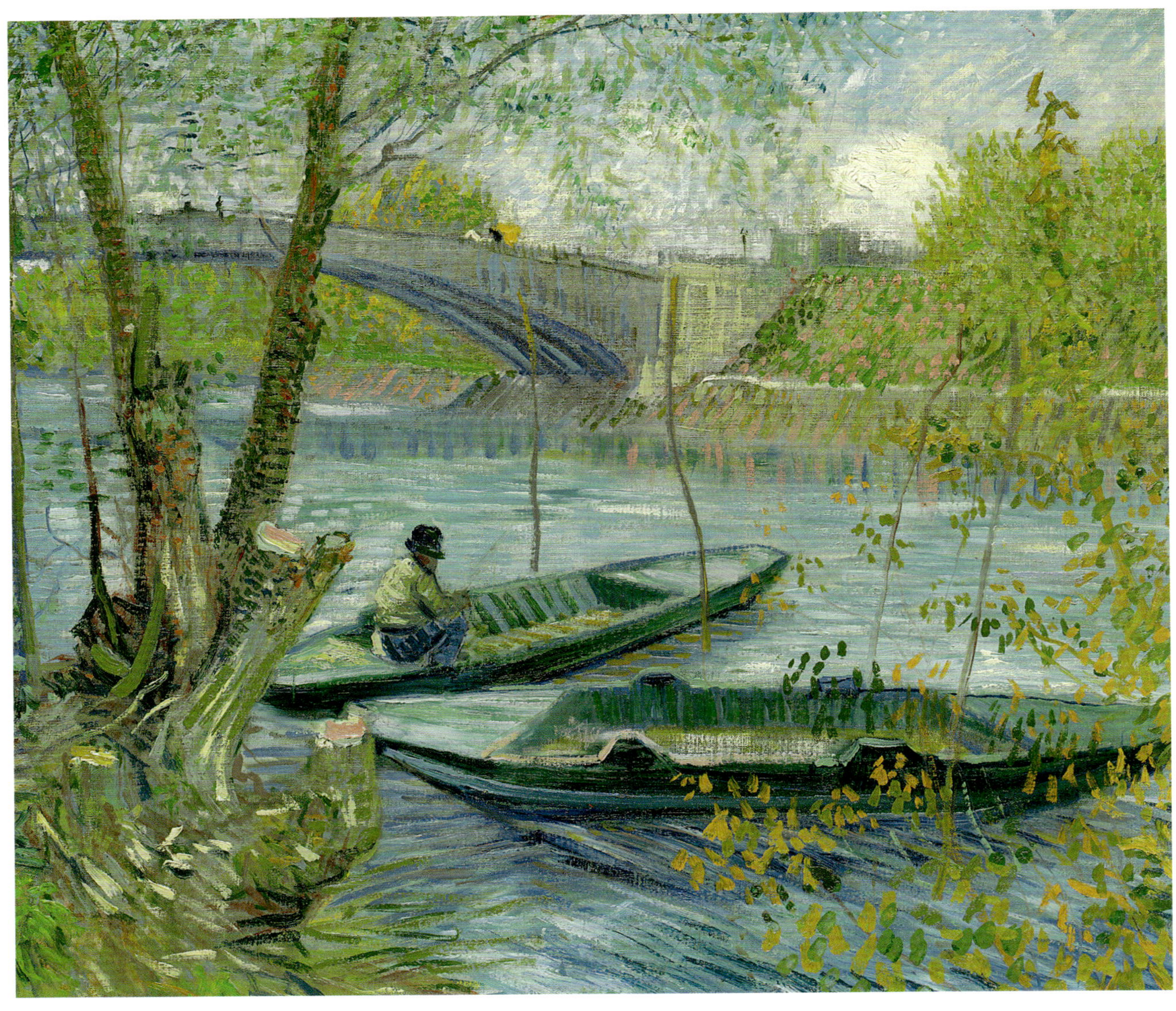

67

Fishing in Spring, the Pont de Clichy (Asnières), 1887

Oil on canvas; 50.5 x 60 cm (19⅞ x 23⅝ in.)
Gift of Charles Deering McCormick, Brooks McCormick, and Roger McCormick, 1965.1169

Fishing in Spring reflects the impact on Vincent van Gogh's art of his friendship, beginning in early 1887, with Paul Signac, whose work, together with that of Georges Seurat, Van Gogh had seen shortly after his arrival in Paris, in May 1886 at the last Impressionist exhibition. Signac was an eloquent spokesman for Seurat's pioneering Neo-Impressionism, explaining it as a natural development of the earlier work of Claude Monet and his colleagues. As this picture attests, under Signac's influence, Van Gogh's palette lightened and brightened; his brushstrokes became more varied, and his subject matter expanded as he simultaneously and directly took on Impressionism and Neo-Impressionism. In May 1887, his brother Theo reported that Vincent was "trying very hard to put more sunlight" into his work.

The setting of *Fishing in Spring* is the Seine River at the Pont de Clichy, near Asnières, where Van Gogh painted on several occasions with Signac. The artist's vantage point was from one of the small islets in the river, which, with their overgrown banks, seemed miles away from the nearby industrial works and provided tranquil spots for fishermen at leisure in their flat-bottomed boats. The Impressionists had favored motifs featuring the banks of the Seine, and Van Gogh was likely aware of a similar composition with fishermen painted by Monet five years earlier (*Fishermen on the Seine at Poissy*, 1882; Neue Galerie in der Stallburg, Vienna). A more immediate precedent was a small picture with a corresponding subject that Seurat exhibited in the 1886 Impressionist exhibition (*Fishermen*, 1883; Musée d'Art Moderne de Troyes). Van Gogh's composition is also related to another of his contemporary paintings, *Banks of the Seine with Pont de Clichy in the Spring* (1887; Dallas Museum of Art), which depicts the other half of the same bridge. Both works are the same size, share the same palette and paint application, and exhibit a painted red border. It is likely that Van Gogh conceived the two as the outer wings of a triptych (he is recorded as having created three triptychs in the spring of 1887).

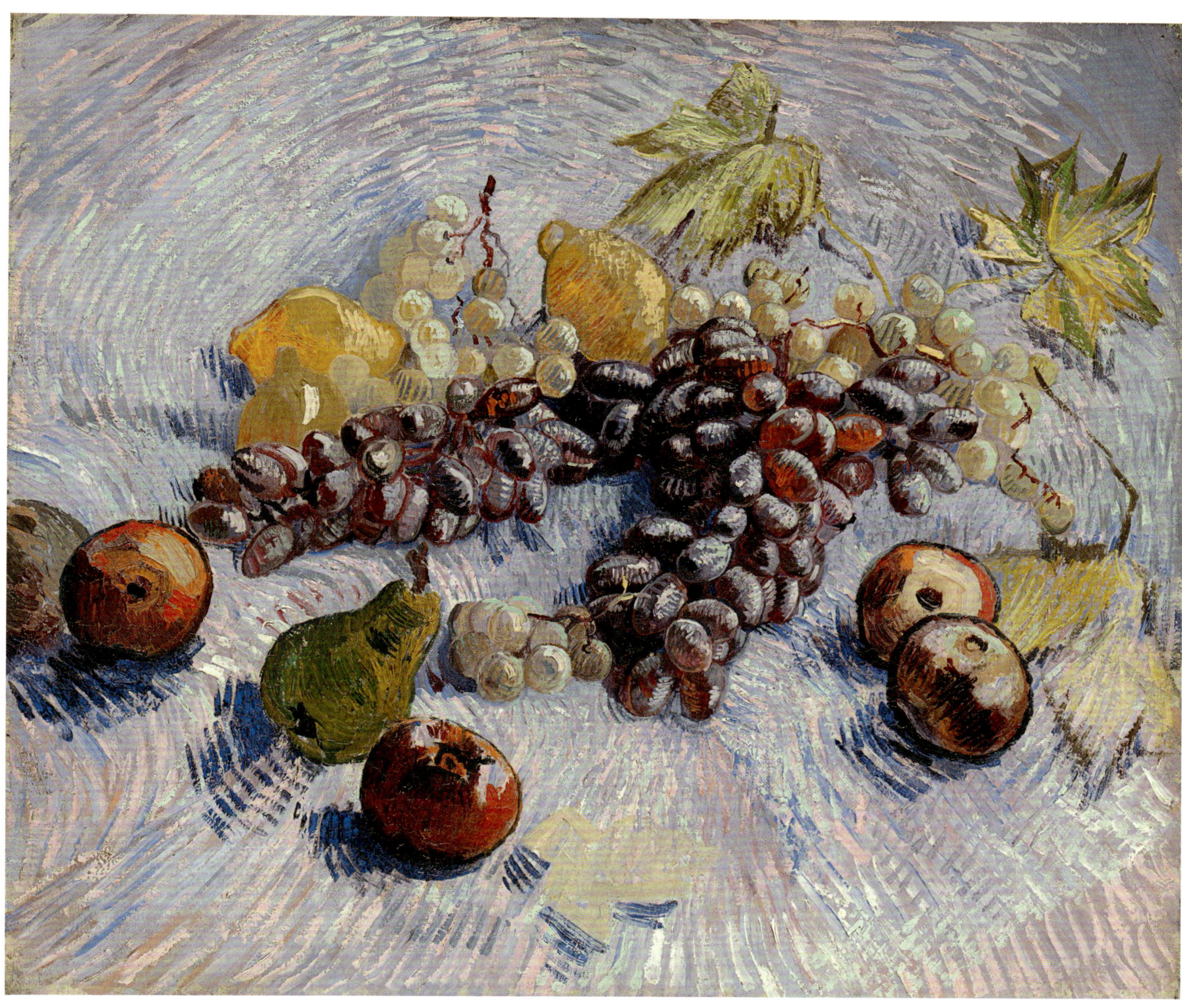

68

Grapes, Lemons, Pears, and Apples, 1887

Oil on canvas; 46.5 x 55.2 cm (18 1/4 x 21 3/4 in.)
Gift of Kate L. Brewster, 1949.215

In the Netherlands, and after he arrived in Paris, Vincent van Gogh made use of still life as a vehicle for technical experimentation. *Grapes, Lemons, Pears, and Apples* is one of a group of related canvases featuring seasonal fruit that the artist painted in the fall of 1887. These compositions reveal his interest in simplifying his palette, employing more vibrant colors and using a thicker, broader paint application than he had in the work of the preceding spring and summer. In the largest of the group (Van Gogh Museum, Amsterdam), which depicts quinces, lemons, pears, and grapes and is dedicated to his brother Theo, the artist explored working within a monochromatic yellow range. In the Art Institute's picture, which has a similarly close-up viewpoint, he pursued a very different exercise, exploring the use of complementary contrasts—yellow and purple, as well as blue and orange, and red and green—in the service of chromatic intensity. This is heightened by the pulsating pattern of purple, pink, and blue directional strokes that define the tablecloth and create a centrifugal force field around the fruit that sits on it. Originally, this aureole was more pronounced, since only the grapes and lemons occupied the compositional center; Van Gogh added the apples, pears, and grape leaves later and then reworked the background. This was probably among the "violent still lifes"—to quote his friend the painter Émile Bernard—that he included in the group exhibition of young avant-garde artists he organized at a local restaurant in November–December 1887. After Van Gogh's death, Theo gave the picture to Bernard, an appropriate gesture since it was his ideas that had, in the fall of 1887, stimulated the artist's experimentations. The canvas was later purchased by the painter Edgar Degas from the legendary dealer Ambroise Vollard.

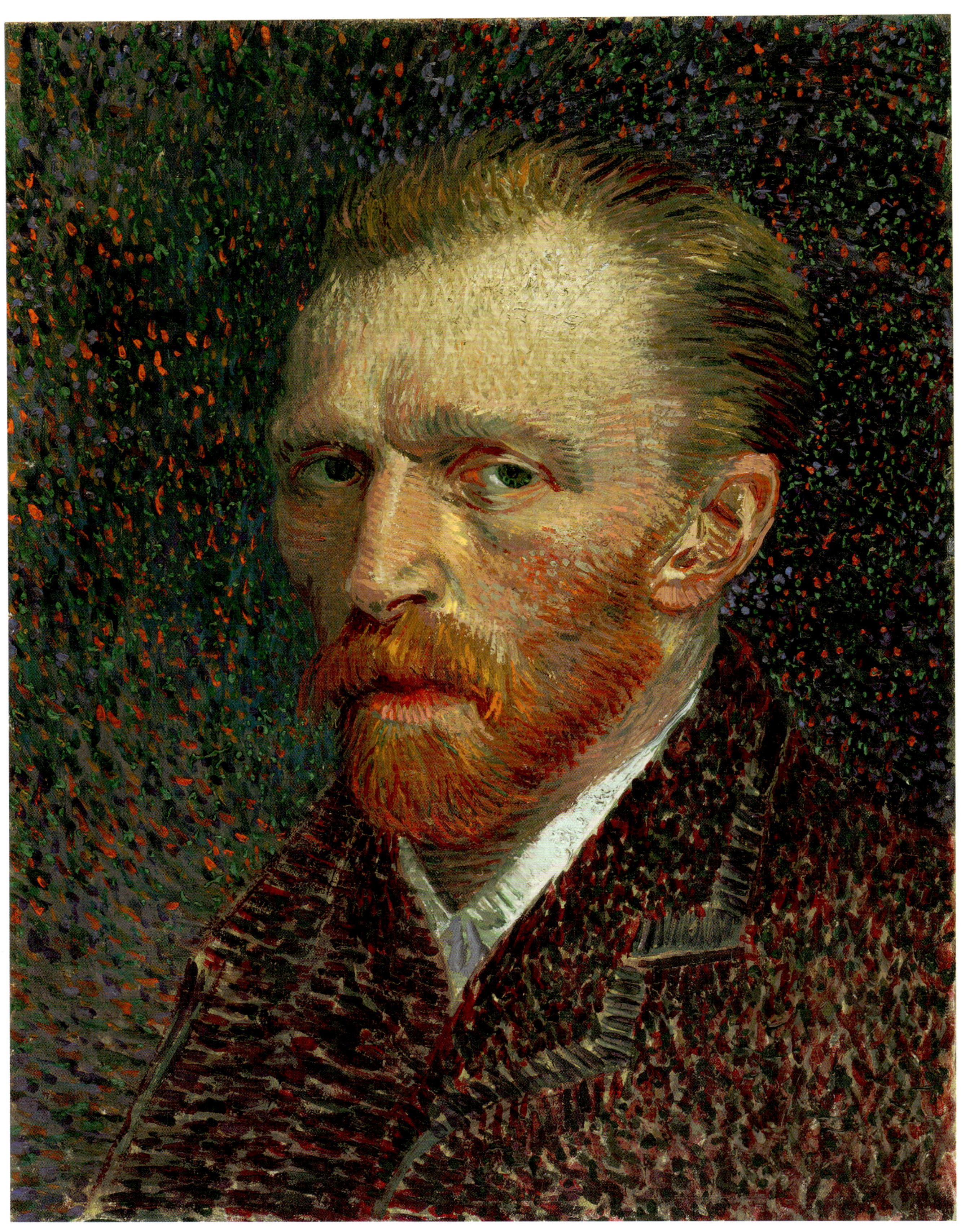

VINCENT VAN GOGH Dutch, 1853–1890

69

Self-Portrait, 1887

Oil on artist's board, mounted on cradled panel; 41 x 32.5 cm (16 ⅛ x 13 ¼ in.)
Joseph Winterbotham Collection, 1954.326

Although Vincent van Gogh had set out to become an artist in 1881, prior to arriving in Paris in early March 1886 he had made no self-portraits that have survived. That he seems never before to have taken the expedient course of depicting his own image is particularly curious given his ambition to be a figure painter and his chronic need for models. His disinclination was perhaps related to his view of himself as a fledgling artist. Indeed, his eventual decision to leave the Netherlands was tied up with a new professional identity and belief in his real potential "to produce and to be something."

His wish to give this symbolic expression informs his first painted self-portrait, which was realized in the spring of 1886 (Van Gogh Museum, Amsterdam). He modeled it on a self-portrait by Rembrandt van Rijn hanging in the Musée du Louvre, Paris, employing the somber palette he had used before coming to Paris. Van Gogh's self-portrait conveys both his resolve to grow as an artist by opening himself up, as his brother urged, to the achievements of modern French artists and his intention to remain true to an artistic vision that he had developed in the Netherlands through a course of self-study shaped, in part, by the Dutch Old Masters, including Rembrandt. Clearly, by the following spring, when Van Gogh painted the Art Institute's self-portrait, his views of art had evolved and he had taken on and personalized the ideas of the Parisian vanguard. Here he portrayed himself not as a follower of the Old Masters but in the radically different stylistic guise of a practicing Pointillist.

The influence of Neo-Impressionist color theory is evident in the way Van Gogh conceived the picture as a study in the contrast of the complementary colors red and green, and blue and orange; the overall blue-green tone of the background serves as the complementary foil to the orange-red of the artist's hair and beard. But however orthodox his Neo-Impressionist technique may appear to be in this portrait and in other works produced at the time of his closest association with the movement's apologist, Paul Signac, Van Gogh was neither as theoretically rigorous nor as painstakingly meticulous as Georges Seurat and Signac. Rather, his interpretation of the new style was personal and idiosyncratic: his touch is more gesturally assertive, and he eschewed ostensible neutrality for a surface that is expressive as well as decorative.

Indeed, the rational surfaces of Neo-Impressionism could not satisfy Van Gogh's desire to plumb the depths of character. The strokes of red and green complementaries that enliven the background swirl stormily around the artist's head, suggesting energy and turbulence, an inner life only hinted at by his baleful stare. This canvas, among the most fully developed or conventionally "finished" of the many self-portraits Van Gogh painted in 1887, anticipates the carefully realized *Self-Portrait at the Easel* (Van Gogh Museum, Amsterdam), with which, in February 1888, he would conclude his two-year stay in Paris. A pointed and newly confident version of his initial self-portrait reprising Rembrandt, this painting translated the moody chiaroscuro of that first self-portrait into vibrant color, demonstrating that the artist had evolved from a "harmonist" into a "colorist." Henceforth, self-portraiture would feature sporadically but prominently in Van Gogh's work.

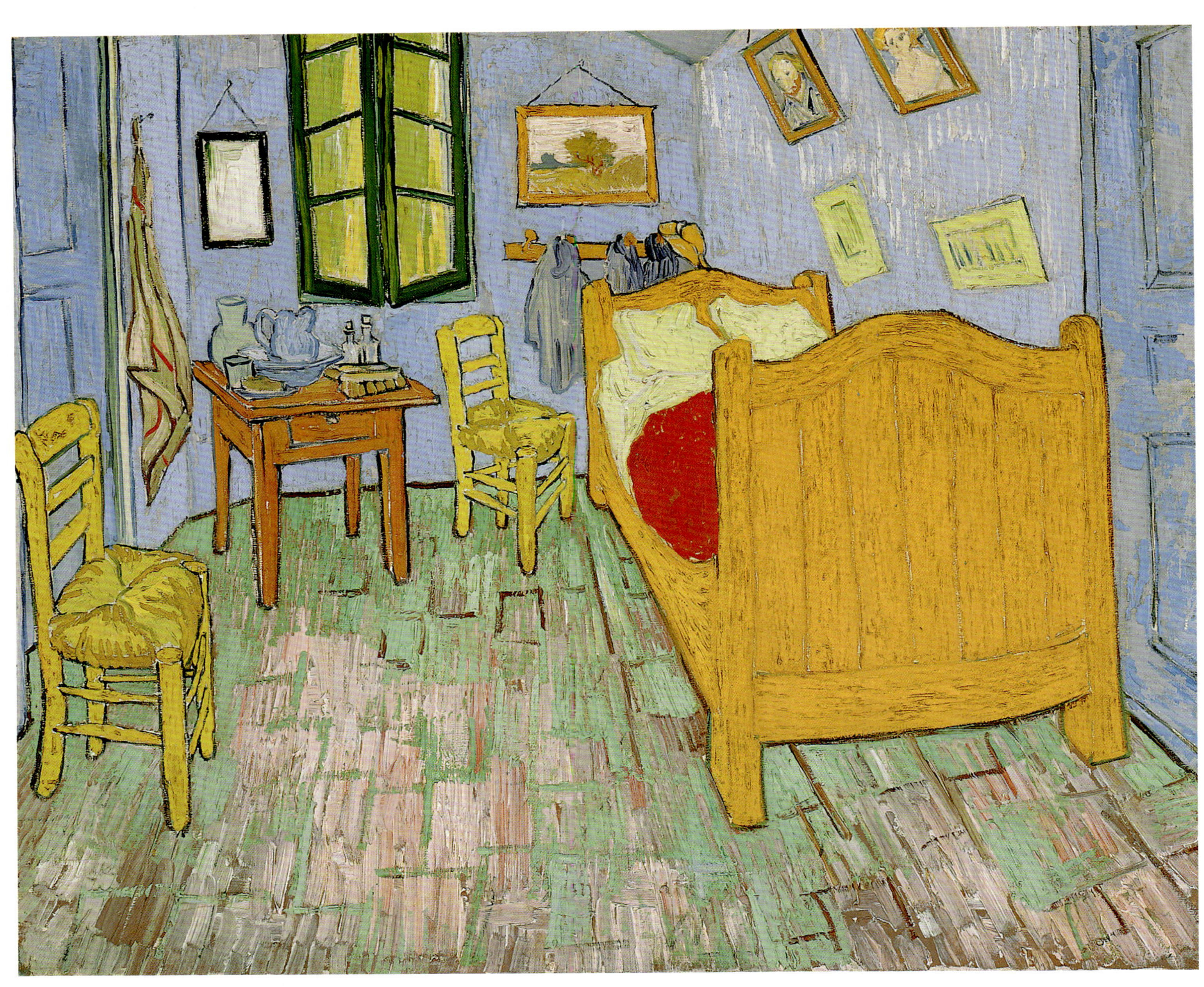

70

The Bedroom, 1889

Oil on canvas; 73.6 x 92.3 cm (29 x 36⅝ in.)
Helen Birch Bartlett Memorial Collection, 1926.417

One of Vincent van Gogh's best-known compositions, *The Bedroom* is the only picture that he made of the interior of the house he rented in the late summer of 1888 on the place Lamartine in Arles. Having lived in furnished rooms in the Provençal city since February, Van Gogh saw the Yellow House as both a long-sought domestic refuge and the embodiment of and headquarters for his dream of a "Studio of the South": a community of like-minded artists working in harmony to create art for the future. Paul Gauguin was his first invited guest, and anticipation of his arrival fueled Van Gogh's efforts to furnish the house and decorate it with his own paintings in order, as he wrote, "to make it really an artist's house."

The first version of *The Bedroom*, which he painted in mid-October (Van Gogh Museum, Amsterdam), was part of this decorative scheme. Upon its completion, the artist described it in letters to both his brother Theo and Gauguin:

> It's just simply my bedroom, only here color is to do everything, and giving by its simplification a grander style to things, is to be suggestive here of *rest* or of sleep in general. In a word, looking at the picture ought to rest the brain, or rather the imagination.... The shadows and the cast shadows are suppressed; it is painted in ... flat tints like Japanese prints.

He had aimed, he noted, for "a Seurat-like simplicity" and an appearance of solidity and durability like that of the big wooden beds he had purchased for the house.

There is, however, an air of disquiet in *The Bedroom*; its distortions—including the bed's exaggerated perspective—can only partially be explained by the room's irregular shape (its south wall was built on a slant). Certainly the mood of "absolute restfulness" that he described to Gauguin failed to materialize with the latter's arrival at the Yellow House later that month. Gauguin occupied the guest bedroom, accessed by the door at the left in Van Gogh's picture, and they shared the studio downstairs on the main floor. After two tense months of working and living together in close quarters, Van Gogh's dream for a Studio of the South exploded in the drama of his self-mutilation on December 23 and Gauguin's immediate flight back to Paris.

When, early in January, Van Gogh returned from the hospital to the Yellow House, he judged *The Bedroom*—which Gauguin especially admired—to be the best of his works there. The artist sent it, along with others, to Theo in Paris in May 1889, just before leaving Arles to live in an asylum at Saint-Rémy. Worried about the picture, he asked Theo to have it relined but then also proposed retouching it. Theo counseled against retouching *The Bedroom* and advised relining it, but—since this was not without risk—only after his brother had taken the precaution of first making a copy, as he had done with other important pictures, including *The Sunflowers*, which Gauguin also esteemed. To this end, Theo sent the canvas back to Vincent, who, in September 1889, made the free translation that is the Chicago painting.

Significantly, in this second version, the artist changed the two pictures hanging above the bed, putting a self-portrait and a painting of a woman in place of the portraits of masculine ideals—*The Lover* (1888; Kröller-Müller Museum, Otterlo) and *The Poet* (1888; Musée d'Orsay, Paris)—that had spoken to his ambitions for partnership with Gauguin. Apparently pleased with the result, Van Gogh made a third, smaller version for his mother and sister Wil (1889; Musée d'Orsay, Paris).

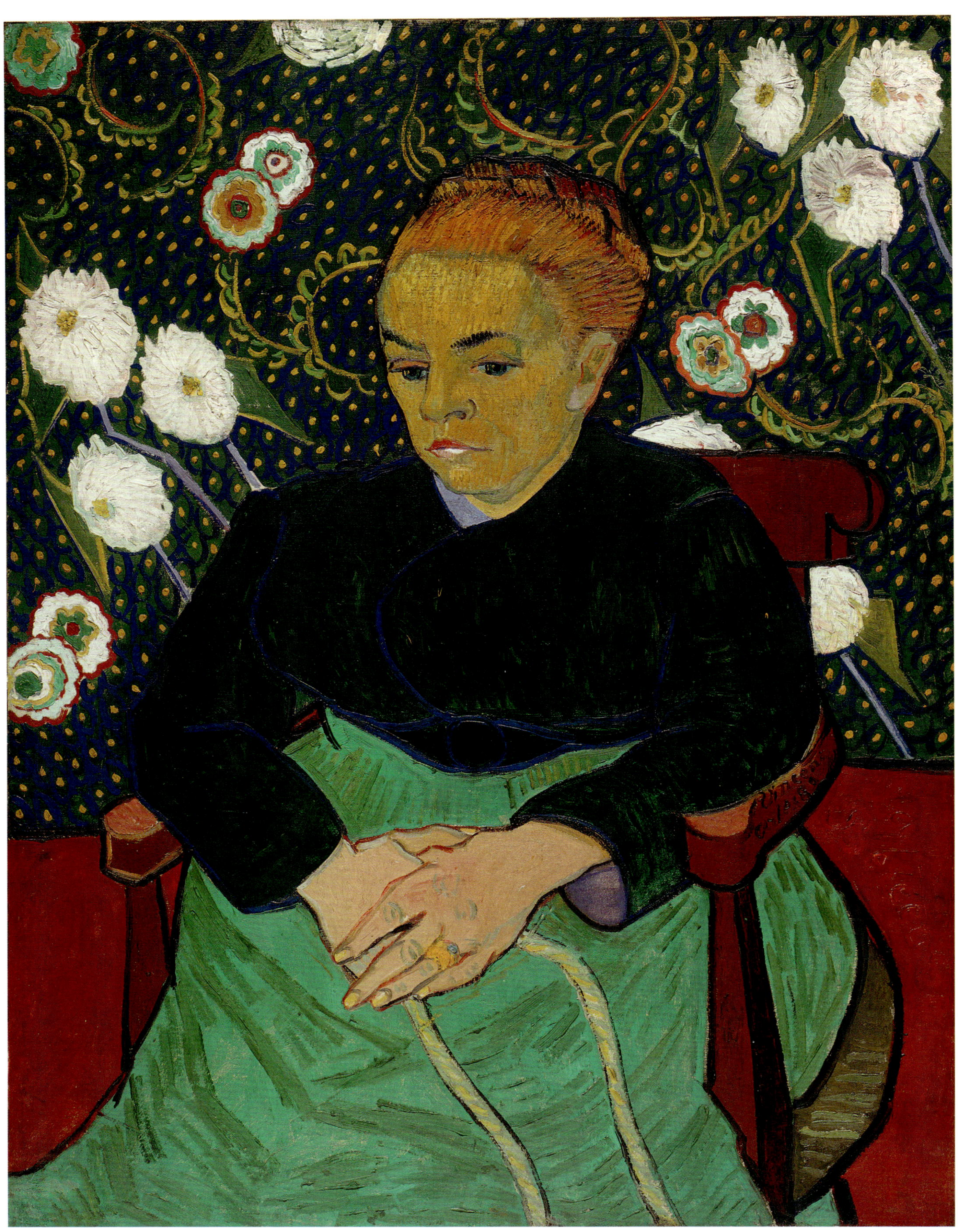

71

Madame Roulin Rocking the Cradle (La Berceuse), 1889

Oil on canvas; 92.7 x 73.8 cm (36 ½ x 29 1⁄16 in.)
Helen Birch Bartlett Memorial Collection, 1926.200

This is the second of five versions that Vincent van Gogh made of a composition featuring Augustine Roulin, the wife of his friend the Arles station postmaster Joseph Roulin, seated and holding a rope with which she rocks the cradle of her baby Marcelle (located outside the picture space). In Van Gogh's oeuvre, the existence of multiple versions signals the significance that the artist attached to a composition. In most cases, as here, this is related to his relationship with Paul Gauguin and his dream of an artistic brotherhood—a "Studio of the South"—based in the yellow house that he had rented in Arles in the late summer of 1888.

Van Gogh began the first version of *Madame Roulin Rocking the Cradle (La Berceuse)* (Boston Museum of Fine Arts) in the second half of December 1888, a time when his relationship with Gauguin had become severely strained and the latter was talking about leaving Arles. Van Gogh had already painted Mme Roulin, whom he associated with the longed-for stability of family life, three times in recent weeks—twice in compositions related to images of the Virgin as Stella Maris (Star of the Sea), the patron of sailors, who offers comfort during stormy weather. With *Madame Roulin Rocking the Cradle*, he consciously continued this symbolism, informed by his association of Gauguin, a former sailor, with the trials of Breton fishermen portrayed in Pierre Loti's 1886 novel *Pêcheur d'islande*. It was to be an image of consolation: "If one were to put the canvas ... in a fishing boat, there would be some ... who would feel they were there, inside the cradle."

Van Gogh had not finished his picture when the dramatic events of December 23—his self-mutilation and hospitalization and Gauguin's flight to Paris—"shipwrecked" his dreams for the Studio of the South and left him "alone on board my little yellow house." During his hallucinatory episodes, as he informed Gauguin in January, when he resumed work on the picture, he had taken comfort in the tunes that "the woman rocking the cradle sang to rock the sailors to sleep." By early February, he had finished the initial canvas, completed two more versions, and embarked on a fourth. One was destined for Gauguin, as was a version of *The Sunflowers*, which Van Gogh had also reprised in January. All this activity speaks to the artist's long-held conviction that painting could be "the raft that will take us safely to shore after the shipwreck."

Van Gogh likened the effects of *La Berceuse* to the inexpensive, unsophisticated colored prints marketed to popular audiences, which communicated their message directly, like music, with the childlike simplicity that he prized. He described his picture to an artist friend as "a woman in a green dress.... The hair is quite orange and in plaits, the complexion is chrome yellow, ... the hands holding the rope of the cradle, the same. At the bottom the background is vermillion.... The wall is covered with wallpaper, which of course I have calculated in conformity with the rest of the colors.... Whether I really sang a lullaby in colors is something I will leave to the critics."

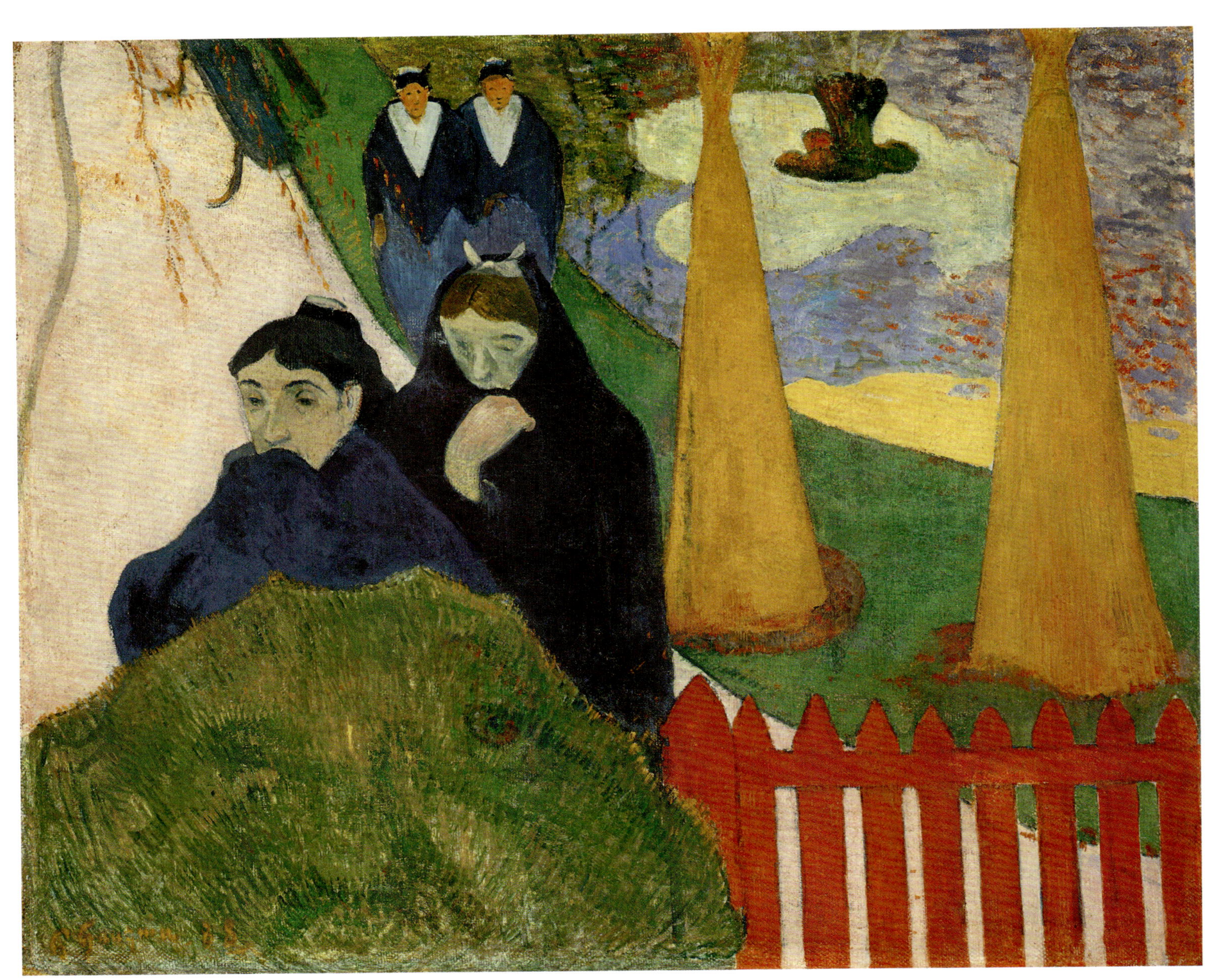

PAUL GAUGUIN French, 1848–1903

72

Arlésiennes (Mistral), 1888

Oil on jute; 73 x 92 cm (28¾ x 36³⁄₁₆ in.)
Mr. and Mrs. Lewis Larned Coburn Memorial Collection, 1934.391
Signed lower left: *P Gauguin. 88*

By the time Paul Gauguin painted this canvas in mid-December 1888, he had been living with Vincent van Gogh in Arles for almost two months. Rain and the strong, cold northwesterly winds of the mistral—an atmospheric phenomenon characteristic of the region—had prevented the artists from working out of doors during the preceding weeks, and their close quarters had fed a growing tension. The setting of *Arlésiennes (Mistral)* is the public park in the place Lamartine, opposite the Yellow House. Van Gogh had idealized the park as the site of the pioneering collaboration he hoped to realize with Gauguin in *The Poet's Garden* (1888; Art Institute of Chicago)—a painting that he created in anticipation of his colleague's arrival. Technical analysis of *Arlésiennes (Mistral)* reveals that Gauguin originally intended to paint a Breton subject but changed his mind and instead undertook this composition, which can be seen as a considered response to Van Gogh and a kind of homage to their work together.

In a contemporary sketchbook, Gauguin planned the principal figures, the details of their headdresses, and their grouping, as well as the fountain, bench, and conical shapes of shrubs wrapped against frost in the park, all of which he could have observed from his bedroom. In his choice of subject and overall composition, the artist responded directly to a painting that Van Gogh had made the previous month, *A Memory of the Garden* (State Hermitage Museum, St. Petersburg). In both works, a curving walkway tilts up to the picture plane, a slightly hunched female figure resembling the raven-haired local café proprietress Mme Ginoux appears at the left, and a planting occupies the foreground. However, Gauguin transformed Van Gogh's floral grouping into a bush in which he consciously embedded forms that suggest eyes and a nose, creating the impression of a strange, watchful presence. This contributes to the somber, reflective mood and mysterious sense of occasion that the artist achieved through the expressions, gestures, and arrangement of the figures. Mme Ginoux clutches her shawl to her mouth against the mistral; this gesture, together with her blank eyes, suggests a stifled grief, reinforcing the sense that she is leading a solemn cortege. As Van Gogh had done in his painting, Gauguin established a feeling of compression by using a steeply rising perspective: there is no glimpse of the sky; the figures' pathway appears blocked by the bush and the red park entrance gate; and the background seems to rise up to the picture surface, flattening out the illusionary three-dimensional space.

There is also a retrospective dimension to the work: it recalls Gauguin's initial enthusiastic comparison of the traditionally costumed Arlésiennes to processional figures on Greek urns. Moreover, the background figures derive from a picture of promenading Arlésiennes at another Arles site, which Gauguin had painted shortly after his arrival and humorously titled *The Three Graces at the Temple of Venus* (1888; Musée d'Orsay, Paris). In quoting Van Gogh's canvas, Gauguin also fashioned a memory of the garden; for one last time, he joined his friend in celebrating the Arlésienne, the symbolic muse of Van Gogh's ambition to create a "Studio of the South." However, a funereal aura pervades the brightly colored but chilly December landscape, as the women exit the pictorial space of the Poet's Garden.

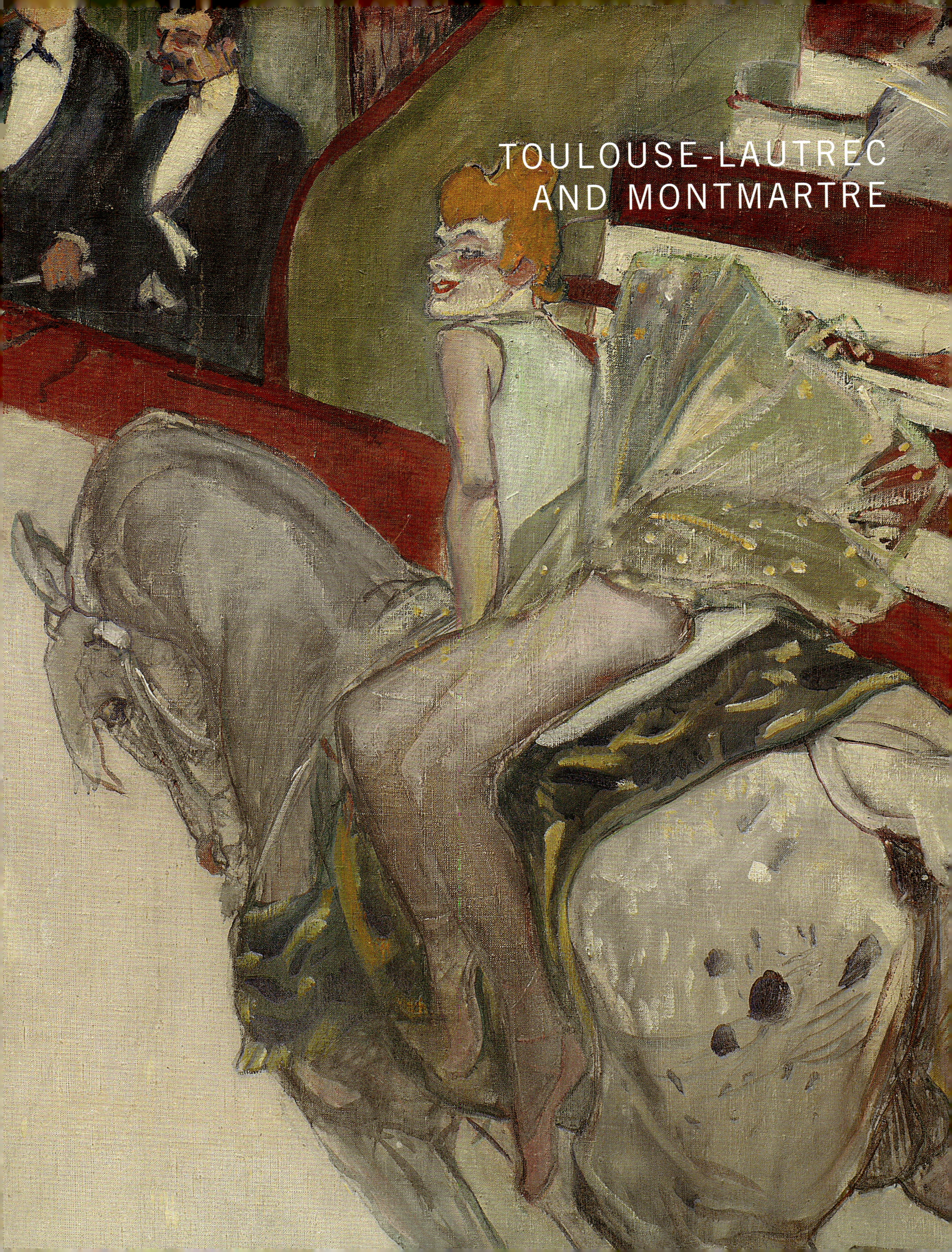

TOULOUSE-LAUTREC AND MONTMARTRE

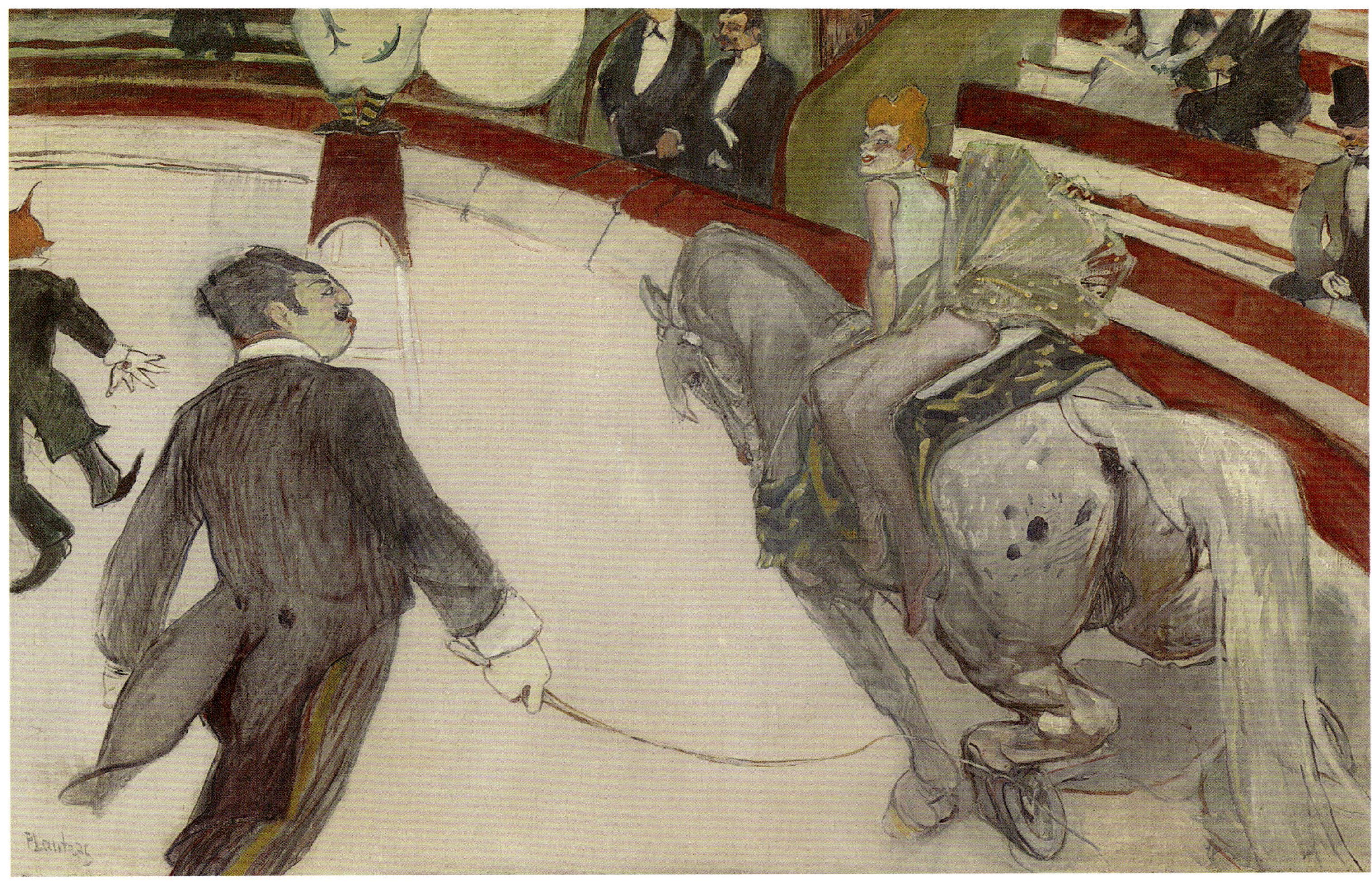

73

Equestrienne (At the Cirque Fernando), 1887–88

Oil on canvas; 100.3 x 161.3 cm (39½ x 63½ in.)
Joseph Winterbotham Collection, 1925.523
Signed lower left: *HT Lautrec*

In the late nineteenth century, the circus—whether in the open air, temporary tents, or like the Cirque Fernando (after 1875), in an enclosed permanent structure—appealed to Montmartre artists and writers both for its perpetual activity and for the colorful spectacles it provided (see cat. 32). Henri de Toulouse-Lautrec became fascinated with the ambiguous nature of such Montmartrois entertainments, which he would continue to explore throughout his short career. Although it is unclear whether *Equestrienne* was a study or later version of a mural-size vertical painting (now lost) also showing a ringmaster and rider, the picture was publicly exhibited in the Moulin Rouge dance hall after it was purchased by the owner of that establishment to decorate the foyer. In the unconventionally cropped, semicircular arena, elongated to fit the horizontal format of the painting, Lautrec captured the frenetic and potentially dangerous moment when the brawny stallion, whipped on by M. Loyal, the circus's well-known ringmaster, gathers sufficient momentum for the rider to stand up and leap through the paper hoop held by a clown.

The model for the garishly made-up rider, who is dressed in a ballet tutu of gauze and sequins, may well have been Suzanne Valadon, a former circus performer, model, and aspiring artist with whom Lautrec would have a nearly three-year relationship. She snarls at M. Loyal, who glares back at her. Indeed, the painting has been titled both *Écuyère* (*Bareback Rider*) and *The Ringmaster*, underscoring these figures' primacy in the somewhat sadistic duet that electrifies the act. Against their coarse, but impassioned performance, Lautrec contrasted the well-dressed, yet seemingly unresponsive bourgeois audience seated at ringside. Given the artist's own aristocratic background, in which horsemanship was considered a privileged gentleman's sport, *Equestrienne*, his first important canvas on a Montmartrois theme, seems an ironic comment on the society he had rejected and on the gritty urban world he had embraced.

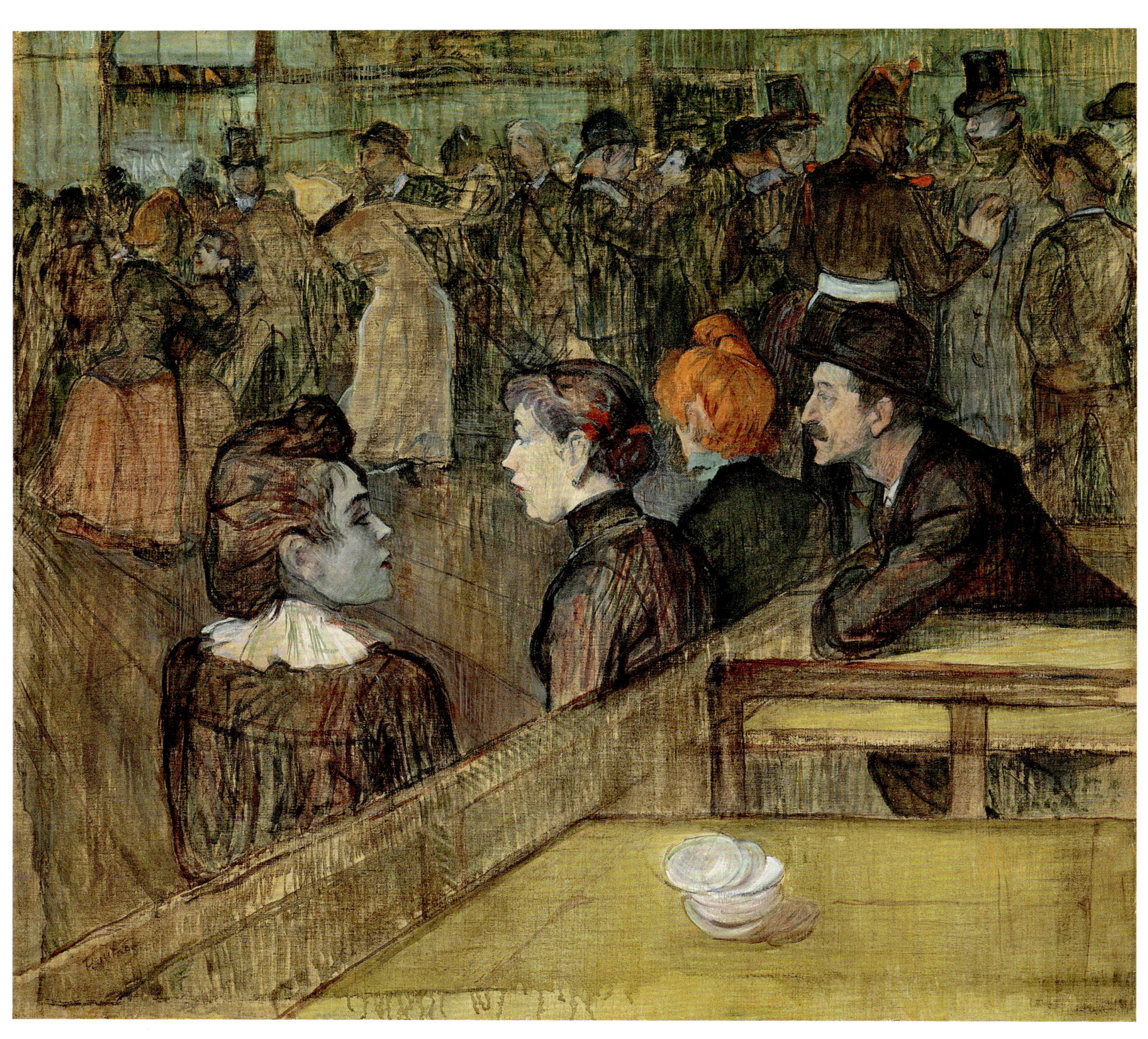

74

Moulin de la Galette, 1889

Oil on canvas; 88.5 x 101.3 cm (35 7/8 x 39 5/8 in.)
Mr. and Mrs. Lewis Larned Coburn Memorial Collection, 1933.458
Signed lower left: *HT Lautrec*

If *Equestrienne (At the Cirque Fernando)* (cat. 73), with its near-caricatural style, marked Henri de Toulouse-Lautrec's first success at elevating popular subjects into fine art, *Moulin de la Galette* confirmed his reputation as a painter-chronicler of Montmartrois dance halls, cafés, and cabarets.

In conceiving this ambitious multifigure composition, Lautrec may have considered Pierre-Auguste Renoir's 1876 masterwork of the same title (Musée d'Orsay, Paris). However, Lautrec's version, painted thirteen years later, represents a complete inversion of Renoir's image of pleasurable sociability, with sun-dappled acacia trees shading bright-eyed men and women who dance and converse. Lautrec instead illustrated the dance hall's interior, a dusty, seedy, dimly lit place where people dance frenetically or are sidelined in boredom and a joyless stupor. The potential danger of this establishment—where the local working poor and the Parisian bourgeoisie mixed to spend their leisure time and, in some cases, earn money—is suggested by the presence of a man in uniform in the upper-right corner, probably a member of the *garde républicaine*.

The painting, which was likely completed by May 1889, when a line drawing of the composition appeared in the illustrated periodical *Courrier français*, seems to have served as the artist's calling card, advertising his new style and subject matter. In September 1889, Lautrec debuted it at the Salon des Indépendents, his first important show in Paris, and he chose to exhibit it again at other notable avant-garde venues in 1890, 1891, and 1893. Critics and reviewers saw in this work a specific narrative, especially in the foreground figures lined up along the diagonal rail that separates participants from onlookers. One contemporary writer described the man in the bowler hat, generally identified as the artist Joseph Albert (presumed to be the painting's first owner), as a pimp with his girls. Another author called him an apache, referring to the dangerous street thugs in the area, and the girls "gigolettes de Butte," locals who earned their living consorting with the wealthier dance-hall customers.

For Lautrec, who specialized in depicting people looking and being looked at, this image of a tawdry dance hall was both an observable reality and a fiction that he set up from drawings made on-site and highly specific oil sketches of models that he posed in his studio. An earlier vertical oil sketch (1889; private collection) does not feature the man in the foreground. By adding him to the composition, the artist underscored the implied sexual availability of the seated women.

Lautrec's inclusion of the tipsy stack of saucers (used to count the number of drinks consumed) suggests his role as an imbiber of both the atmosphere and the house specialty: cheap mulled wine. Even the technique of adding turpentine to thin his paint (*peinture à l'essence*), which he applied in loose washes, resulted in a seemingly unfinished, messy quality that conveys not only a sense of immediacy and spontaneity, but also the dinginess of this working-class establishment. Despite the painting's notoriety, within a year, Lautrec shifted his allegiance to a more upscale Montmartre dance hall, the Moulin Rouge (see cat. 75).

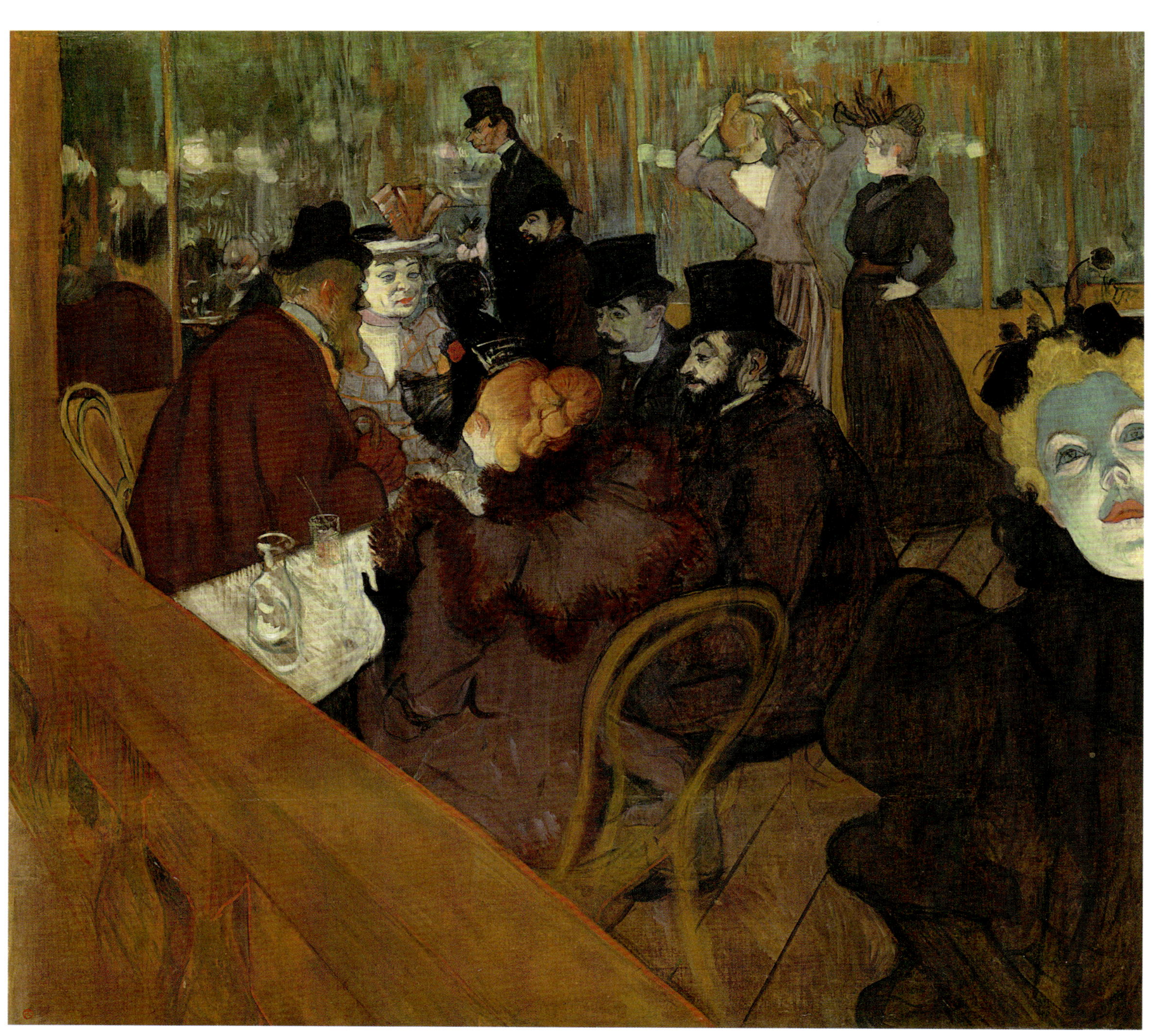

75

At the Moulin Rouge, 1892/95

Oil on canvas; 123 x 141 cm (48 7/16 x 55 1/2 in.)
Helen Birch Bartlett Memorial Collection, 1928.610
Stamped lower left with monogram

No artist understood the role of celebrity culture in fin-de-siècle Paris better than Henri de Toulouse-Lautrec. His posters, lithographs, and paintings of dance-hall performers kept their faces in the public eye, helping them to achieve superstar status and simultaneously making his reputation. Primary to his success was the Moulin Rouge dance hall and café, which was famous for performers such as Jane Avril, La Goulue, and La Macarona. Lautrec's association with this nightspot began with its inauguration in 1889, when its owner bought the artist's *Equestrienne* (cat. 73) for the foyer. Two years later, Lautrec produced his unforgettable poster of La Goulue dancing the cancan and soon after painted *At the Moulin Rouge*, which immortalized his intimate relationship with performers and other cabaret luminaries and intensified his connection to the dance hall.

As in his earlier picture *Moulin de la Galette* (cat. 74), Lautrec organized this composition along the rushing diagonal of a wood railing that separates the dance hall from the café area. In the earlier canvas, the spectators look out toward the dance hall, but *At the Moulin Rouge* shows only the café, with its mirrored paneling. In both compositions, Lautrec emphasized the diagonal thrust by including heads lined up and in profile. In *Moulin de la Galette*, he arranged three female heads along the balustrade, while in this later canvas, four male heads—beginning with that of the wine merchant and amateur artist Maurice Guibert, the man in a top hat at the right—move vertically toward the photographer Paul Sescau and the center of the canvas. There Lautrec included his own stunted figure, accompanied by that of the physician Gabriel Tapié de Céleyran, his cousin and companion. Although the artist's status as a habitué of the Moulin Rouge afforded him a permanently reserved table, here he presented himself as a tourist, seemingly oblivious to La Goulue to the right of him and unnoticed by his friends, who are seated at what may have been his table. As with his posters, Lautrec emphasized the telling details of these regulars—the heavy-lidded eyes of Guibert; the flowing whiskers and hooked cane of the Symbolist poet, novelist, and publisher Édouard Dujardin; the manly, square-jawed face of La Macarona at Dujardin's left; and, to his right, with her back turned toward the viewer, the red-haired Jane Avril, with her signature fur-trimmed coat and extravagantly plumed hat.

In 1902, when this painting was first photographed, it consisted of only this grouping, without the L-shaped strip of canvas (about ten inches wide) that now appears along the bottom and right side. Titled *A Table at the Moulin Rouge*, this version conveyed a certain "end-of-the-party" melancholy that may have had something to do with Lautrec's diminishing interest in this haunt as he broadened his focus both artistically and geographically to more mainstream performances closer to the city center. At some point, the artist, or perhaps his dealer, Maurice Joyant, cut the original painting down; why this was done can only be surmised. Perhaps it was because the depiction of the notorious English performer May Milton along the right edge of the picture was deemed too disturbing, rendering the painting less saleable. In any case, by 1914 the missing piece was rejoined to the canvas. Although this nightmarish image of Milton—with her skeletal eye sockets, greenish blue skin, and antennae-like hat—is something of a mystery, she was definitely painted on the original canvas as part of Lautrec's composition and cut off at some later point. Without her, there is no frisson—she provides the glamour, danger, and artificial gaiety associated with the Moulin Rouge. Indeed, her masklike, starkly lit face infuses the painting with a confrontational, immediate, and haunting presence.

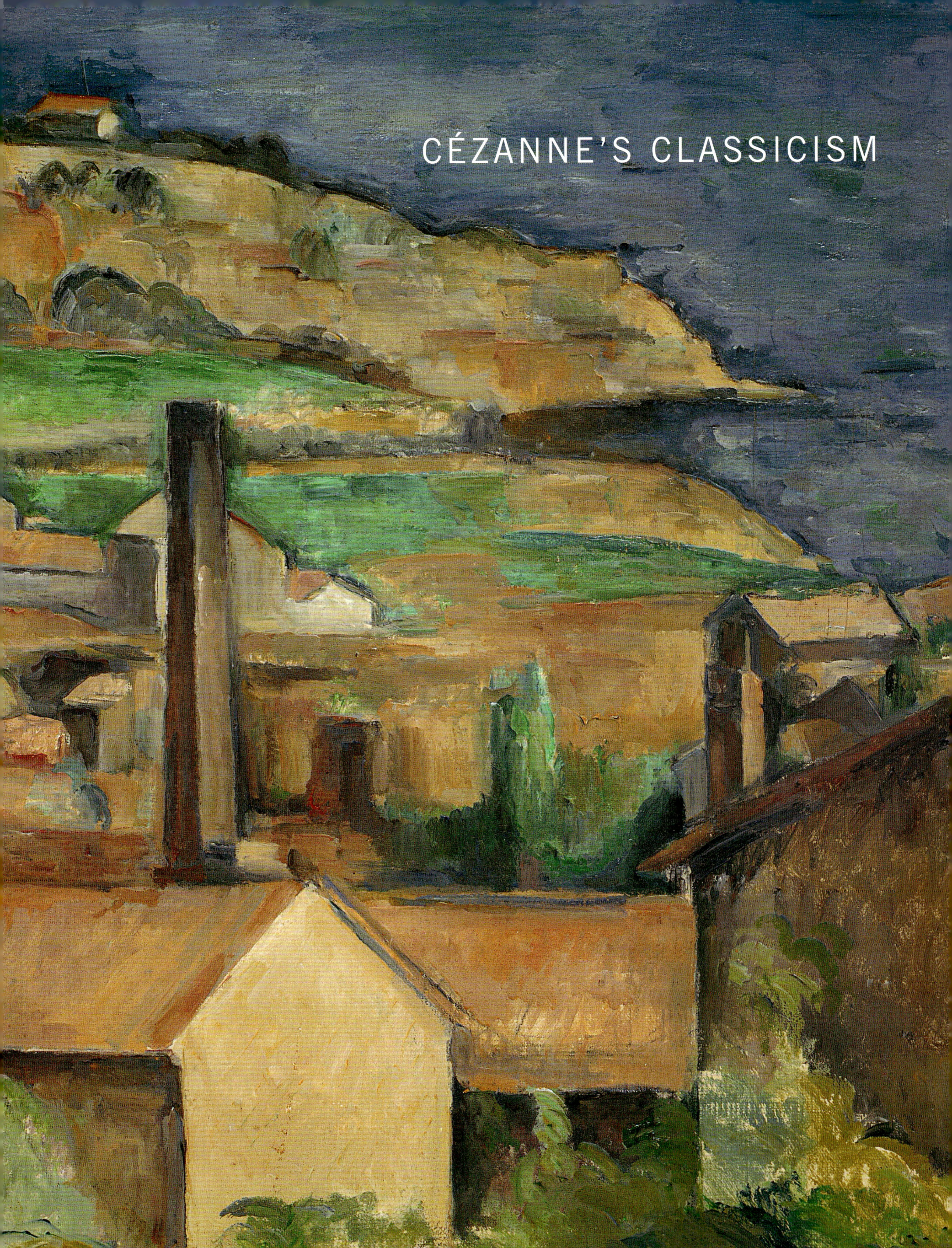
CÉZANNE'S CLASSICISM

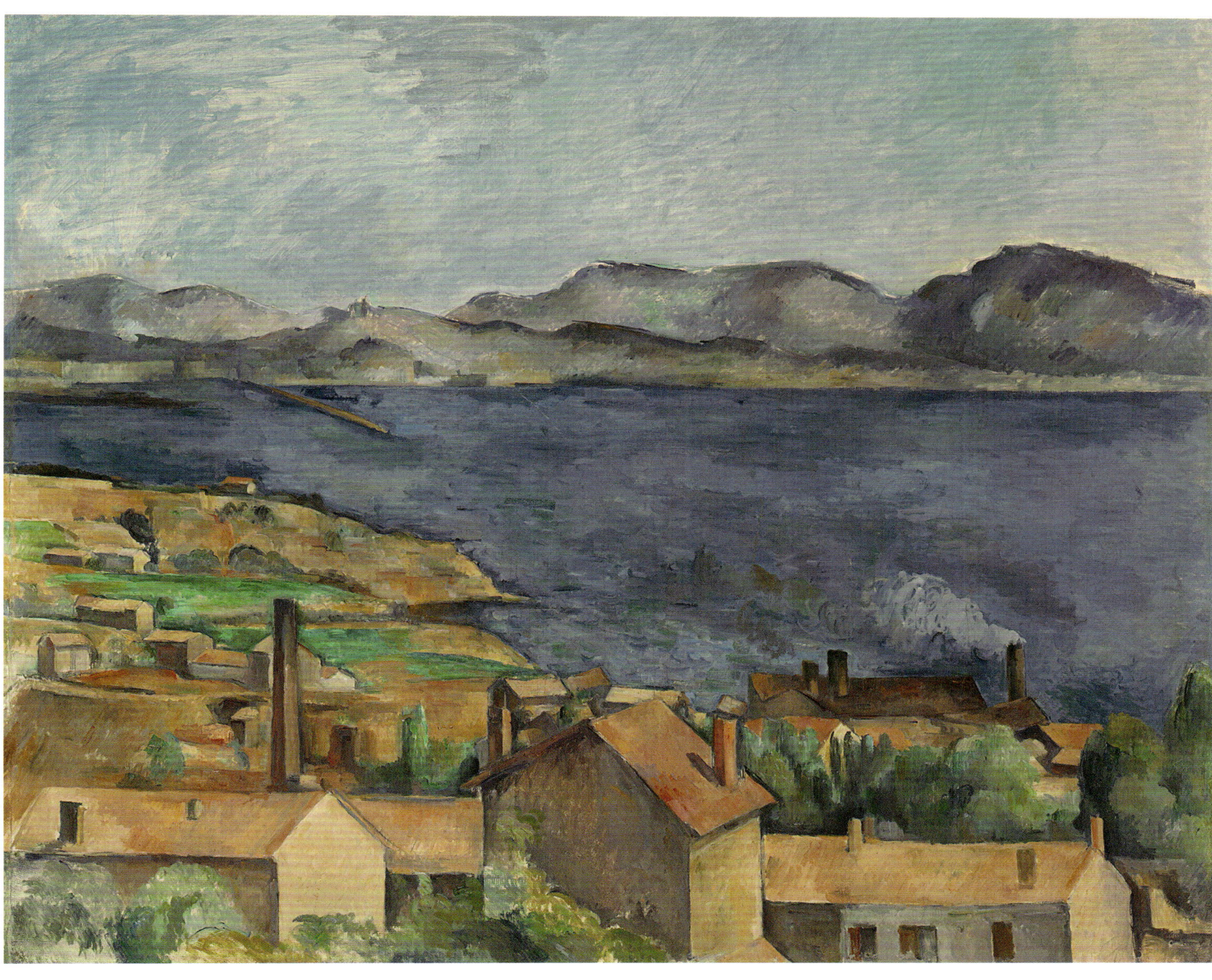

76

The Bay of Marseilles, Seen from L'Estaque, c. 1885

Oil on canvas; 80.2 x 100.6 cm (31⅝ x 39⅝ in.)
Mr. and Mrs. Martin A. Ryerson Collection, 1933.1116

In scale and resolution, *The Bay of Marseilles, Seen from L'Estaque* can be considered the culminating work of a group of landscapes that Paul Cézanne painted in the 1880s at L'Estaque, a picturesque fishing village a few miles from the port city of Marseilles. The artist first visited L'Estaque, where his mother had long rented a summer home, in 1864, and he returned to the village a number of times, including during the Franco-Prussian War (1870–71), when he stayed there to escape being drafted. In the early 1880s, he needed to be near his mother and sister in Aix-en-Provence as well as his mistress, Emélie-Hortense Fiquet, and their school-age son, Paul, in Marseilles. L'Estaque provided a geographical and emotional refuge; it also served as the setting for some of his grandest landscapes, second only to his views of Mont Sainte-Victoire. Writing to his childhood friend the author Émile Zola in 1883, Cézanne remarked that he was renting a house and had found some beautiful views, although he was still looking for "motifs." He would eventually discover one in the view seen in this painting, from a hillside adjacent to the village, looking down on its irregular coastline and toward Marseilles. Across the bay, at the bottom right, he depicted a chimney whose unexpected puff of smoke does not so much rise as blow sideways in the direction of the jetty at the upper left, suggesting an imaginary diagonal that divides the composition into sea, mountains, and sky on one side, and sea and houses nestled among trees and rocks on the other. Cézanne used a variety of brushstrokes—from the thickly banded marks of the sea to the wispy brushing in of the sky—and a palette of subtly modulated ochers and blues to convey what the scholar Meyer Schapiro deemed "a marvelous peace and strength . . . the true feeling of the Mediterranean."

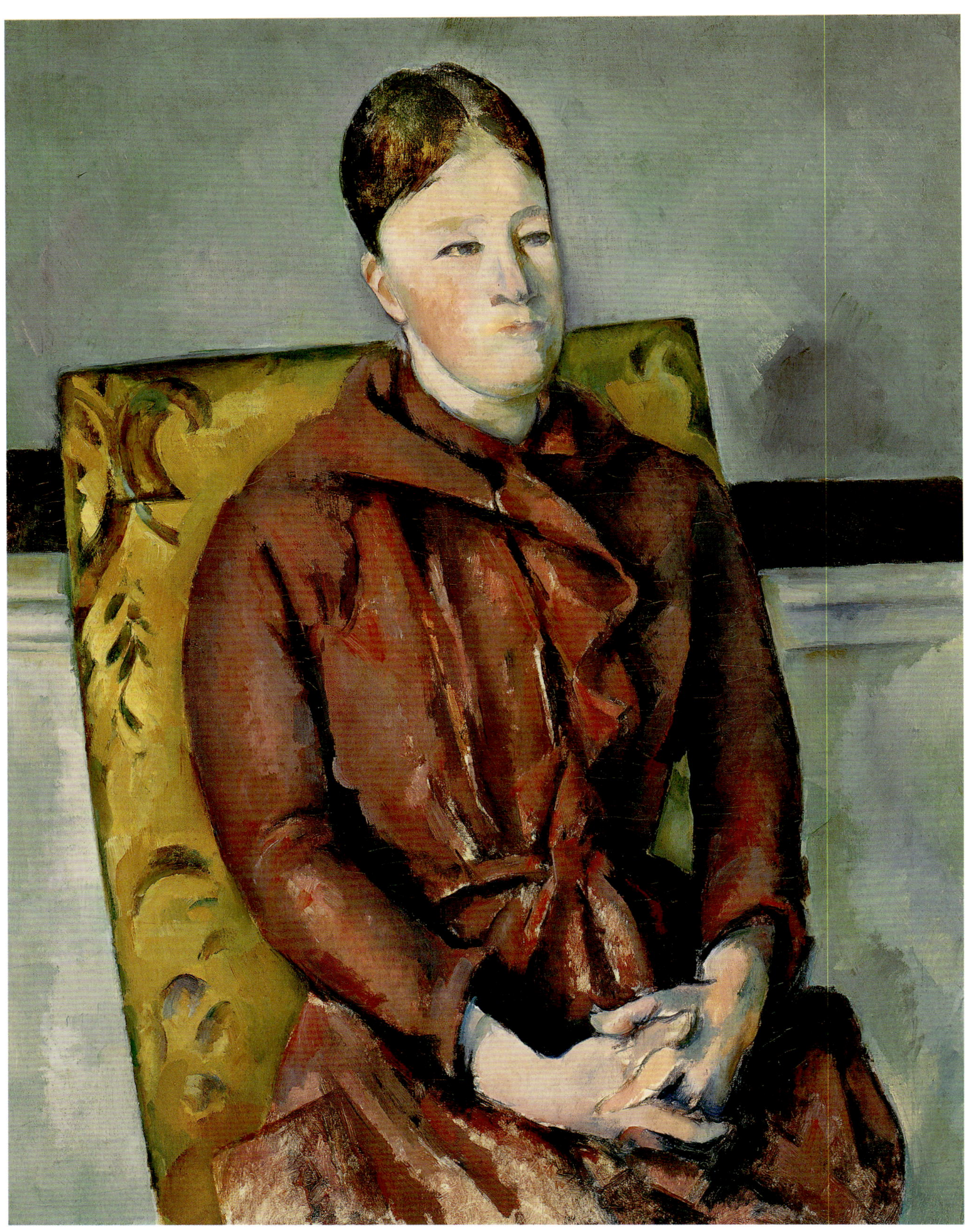

77

Madame Cézanne in a Yellow Chair, 1888–90

Oil on canvas; 80.9 x 64.9 cm (31 13/16 x 25 9/16 in.)
Wilson L. Mead Fund, 1948.54

Ambroise Vollard, the art dealer who commissioned Paul Cézanne to paint his portrait in 1899 (Musée des Beaux-Arts, Petit Palais, Paris), later claimed that it took the artist over one hundred sittings to finish the work. Irritated at Vollard's inability to stay awake during this process, the painter admonished him to sit still, "like an apple." However apocryphal, Vollard's reminiscence of the scrutiny to which he was subjected underscores Cézanne's need—be it for portrait, still life, or landscape—to achieve pictorial resolution through structure and carefully orchestrated color. It also helps to explain why Cézanne generally refused to take on commissioned portraits, preferring to paint his friends, family members, and above all, Emélie-Hortense Fiquet, a model eleven years his junior, whom he had met in Paris in 1869. Fiquet soon became the artist's mistress, and in 1872 their son, Paul, was born; they were married in 1886.

By the time Cézanne painted the Art Institute's portrait, along with two others—all of which share the same title and date and show Fiquet wearing the same carmine dress and seated in a gold damask chair—the family was largely living off the inheritance left to them by Cézanne's father, who had died in 1886. The grandest of these three (Metropolitan Museum of Art, New York), includes elaborately patterned drapery, the edge of a mirror, and fire tongs that correspond to the interior of the Paris apartment at 15, quai d'Anjou on the Île Saint-Louis, where the Cézannes lived from the end of 1888 until the spring of 1890.

In the two smaller portraits—the Art Institute's and one in the collection of the Fondation Beyeler, Riehen/Basel—these details are absent, but the heavy chair and the violet-black molding above the turquoise wainscoting confirm the setting and thus the paintings' dates. Cézanne's reason for making these portraits, which are among a total of approximately thirty showing his wife, may have been to acknowledge their new urban residence and possibly a new chapter in their marriage, during which they had mostly lived apart. Having been guaranteed one-third of her husband's monthly allowance, Mme Cézanne could finally indulge her consumerist desires (to the extent that by 1891 Cézanne was complaining about her overspending). It is likely that the frock she modeled in this series was a new Parisian acquisition.

Of the three related portraits, the Art Institute's is the most austere and compelling. Stripped of a descriptive setting, it offers few physiognomic clues to Mme Cézanne's personality. The illusion of stability provided by the self-contained and closed geometry of her oval head and rounded arms is skewered by her awkward placement on the oddly sloping chair, prompting doubt as to whether she is sitting, standing, or sliding downward.

Most dramatic is the artist's treatment of her face and hands. Despite nineteenth-century portrait traditions that considered the eyes and hands expressive of a person's true character, Mme Cézanne's face is masklike, her eyes abstracted into two almond shapes. Heavily worked in colors that reprise those used throughout the rest of the composition, her visage glows and shimmers but gives nothing away. Offsetting her impassivity are her agitated, clasping hands, with squidlike fingers that are barely sketched in—perhaps a visual metaphor for the artist's unresolved and ambiguous feelings toward his model's stoic, yet seemingly indifferent participation.

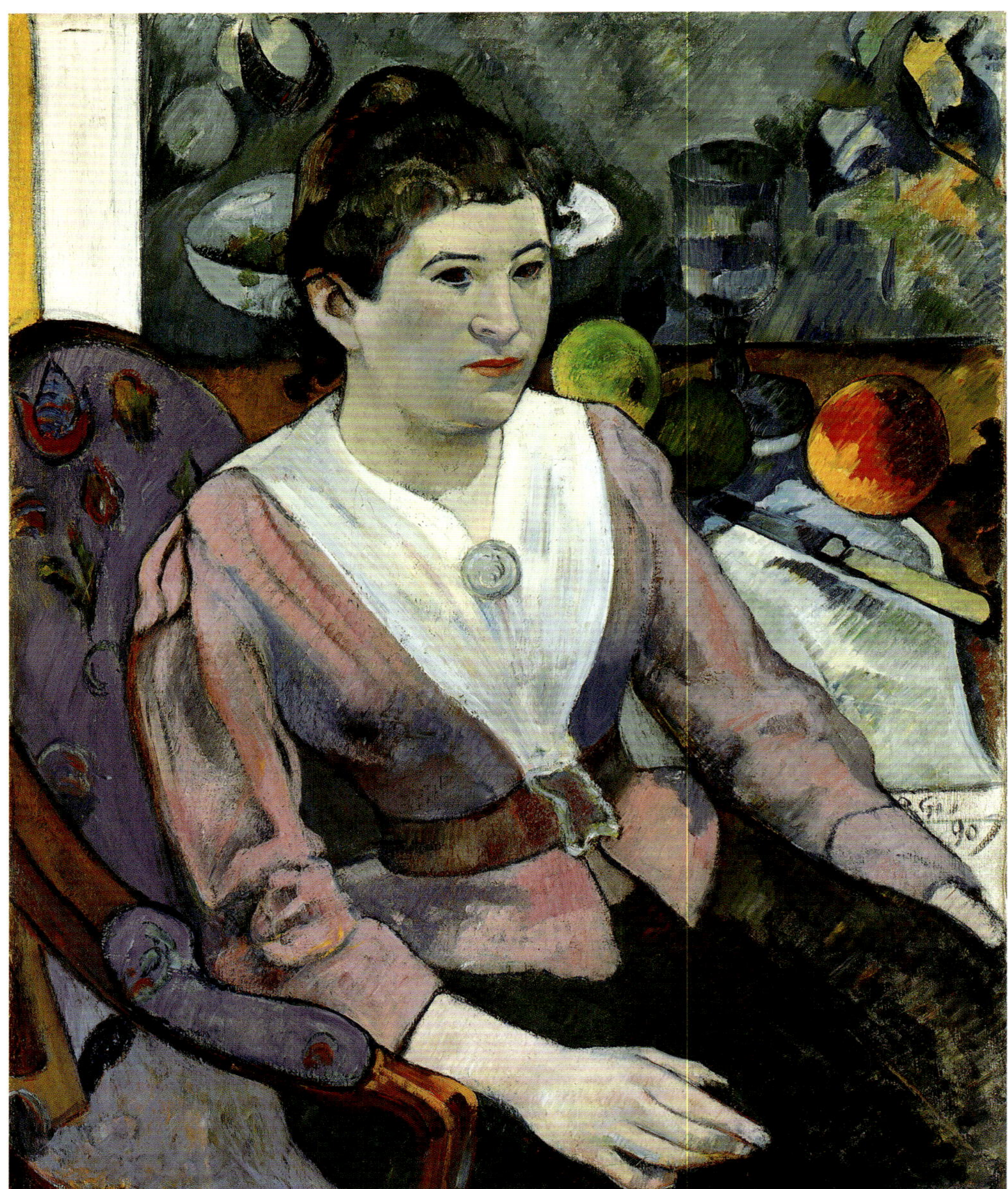

78

Woman in Front of a Still Life by Cézanne, 1890

Oil on canvas; 65.3 x 54.9 cm (25 11/16 x 21 5/8 in.)
Joseph Winterbotham Collection, 1925.753
Signed lower right: *P. Go. / 90*

Although Paul Gauguin established himself as the leader of an avant-garde group of younger painters in Brittany, he continued to measure his work against that of his contemporaries. In 1891 he made a copy of Édouard Manet's *Olympia* (1863; Musée d'Orsay, Paris), and in this picture of an unidentified female sitter, he included Paul Cézanne's 1879–80 *Still Life with Fruit Dish* (Museum of Modern Art, New York). The painting was part of his own collection, and he signed his name prominently at the bottom right of its white frame. Although Gauguin's version of the still life is nearly to scale with the original, it is more a translation than a copy. Its rhythmical arabesques have less to do with Cézanne's constructivist strokes than with Gauguin's own emotive line and color. Only its Impressionist white frame—typical of those first employed by Edgar Degas, Camille Pissarro, and the Neo-Impressionists—distinguishes it as a work of art and not a segment of the highly stylized wallpaper that Gauguin used to suggest dreams and the unconscious.

The sitter, too, is more fiction than fact. X-radiographs show that, while Gauguin made few changes to the still life, the figure underwent many alterations, including a generalization of what were probably more individualized features and a repositioning of both the figure and the chair on the diagonal. These changes brought the work even closer to Cézanne's roughly contemporary portraits of his wife; it is tempting to think that Gauguin may have known at least one of the series that Cézanne painted in Paris between 1888 and 1890 (see cat. 77), when Gauguin himself was intermittently in the capital.

Clearly Gauguin wanted his name to be associated with the master of Aix and, in particular, with this still life. Out of the five or six Cézannes that he acquired while still a banker, this was the work he claimed he would never part with "except in a case of direst necessity." Ten years later, in 1898, he was forced to do just that: desperately ill in Tahiti and without money for hospitalization, he had to sell the painting.

79

The Vase of Tulips, c. 1890

Oil on canvas; 59.6 x 42.3 cm (23½ x 16⅝ in.)
Mr. and Mrs. Lewis Larned Coburn Memorial Collection, 1933.423

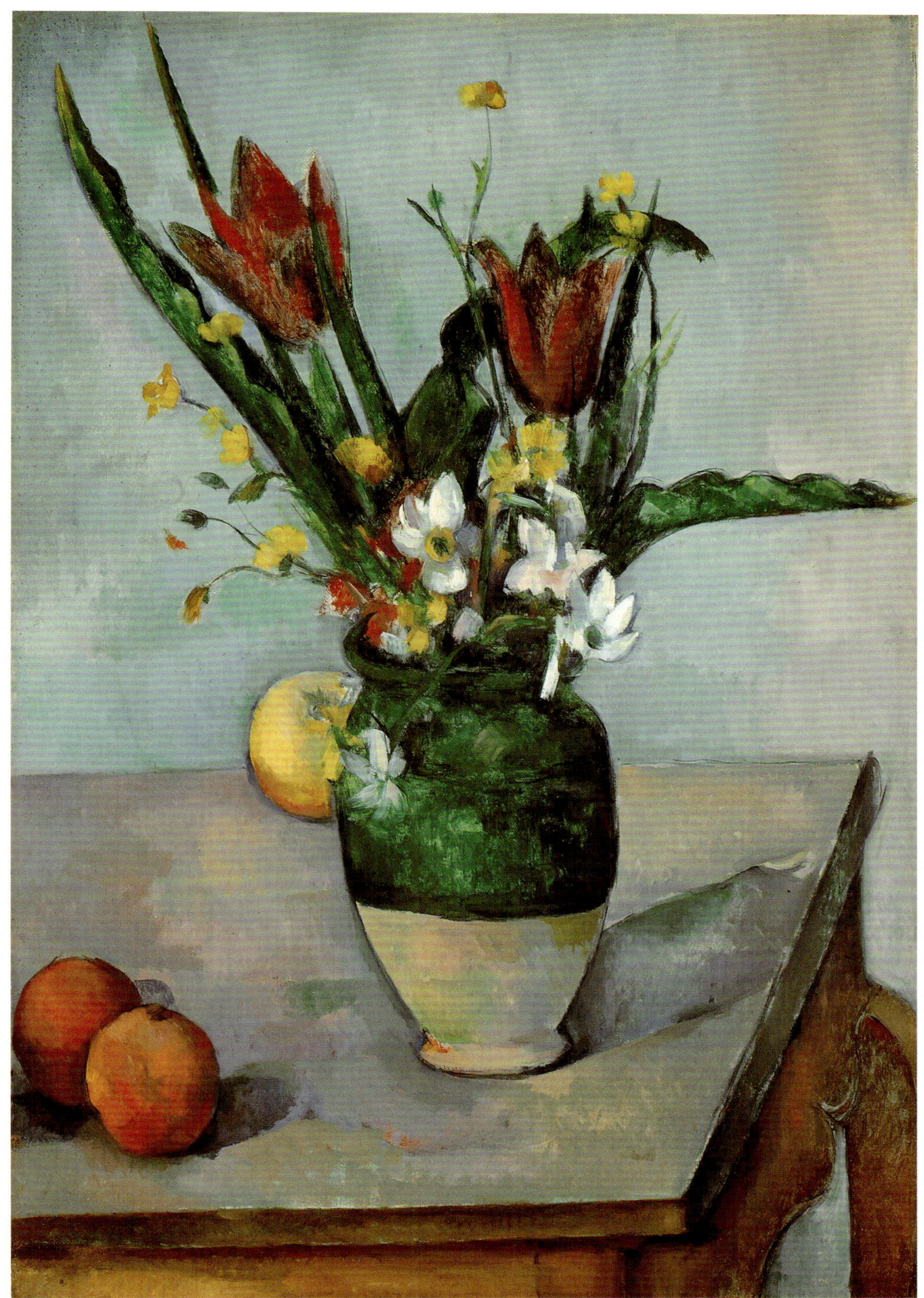

Although Paul Cézanne left Paris at the end of 1885 to return permanently to his native Provence, he did go back to the capital in 1888 and again for several months in 1889 and 1890. *The Vase of Tulips* is part of a group of paintings showing the same wood table with pronounced curves, although scholars do not agree about which of the artist's residences housed this piece of furniture. He made very few fruit and flower pictures, and the Art Institute's is one of only two compositions showing fruit with tulips (the other is *Tulips in a Vase*, 1888–90; Norton Simon Museum, Pasadena). The Norton Simon painting is more columnar in format and, despite its larger scale, may have preceded the Art Institute's canvas. This chronology is supported by pentimenti, or traces, of at least three other fruits (presumably oranges) in the bottom-left corner of the Art Institute's work that were largely retained in the Norton Simon composition. It seems likely that Cézanne used a watercolor approach in that picture, which was made on paper rather than canvas and was thus more difficult to scrape down and alter. By adding an apple at the edge of the table in the Chicago painting and reducing the fruit to a pair of oranges—one of which projects an imaginary diagonal across to the vase and its shadow—the artist energized the composition and increased the aura of solidity and instability. Erupting from the vase are lily-flowered tulips whose spiky tips and stems contrast with the rounded fruits and the petals of the nearby buttercups and daffodils. One yellow petal just below the vase's mouth draws us to the solitary apple rising like a solar orb. Despite its seemingly straightforward subject, the overall effect of this still life is one of logical and unnerving oppositions, a struggle between forms held in abeyance only by their carefully considered spatial relationships.

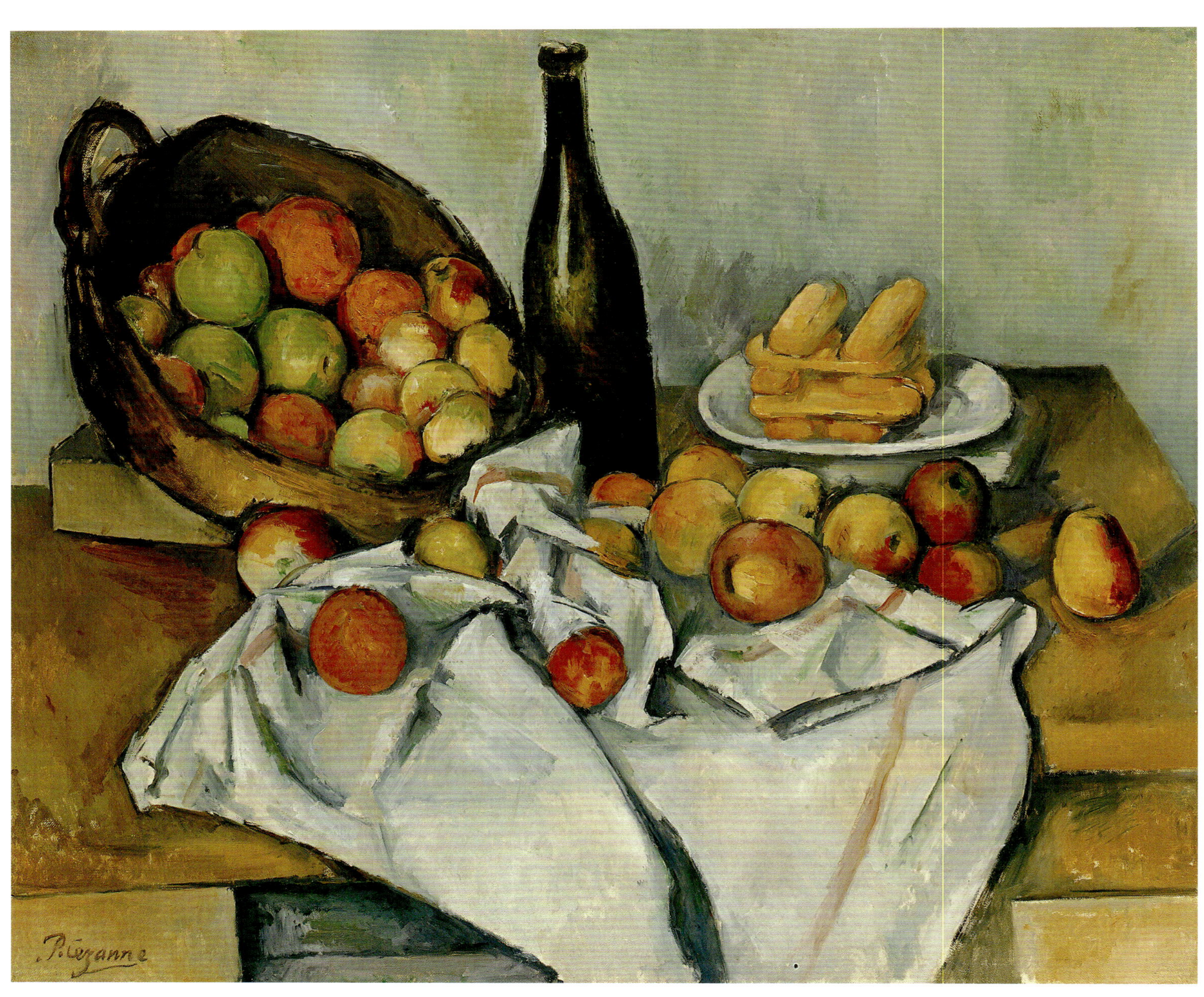
P.Cezanne

80

The Basket of Apples, c. 1893

Oil on canvas; 65 x 80 cm (25 7/16 x 31 1/2 in.)
Helen Birch Bartlett Memorial Collection, 1926.252
Signed lower left: *P. Cézanne*

Paul Cézanne probably signed this still life before sending it to his first one-man exhibition, in November 1895, which was organized by the fledgling art dealer Ambroise Vollard. The show provided artists and collectors with their first opportunity to appreciate the development of the reclusive artist working in Provence, who, for the most part, had turned away from the Paris art scene nearly twenty years earlier and whose works were only known through a few select collections. Even Cézanne's former colleagues, like Camille Pissarro, who owned a number of his paintings from the 1870s, found the show revelatory. Pissarro referred in particular to the "astonishing" and "irreproachable" perfection of the still lifes.

In *The Basket of Apples*, Cézanne's fascination with apples as three-dimensional forms is his true subject. The publisher, journalist, and collector Thadée Natanson probably had this work in mind when he reviewed the exhibition and noted that "[Cézanne] is and remains a painter of apples—apples that are smooth, round, fresh, ponderous, dazzling, of shifting color, not the ones you'd like to eat . . . but rather of forms that ravish. . . . He has made apples his own." No less than thirty of these seemingly uncontrollable geometric spheres populate the composition, beginning at the upper left and cascading down to the lower right, where a sole apple with a flattened side abruptly halts the diagonal movement.

The pieces of fruit appear to fall out of the tilted basket, which sits precariously on a wood slab or book, only to be checked and held in suspension by the deep valleys and peaks of the dish cloth crumpled on the slanting tabletop. Although this stiff, sculptural piece of fabric blocks movement and conveys a sense of permanence, it does little to counteract the overall implication of shifting and descending forms. Even the wine bottle, which appears at first to serve as a vertical axis that anchors the composition, lists slightly; it recalls the odd tilt of Mme Cézanne in the Art Institute's portrait of her (cat. 77) and contributes to an overriding sense of instability, of things momentarily suspended in place.

The precarious balance of elements in this not-still still life is particularly apparent in the ladyfinger biscuits, carefully layered on the plate at the right and set against a darker blue patch that distinguishes them from the turquoise background. Their shadow appears to connect with the wine bottle (already a tilting object), and their ability to maintain the latticelike arrangement seems physically impossible outside of art. Cézanne's balancing act of contradictories extends to the palette, which is dominated by blues and oranges.

His use of pronounced contours in some places and sketchy and "broken" ones in others, along with the fact that the tabletop emerges on the right side at a different level than on the left, adds to the quality of impermanence and, most importantly, underscores the deliberative nature of art making. It is clear that here, and in other compositions of this time, Cézanne was involved in a critical rethinking of form, space, and perception. It was these experimentations with fragmenting reality that led Pablo Picasso to declare that the older artist was "my one and only master . . . the father of us all."

The Basket of Apples was the first work by Cézanne to enter to the Art Institute's collection. It was also singled out early on as one of the artist's masterpieces when Maurice Denis included it, along with a portrait of Cézanne, in his mural decoration *History of the Arts in France*, for the Dutuit dome in the Petit Palais, Paris (1924/25).

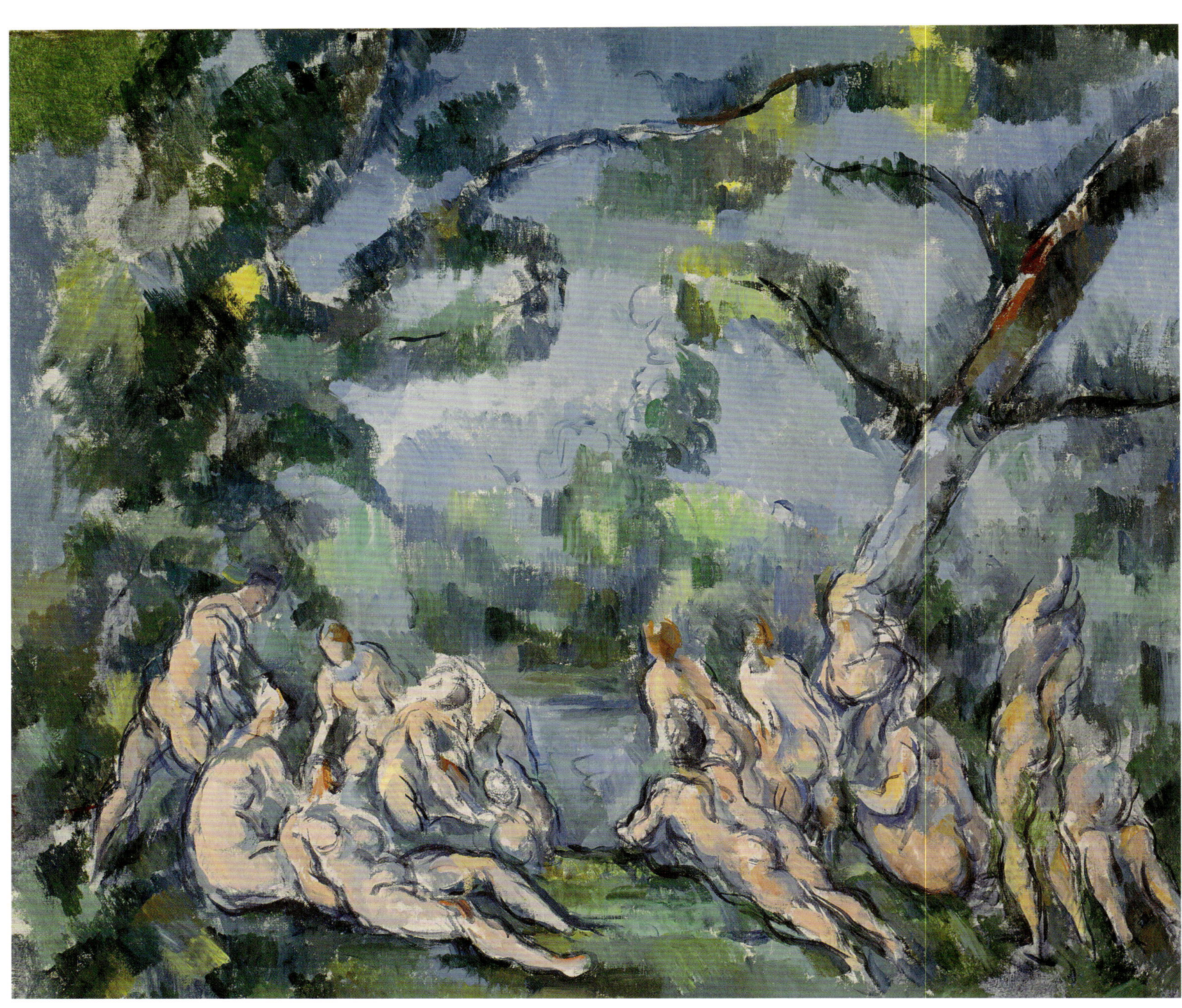

81

The Bathers, 1899/1904

Oil on canvas; 51.3 x 61.7 cm (20 3/16 x 24 1/4 in.)
Amy McCormick Memorial Collection, 1942.457

In the 1870s, Paul Cézanne made his first attempts to depict nudes out of doors, initiating a meditation on this traditional subject that would preoccupy him on and off over the next three decades. Although he painted a few mythological scenes with nudes, he dealt with this theme primarily in his *Bathers* canvases, which rarely show figures actually bathing. Instead, he struggled to achieve a pictorial resolution—based on composition, construction, and palette—between classical iconography and his modernist viewpoint.

The Art Institute's *The Bathers* belongs to the last of Cézanne's three chronological phases of work on the theme: the first focused on single figures; the second, on male or female figures grouped closely together; and the third, beginning in the 1890s, on large and complex multifigure compositions. Among the paintings from this last phase are two monumental canvases that were considered unfinished at the artist's death in 1906: *Large Bathers*, in the National Gallery of London (1894–1905); and an even larger canvas of the same title in the Philadelphia Museum of Art (1906). Both include several of the female figures that appear in the much smaller and sketchier Chicago painting.

Although this canvas has been described as an intermediary study for the larger compositions, it is also very much an independent picture, with freer and more lighthearted brushwork that sets it apart from the laboriously worked larger versions. It shares with them the general setting and the group of females lying, bending, stooping, and standing in the foreground, but it has none of their ponderous gravitas. It is as if the artist lightly skipped his brush over the surface, patching in areas of foliage in parallel strokes and dabbing the flesh tones for the female figures, whose contours are barely indicated by the agitated, broken blue lines. Indeed, in some cases, the gender of these figures would be difficult to determine were it not for the comparison with the other larger canvases, which show the women's cascading hair and solidly defined torsos. Common to all three compositions are the lunging female at the left, two red-haired figures just right of center, who seem ready to plunge into the water, and a woman lying on her belly to the right of the center.

Only the Chicago picture, however, includes the sprawling female third from the left, who does not fit into the iconography of any of the other *Bathers* paintings. She holds herself up on her forearms in a pose recalling Édouard Manet's *Olympia* (1863; Musée d'Orsay, Paris)—the highly charged depiction of a prostitute that had already inspired earlier paintings by Cézanne. The woman's pose could also have been drawn from any number of reproductions the artist owned or drawings he had made in the Musée du Louvre, Paris, as a student. For, unlike his still lifes, portraits, and landscapes, Cézanne conceived of and created his *Bathers* from his mind and memory, treating them as pictorial symbols evoking the Old Masters he so admired, to be integrated and harmonized into the familiar landscape of Provence.

The Chicago painting, for all its compositional complexity, evokes the lightness of a watercolor, especially in the thin parallel strokes and dashes and the ample areas of white-primed canvas that Cézanne allowed to show through. Although clearly related, it is not a study for either monumental composition but rather an exploratory work, similar to Georges Seurat's small oil on panel studies (see cats. 61–62). In Cézanne's case, he was still working on the final resolution at his death, so it is in his small oil paintings and watercolors, conceived en route to the large *Bathers* canvases, that one can appreciate the artist's quest to rethink classical iconography in a modern visual idiom.

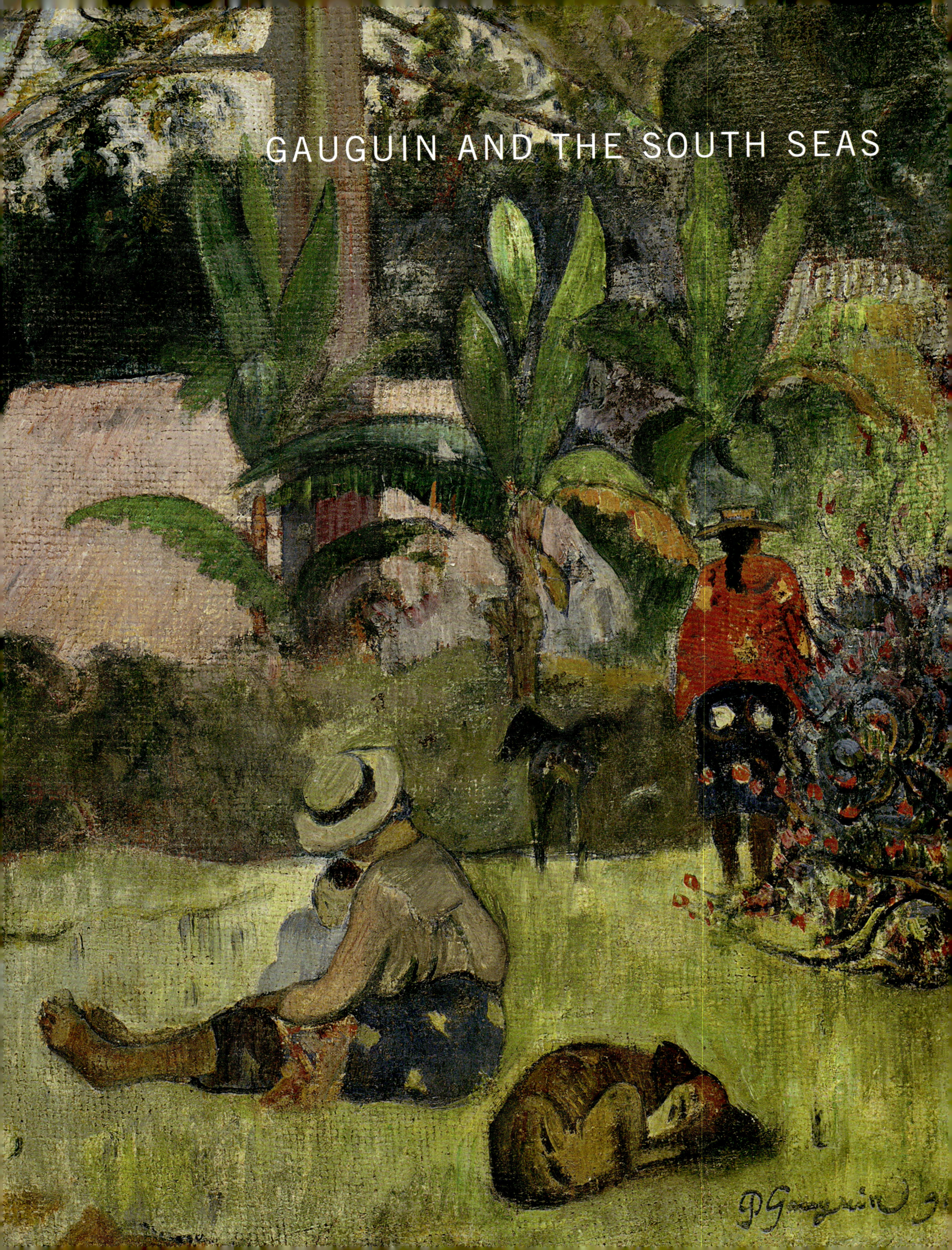
GAUGUIN AND THE SOUTH SEAS
P Gauguin 9

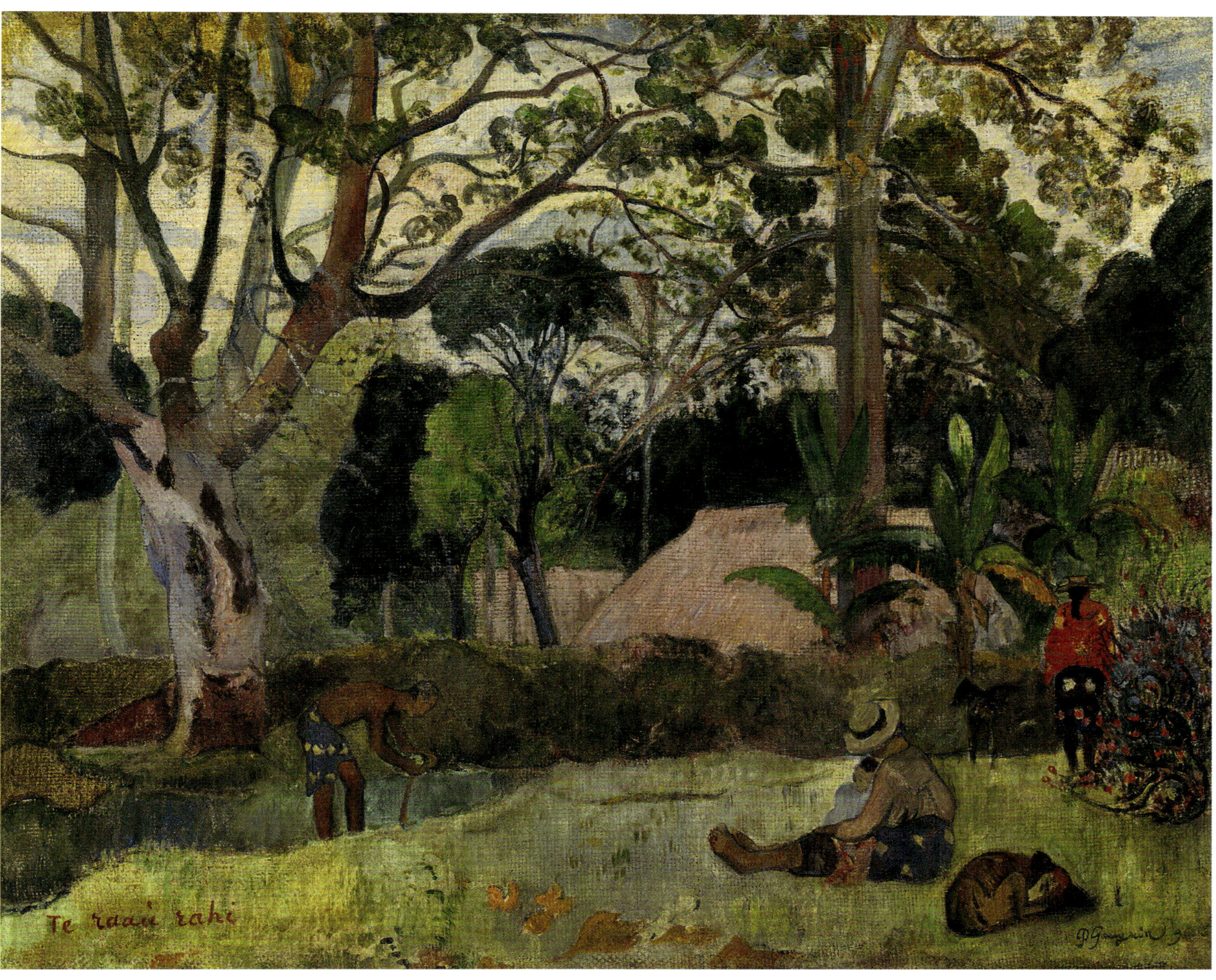

82

The Big Tree (Te raau rahi), 1891

Oil on jute; 73 x 91.5 cm (28¾ x 36 in.)
Gift of Kate L. Brewster, 1949.513
Signed lower right: *P Gauguin 91*
Inscribed lower left: *Te raaù rahi*

Paul Gauguin painted this landscape in the fall of 1891 in Tahiti, where he had arrived in June, using a coarse jute support and a range of paint applications, from thin washes of color to low impasto in the sky and foliage. The picture grew out of the artist's initial period of study of local flora and fauna, which is reflected in his drawings and echoed in his early reports home. Rather than painting, he explained, he was carrying out "a pile of research that will bear fruit, many documents that will serve me for a long time." Such research informs *The Big Tree*, which, though picturesque, reveals Gauguin's attention to local nature and practices. It features, at left, a violet-trunked *hotu* tree and, between the huts, a tall, thin mango tree and an even taller, spindly coconut (*haari*); large green leaves of banana (*tunu maia*) trees form a screen at the right, behind which rises a majestic tropical almond (*auteraa*); at the right edge, the red blossoms of a peacock-like hibiscus shrub add a note of color, and breadfruit (*uru*) leaves dot the foreground. A native man husks a coconut, and one woman looks after a child while another performs chores in the background. *Te raau rahi*, the Tahitian title that Gauguin inscribed at the lower left, means "the big tree"—the translation that the artist supplied to his wife, Mette. It also refers to the use of plants for medicinal purposes, suggesting the artist's awareness of the role of the natural setting in the Tahitian domestic narrative: how the indigenous people used the nuts and leaves of the *auteraa* tree and the pods and flowers of the *hotu* tree as remedies. Here Gauguin rendered both varieties with an exactitude that is remarkable given his parallel interest in overall decorative effect.

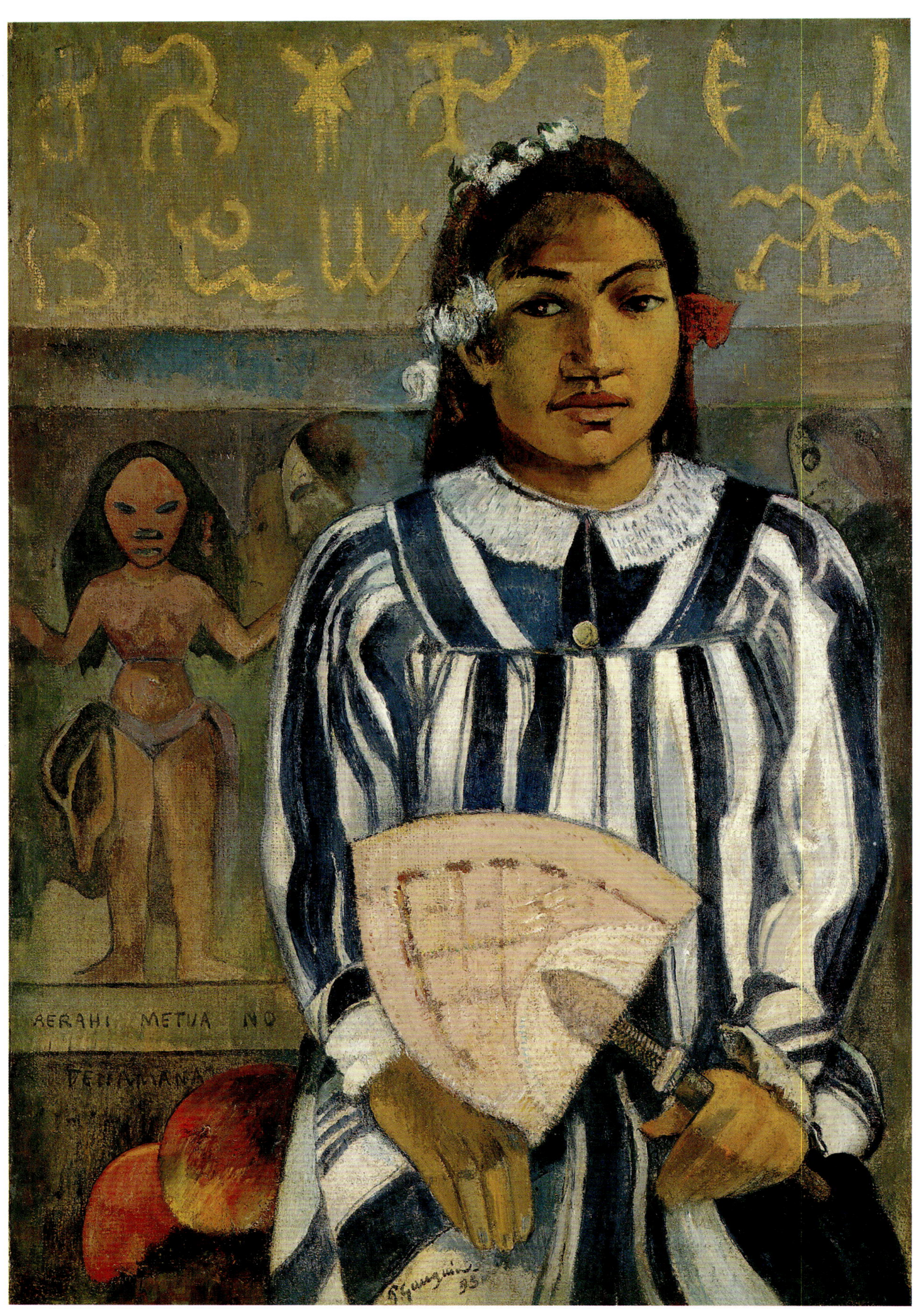
AERAHI METUA NO

83

The Ancestors of Tehamana, or *Tehamana Has Many Parents* (*Merahi metua no Tehamana*), 1893

Oil on canvas; 76.3 x 54.3 cm (30 1/16 x 21 3/8 in.)
Gift of Mr. and Mrs. Charles Deering McCormick, 1980.613
Signed lower center: *P. Gauguin. / 93*
Inscribed lower left: *MERAHI METUA NO / TEHAMANA*

Paul Gauguin painted *The Ancestors of Tehamana* during his last months in Tahiti before leaving for France in July 1893. It is a remarkable picture, at once a compendium of the artist's experiences and ideas about Tahitian culture and a portrait of the teenage girl he claimed was his link to it. He felt he needed one, for upon arrival in Papeete, Tahiti, in 1891, he had immediately recognized that it was too late to fulfill his fantasy to "immerse myself in virgin nature, see no one but savages, live their life": colonization was rendering Tahiti "completely French," and missionaries had imported "much hypocrisy and are sweeping away part of the poetry," including knowledge of the island's culture and the artifacts reflecting it. The artist sought to achieve cultural immersion through relationships with native women. Having broken with his first companion because she was "glossy from contact with Europeans," Gauguin met a young woman who fulfilled his expectations of the country's "female type." He would identify her as Tehamana in the first draft of *Noa noa*, the pseudo-memoir of his Tahitian experience, which describes his spiritual and artistic rejuvenation through contact with the primitive "other." (In the second draft, he changed her name to Tehura.)

In this painting, Tehamana wears the prim, high-collared, Mother Hubbard–style dress imposed on native women by missionaries for the sake of propriety. Despite her body covering and her poised comportment, Tehamana's sexual availability is suggested by the flowers in her hair: the red blossom over her ear and the fragrant white frangipani. She holds an antique plaited fan, a symbol of superior social rank that, together with the calm dignity of her face, recalls Gauguin's observation in *Noa noa* that the features of Tahitian women are "cast . . . for wearing dignity. Ancient memories of great chieftains (a race that has had such a feudal past)."

The Tahitian title that Gauguin inscribed on the canvas has recently been translated as *Tehamana Has Many Parents* and can be understood in terms of the Tahitian custom of sharing children between real and foster parents. However, the French title that Gauguin assigned the work in the catalogue accompanying his one-man show at the Durand-Ruel Gallery in 1893—*Les Aïeux de Tehamana* (*The Ancestors of Tehamana*)—stresses the sitter's larger cultural legacy and the belief that Tahitians descended from the union of the ancient deities Ta'aroa and Hina. This link to the past informs the background of the painting, which is made up of three horizontal zones alluding to the physical, spiritual, and intellectual realms.

In the absence of archeological evidence of Tahiti's past, Gauguin drew upon books, especially Jacques-Antoine Moerenhout's two-volume *Travels to the Islands of the Pacific Ocean* (1837), as well as non-Tahitian visual sources, to invent "ancestors" for Tehamana. At the lower left, two ripe mangoes symbolize the abundance of the land and perhaps also the fertility and sensuality of Tahitian women (Tehamana became pregnant with Gauguin's child at around this time). In the middle range, the artist depicted figures from Polynesian mythology: most prominent is the goddess Hina, who represents the female principle that so fascinated the artist and assumes a posture drawn from photographs of Hindu sculpture. Tehamana's connection to Hina is suggested by the red flower in the idol's hair. Above, the yellow glyphs surrounding Tehamana's head derive from ancient *rongorongo* tablets, or "talking boards," found on Easter Island, which Gauguin may have seen both at the 1889 Exposition Universelle in Paris and in a collection in Papeete. In short, the picture is less the portrait of a particular individual than a representation of Gauguin's Tahitian experience.

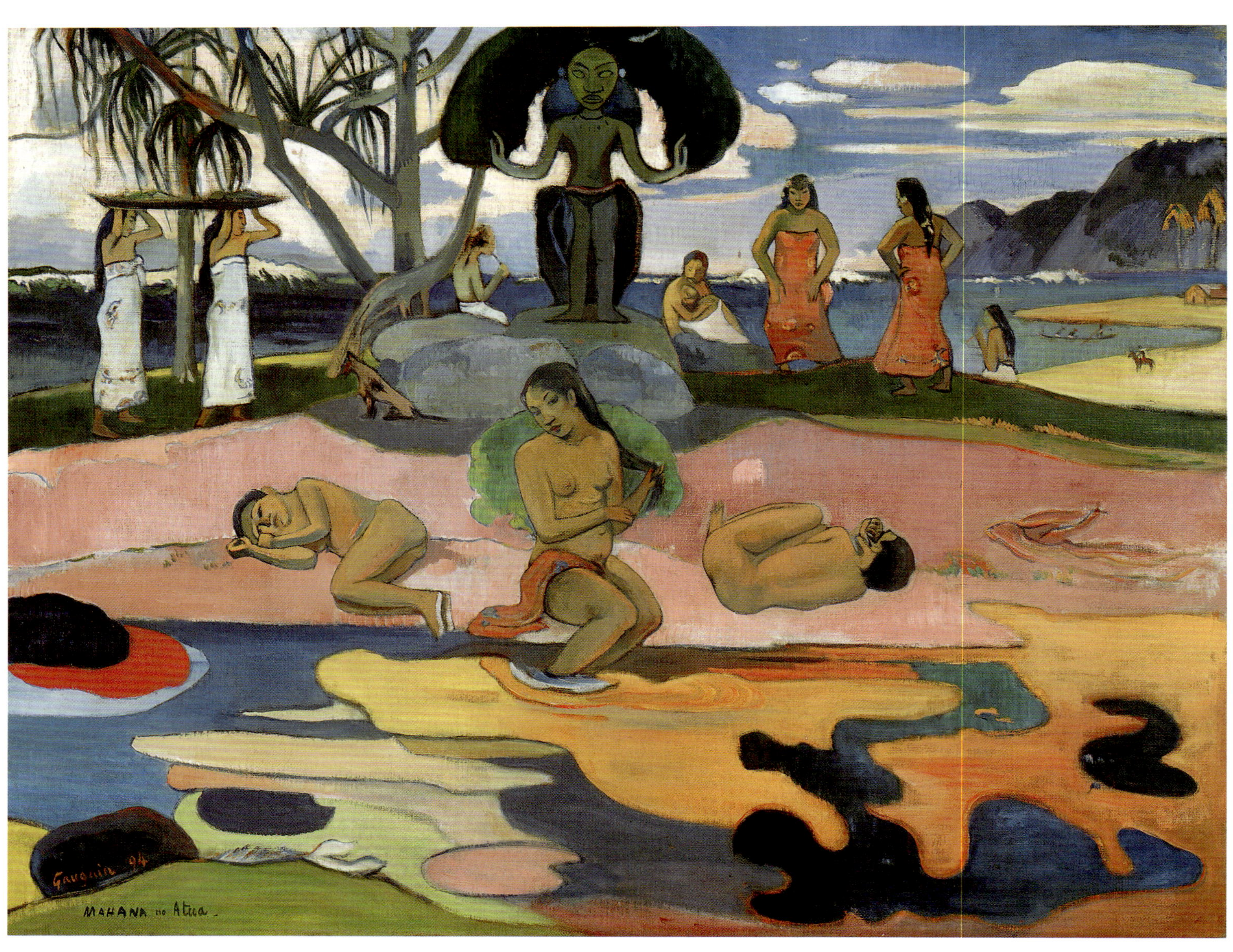
Gauguin 94
MAHANA no Atua

84

Day of the God (Mahana no Atua), 1894

Oil on canvas; 68.3 x 91.5 cm (26 7/8 x 36 in.)
Helen Birch Bartlett Memorial Collection, 1926.198
Signed lower left: *Gauguin 94*
Inscribed lower left: *MAHANA no Atua.*

Day of the God is one of a small number of canvases featuring Tahitian subjects that Paul Gauguin painted after returning to France in late August 1893 and before setting sail again for the South Pacific in July 1895. He devoted most of his energy over these months to making works on paper, including drawings and woodcuts designed to be part of the eventual publication of *Noa noa*, the first draft of which he began in October 1893. Painted the following year, *Day of the God* can be regarded as a parallel endeavor to synthesize his Tahitian experience. This literally brilliant fabrication, pieced together using motifs from books on the South Pacific, photographs, and his own current graphic work, exceeds, in terms of its mythic ambition, anything the artist had attempted in Tahiti.

Monumental in effect, though not large in scale, *Day of the God* is a lush evocation of a Tahitian golden age, a South Pacific equivalent of the decorative, nostalgic reveries of the classical Western past realized by the muralist Pierre Puvis de Chavannes, whom Gauguin greatly admired. Gauguin concentrated his imagery within a formally and thematically complex composition organized on three horizontal levels. At the top, the scene is dominated by a large idol of Hina, similar to that seen in *Tehamana* (cat. 83) but now embellished with a fan-shaped, featherlike decoration. To the left of Hina, under a pandanus tree, two figures in white bear a large platter with food or offerings to her on their heads, while a seated figure plays the flute. To the right of the goddess, a seated couple makes love, and two figures in red dance the *upaupa*, the sexually suggestive ancient Tahitian dance whose performance missionaries and colonial authorities had tried to suppress. In the distance, beyond a second flutist, is a stretch of beach, its sole occupant a figure on horseback who may be observing the native canoe near the shore. In a middle ground of pink sand, sitting at the god's feet, is a female bather, flanked by two ambiguously gendered figures lying on their sides, one facing front, the other back. Although the arrangement of these figures seems symbolic—perhaps of birth, life, and death—their meaning is by no means clear. The trajectory toward mystery continues in the canvas's lower third, which features a pool of water whose surface movements and reflections Gauguin presented as an abstract pattern of interlocking zones of color, a resplendent demonstration of the theories relating to color, pattern, and subjectivity that he had formulated over the preceding decade.

Day of the God is stylized in a way that distinguishes it from the paintings Gauguin produced in Tahiti, which are ultimately rooted in their setting and thus display a degree of naturalism here vacated for maximum decorative effect. He evidently showed the painting in the weeklong exhibition including recent works that he held in his Paris studio on the rue Vercingétorix in early December 1894. Edgar Degas, whose art Gauguin revered, visited the studio and purchased the picture.

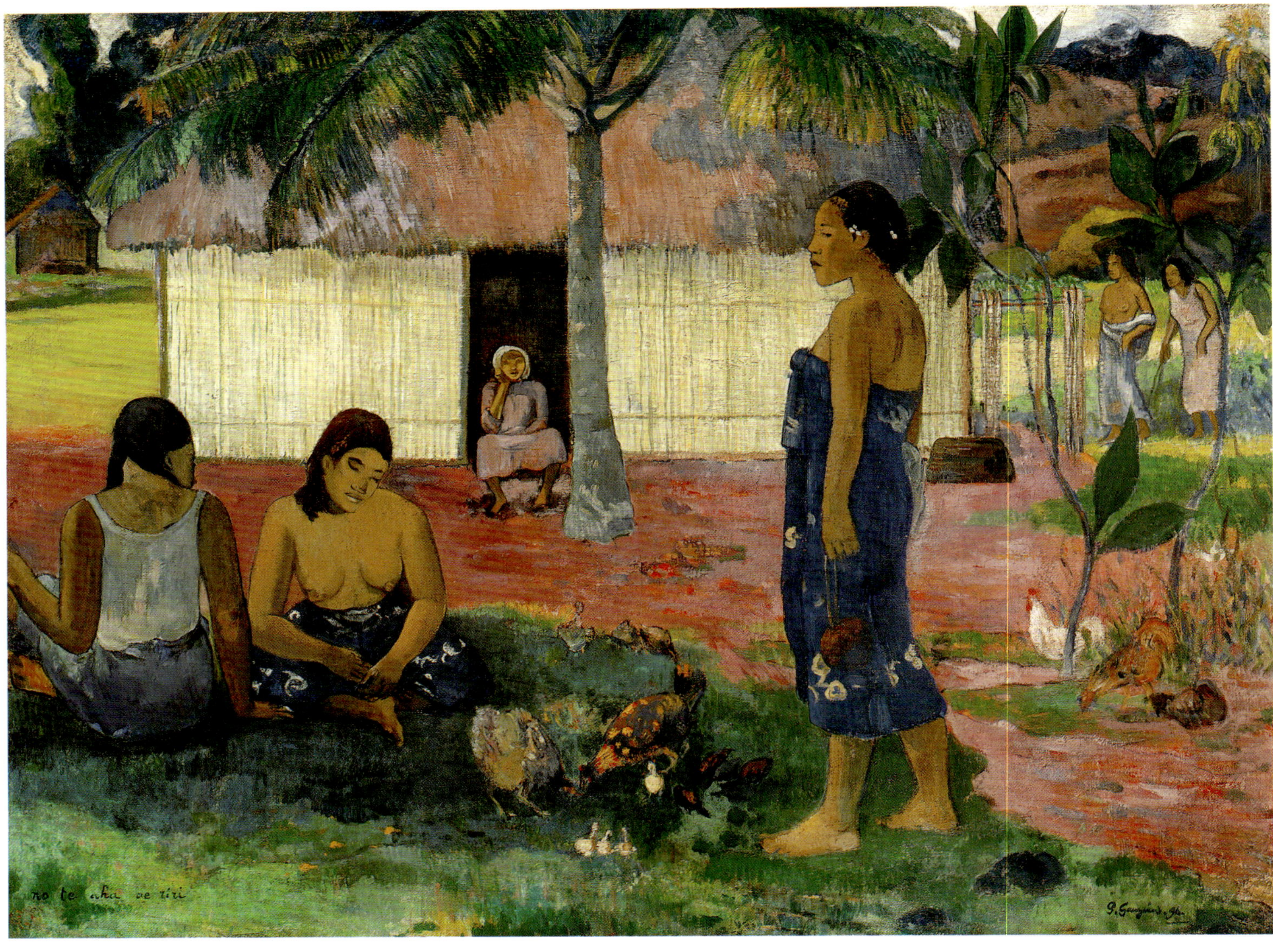

85

Why Are You Angry? (No te aha oe riri), 1896

Oil on canvas; 95.3 x 130.6 cm (37 ½ x 51 ⅜ in.)
Mr. and Mrs. Martin A. Ryerson Collection, 1933.1119
Signed lower right: *P. Gauguin. 96.*
Inscribed lower left: *no te aha oe riri*

Returning to Tahiti in the fall of 1895, Paul Gauguin was soon beset by physical ailments and financial difficulties. Despite this, between 1896 and 1897, he realized a group of impressive canvases in a notably larger format than he customarily employed. *Why Are You Angry?* is unique among these works because it was closely based on an earlier Tahitian composition—a picture to which the artist assigned the same title as a contemporary Art Institute landscape (cat. 82): *Te raau rahi (The Big Tree)* (1891; Cleveland Museum of Art). Although elements of the two related compositions—the landscape with the hut and the three main figures—are similar, the pictures exhibit significant differences that allow us to consider Gauguin's changing priorities. The earlier composition, like the Art Institute's work of the same title, reflects the artist's interest in capturing specific details of the island and its people as they go about their daily activities. In *Why Are You Angry?*, he reduced the landscape's prominence and complexity, establishing a symmetrical composition with a palm tree in the center. The principal figures are larger and are disengaged from one another, their postures and characters more difficult to interpret. The interrogative title encourages us to seek some sort of narrative, but the imagery resists a definitive reading.

As scholars have observed, the imposing, stilled figure of the standing woman at the right of the painting has an affinity with the promenading Parisienne who occupies an analogous position in Georges Seurat's magisterial *A Sunday on La Grande Jatte—1884* (cat. 63). This canvas had dominated the final Impressionist exhibition (May 1886), in which Gauguin participated with little critical or financial reward. His ambition to create a work that rivaled *La Grande Jatte* would culminate in his own monumental masterpiece *Where Do We Come From? What Are We? Where Are We Going?* (1897–98; Museum of Fine Arts, Boston).

86

Polynesian Woman and Children, 1901

Oil on canvas; 97.1 x 74.2 cm (38 ¼ x 29 ¼ in.)
Helen Birch Bartlett Memorial Collection, 1927.460
Signed upper left: *Paul Gauguin / 1901*

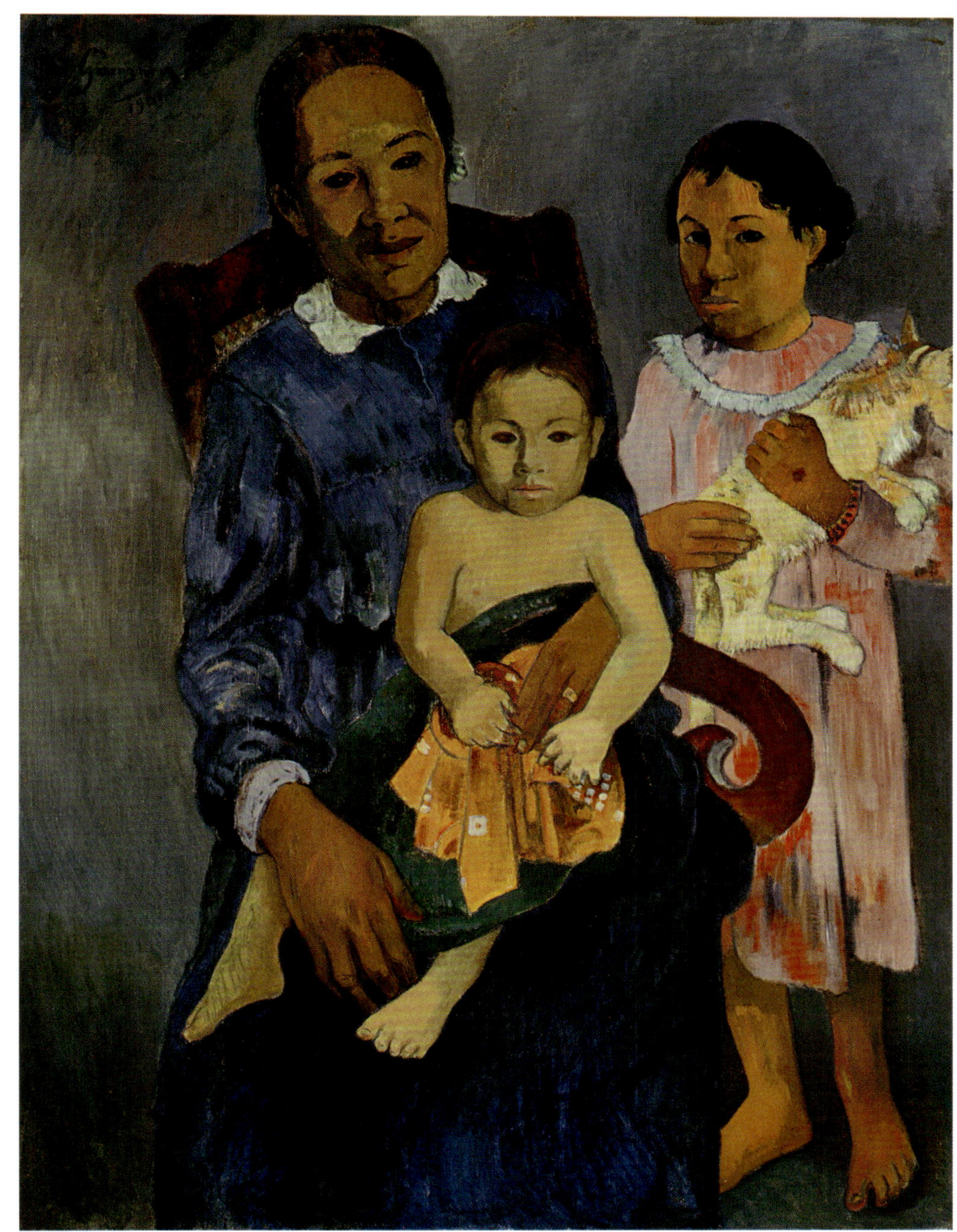

Throughout his career, Paul Gauguin occasionally painted portraits, and not long before realizing this canvas, he created an image of two Tahitian women against a landscape background in which the quality of portraiture is emphatic (*Two Tahitian Women*, 1899; Metropolitan Museum of Art, New York). In *Polynesian Woman and Children*, the neutral background compounds this quality, but while the canvas is generic in format, it is inscrutable in content. We do not know exactly when in 1901 this painting was made or whom it depicts: scholars have suggested that the boy may be Gauguin's son—born to his current Tahitian lover, Pahura, in March 1899 and named Emil after his eldest legitimate child—and that the older woman is this boy's grandmother.

The composition recalls a pervasive Christian prototype: the Madonna with the Christ Child and young Saint John the Baptist. Here, however, the older child is clearly a girl; she looks warily at the viewer and holds a startlingly yellow cat. Five years earlier, the artist had fashioned a Tahitian nativity that he titled *The Child of God* (*Te tamari no atua*) (Bayerische Staatsgemäldesammlungen, Neue Pinakothek, Munich); it has been interpreted with reference to the birth of an earlier child by Pahura who died in infancy. The Chicago picture may be that which Gauguin's dealer, Ambroise Vollard, exhibited in 1910 as *The Family*. In any event, the artist's Tahitian family would suffer the same fate as its European counterpart: in September 1901, Gauguin abandoned Tahiti for the remote islands of the Marquesas, where he would live out his final years.

Remarkable in this canvas is the artist's interest in the play of complementary colors—orange and blue, red and green, yellow and violet—which speaks to his admiration for the work of the French Romantic painter Eugène Delacroix.

Late Monet: The Series Paintings

GIVERNY

OUTSIDE FRANCE

WATER LILIES

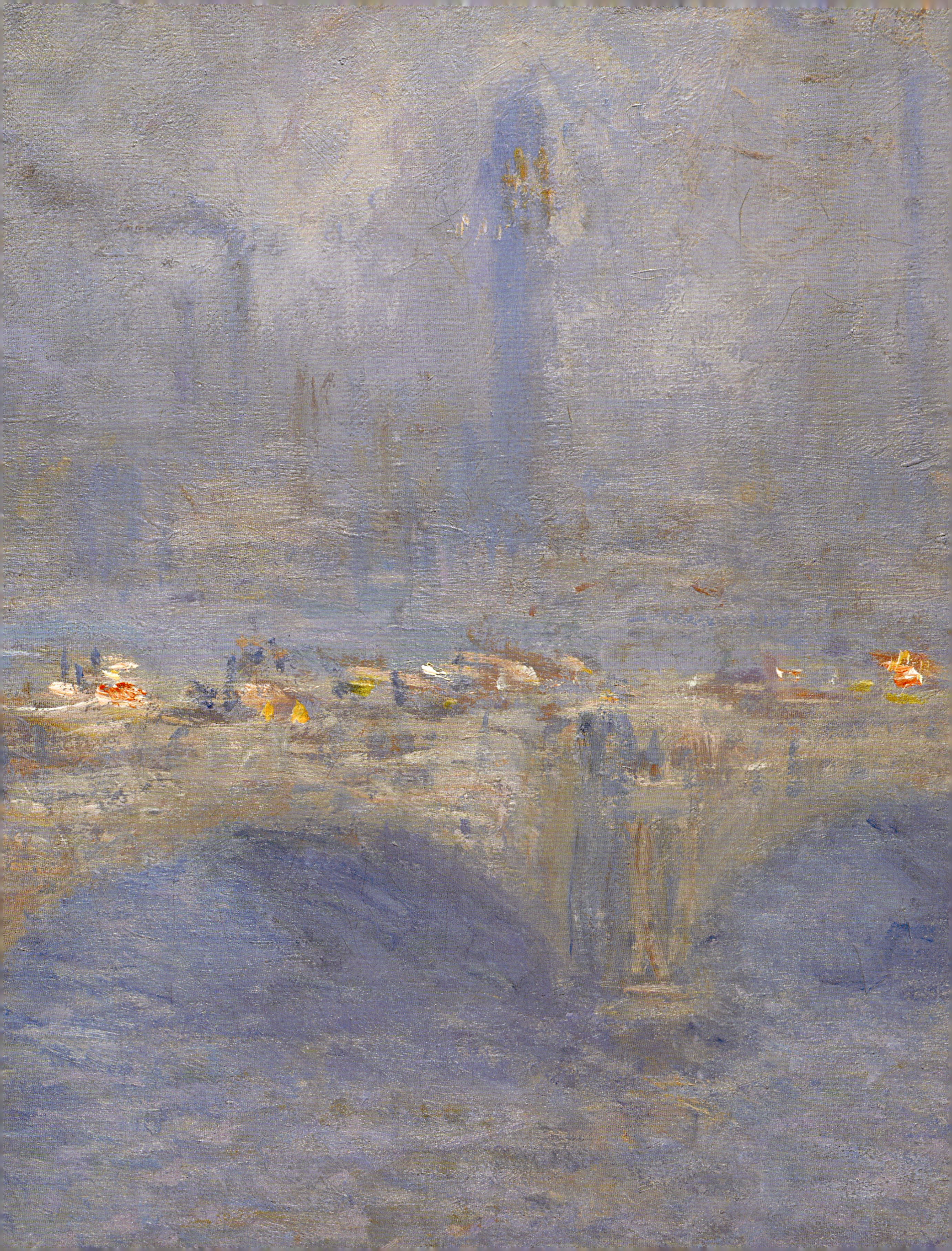

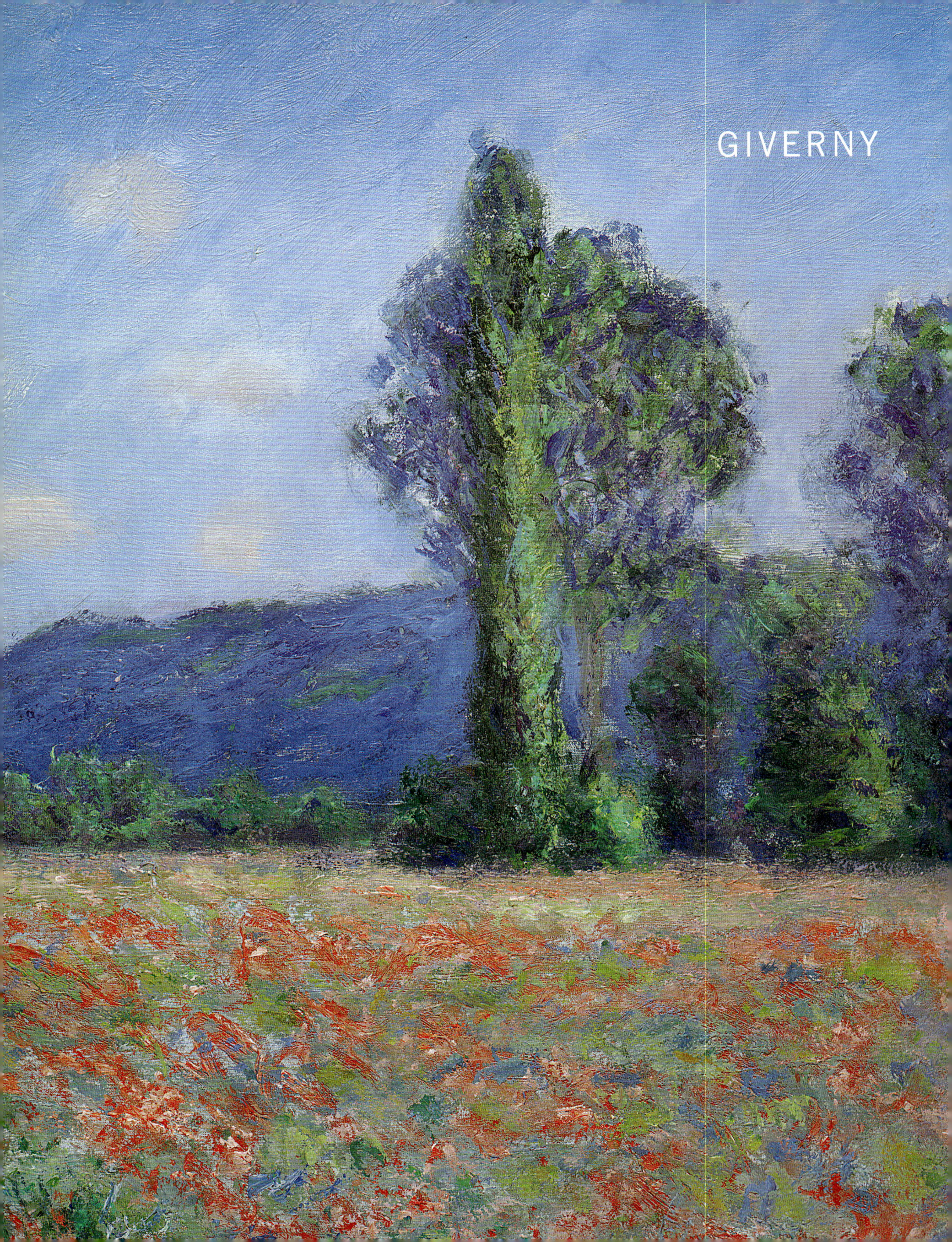

GIVERNY

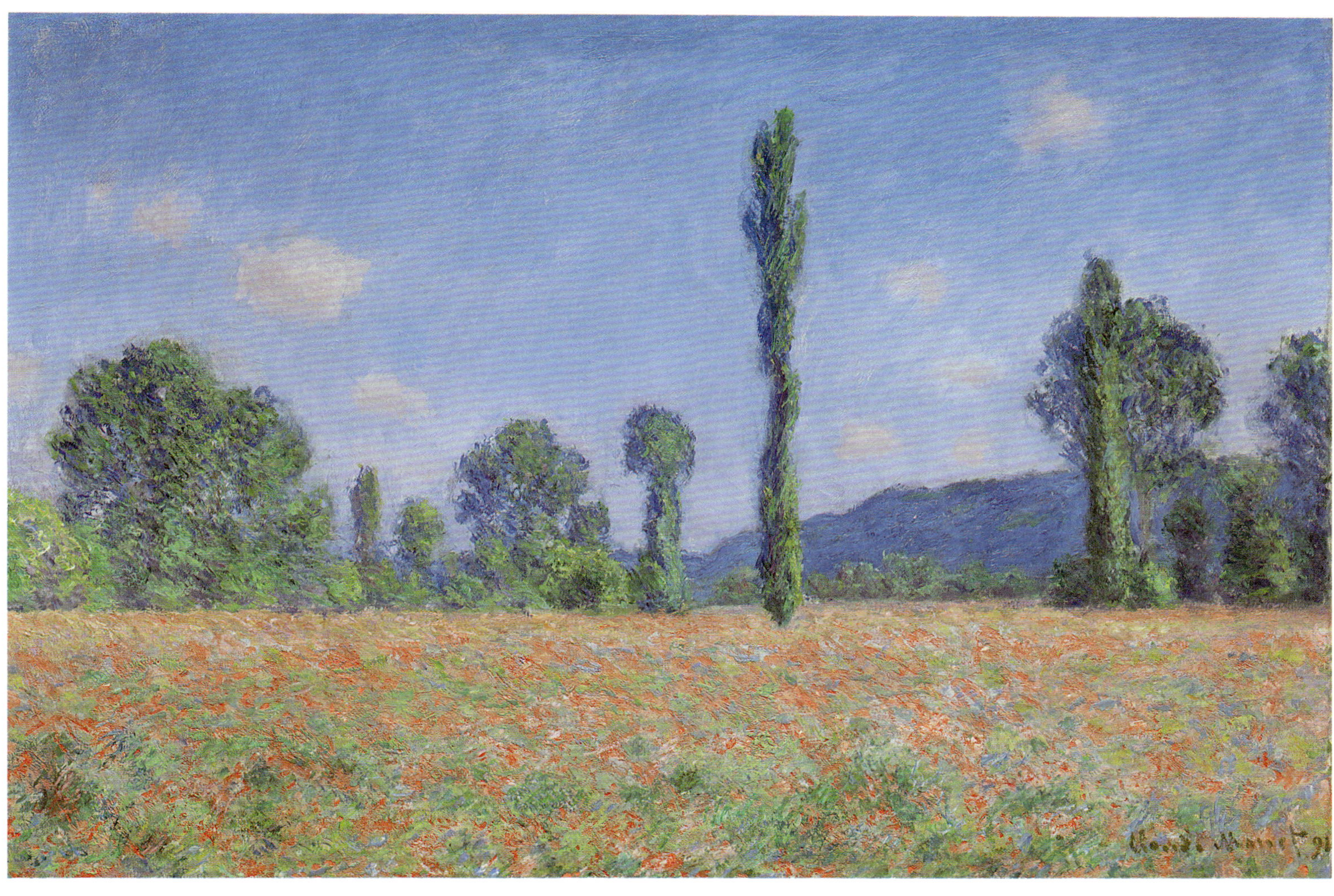

87

Poppy Field (Giverny), 1890–91

Oil on canvas; 61.2 x 93.1 cm (24 1/16 x 36 5/8 in.)
Mr. and Mrs. W. W. Kimball Collection, 1922.4465
Signed lower right: *Claude Monet 91*

In 1887 Claude Monet began painting subjects that were visible from his backyard in Giverny. These included a few stacks of wheat (1888–89), a pond (1887–89), and poppy fields, which he depicted in four almost identically scaled canvases undertaken in July 1890. Although they are compositionally and chromatically similar, the artist did not consider the poppy-field pictures serial works in the same way as the twenty-five paintings of stacks of wheat that he began shortly after the harvest that same summer. What this miniseries did reveal, however, was his growing interest in expressing nature using relatively homogenous touches and developing several canvases at once. Monet's future biographer, the politician and journalist Georges Clemenceau, who visited the artist while he was at work on these canvases, believed that they constituted "a new way of seeing, of feeling, of expression—a revolution."

Monet was now not just painting variants of a subject but rather the same motif from the same viewpoint, its differences nuanced only by changes in light. Here the varied light effects color the poppies orange, orange-yellow, and fiery red, contrasting them with the green trees fringing the horizon and the blue hills at the right. Conceived to translate a particular temporal condition, this painting bears little resemblance to Monet's sketchlike and more freely brushed landscapes of the 1870s. Instead, the surface has a tapestry-like materiality that recalls Georges Seurat's use of divided color in his canvases from the mid-1880s (see cats. 61–63). *Poppy Field*'s dense and reworked surface, along with the fact that the artist dated it 1891, suggests a long gestation period. This is typical of his later major series, in which he explored the possibilities of painting a simple motif from the same viewpoint with varying degrees of surface complexity.

88

Stacks of Wheat (End of Summer), 1890/91

Oil on canvas; 60 x 100 cm (23 5/8 x 39 3/8 in.)
Gift of Arthur M. Wood, Sr., in memory of Pauline Palmer Wood, 1985.1103
Signed lower left: *Claude Monet 91*

89

Stacks of Wheat (End of Day, Autumn), 1890/91

Oil on canvas; 65.8 x 101 cm (27 7/8 x 39 3/4 in.)
Mr. and Mrs. Lewis Larned Coburn Memorial Collection, 1933.444
Signed lower left: *Claude Monet 91*

90

Stacks of Wheat (Sunset, Snow Effect), 1890/91

Oil on canvas; 65.3 x 100.4 cm (25 11/16 x 39 1/2 in.)
Potter Palmer Collection, 1922.431
Signed lower right: *Claude Monet 91*

91

Stack of Wheat (Snow Effect, Overcast Day), 1890/91

Oil on canvas; 66 x 93 cm (26 x 36 5/8 in.)
Mr. and Mrs. Martin A. Ryerson Collection, 1933.1155
Signed lower right: *Claude Monet 91*

92

Stack of Wheat, 1890/91

Oil on canvas; 65.6 x 92 cm (25 13/16 x 36 1/4 in.)
Restricted gift of the Searle Family Trust; Major Acquisitions Centennial Endowment; through prior acquisitions of the Mr. and Mrs. Martin A. Ryerson and Potter Palmer collections; through prior bequest of Jerome Friedman, 1983.29
Signed lower left: *Claude Monet 91*

93

Stack of Wheat (Thaw, Sunset), 1890/91

Oil on canvas; 64.9 x 92.3 cm (25 9/16 x 36 3/8 in.)
Gift of Mr. and Mrs. Daniel C. Searle, 1983.166
Signed lower left: *Claude Monet 91*

Claude Monet's work on his *Poppy Field* paintings in the summer and fall of 1890 coincided with his move toward a theme that was to become a turning point in his art and the history of art in general: *les meules* (stacks). Although he had previously worked on and even exhibited groups of canvases with similar motifs, this ambitious series was an entirely new undertaking. The subject—piles of threshed wheat thirteen to sixteen feet wide with thatched crowns for protection against inclement weather—captivated the artist, who, at some point in the process, began to develop his canvases cumulatively.

Monet's shift from his efforts of the previous decade, during which he searched for increasingly exotic and challenging motifs, may have had something to do with his growing attachment to his property in Giverny, which he purchased in November 1890. But his decision to paint serially came from a need to find a method commensurate with his artistic quest. As Monet explained in a letter to Gustave Geffroy dated October 7, 1890:

> I've been really slaving away, doggedly doing a series of different effects (stacks).... I've become so slow at working that I despair, but the more I go along, the more I see that I need to work a great deal to capture what I'm trying to get across: "instantaneity," especially the envelope, the same light spreading everywhere.

Left unmentioned in this explanation was Monet's need to finish (what Geffroy called "harmonize") the works together in the studio, away from his subject.

The series format allowed the artist to resolve the paradox that the more nuances his eye perceived as he painted a moment's view, the longer it took him to complete the canvas. Monet worked without complaint on this series in the comfort of his own home, praising the "superb weather" and finishing a remarkable group of twenty-five canvases by the spring of 1891. The display of fifteen *Stacks* at Paul Durand-Ruel's gallery in Paris from May 4 until May 16, 1891, marked the first time he had publicized a predetermined series of works and shown it together in one room. Collectors flocked to the May show, but the paintings were largely bought by dealers and by the Chicagoan Bertha Honoré Palmer, who by 1892 owned at least eight *Stacks*.

It is impossible to know exactly how the works were installed in the exhibition, although the Dutch writer Willem G. C. Byvanck highlighted their sequential, temporal nature, "from the purple scarlet of summer to the chilly gray of a winter evening's dying glow." However they were installed, these pictures resonated as compelling works of art. In their very simplicity, they were recognizable yet abstract shapes filled with color, appealing forms as well as conveyers of mood. Moreover, Monet's choice of subject—monumental, dwelling-like stacks of wheat that resisted the wind, rain, and snow—held deeper significance for him. Not only did they embody the way humans work with and harness nature (something that the artist tried to evoke in earlier painting campaigns and would more fully achieve with his water-lily garden), but they were also symbols of shelter, solidity, and abundance, underscoring France's rich and enduring agrarian life. For Monet the *Stacks* were both the beginning of a new way of thinking about painting and a tribute to the region that he had adopted as his home and where he would remain for the rest of his life.

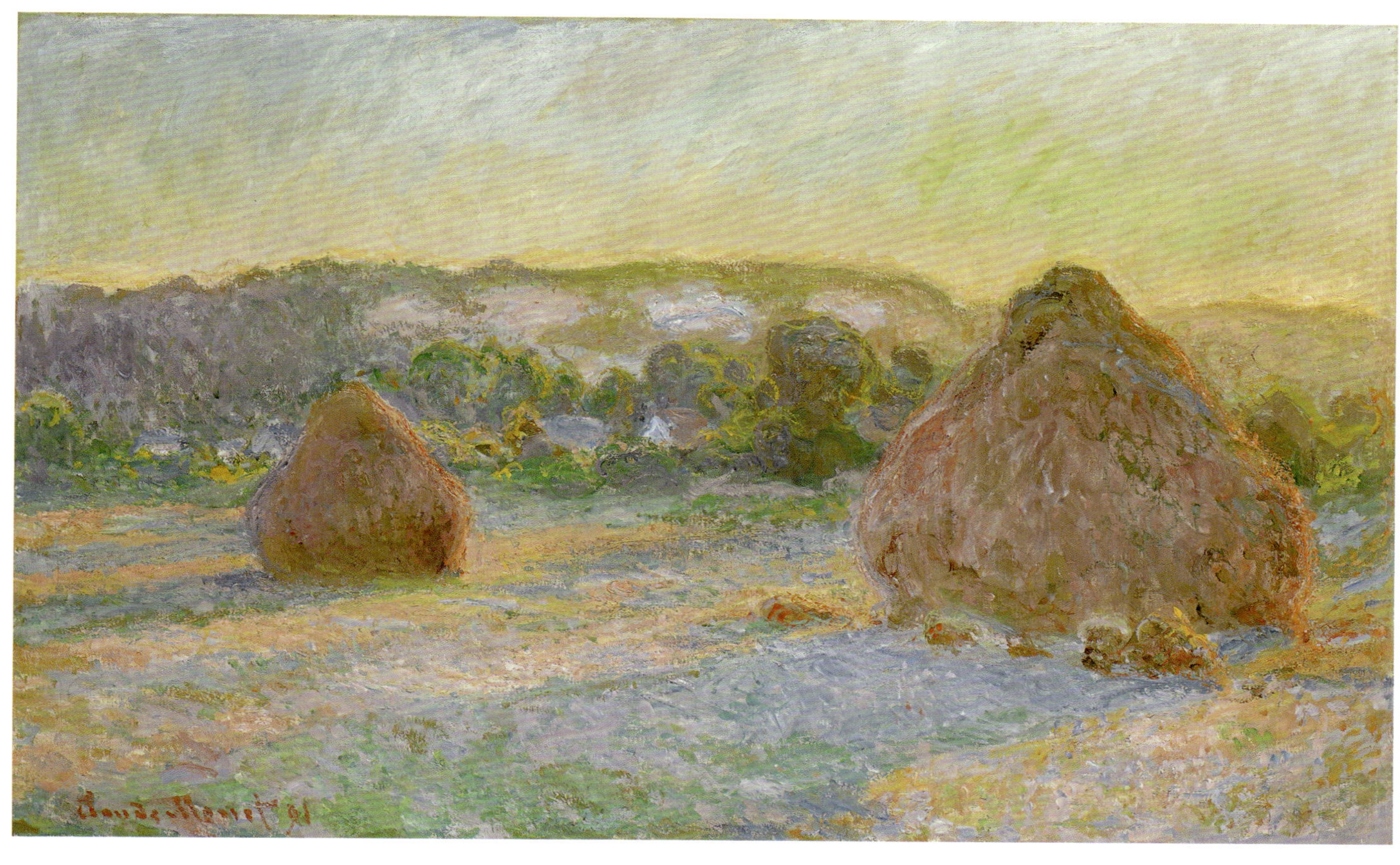

88

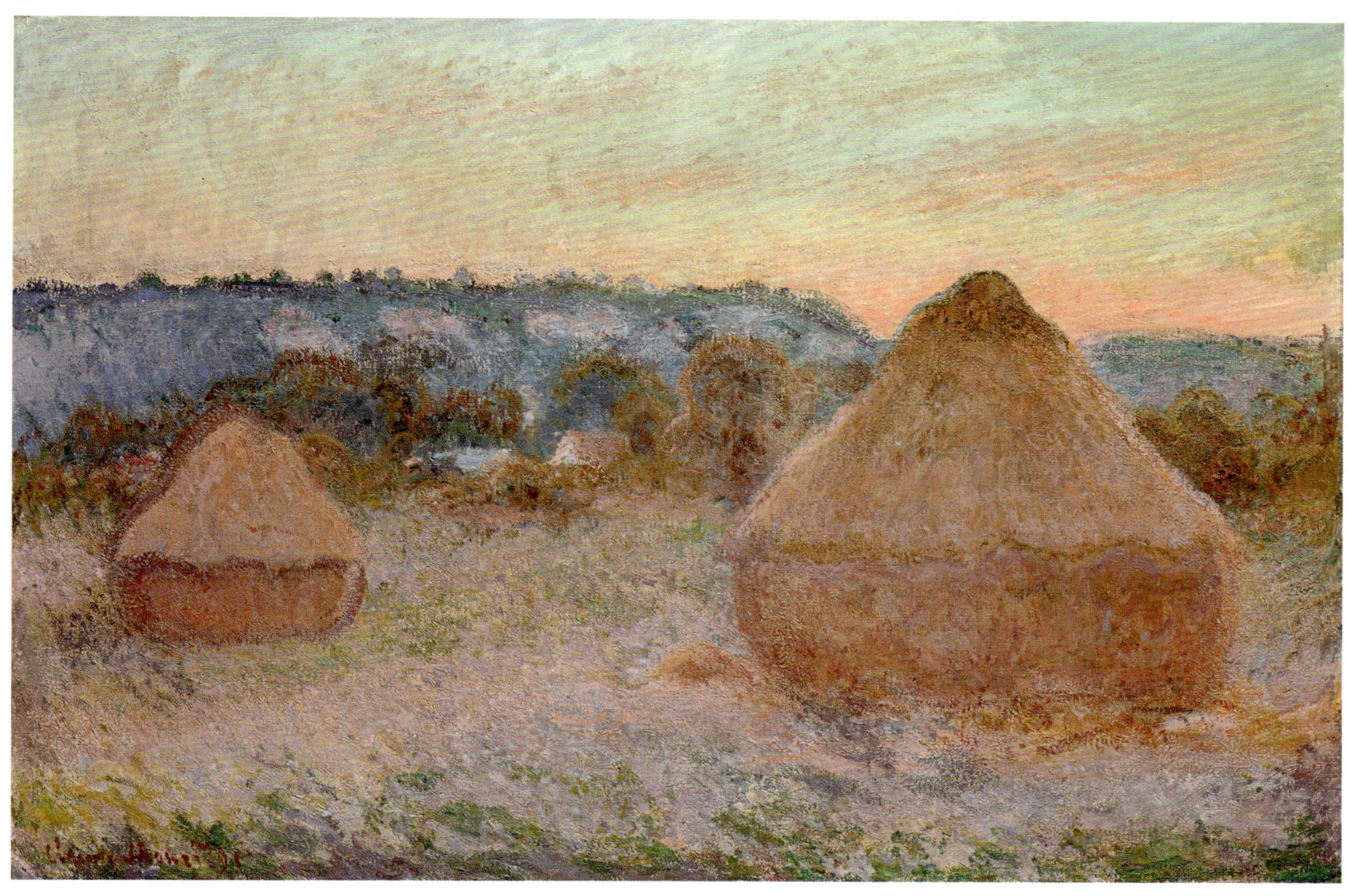

89

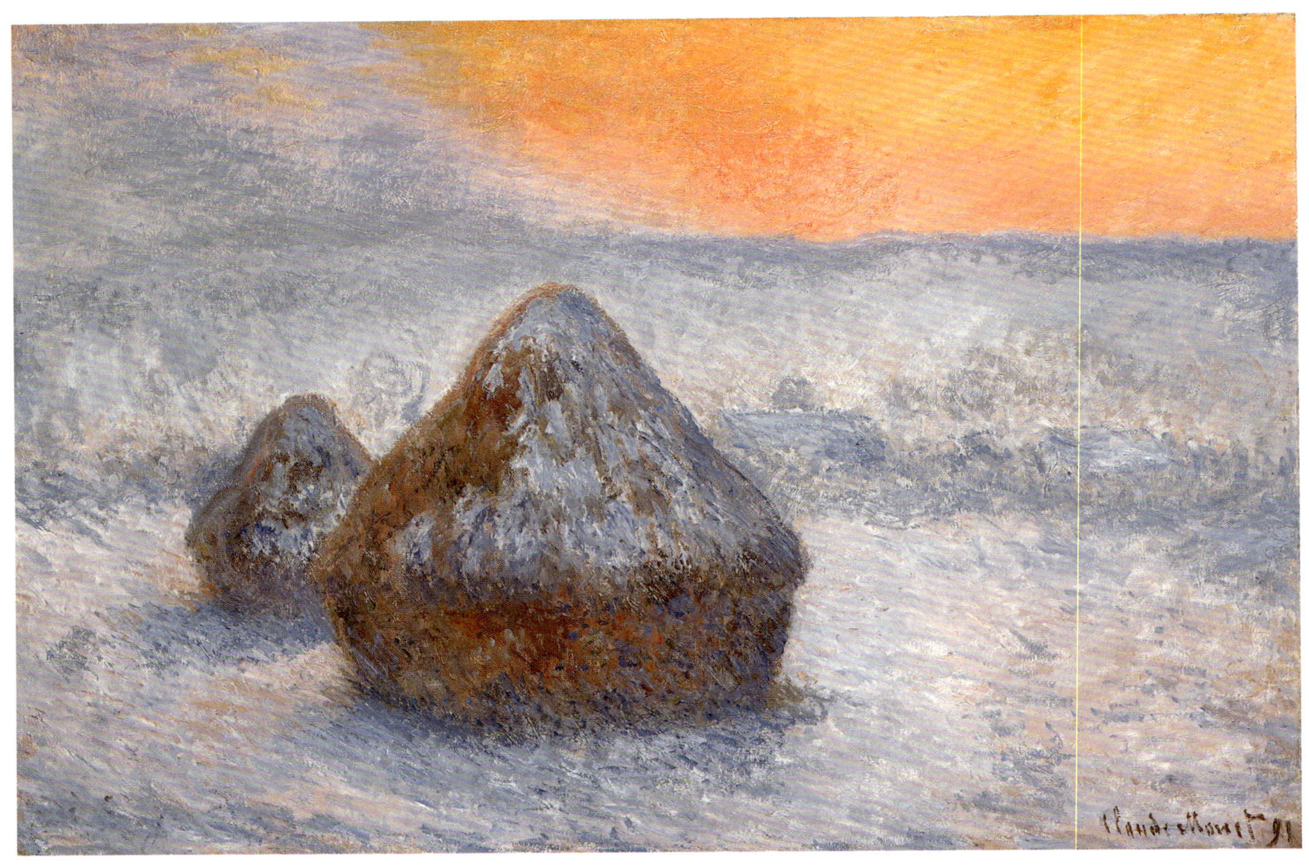

90

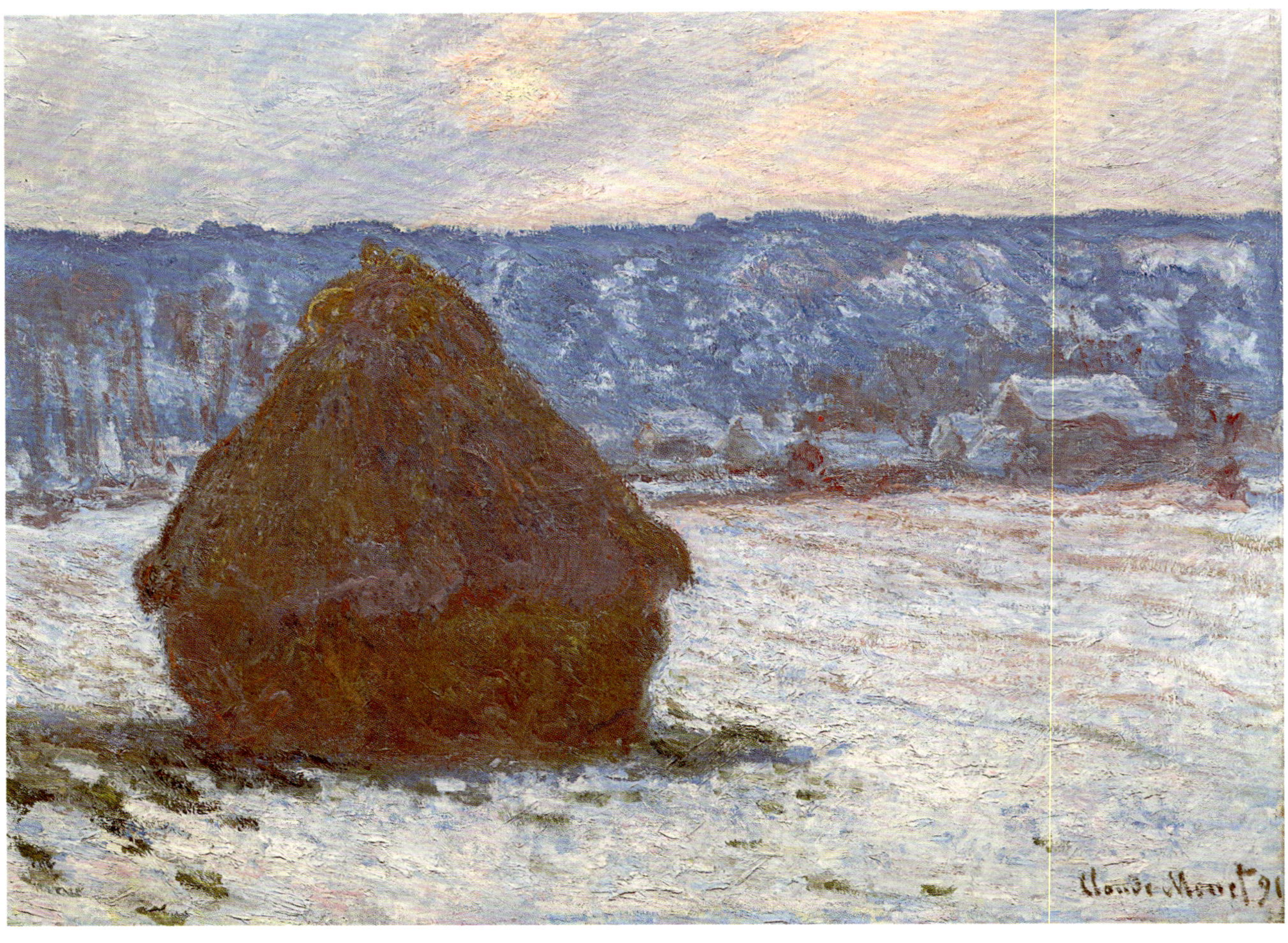

91

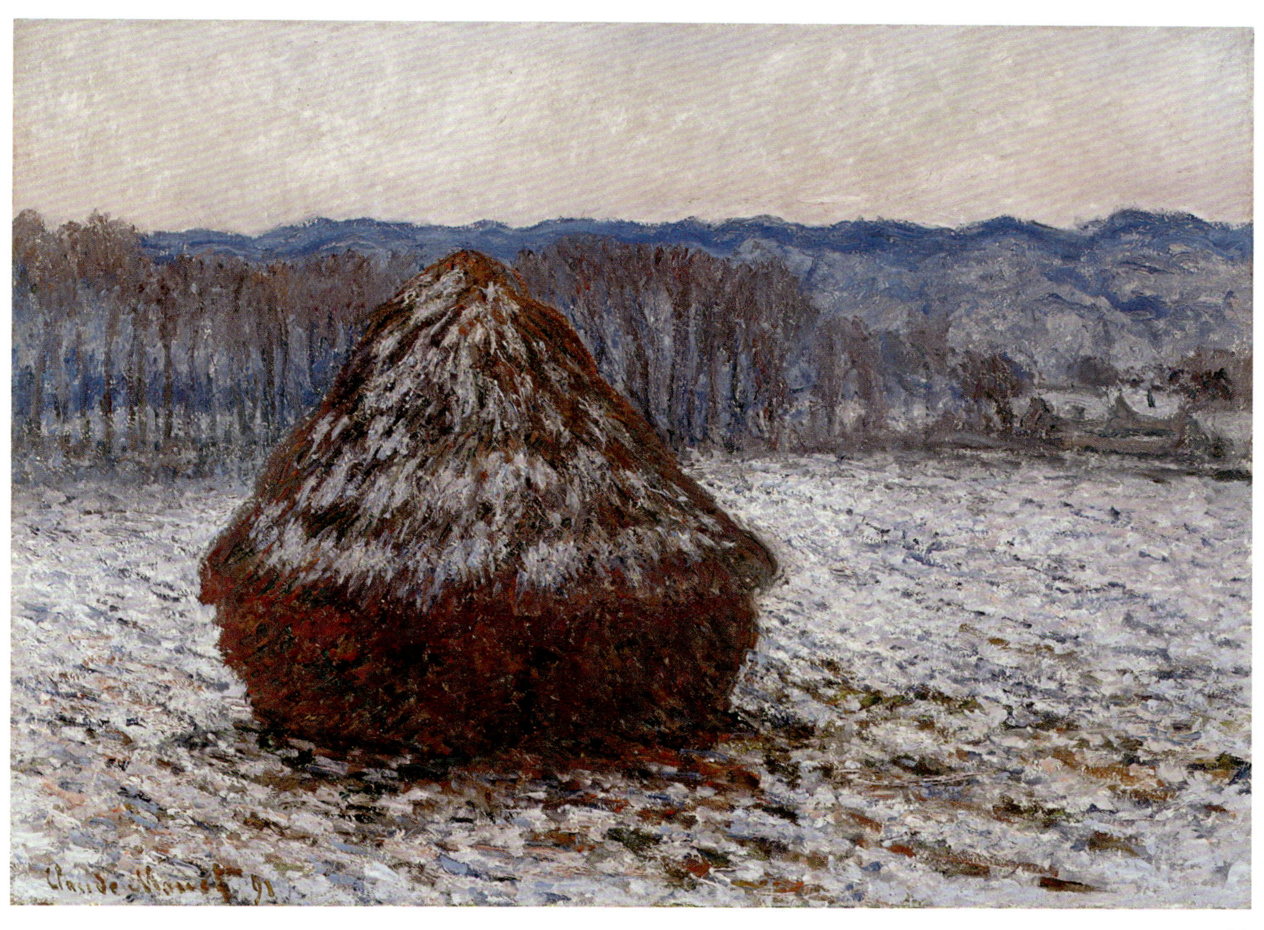

92

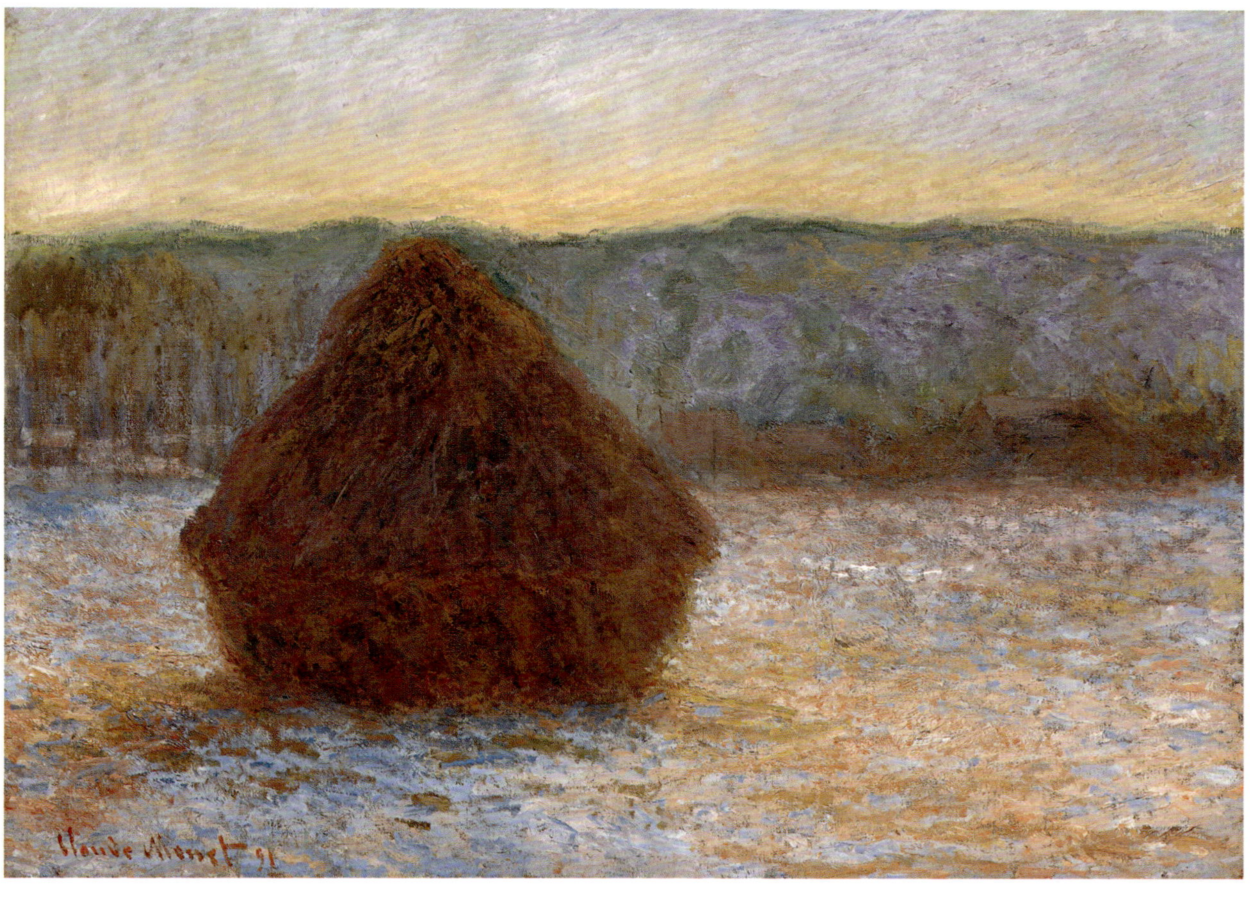

93

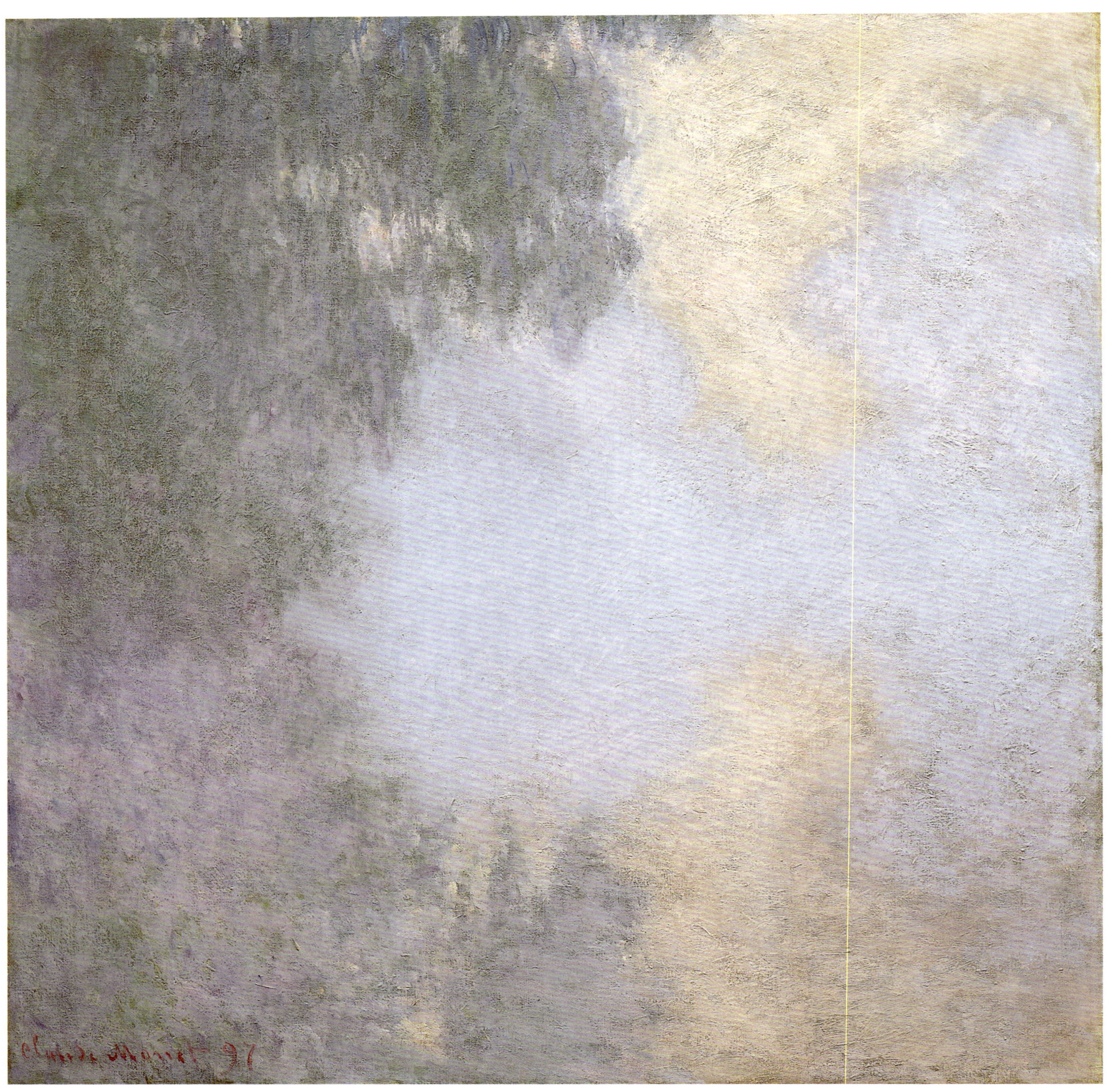
Claude Monet 97

94

Branch of the Seine near Giverny (Mist), from the series *Mornings on the Seine*, 1897

Oil on canvas; 89.9 x 92.7 cm (35 3/8 x 36 1/2 in.)
Mr. and Mrs. Martin A. Ryerson Collection, 1933.1156
Signed lower left: *Claude Monet 97*

Following the unqualified success of his *Stacks of Wheat* exhibition in 1891, Claude Monet increasingly painted series, a task that necessitated longer investments of time and money. In June 1898, at the fashionable Georges Petit Gallery, Paris, he showed the series *Rouen Cathedrals* (1893), *Cliffs at Pourville* (1896/97), *Chrysanthemums* (1897), *Cliffs near Dieppe* (1897), and eighteen canvases from his most recently completed suite, *Mornings on the Seine*. While viewers had become attuned to the inventiveness of Monet's serial canvases, they may have been surprised by the *Mornings* series. When compared to the solidity of his cathedrals and cliffs, this series—showing reflections of foliage shimmering in the absolutely still water of a riverbank overhung with trees—constituted a dramatic change in subject and technique. Instead of thickly scumbled and impastoed surfaces, the artist obtained more tonal, subtle hues by painting with smoother, integrated strokes.

Two months before the exhibition opened, the writer and journalist Maurice Guillemot published a description of his visit to the artist's flat-bottomed boat, which was anchored to the riverbank where the Epte River flows into the Seine River. There, as the light changed from dawn to day, Monet worked on fourteen stretched canvases, which were kept in grooves built into the boat and handed to him by the local gardener, whom the artist had enlisted for his painting expeditions. According to Guillemot's account, the canvases were also numbered, which would have enabled Monet to concentrate on the light effects without worrying about the specific order. Indeed, of all the series paintings, the *Mornings* were the most time specific. For the 1898 exhibition, they were undoubtedly hung in order from the least legible images of predawn fog and mist to the more comprehensible riverbank painted in near daylight. The Art Institute's canvas, one of five from the 1898 exhibition that have the word *mist* in the title, would have been hung early in the series. Not only are the outlines for foliage and horizon suggested rather than indicated, but the work is also among the most nuanced, least contrasted of the series and is equally legible upside down. This interchangeability is compounded by Monet's choice of nearly square canvases for the group, a new format normally associated with decorative paintings, and one he would use continuously in his series from the first decade of the twentieth century (see cats. 95–96 and 103–04).

Paradoxically, although the location and temporal conditions are clearly indicated in the individual titles, the works themselves appear subjectless. Not until his *Water Lilies* series would Monet again achieve the near-abstract quality of these pictures, in which evocative atmosphere and mood combine to form the all-important "envelope" containing the subject. The artist was firmly planted on the skiff, moored to a bank, but this vantage point offers the viewer no sense of grounding. Thus the *Mornings* series requires a slow, contemplative kind of looking, and the works suggest a mood of timelessness as well as reverie. Several contemporary critics pointed out this quality and compared the misty poetry of the series to the work of Camille Corot, whose landscapes combine modern Realism and Neoclassical idealism. At the same time, reviewers and artists attending Monet's 1898 exhibition compared the open-ended and subjective meaning of the *Mornings* series to the anti-naturalist aims of Symbolist art and literature. Monet, who acknowledged Corot as among the greatest landscape painters, and who also counted many friends in the Symbolists' circle, would no doubt have appreciated the perceived dual citizenship of these works—adhering to both venerable landscape traditions and avant-garde artistic ideas.

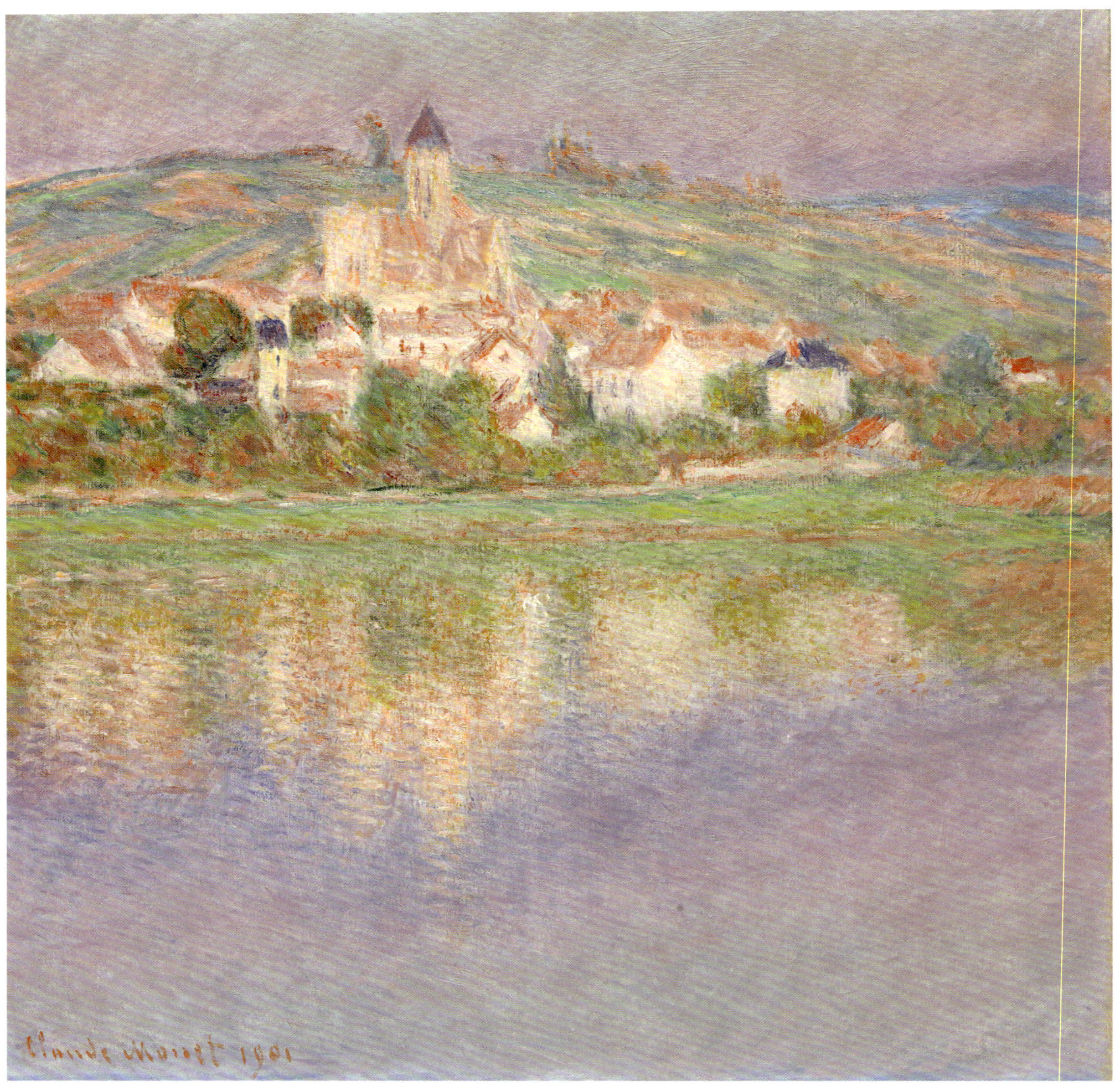

95

95

Vétheuil, 1901

Oil on canvas; 90.2 x 93.4 cm (35 ½ x 36 ¾ in.)
Mr. and Mrs. Lewis Larned Coburn Memorial Collection, 1933.447
Signed lower left: *Claude Monet 1901*

96

Vétheuil, 1901

Oil on canvas; 88.3 x 91.5 cm (34 ¾ x 36 in.)
Mr. and Mrs. Martin A. Ryerson Collection, 1933.1161
Signed lower left: *Claude Monet 1901*

Claude Monet began fifteen canvases depicting the village of Vétheuil, seven miles from his Giverny home, in July 1901. As he wrote to his dealer Paul Durand-Ruel, the heat in his studio was unbearable by July, which may have prompted him to rent a small pavilion in nearby Lavacourt with a balcony view looking directly across the Seine River to Vétheuil.

Characteristically, what began as a simple experiment became something complex and time-consuming. "I have undertaken a series of *Views of Vétheuil*," he explained to Durand-Ruel in a letter on October 19, "that I thought I would be able to finish quickly and that have taken me all summer." In depicting Vétheuil, the artist returned to the site where he had earlier painted landscapes and views of the imposing Church of Notre-Dame, as well as a portrait of Camille, his first wife, on her deathbed. Now it was as a world-famous artist that he settled across the river, furnishing the pavilion so that his wife, Alice, and his extended family could enjoy a second home. Sometimes they brought with them a rowboat, perhaps the small skiff seen in three of the Vétheuil canvases. In general, however, Monet's views of the village are uninflected by river traffic, and only the first five of the series include a clump of grass at the bottom right to help orient the composition. In contrast to his earlier representations of Vétheuil and the church, with its ornate Renaissance facade (for example,

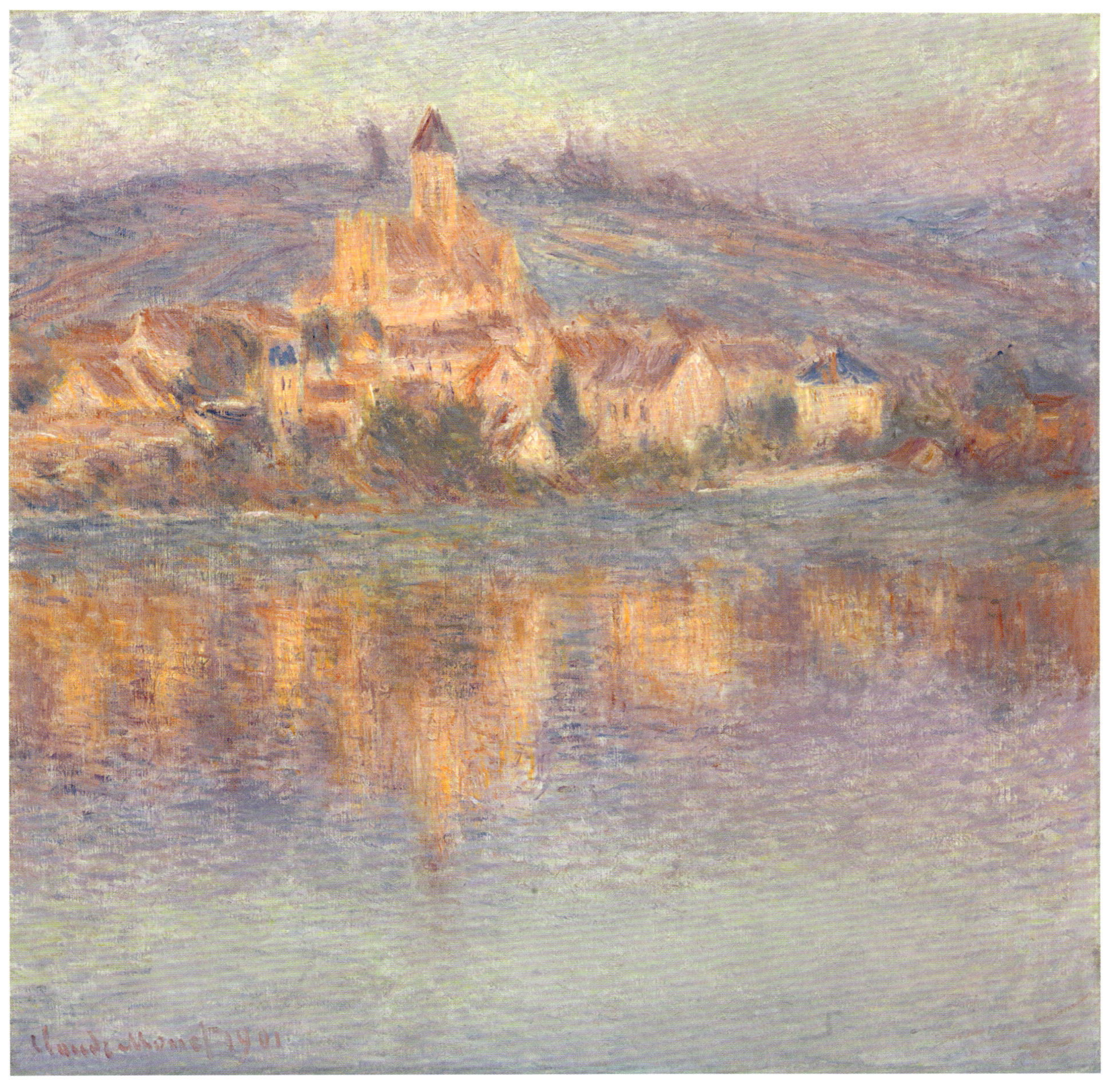

96

Vétheuil in Summer, 1879; Art Gallery of Ontario, Toronto), in his later views, decorative effects take precedence, so that the subject is really the inverted image of the village on the water. Painted on the same nearly square canvases as the *Mornings on the Seine* paintings (see cat. 94), and similarly divided horizontally, this series is nonetheless quite different. The band of landscape between village and water in the *Vétheuil* works disrupts the reflections that are so seamlessly merged with the horizon in the *Mornings* series. In contrast to the smooth, integrated brushwork of these earlier river scenes, which convey a quiet, meditative quality, the *Vétheuil* canvases sparkle and flicker with agitated and quite visible brushstrokes.

By November, Monet was still working on the *Vétheuil* series, with the promise to show it in February 1902 at an exhibition entitled *Recent Works by Camille Pissarro and a New Series by Claude Monet*, organized by the gallery owners Josse and Gaston Bernheim-Jeune. Around a dozen of the *Vétheuil* paintings were shown, including the two in the Art Institute's collection: one depicting midday (cat. 95) and the other sunset (cat. 96). When he first began thinking about the exhibition, Monet shied away from specific descriptive titles, but by February 14, 1902, a few days before the show was to open, he had changed his mind. He titled three canvases that he sent at the last minute *Misty Day*, *Autumn Afternoon*, and *At Sunset*. The last title may well refer to the painting from the Martin A. Ryerson Collection (cat. 96), which was several times exhibited and published as *Sunset*. As he had done with his *Stacks* series, Monet provided his own frames for these works—undoubtedly to emphasize the importance of the series as a decorative unit. These were quickly returned to the artist after the show, however, and the sold paintings (at least ten) were likely put into more sumptuous surrounds. Despite its public success, the *Vétheuil* series would be Monet's last engagement with French sites outside his Giverny property before his great cycle of water lilies (see cats. 103–05).

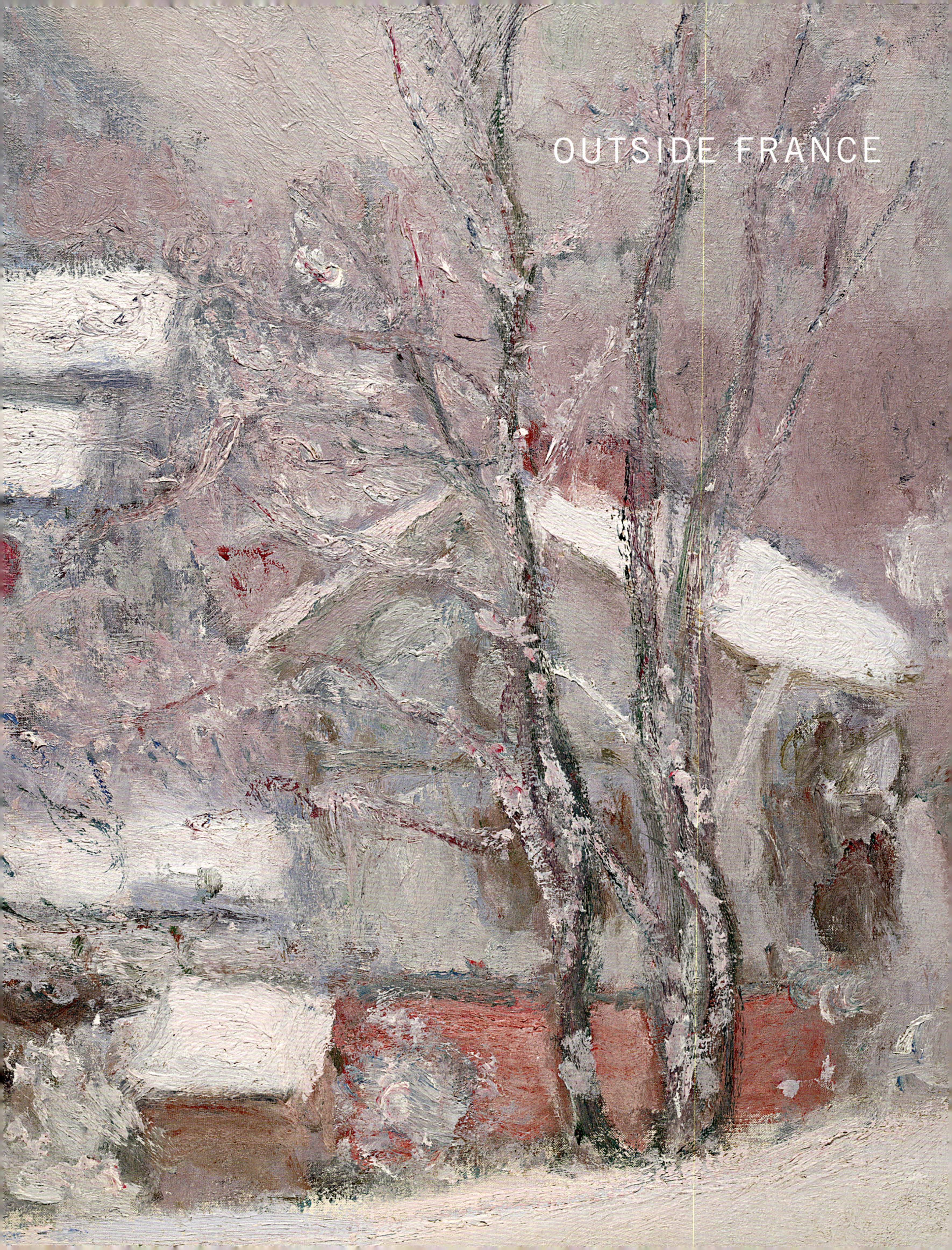

OUTSIDE FRANCE

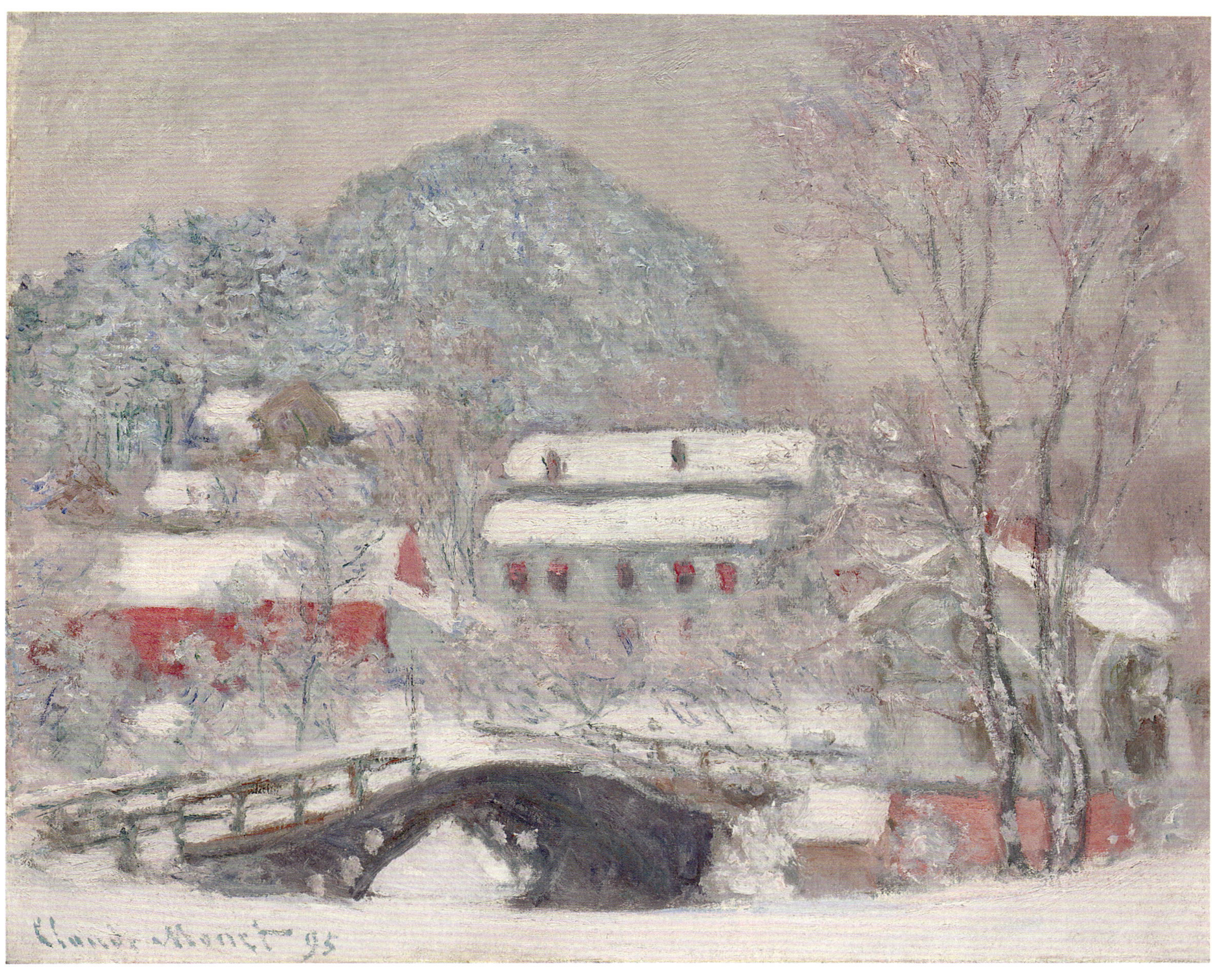

97

Sandvika, Norway, 1895

Oil on canvas; 73.4 x 92.5 cm (28 7/8 x 36 3/8 in.)
Gift of Bruce Borland, 1961.790
Signed lower left: *Claude Monet 95*

Among Claude Monet's most physically taxing and unusual painting campaigns was his trip to Norway. Over two months, he painted twenty-nine canvases, including at least six views of the village of Sandvika. With his stepson Jacques Hoschedé, who had resided in Christiania (now Oslo) since June 1894, as cicerone, Monet toured the snowbound landcapes, awe-struck and then frustrated in his struggle to find a theme amid the snow. He finally settled in Sandvika, a village less than an hour from Christiania, and painted the blue and red houses with snow-covered roofs and the iron bridge of Lokken—the latter reminiscent of the Japanese-style bridge on his property at Giverny, which he had depicted covered in snow a few weeks before departing for Norway.

The Art Institute's canvas, dominated by pinks and whites, was probably sufficiently finished before the inevitable thaw, which Monet dreaded because of how it would transform his snowy motifs. Returning to Giverny at the beginning of April, the artist bypassed his customary studio reworking and allowed eight canvases—six views of Mount Kolsaas and two of Sandvika (including this one)—to be shown a month later with scenes from Normandy and his views of Rouen Cathedral. Although Monet would insist that his Norwegian subjects were unfinished, *Sandvika* is signed, dated, and solidly painted. It is possible that he continued to work on it, but by 1899 Monet considered the painting "the best thing" he owned and donated it to an auction benefiting the family of Alfred Sisley, who had died that year. The rest of the works from this series remained with the artist: indeed, *Sandvika*, given to the Art Institute in 1961, was the first of Monet's Norwegian paintings to enter a public institution.

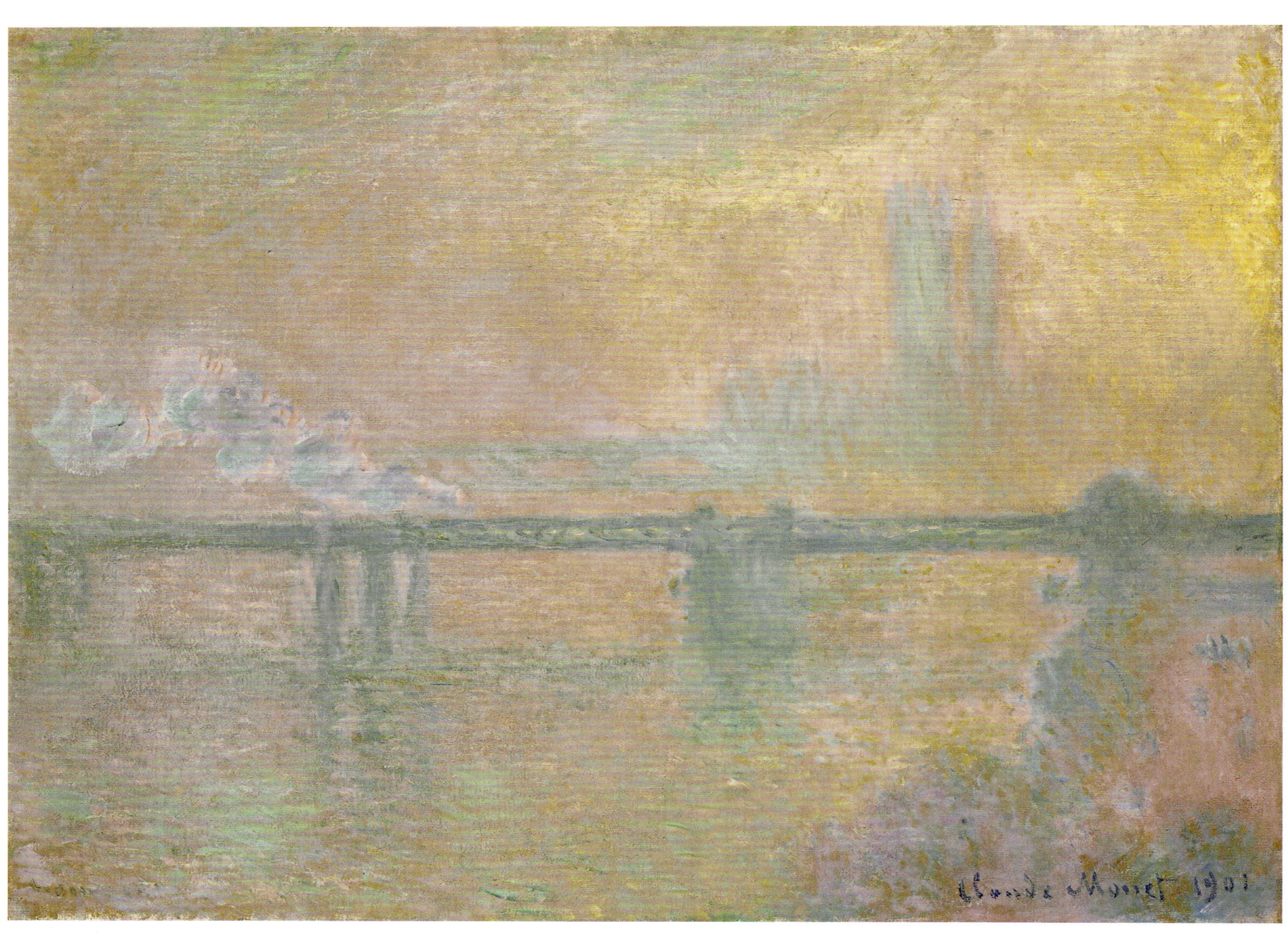
Claude Monet 1901

98

Charing Cross Bridge, London,

1901

Oil on canvas; 63.5 x 91.4 cm (25 x 36 in.)
Mr. and Mrs. Martin A. Ryerson Collection, 1933.1150
Signed lower right: *Claude Monet 1901*

Claude Monet was almost fifty-nine years old when, in September 1899, he began what was to become a group of nearly one hundred canvases of London scenes. Five years later, he allowed thirty-seven of these to be exhibited. His first stay with his wife, Alice, at the exclusive and centrally located Savoy Hotel in London in 1899 was followed by two solo trips in 1900 and 1901, made so that he could continue his depictions of the Charing Cross and Waterloo bridges, both of which he had begun painting from the balcony terrace of his room. In many ways, the London series, to which he added the *Houses of Parliament* in 1900 (see cat. 101), represents the logical development from his *Mornings on the Seine* and *Vétheuil* series (see cats. 94 and 95–96), both of which had to do with atmospheric effects playing off a large expanse of water.

With the *Vues de la Thamise à Londres* (*Views of the Thames in London*), as he titled the series in 1904, Monet challenged himself to express sunlight seen through a dense screen of mist, fog, and steam. Although he had never encountered anything similar, he would have known of Joseph Mallord William Turner's atmospheric visions of the river Thames created decades earlier. As always, the artist's initial enthusiasm turned to frustration as he struggled with elements outside of his control; he was particularly disappointed to find that on Sunday reduced trains and closed factories altered the dense atmospheric effects he sought. Of his three London subjects, Monet's starting point seems to have been the steel bridge that takes trains into the Charing Cross station. Not only are these canvases the most colorful, but they are also the most ethereal of the series, with the bridge's rectilinear skeleton creating an elegant divide—reminiscent of bridges in Japanese prints, which the artist collected—between the water and the ghostlike silhouette of the Houses of Parliament behind. In these works, Monet's approach was not to convey the feeling of immediacy that he had sought in his paintings of the Gare Saint-Lazare (see cat. 22), where smoke and steam mingle with people and machines and one senses the artist's participatory role as on-the-spot observer.

In the Art Institute's *Charing Cross Bridge*—possibly inspired by the pastels on this subject that he undertook in January 1901, while he was awaiting the arrival of crates of canvases—soft yellows, blues, and pinks obscure the sharpness of the modern railway bridge and Neo-Gothic architecture. The shimmering, cloudlike form at the bottom right, representing part of the Victoria Embankment, recalls the reflections of foliage in *Mornings* and serves to soften the reality of the gritty metropolis. By including the puff of steam from the invisible engine along the bridge, behind which lie the towers and pinnacles of the Houses of Parliament, Monet created the illusion of speed and immediacy. In all of the London canvases—resulting from compositions made quickly on the spot according to specific weather conditions, laboriously reworked from memory in his Giverny studio over a protracted period of time, and finally studied as a totality—Monet was able to marry the notion of a modern, industrial London to a sense of the city's past, at once timeless and historic.

Although not among the eight canvases of the subject shown in 1904 at the Durand-Ruel Gallery, Paris, the Art Institute's *Charing Cross Bridge* was purchased the following year by Paul Durand-Ruel and sold to the Prince de Wagram, who already owned Monet's *Water Lily Pond* (cat. 103).

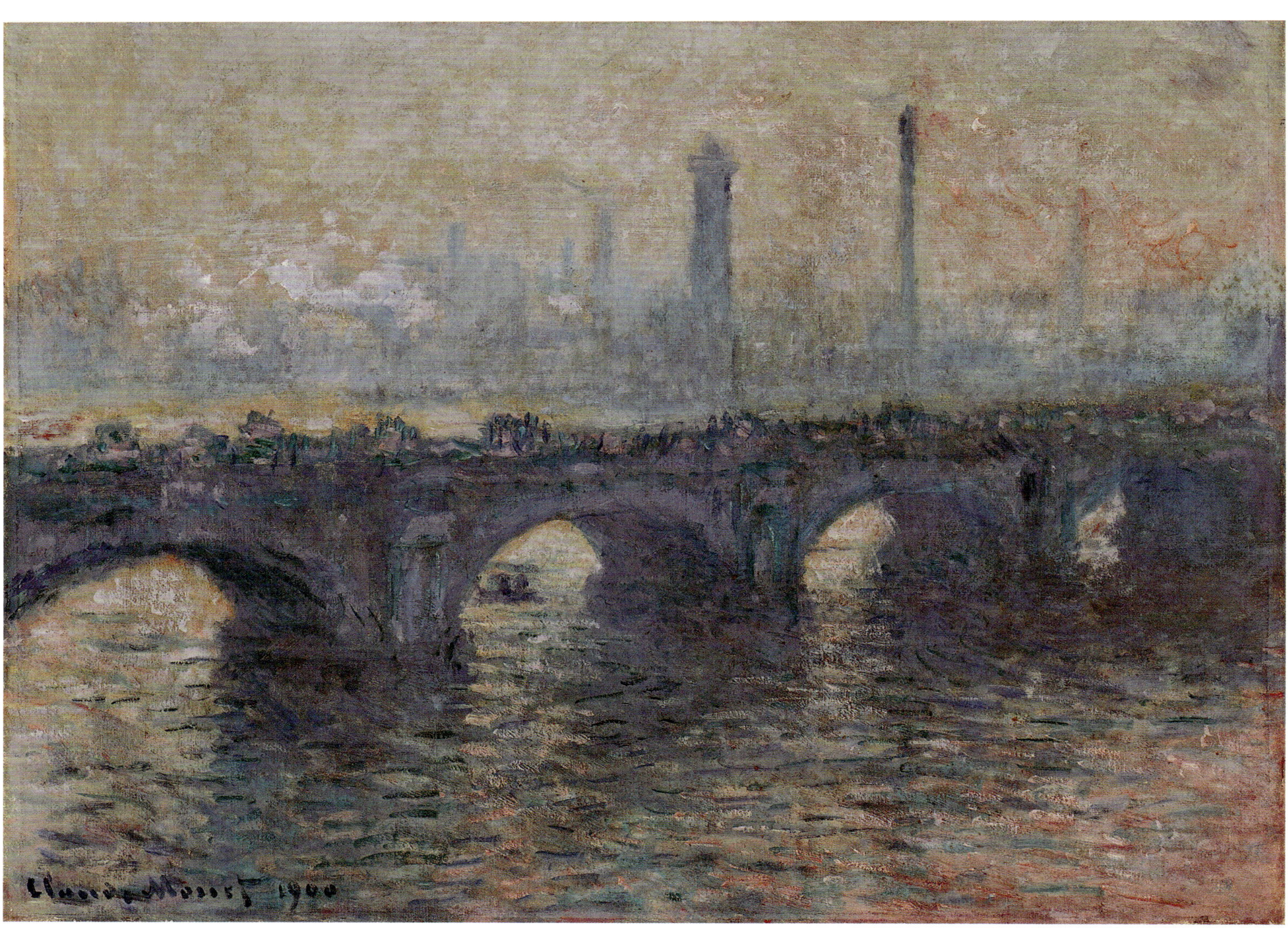

99

99

Waterloo Bridge, Gray Weather, 1900

Oil on canvas; 65.4 x 92.6 cm (25¾ x 36⅜ in.)
Gift of Mrs. Mortimer B. Harris, 1984.1173
Signed lower left: *Claude Monet 1900*

100

Waterloo Bridge, Sunlight Effect, 1903

Oil on canvas; 65.7 x 101 cm (25⅞ x 39¾ in.)
Mr. and Mrs. Martin A. Ryerson Collection, 1933.1163
Signed lower right: *Claude Monet 1903*

In choosing to stay in London for his second and third campaigns during the winters of 1900 and 1901—the most inclement and least tourist-friendly months to visit the city—Claude Monet acted in accordance with his twenty-year quest to paint the envelope of atmosphere for a given motif. In London it was the wintry light filtered through fog that he loved. As he later told the dealer René Gimpel, without fog, "London wouldn't be a beautiful city. It's the fog that gives it its magnificent breadth."

Arriving at the beginning of February 1900, he had about sixty-five canvases in progress by late March but complained that they "were not London enough." He returned the following year in late January and stayed until the end of March, bringing home more than ninety canvases that he worked on over the next three years. To achieve this feat, Monet rose daily at 6:00 a.m. in order to capture the sunlight as it appeared behind Waterloo Bridge, which he could see from his fifth-floor window at the Savoy Hotel, and then shifted to illuminate the side of Charing Cross Bridge, which he painted at midday and in the afternoon. Although he was attracted to the slender but insistently perpendicular geometry of Charing Cross Bridge, Waterloo Bridge's looping granite arches actually inspired the largest sub-series (forty-one works as opposed to thirty-four *Charing Cross* canvases) among his London paintings.

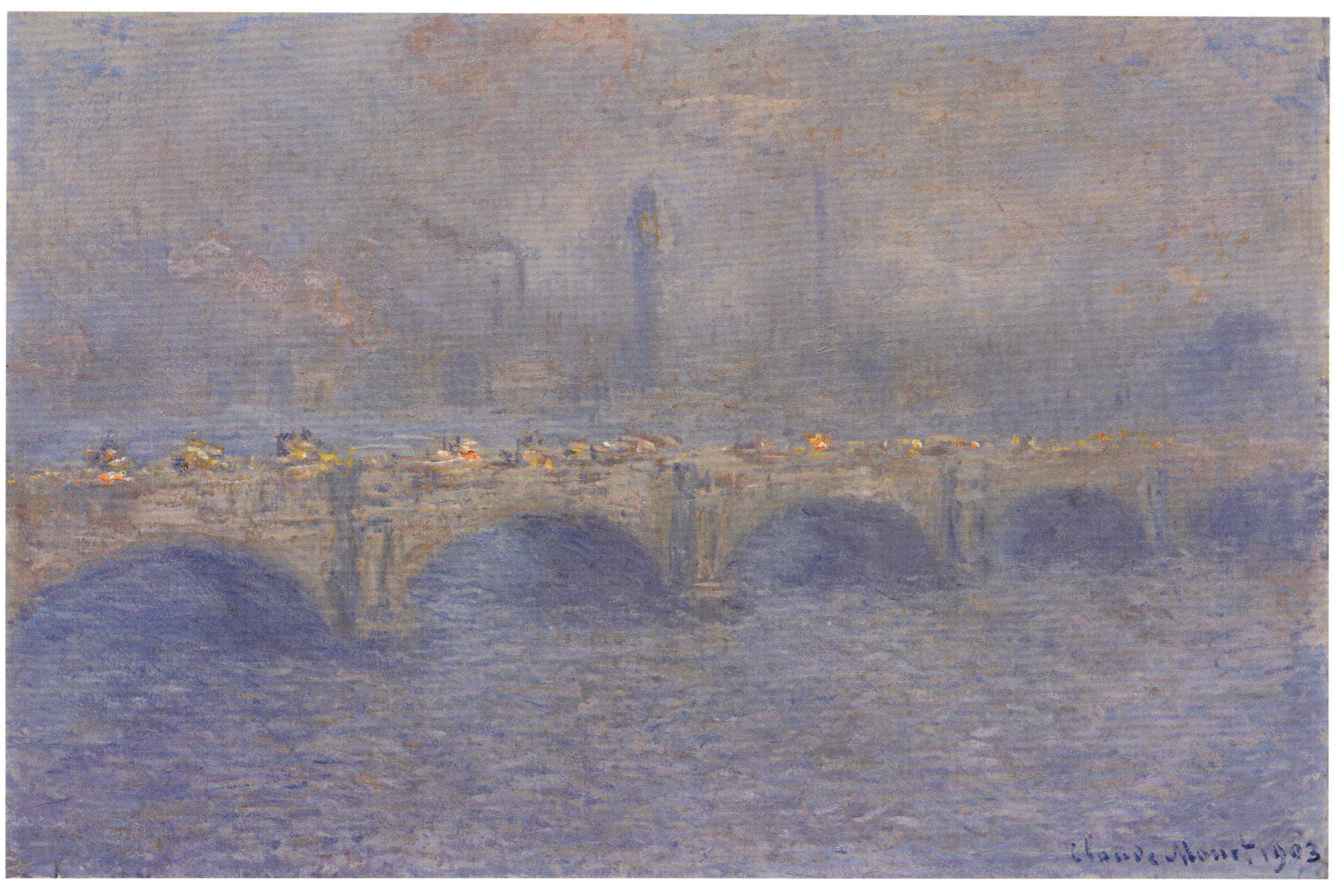

100

The two pictures in the Art Institute's collection are dated 1900 (cat. 99) and 1903 (cat. 100), but both were likely begun in 1900 and dated only when Monet felt them to be sufficiently advanced, if not completely finished. Just as he no longer sought to imitate the elusive effects of light at any given time on a specific canvas, he did not worry about finishing his paintings on the spot. Returning to Giverny in April 1901, Monet began to rework the entire group, relying on his memory of the London light and the immediate light in his studio. To Paul Durand-Ruel's persistent demands that the artist send him some of the London canvases already signed and finished, Monet responded no less adamantly that he could not work on one without seeing the others. So fixated was he on the ensemble that he could no longer distinguish a painting's singular merit, to the point that he requested that Durand-Ruel come to his studio to choose which of the group to exhibit, since several "are redundant." In the Art Institute's pair, subtle yet telling differences are conveyed by mood and atmosphere, from the blue-purple mist to the monochromatic blue-gray fog that creates an even more dramatic backdrop for the towering industrial buildings in the background. If the *Charing Cross* series emphasized railway traffic, with two of the works titled *Trains Crossing* (1902; private collection) and *Trains Passing* (1904; private collection), the *Waterloo Bridge* scenes are predominantly about sun, fog, and *temps couvert* (gray weather), when sunlight is blocked. The splotches of highly impastoed orange and yellow dotting the bridge in *Waterloo Bridge, Sunlight Effect* do not suggest artificial illumination from vehicles but rather the effects of natural light glancing off them. These reflections are totally absent in *Waterloo Bridge, Gray Weather*.

Both pictures were included among the eighteen depictions of Waterloo Bridge shown in 1904 at the Durand-Ruel Gallery, Paris, and both were immediately bought from the dealer. Indeed, this exhibition was a critical and monetary success for Monet, as was a smaller show held later that same year at the Cassirer Gallery, Berlin, in which *Waterloo Bridge, Gray Weather* was again included.

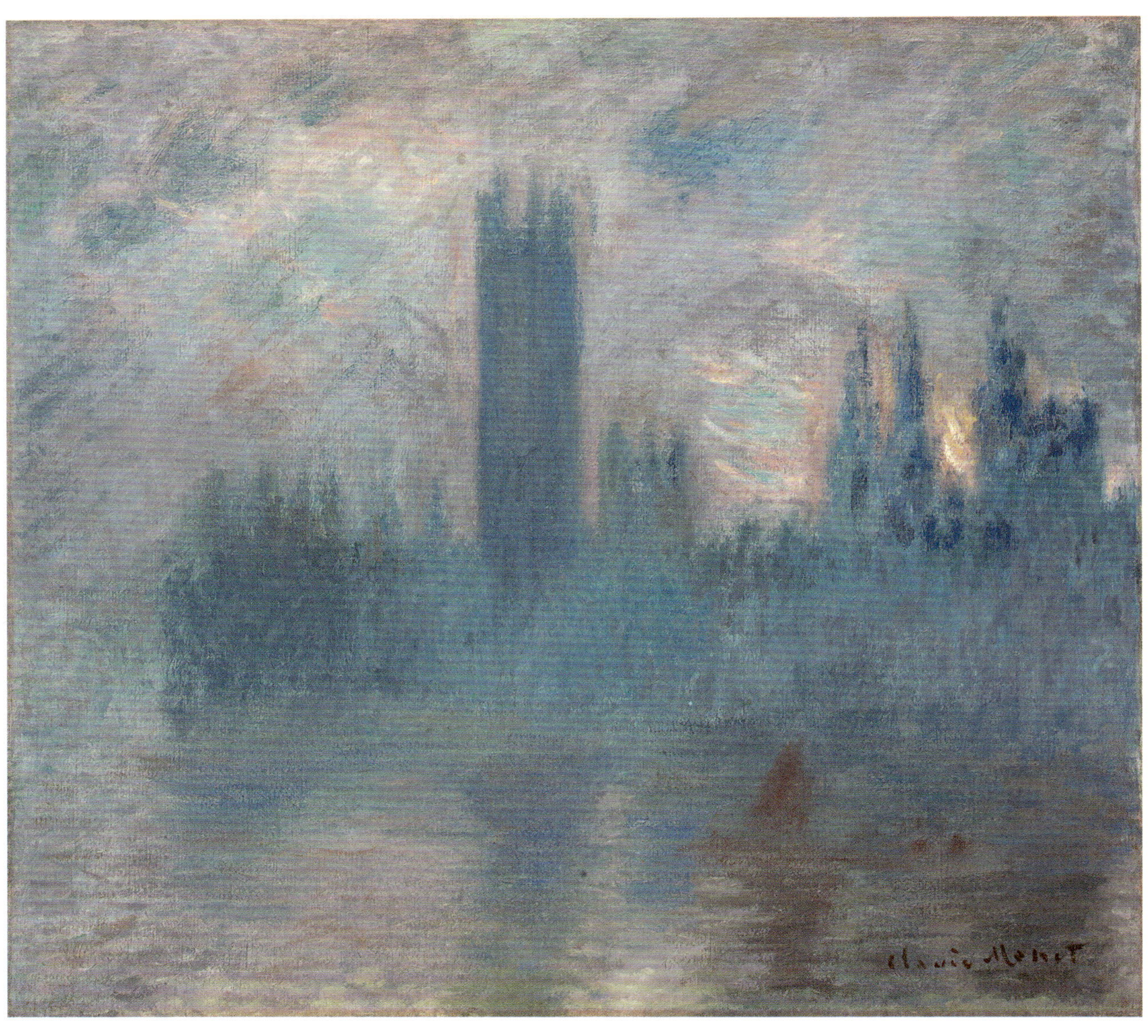

101

Houses of Parliament, London, 1900–01

Oil on canvas; 81 x 92 cm (31 7/8 x 36 1/4 in.)
Mr. and Mrs. Martin A. Ryerson Collection, 1933.1164
Signed lower right: *Claude Monet*

Claude Monet began his series on the fantastical Neo-Gothic Houses of Parliament at the beginning of his second trip to London. On February 14, 1900, he reported to his wife, Alice, that he "had started work at the hospital. If only you could see how beautiful it was." The hospital he referred to was St. Thomas, where, thanks to Mary Hunter—the English collector whom he had met through the American painter John Singer Sargent—and her friend Dr. Joseph Payne, he had access to a large room and terrace on the opposite bank of the river Thames from the Savoy Hotel, close to Westminster Bridge. As always, Monet's excitement about this new prospect was mitigated by anticipated difficulties, but in actuality these paintings seem to have caused him few problems and were apparently the most satisfactory of all his London series. Not only did he exhibit a larger proportion of these canvases at the Durand-Ruel Gallery in 1904, but he also asked 20,000 francs for them rather than the 15,000 francs at which the other works in the exhibition were priced. The Art Institute's *Houses of Parliament* was not shown among these, although it displays no signs of having been reworked at a later stage. Monet painted all the *Parliament* canvases in the late afternoon or at sunset, so that the backlit pinnacles and towers convey an immutable, iconic quality in contrast to the rushing trains and carriages that animate and modernize his depictions of bridges. The artist was undoubtedly thinking of the poetic *Nocturnes* of James McNeill Whistler, as well as the famous *Parliament Houses* of Joseph Mallord William Turner, both of which dissolved objective references with sweeping chromatic harmonies. But the apparitional quality of Monet's Neo-Gothic buildings, which he painted in closely ranged hues that make them appear to loom out of the fog, also shows his assimilation of contemporary Symbolist aesthetics, which championed mood, mystery, and emotional expression over description.

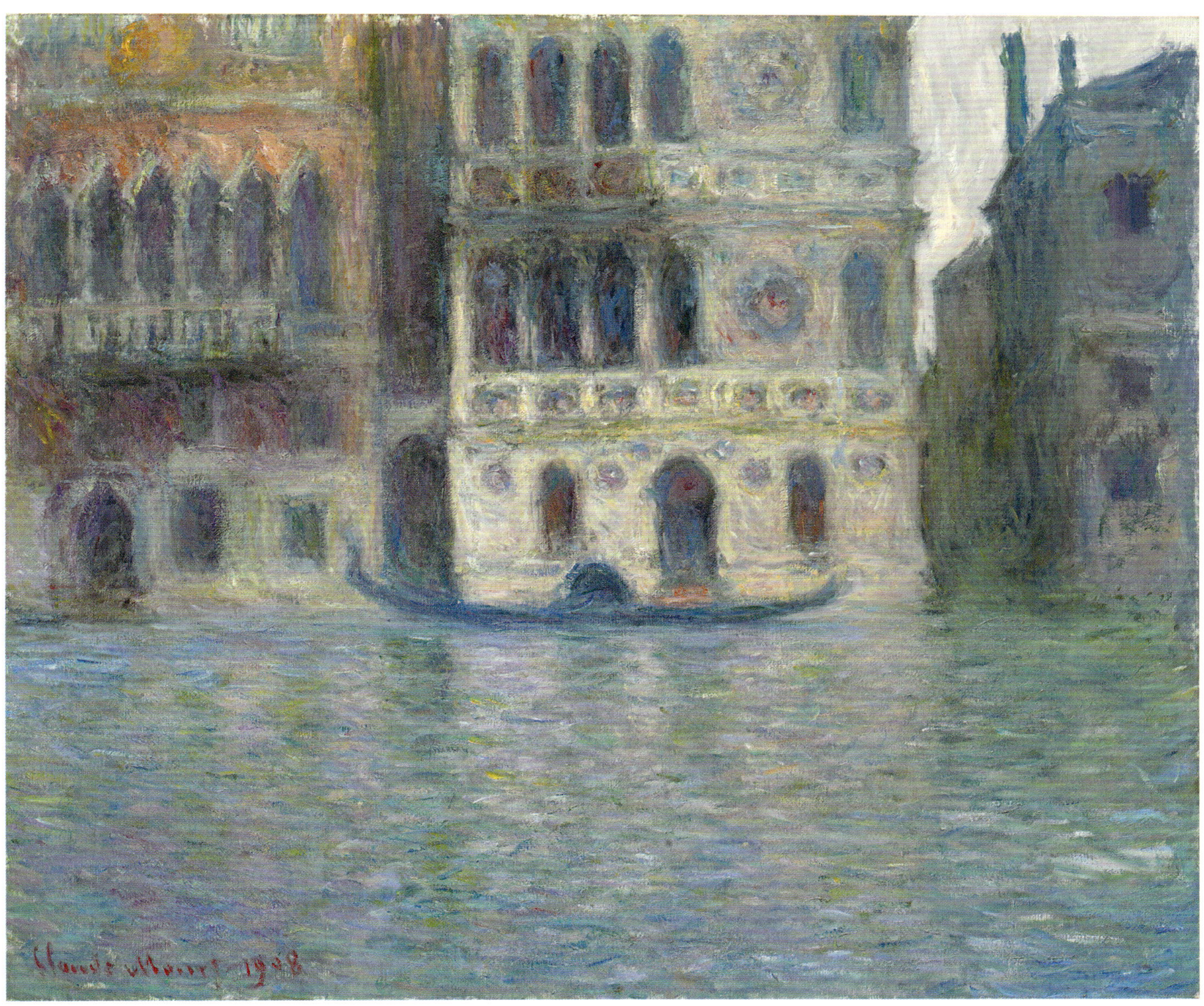

102

Venice, Palazzo Dario, 1908

Oil on canvas; 64.8 x 78.8 cm (25½ x 31 in.)
Mr. and Mrs. Lewis Larned Coburn Memorial Collection, 1933.446
Signed lower left: *Claude Monet 1908*

Claude Monet's final major thematic series of easel paintings was the result of his trip to Venice, where he and his wife, Alice, had been invited by Mary Hunter, who eight years earlier had helped arrange for the artist's use of a terrace at St. Thomas Hospital in London (see cat. 101). Although Monet had visited London several times before his 1899–1901 campaigns, in Venice he was a tourist, following in the footsteps of John Singer Sargent, Joseph Mallord William Turner, and James McNeill Whistler, who had already painted its architecture, water, and brilliant light. Perhaps because he was exploring Venice while painting it, the artist chose ten different motifs for which he realized a total of thirty-seven paintings. Among these are the palazzi along the Grand Canal, including that of Giovanni Dario, secretary of the Venetian Senate, whose richly decorative fifteenth-century residence is the subject of this and three other canvases. Although Monet's painting of the palace shares with the London series similar elements of architecture, water, and mist, his aims were quite different here. Instead of dissolving the stone with broad directional strokes, he used smaller brushes and thicker pigments to highlight the prismatic marble facing that was the structure's distinguishing feature. While placing the palazzo off center, he put a gondola directly in front of its entryway. Like a gentle smile articulating the water's edge, the boat's bulbous cabin echoes the curved windows, whose deep shadows prevent any glimpse into the building's interior. Monet showed this and twenty-eight other Venetian scenes at the Bernheim-Jeune Gallery, Paris, in May 1912, but he remained dissatisfied with the series, in part because Alice's long illness (and death in May 1911) made it impossible for him to return to Venice and to the subject. He would freely admit, however, that his Venice paintings provided an important breakthrough for an entirely new kind of series: *Water Lilies*.

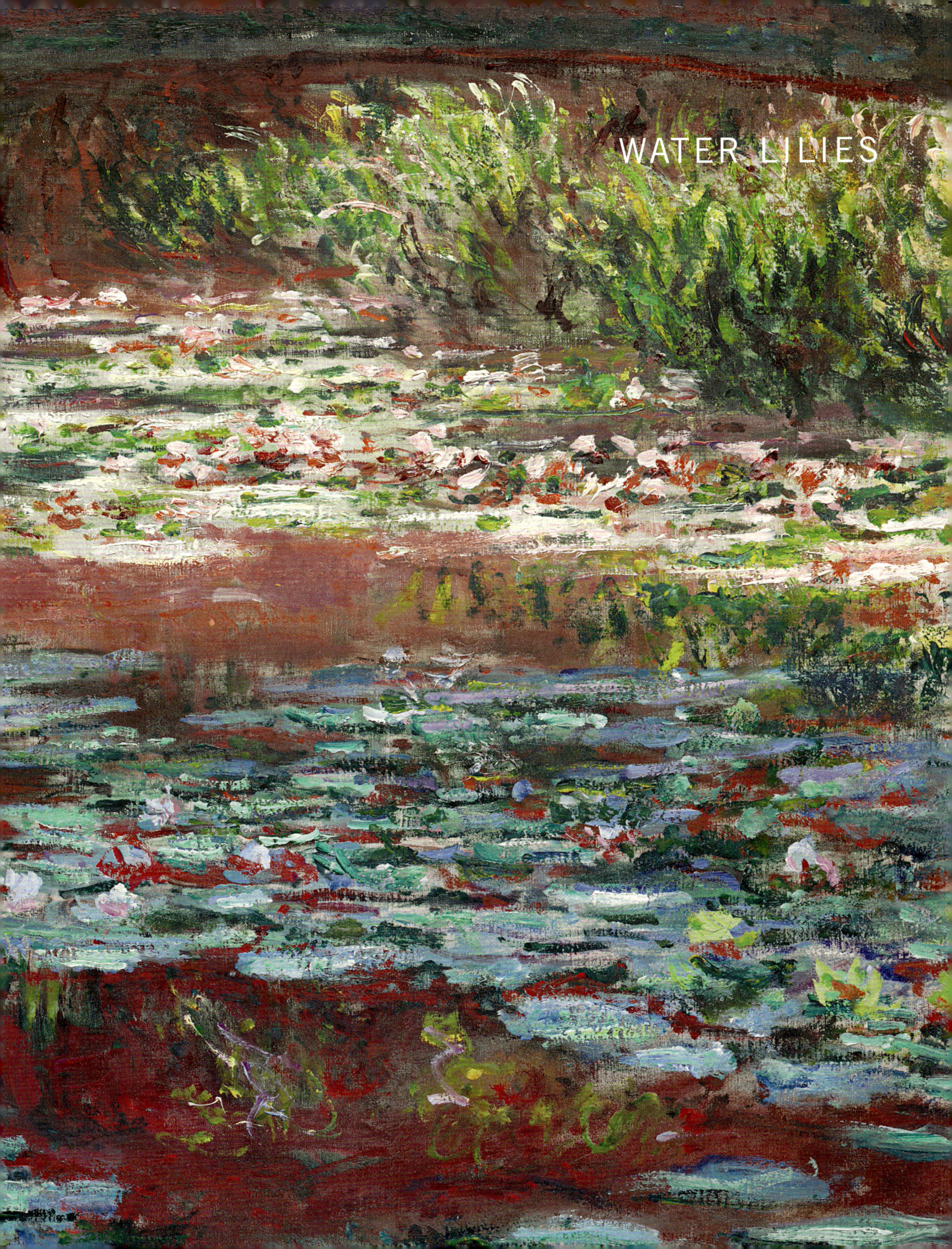
WATER LILIES

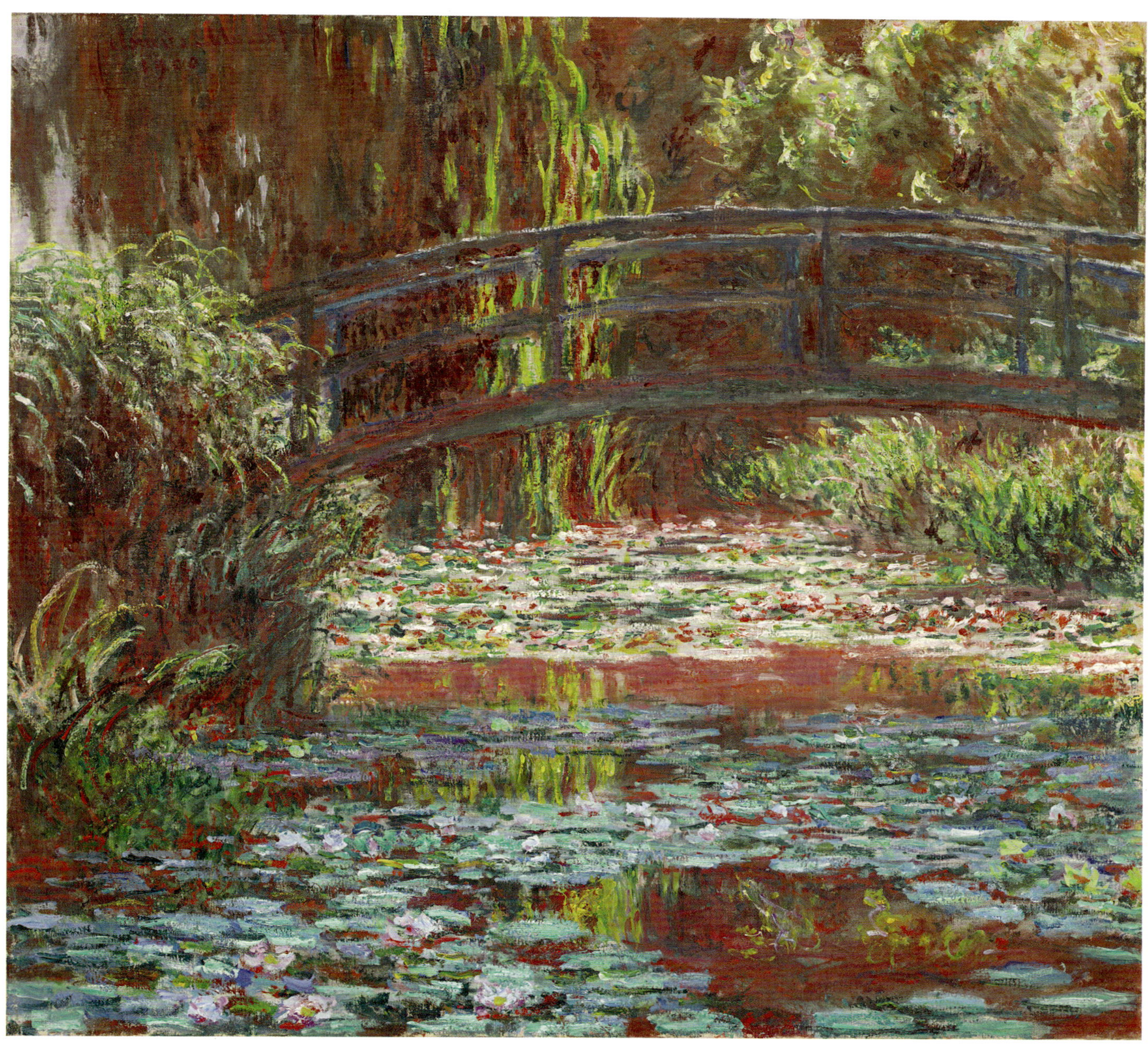

103

Water Lily Pond, 1900

Oil on canvas; 89.8 x 101 cm (35 3/8 x 39 3/4 in.)
Mr. and Mrs. Lewis Larned Coburn Memorial Collection, 1933.441
Signed upper left: *Claude Monet / 1900*

In 1893, three years after buying property at Giverny, Claude Monet began transforming the marshy ground behind his home into a pond, on the narrow end of which he built a Japanese-style, arched wooden bridge. Adding both exotic and domestic plantings, including his famous water lilies, he set out to create the ideal garden, which would be among his principal subjects until his death in 1926. The Art Institute's *Water Lily Pond*, showing the green-painted bridge cut off at the right so that it seems to float across the pool of lilies, was among eighteen similar versions of the subject that the artist made between 1899 and 1900, twelve of which he showed in November–December 1900 at the Durand-Ruel Gallery. Although not included in this exhibition, the painting was signed, dated, and sold in December 1900, suggesting that Monet considered it complete and simply chose not to exhibit it. By 1900 he had added more plants to his pond, swelling the vegetation that hung over the water along the embankments so that its reflection is confused with those of the aquatic plants that surge up toward the surface. It was this seamless continuum of surface and depth that the Belgian Symbolist poet Émile Verhaeren noted upon seeing the *Water Lilies* canvases. For him, Monet had created an alternative universe: "One senses the subterranean life at the bottom of the pool, the thick growth of roots; the intertwining of the stems, of which the flowers, massed on the surface, are only the continuation." In 1901 Monet enlarged the pond but abandoned the bridge motif (which he only took up again in 1918) to focus on the water lilies and their reflections.

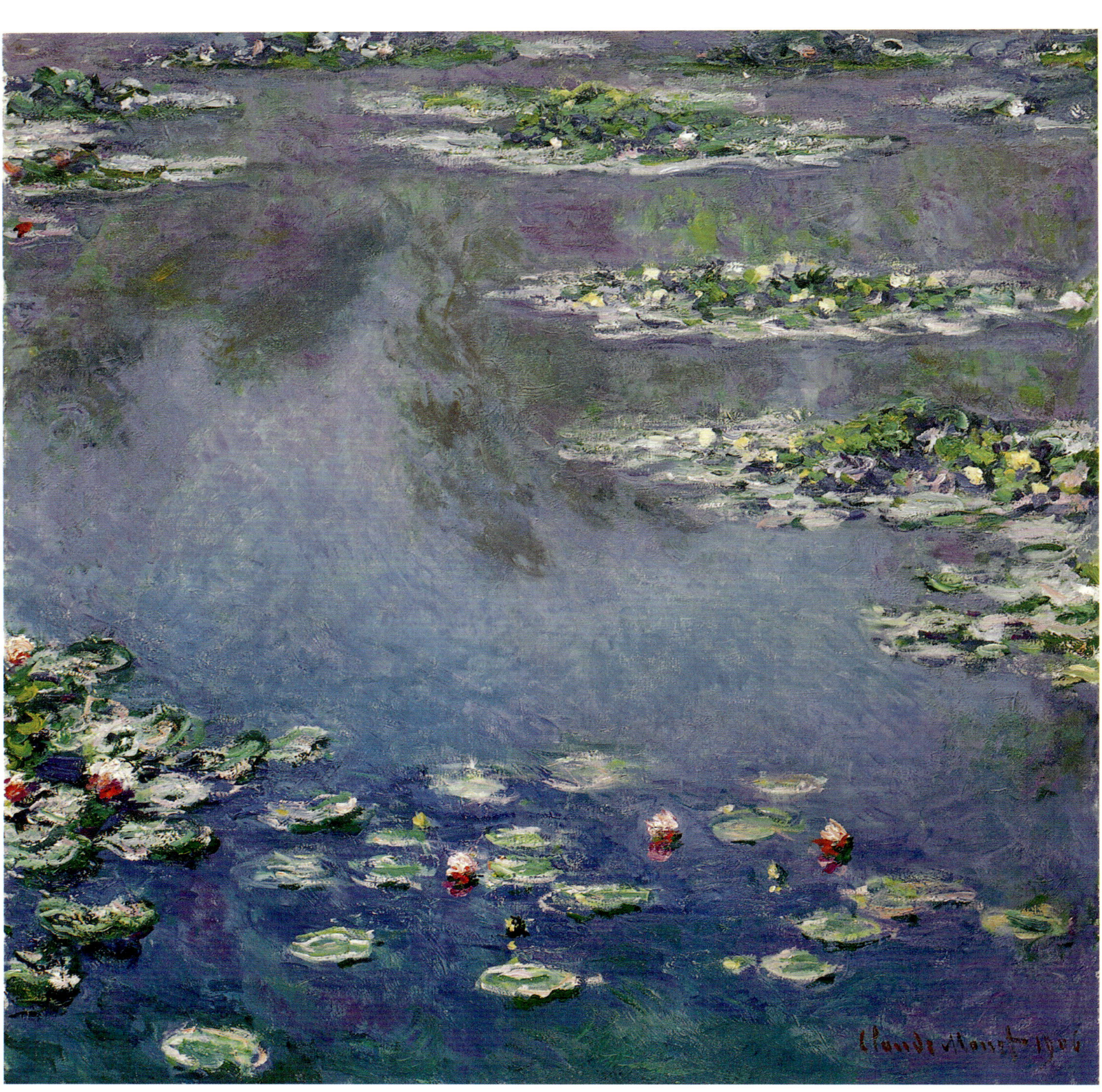
Claude Monet 1906

104

Water Lilies, 1906

Oil on canvas; 87.6 x 92.7 cm (34 ½ x 36 ½ in.)
Mr. and Mrs. Martin A. Ryerson Collection, 1933.1157
Signed lower right: *Claude Monet 1906*

> Know that I am absorbed by my work. These landscapes of water and reflections have become an obsession. It is beyond my power as an old man, and yet I want to manage to render what I feel. I have destroyed some.... Some I've begun again ... and I hope that out of so many efforts, something will emerge.

Thus wrote Claude Monet to his friend Gustave Geffroy in August 1908, nine months before the May opening of his exhibition *Water Lilies: Series of Water Landscapes*. The "something" that came out included the series of forty-eight works begun in 1903 and listed in the show's catalogue only by dates and numbers rather than by individual titles.

Monet claimed to have destroyed thirty or more other canvases "much to my satisfaction" during his struggle to paint the surface and reflections of the water-lily pond. Fortunately, the 1906 canvas in the Art Institute's collection escaped this mass destruction and was shown in his 1909 exhibition, along with four more of the same nearly square format. These and the others from the series—on vertical, rectangular, square, and oval canvases—showed flotillas of pink and white blossoms floating on a surface described by the critic Roger Marx as having "no more earth, no more sky, no limits now.... [Monet] wants attention diffused and scattered everywhere." With these words, Marx defined the artist's evolving aesthetic, in which overall patterns and the placement of forms and colors on canvas took precedence over the description of a particular time of day or year. Instead of a sense of spontaneity, Monet conveyed timelessness; instead of natural effects, he expressed harmony between forms and colors, or what contemporary artists called *le décoratif*.

On these easel-size canvases, Monet began what would be a much grander quest—to find a way of conceiving a composition so that the painted surface itself elicits a sustained emotional response. He chose the collective title for the series in order to pay homage to the Realist artist Gustave Courbet, whose *Sea Landscapes*, shown in the early 1870s, referred to his highly reductive images of sand, sea, and sky. Monet, however, took Courbet's abstractions of nature much further. By eliminating the horizon, he changed his works' viewpoint: no longer just pictures of nature, they depict a surface of plants and their watery reflections. The artist's fitful production signals the self-doubt, boredom, and eye problems he experienced during these years, as well as his inability to "render what I feel." Although he had created and cultivated his subject, he remained hostage to its mutability. As his wife, Alice, wrote in 1906, "The water lilies, which are superb now, are never the same from one moment to another; they perpetually change under the wind."

Firmly drawn and painted, the Art Institute's *Water Lilies*, which Monet probably began in the summer of 1906, lacks the sketchy quality that characterizes his later canvases of this motif. Its aquamarine surface reads as both beautifully still and texturally agitated: the underlying brushstrokes show through the top layers depicting water, while thinner passages suggesting reflected foliage are dotted with thickly impastoed blossoms. Despite the success of this picture (it was acquired jointly by the dealers Paul Durand-Ruel and Josse and Gaston Bernheim-Jeune and sold immediately to the playwright Henri Bernstein) and the exhibition in general, it would be five more years before Monet resumed painting his pond and undertook a group of murals, his most ambitious water-lilies project.

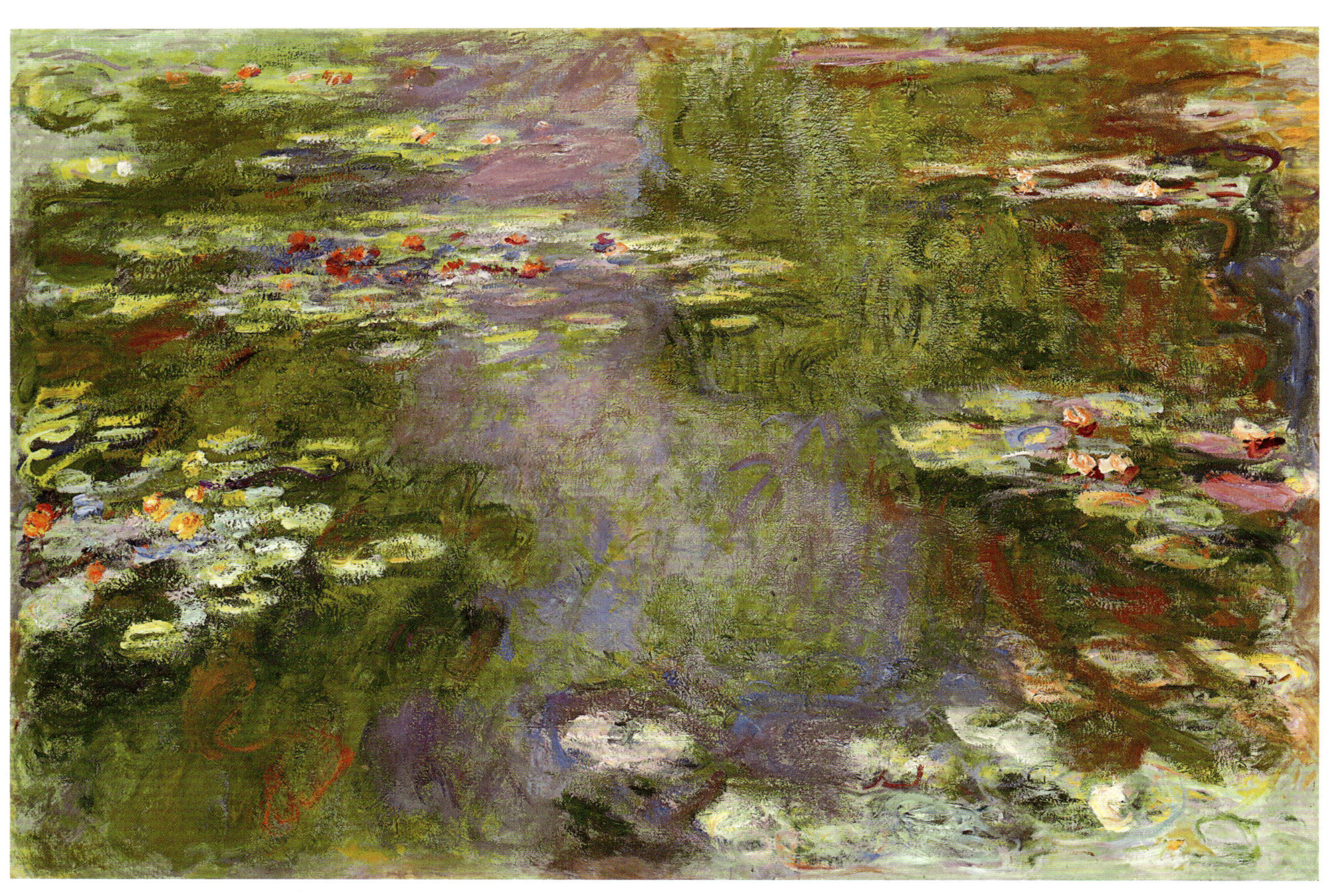

105

Water Lily Pond, 1917–22

Oil on canvas; 130.2 x 201.9 cm (51 ½ x 79 ½ in.)
Gift of Mrs. Harvey Kaplan, 1982.825

Following the outbreak of World War I, Claude Monet, who had not been able to work for several years because of his deteriorating health and his grief over the death of his wife, Alice, became immensely productive. Building a large studio and improving his garden, he entered an intense period of work focused on the monumental water-lilies cycle that he would later offer to the French state. Over the next twelve years, these canvases were extensively documented by journalists, photographers, collectors, and celebrities who paid homage to the Giverny master. Less well known are the nineteen smaller canvases that he painted between 1917 and 1922. These works, including the Art Institute's *Water Lily Pond*, occupy a pivotal role between the easel paintings that he completed by 1909 (see cat. 104) and the enormous murals on which he would embark in 1914. Monet envisioned the latter exhibited in elliptical rooms, an installation realized only in 1927 at the Orangerie in the Tuileries Gardens, Paris.

Although Monet worked on the Art Institute's painting and other canvases from this series while he was also making pictures double and triple them in size, the smaller compositions are not directly preparatory to his larger ones. In the smaller works, the artist moved from depicting single water lilies, willows, clouds, and their reflections to more personal, decorative compositions, in which the water-lily reflections are densely rendered and repeated rather than made to fit coloristically and compositionally with one another. There is evidence—including a few photographs that show Monet working by the pond—that these independent paintings were conceived out of doors and then reworked in the studio. In all of them, the sense of light, shade, and subaqueous vegetation surging upward seems as closely observed as in the earlier *Water Lilies* paintings, which are known to have been executed in part outside.

In the Art Institute's canvas, the fluid surface of the underlying water is interrupted with broad swirls of scumbled pigments similar to those found in other works in this series, such as *Water Lilies* (1919), in the Metropolitan Museum of Art, New York. It is as if the artist used this series of easel paintings to experiment with ways of transforming a carefully studied fragment of nature into a large artistic statement. Perhaps because of their personal nature and significance as an experimental detour from his larger mural project, Monet was reluctant to release them to dealers and collectors, allowing only five of the nineteen works to leave his studio during his lifetime. Signed and dated, the five attest to the artist's habit of personalizing his paintings as he sold or gave them away. At this time, Monet also "finished" (filled in) the compositions' edges (usually the bottom right) as an authorial sign-off, which, according to the artist, made no difference to the artwork but was expected by the buyer. The Art Institute's unsigned and undated *Water Lily Pond* has an unfinished edge, as do other canvases remaining in his possession at his death.

Only in the 1950s were these works eagerly pursued, at the moment when their large-scale, gestural brushwork would have appealed to collectors and curators who saw them as precursors to Abstract Expressionism. Unlike those post–World War II artists, whose aim was to express the subconscious through abstraction, Monet's final pictorial testaments—his water-lilies paintings and murals—were based entirely in nature. However, the distinction between indoors and outdoors, observation and memory, had become meaningless for the artist in the last, inspired decade of his life.

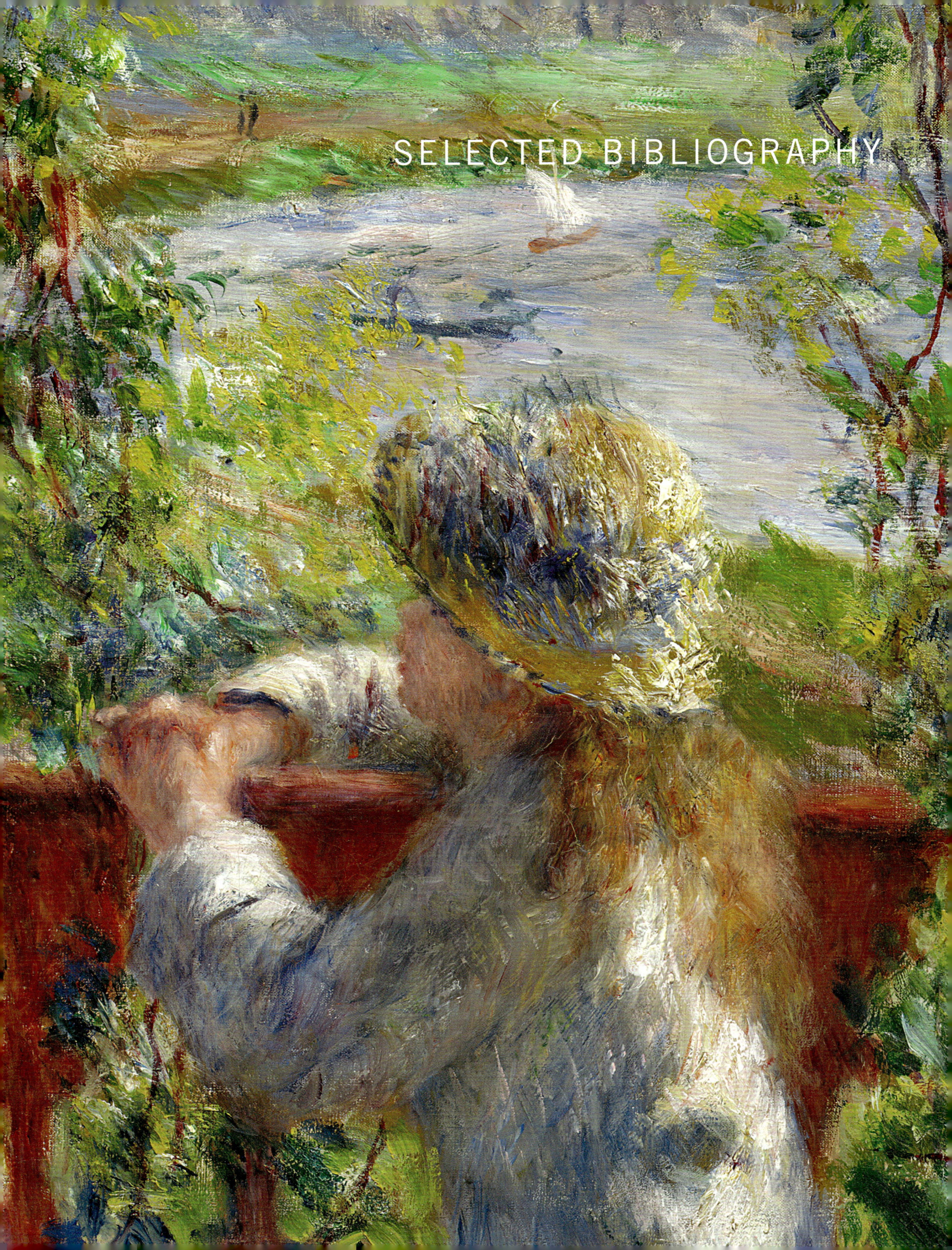

SELECTED BIBLIOGRAPHY

All references to the Art Institute of Chicago as publisher are listed below as AIC.

BOOKS ON THE ART INSTITUTE'S HISTORY AND COLLECTION

Art Institute of Chicago. 1986. *The Helen Birch Bartlett Memorial Collection. Museum Studies* 12, 2.

———. 1986. *The Joseph Winterbotham Collection: A Living Tradition*. AIC.

———. 1988. *The Architecture of the Art Institute of Chicago. Museum Studies* 14, 1.

———. 1993. *One Hundred Years at the Art Institute: A Centennial Celebration. Museum Studies* 19, 1.

———. 2000. *Impressionism and Post-Impressionism in the Art Institute of Chicago*. AIC//Hudson Hills Press, Inc.

———. 2003. *Graphic Modernism: Selections from the Francey and Dr. Martin L. Gecht Collection at the Art Institute of Chicago*. Exh. cat. AIC/Hudson Hills Press, Inc.

———. 2006. *Master Paintings in the Art Institute of Chicago*. AIC/Yale University Press.

Boggs, Jean Sutherland. 1996. *Artists in Focus: Degas*. AIC/Harry N. Abrams, Inc.

Brettell, Richard R. 1987. *French Impressionists*. AIC/Harry N. Abrams, Inc.

———. 1987. *Post-Impressionists*. AIC/Harry N. Abrams, Inc.

Brettell, Richard R., and Suzanne Folds McCullagh. 1984. *Degas in The Art Institute of Chicago*. Exh. cat. AIC/Harry N. Abrams, Inc.

Druick, Douglas W. 1997. *Artists in Focus: Renoir*. AIC/Harry N. Abrams, Inc.

Forge, Andrew. 1995. *Artists in Focus: Monet*. AIC.

McCullagh, Suzanne Folds, ed. 2006. *Drawings in Dialogue: Old Master through Modern, the Harry B. and Bessie K. Braude Memorial Collection*. AIC/Yale University Press.

Rich, Daniel Catton. 1938. *Catalogue of the Charles H. and Mary F. S. Worcester Collection of Paintings, Sculpture, and Drawings*. Lakeside Press.

Salvesen, Britt, et al. 2001. *Artists in Focus: Gauguin*. AIC/Harry N. Abrams, Inc.

Thomson, Belinda. 2001. *Artists in Focus: Van Gogh*. AIC/Harry N. Abrams, Inc.

GENERAL BOOKS ON THE PERIOD

Brettell, Richard R., et al. 1984. *A Day in the Country: Impressionism and the French Landscape*. Exh. cat. Los Angeles County Museum of Art/Harry N. Abrams, Inc.

———. 2000. *Impression: Painting Quickly in France, 1860–1890*. Exh. cat. Sterling and Francine Clark Art Institute/Yale University Press.

Brettell, Richard R., with Natalie H. Lee. 1999. *Monet to Moore: The Millennium Gift of Sara Lee Corporation*. Yale University Press.

Gamboni, Dario. 2002. *Potential Images: Ambiguity and Indeterminacy in Modern Art*. Reaktion Books.

Herbert, Robert L. 1968. *Neo-Impressionism*. Exh. cat. Solomon R. Guggenheim Museum.

———. 1988. *Impressionism: Art, Leisure, and Parisian Society*. Yale University Press.

Johnston, Sona, ed. 1999. *Faces of Impressionism: Portraits from American Collections*. Exh. cat. Baltimore Museum of Art/Rizzoli.

Moffett, Charles, et al. 1986. *The New Painting: Impressionism, 1874–1886*. Exh. cat. 2nd ed. Fine Arts Museums of San Francisco.

Rabinow, Rebecca A., ed. 2006. *Cézanne to Picasso: Ambroise Vollard, Patron of the Avant-Garde*. Exh. cat. Metropolitan Museum of Art/Yale University Press.

Schapiro, Meyer. 1997. *Impressionism: Reflections and Perceptions*. George Braziller.

Smith, Edward Lucie. 1989. *Impressionist Women*. Weidenfeld and Nicolson.

Smith, Paul. 1995. *Impressionism: Beneath the Surface*. Harry N. Abrams, Inc.

Sondergaard, Sidsel Maria, ed. 2006. *Women in Impressionism: From Mythical Feminine to Modern Woman*. Exh. cat. Ny Carlsberg Glyptotek/Skira.

Sturgis, Alexander, et al. 2006. *Rebels and Martyrs: The Image of the Artist in the Nineteenth Century*. Exh. cat. National Gallery Company Ltd./Yale University Press.

Tinterow, Gary, and Henri Loyrette. 1994. *Origins of Impressionism*. Exh. cat. Metropolitan Museum of Art/Harrry N. Abrams, Inc.

Torsten, Gunnarsson, et al. 2003. *Impressionism and the North: Late 19th-Century French Avant-Garde Art and Art in the Nordic Countries, 1870–1920*. Exh. cat. Nationalmuseum Stockholm.

BOOKS ON THE ARTISTS

BAZILLE

Jourdan, Aleth. 1992. *Frédéric Bazille: Prophet of Impressionism*. Exh. cat. Translated by John Goodman. Brooklyn Museum.

Pitman, Diane W. 1998. *Bazille: Purity, Pose and Paintings in the 1860s*. Pennsylvania State University Press.

BOUDIN

Hamilton, Vivien. 1992. *Boudin at Trouville*. Exh. cat. John Murray/Glasgow Museums.

CAILLEBOTTE

Distel, Anne, et al. 1995. *Gustave Caillebotte: Urban Impressionist*. Exh. cat. Réunion des Musées Nationaux/AIC/Abbeville Press.

Varnedoe, Kirk. 1987. *Gustave Caillebotte*. Yale University Press.

CÉZANNE

Adriani, Götz. 1995. *Cézanne Paintings*. Translated by Russell Stockman. Harry N. Abrams, Inc.

Buren, Ann H. van. 1966. “Mme Cézanne's Fashions and the Dates of Her Portraits.” *Art Quarterly* 9, 2, pp. 111–27.

Cachin, Françoise. 1996. *Cézanne*. Exh. cat. Harry N. Abrams, Inc./Philadelphia Museum of Art.

Conisbee, Philip, et al. 2006. *Cézanne in Provence*. Exh. cat. National Gallery of Art/Yale University Press.

Howard, Michael. 1990. *Cézanne*. Bison Group.

Reff, Theodore. 1977. “Cézanne's Late Bather Paintings.” *Arts Magazine* 52, 2 (October), pp. 116–19.

Rewald, John, Walter Feilchenfeldt, and Jayne Warman. 1996. *The Paintings of Paul Cézanne: A Catalogue Raisonné*. Harry N. Abrams, Inc.

R. M. F. 1926. “Cézanne, Rousseau, Picasso.” *Art Institute of Chicago Bulletin* 20, 5 (May), pp. 61–64.

Shiff, Richard. 1978. “Seeing Cézanne.” *Critical Inquiry* 4, 4 (Summer), pp. 769–808.

Verdi, Richard. 1990. *Cézanne and Poussin: The Classical Vision of Landscape*. Exh. cat. National Galleries of Scotland.

———. 1992. *Cézanne*. Thames and Hudson.

CROSS

Compin, Isabelle. 1964. *H. E. Cross*. Quatre Chemins-Editart.

Rewald, John. 1951. *Henri-Edmond Cross*. Exh. cat. Fine Arts Associates.

DEGAS

Baumann, Felix, and Marianne Karabelnik, eds. 1994. *Degas Portraits*. Exh. cat. Kunsthaus Zurich/Merrell Holberton Publishers.

Boggs, Jean Sutherland, et al. 1988. *Degas*. Exh. cat. Metropolitan Museum of Art/National Gallery of Canada.

Bomford, David, et al. 2004. *Art in the Making: Degas*. Exh. cat. National Gallery Company Ltd./Yale University Press.

DeVonyar, Jill, and Richard Kendall. 2002. *Degas and the Dance*. Exh. cat. American Federation of Arts/Harry N. Abrams, Inc.

Dumas, Ann, et al. 1997. *The Private Collection of Edgar Degas*. Exh. cat. Metropolitan Museum of Art/Harry N. Abrams, Inc.

———. 2002. "Degas: Sculptor/Painter." In Joseph S. Czestochowski and Anne Pingeot, *Degas Sculptures: Catalogue Raisonné of the Bronzes*, pp. 39–47. International Arts/Torch Press.

Kendall, Richard. 1996. *Degas: Beyond Impressionism*. Exh. cat. National Gallery Publications/AIC/Yale University Press.

Reff, Theodore. 1968. "Some Unpublished Letters of Degas." *Art Bulletin* 50, 1 (March), pp. 87–94.

Robins, Anna Gruetzner, and Richard Thomson. 2005. *Degas, Sickert, and Toulouse-Lautrec: London and Paris, 1870–1910*. Exh. cat. Tate Publishing.

FANTIN-LATOUR

Druick, Douglas, and Michel Hoog. 1983. *Fantin-Latour*. Exh. cat. National Gallery of Canada/National Museums of Canada.

GAUGUIN

Brettell, Richard R., et al. 1988. *The Art of Paul Gauguin*. Exh. cat. National Gallery of Art.

Druick, Douglas W., and Peter Kort Zegers, et al. 2001. *Van Gogh and Gauguin: The Studio of the South*. Exh. cat. AIC/Thames and Hudson.

Laudon, Paule. 2003. *Tahiti-Gauguin: Mythe et vérités*. Adam Biro.

Shackelford, George T. M., and Claire Frèches-Thory, et al. 2004. *Gauguin Tahiti*. Exh. cat. Museum of Fine Arts, Boston.

Wildenstein, Daniel, et al. 2001. *Gauguin: Premier itinéraire d'un sauvage, catalogue de l'oeuvre peint (1873–1888)*. 2 vols. Skira/Wildenstein Institute.

Wildenstein, Georges. 1964. *Gauguin*. Beaux-Arts.

VAN GOGH

Cachin, Françoise, and Bogomila Welsh-Ovcharov. 1988. *Van Gogh à Paris*. Exh. cat. Réunion des Musées Nationaux.

Dorn, Roland, George S. Keyes, and Joseph J. Rishel, et al. 2000. *Van Gogh Face to Face: The Portraits*. Exh. cat. Detroit Institute of Arts/Thames and Hudson.

Druick and Zegers, et al. 2001. *Van Gogh and Gauguin* (see Gauguin).

Hendriks, Ella, and Louis van Tilborgh. 2006. "New Views on Van Gogh's Development in Antwerp and Paris: An Integrated Art Historical and Technical Study of His Paintings in the Van Gogh Museum." 2 vols. Ph.D. diss., Proefschrift Universiteit van Amsterdam.

Hulsker, Jan. 1996. *The New Complete Van Gogh: Paintings, Drawings, Sketches; Revised and Enlarged Edition of the Catalogue Raisonné of the Works of Vincent van Gogh*. J. M. Meulenhoff/John Benjamins.

Pickvance, Ronald. 2000. *Van Gogh*. Exh. cat. Fondation Pierre Gianadda.

Uitert, Evert van, Louis van Tilborgh, Sjraar van Heugten. 1990. *Vincent van Gogh: Paintings*. Exh. cat. Rijksmuseum Vincent van Gogh/Rizzoli.

GONZALÈS

Grant, Carol Jane. 1994. "Eva Gonzalès (1849–1883): An Examination of the Artist's Style and Subject Matter." 2 vols. Ph.D. diss., Ohio State University.

GUILLAUMIN

Fondation de L'Hermitage. 1996. *Armand Guillaumin, 1841–1927: Un Maître de l'impressionisme français.* Exh. cat. Bibliothèque des Arts.

Gray, Christopher, and Gilles Kraemer. 1997. *Armand Guillaumin: De la lumière à la couleur.* Exh. cat. Musée d'Art et d'Histoire.

JONGKIND

Sillevis, John, et al. 2003. *Johan Barthold Jongkind*. Exh. cat. Waanders Uitgevers/Gemeentemuseum Den Haag.

MANET

Armstrong, Carol. 2002. *Manet Manette*. Yale University Press.

Hanson, Anne Coffin. 1966. *Édouard Manet, 1832–1883*. Exh. cat. Philadelphia Museum of Art/AIC.

Reff, Theodore. 1982. *Manet and Modern Paris*. Exh. cat. National Gallery of Art.

Tinterow, Gary, and Geneviève Lacambre, eds. 2003. *Manet/Velázquez: The French Taste for Spanish Painting*. Exh. cat. Metropolitan Museum of Art/Yale University Press.

Wilson-Bareau, Juliet. 1998. *Manet, Monet, and the Gare Saint-Lazare*. Exh. cat. Réunion des Musées Nationaux/Yale University Press.

Wilson-Bareau, Juliet, and David Degener. 2003. *Manet and the Sea*. Exh. cat. Philadelphia Museum of Art.

MILLET

Herbert, Robert L. 1962. *Barbizon Revisited*. Exh. cat. Clarke & Way.

Jones, Kimberly. 2008. *In the Forest of Fontainebleau: Painters and Photographers from Corot to Monet.* Exh. cat. National Gallery of Art/Museum of Fine Arts, Houston/Yale University Press.

MONET

Baillio, Joseph, ed. 2007. *Claude Monet (1840–1926): A Tribute to Daniel Wildenstein and Katia Granoff*. Exh. cat. Wildenstein.

Clarke, Michael, and Richard Thomson. 2003. *Monet: The Seine and the Sea, 1878–1883*. Exh. cat. National Galleries of Scotland.

Hellandsjø, Karin, et al. 1995. *Monet in Norway: Exhibition to Mark the Centenary of Claude Monet's Visit to Norway During the Winter of 1895*. Exh. cat. Utenriksdepartementet.

House, John. 1986. *Monet: Nature into Art*. Yale University Press.

———, et al. 2005. *Monet's London: Artists' Reflections on the Thames, 1859–1914*. Exh. cat. Museum of Fine Arts, St. Petersburg, Florida/Snoeck.

Isaacson, Joel. 1978. *Claude Monet: Observation and Reflection*. Phaidon.

Kendall, Richard, ed. 1989. *Monet by Himself.* Mcdonald Orbis.

Koja, Stephan. 1996. *Claude Monet*. Exh cat. translated by John Brownjohn. Österreichische Galerie/Prestel.

Lemonedes, Heather, Lynn Federle Orr, David Steel, et al. 2006. *Monet in Normandy*. Exh. cat. Fine Arts Museums of San Francisco/Rizzoli.

Moffett, Charles. 1981. "Monet's Haystacks." In *Aspects of Monet: A Symposium on the Artist's Life and Times*, edited by John Rewald and Frances Weitzenhoffer, pp. 142–59. Harry N. Abrams, Inc.

Pissarro, Joachim. 1997. *Monet and the Mediterranean*. Exh. cat. Kimbell Art Museum/Rizzoli.

Seiberling, Grace. 1976. "Monet's Series." Ph.D. diss., Yale University.

Stuckey, Charles F., ed. 1985. *Monet: A Retrospective*. Hugh Lauter Levin Associates.

———. 1995. *Claude Monet, 1840–1926*. Exh. cat. AIC/Thames and Hudson.

Tucker, Paul Hayes. 1989. *Monet in the '90s: The Series Paintings*. Exh. cat. Museum of Fine Arts, Boston/Yale University Press.

———. 1996. *Monet in Norway*. Exh. cat. Ordrupgaard.

———, et al. 1998. *Monet in the 20th Century*. Exh. cat. Yale University Press.

Wildenstein, Daniel. 1996. *Monet*. 4 vols. Taschen.

Wilson-Bareau. 1998. *Manet, Monet, and the Gare Saint-Lazare* (see Manet).

MORISOT

Higonnet, Anne. 1992. *Berthe Morisot's Images of Women.* Harvard University Press.

Patry, Sylvie, et al. 2002. *Berthe Morisot, 1841–1895*. Exh. cat. Réunion des Musées Nationaux.

Rouart, Denis. 1986. *The Correspondence of Berthe Morisot with Her Family and Her Friends*. Camden Press.

PISSARRO

Adler, Kathy. 1986. "Camille Pissarro: City and Country in the 1890s." In *Studies on Camille Pissarro*, edited by Christopher Lloyd, pp. 99–116. Routledge & Kegan Paul.

Bailly-Herzberg, Janine, ed. 1988. *Correspondance de Camille Pissarro*. Vol. 3. Presses Universitaires de France.

Brettell, Richard R. 1990. *Pissarro and Pontoise: The Painter in a Landscape*. Yale University Press.

Brettell, Richard R., and Joachim Pissarro. 1992. *The Impressionist and the City: Pissarro's Series Paintings*. Exh. cat. Dallas Museum of Art/Yale University Press.

Pissarro, Joachim. 1992. *Camille Pissarro*. Rizzoli.

Rewald, John, ed. 2002. *Camille Pissarro: Letters to His Son Lucien*. Translated by Lionel Abel. Artworks.

Thomson, Richard. 1990. *Camille Pissarro: Impressionism, Landscape, and Rural Labour*. Exh. cat. South Bank Centre.

Ward, Martha. 1996. *Pissarro, Neo-Impressionism, and the Spaces of the Avant-Garde*. University of Chicago Press.

RENOIR

Bailey, Colin B., et al. 1997. *Renoir's Portraits: Impressions of an Age*. Exh. cat. Yale University Press/National Gallery of Canada.

———, et al. 2007. *Renoir Landscapes, 1865–1883*. Exh. cat. National Gallery Company Ltd.

SEURAT

Herbert, Robert L., et al. 2004. *Seurat and the Making of "La Grande Jatte."* Exh. cat. AIC/University of California Press.

SIGNAC

Bocquillon-Ferretti, Marina. 2001. *Signac, 1863–1935*. Exh. cat. Metropolitan Museum of Art/Yale University Press.

Cachin, Françoise, et al. 2003. *P. Signac*. Exh. cat. Fondation Pierre Gianadda.

SISLEY

Stevens, Mary Anne, ed. 1992. *Alfred Sisley*. Exh. cat. Royal Academy of Arts/Yale University Press.

TOULOUSE-LAUTREC

Murray, Gale B. 1991. *Toulouse-Lautrec: The Formative Years, 1878–1891*. Clarendon Press.

Robins and Thomson. 2005. *Degas, Sickert, and Toulouse-Lautrec* (see Degas).

Stuckey, Charles F. 1979. *Toulouse Lautrec: Paintings*. Exh. cat. AIC.

Sweetman, David. 1999. *Explosive Acts: Toulouse-Lautrec, Oscar Wilde, Félix Fénéon, and the Art and Anarchy of the Fin de Siècle*. Simon & Schuster.

Thomson, Richard, et al. 2005. *Toulouse-Lautrec and Montmartre*. Exh. cat. National Gallery of Art/Princeton University Press.

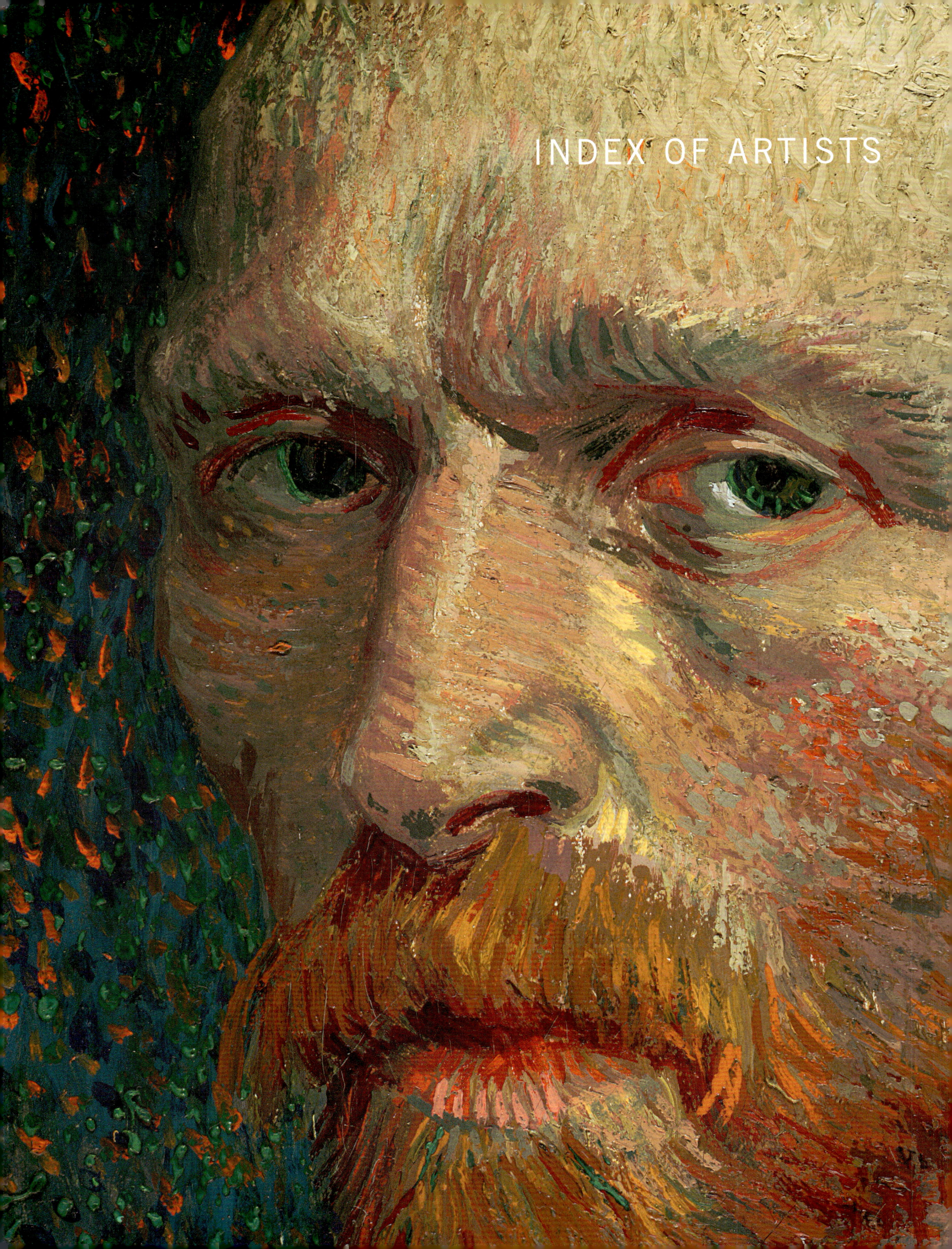
INDEX OF ARTISTS

PHOTOGRAPHY CREDITS

Unless otherwise noted, all photographs of the works in the catalogue were made by the Department of Imaging of the Art Institute of Chicago, Christopher Gallagher, Director of Imaging, and are copyrighted by the Art Institute of Chicago.

Unless otherwise noted, photographs in the chronology are courtesy of the Art Institute of Chicago.

Every effort has been made to contact and acknowledge copyright holders for all reproductions; additional rights holders are encouraged to contact the Art Institute of Chicago. The following credits apply to all images in this catalogue for which separate acknowledgment is due.

Page 12 (upper right): Collection of the Union League Club of Chicago.

Page 15 (upper left): Courtesy of Libby Bartlett Sturges.

Page 16 (lower right): Courtesy of Colonel Robert R. McCormick Research Center.

Page 17 (upper center): © 2010 Man Ray Trust/Artists Rights Society (ARS), NY/ ADAGP, Paris.

Page 17 (lower center): Koehne Photo.

Page 19 (upper left): AP Photos.

Page 19 (lower right): Courtesy of *Chicago American*.

Page 21 (lower center): Photograph by Karen Engstrom, courtesy of *Chicago Tribune*.

Page 21 (lower right): Paul Hansen Photography.

Page 22 (left): Photograph by Faye Wrubel.

Page 23 (lower left): Photograph by Robert Lifson, Department of Imaging, Art Institute of Chicago.

Page 24 (upper left): Photograph by Gloria Groom.

Page 24 (upper right): Photograph by Susan Huang, Department of Imaging, Art Institute of Chicago.

Page 24 (lower left): © Robert Carl.

Page 25 (upper left): © Kurt Gerber.

Page 25 (lower left): Photograph by Susan Huang, Department of Imaging, Art Institute of Chicago.